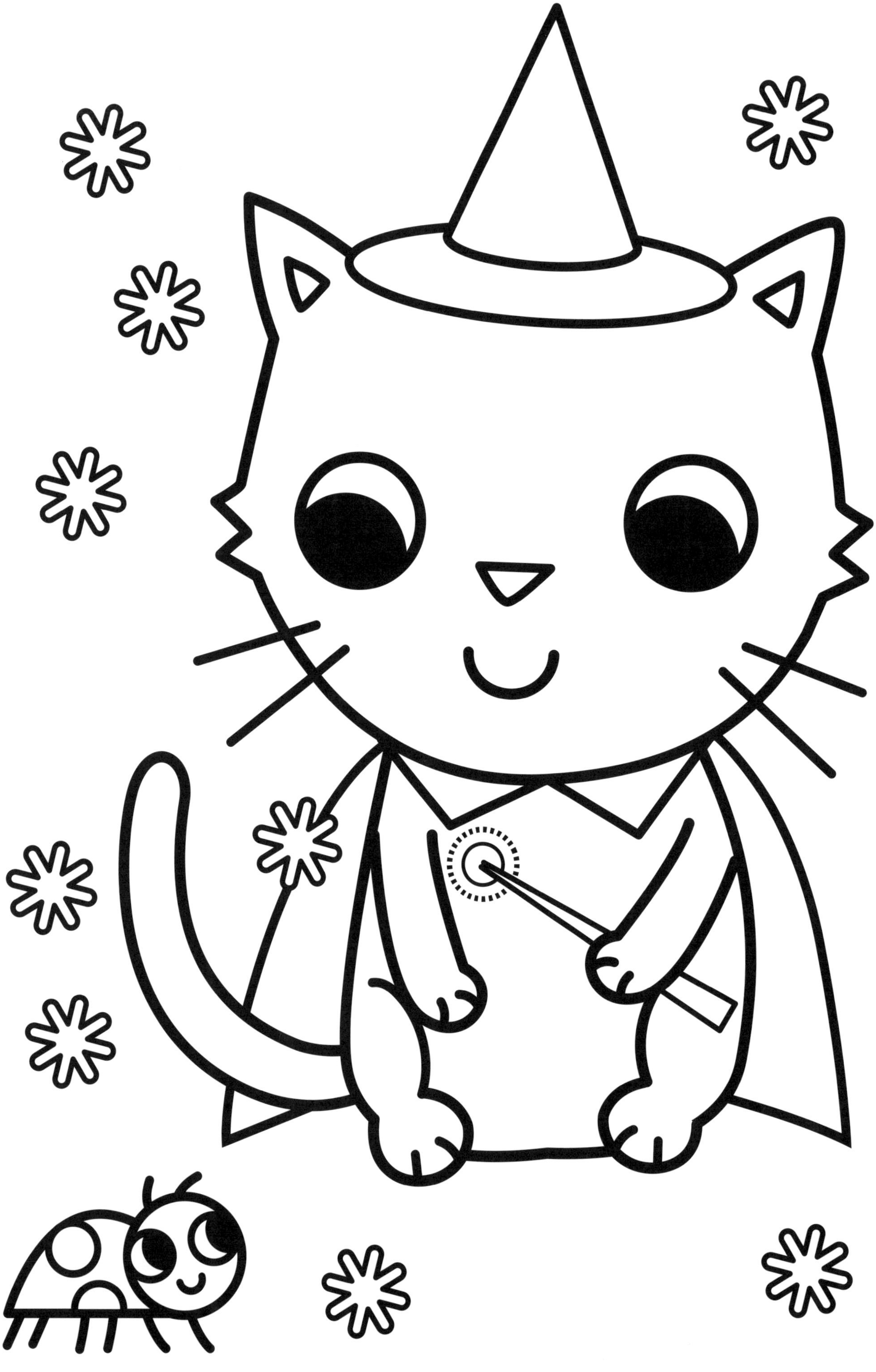

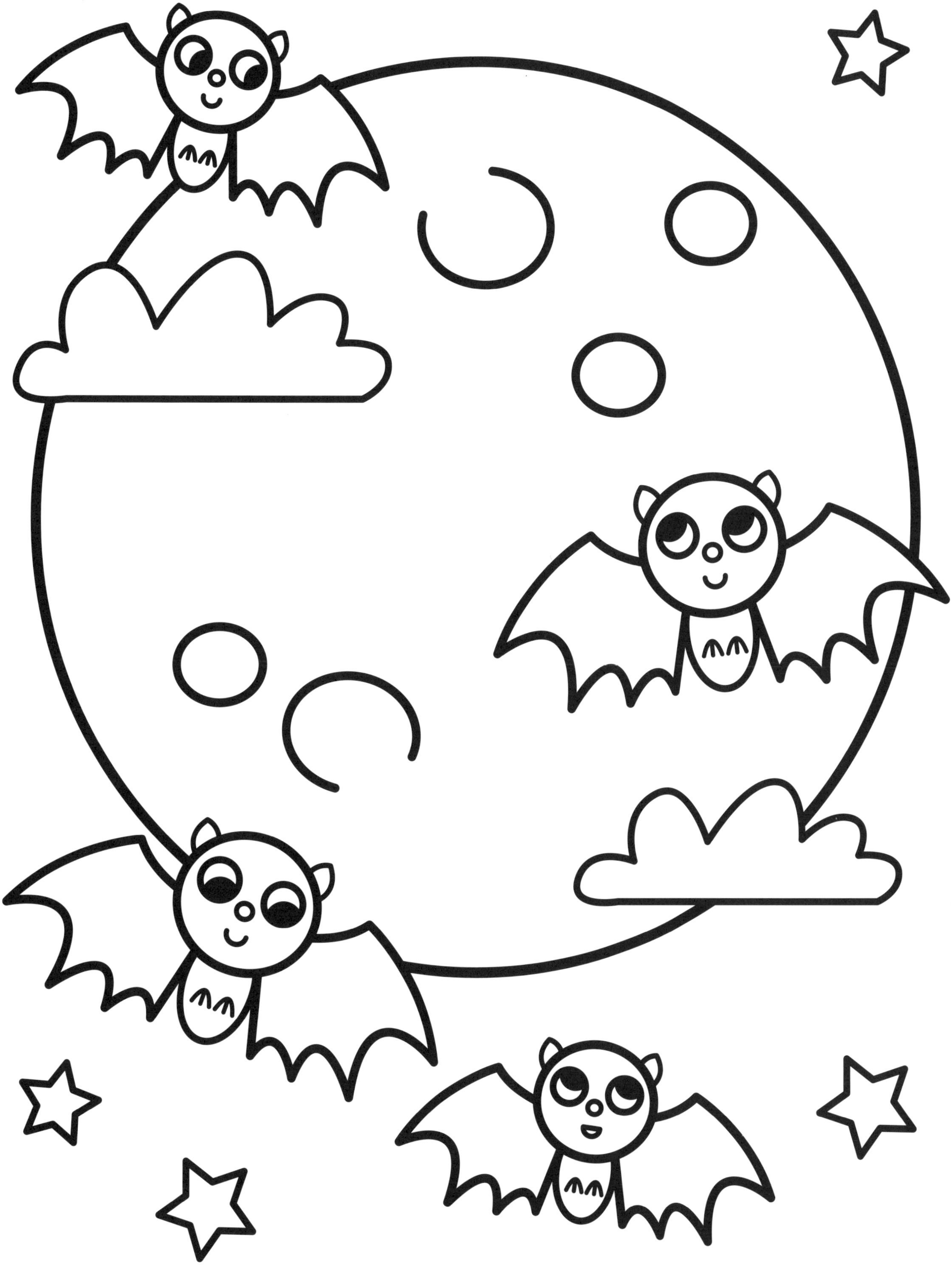

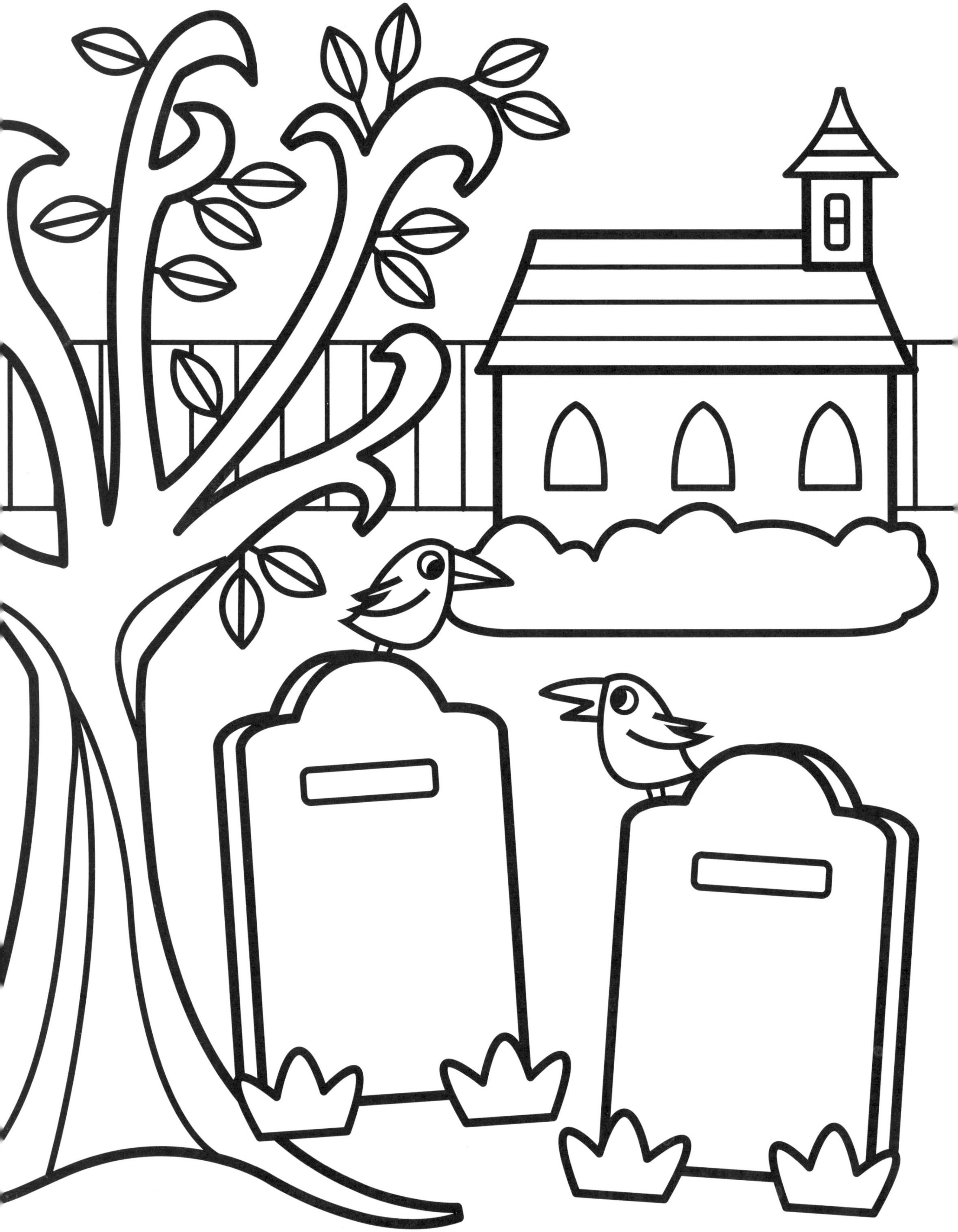

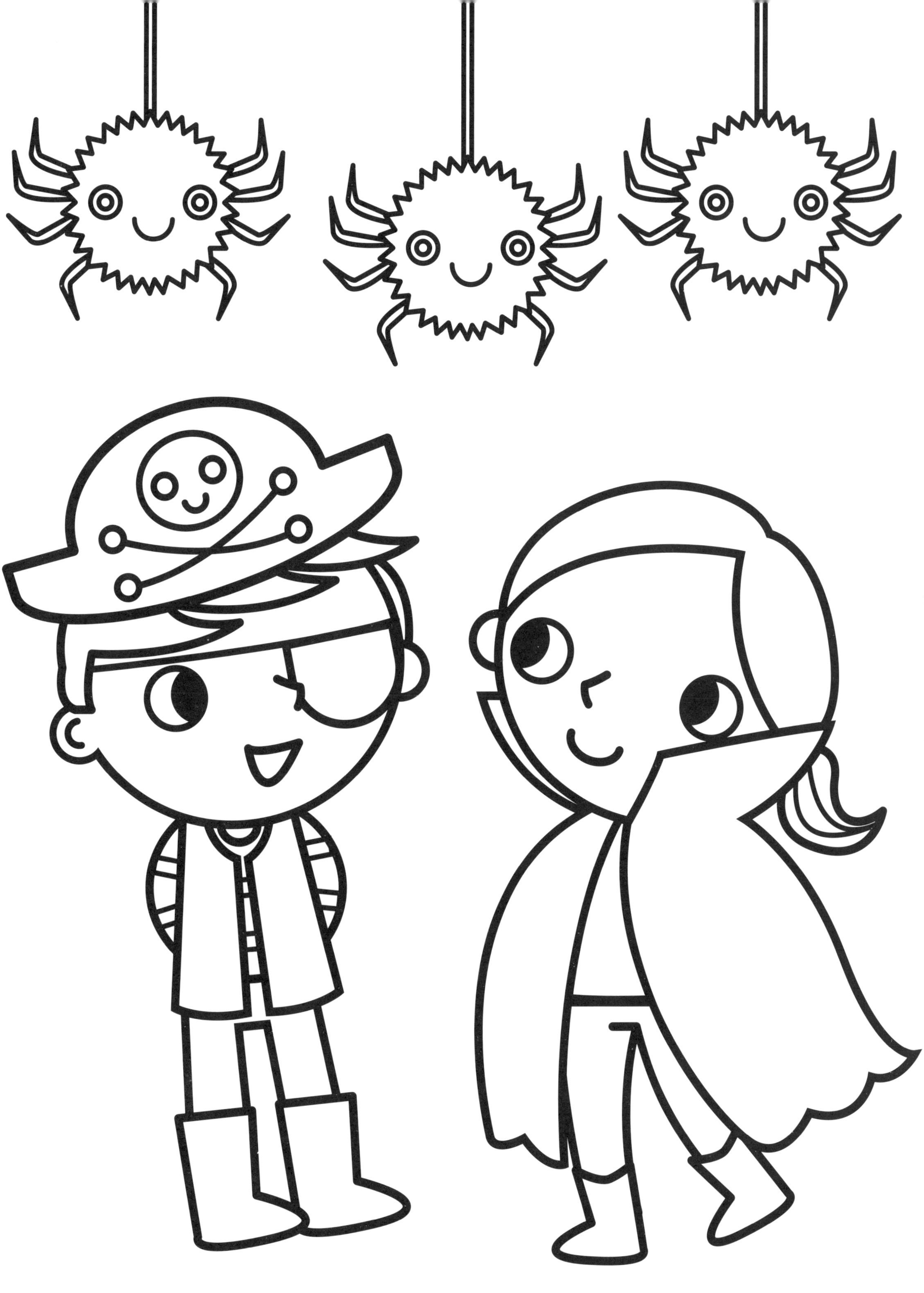

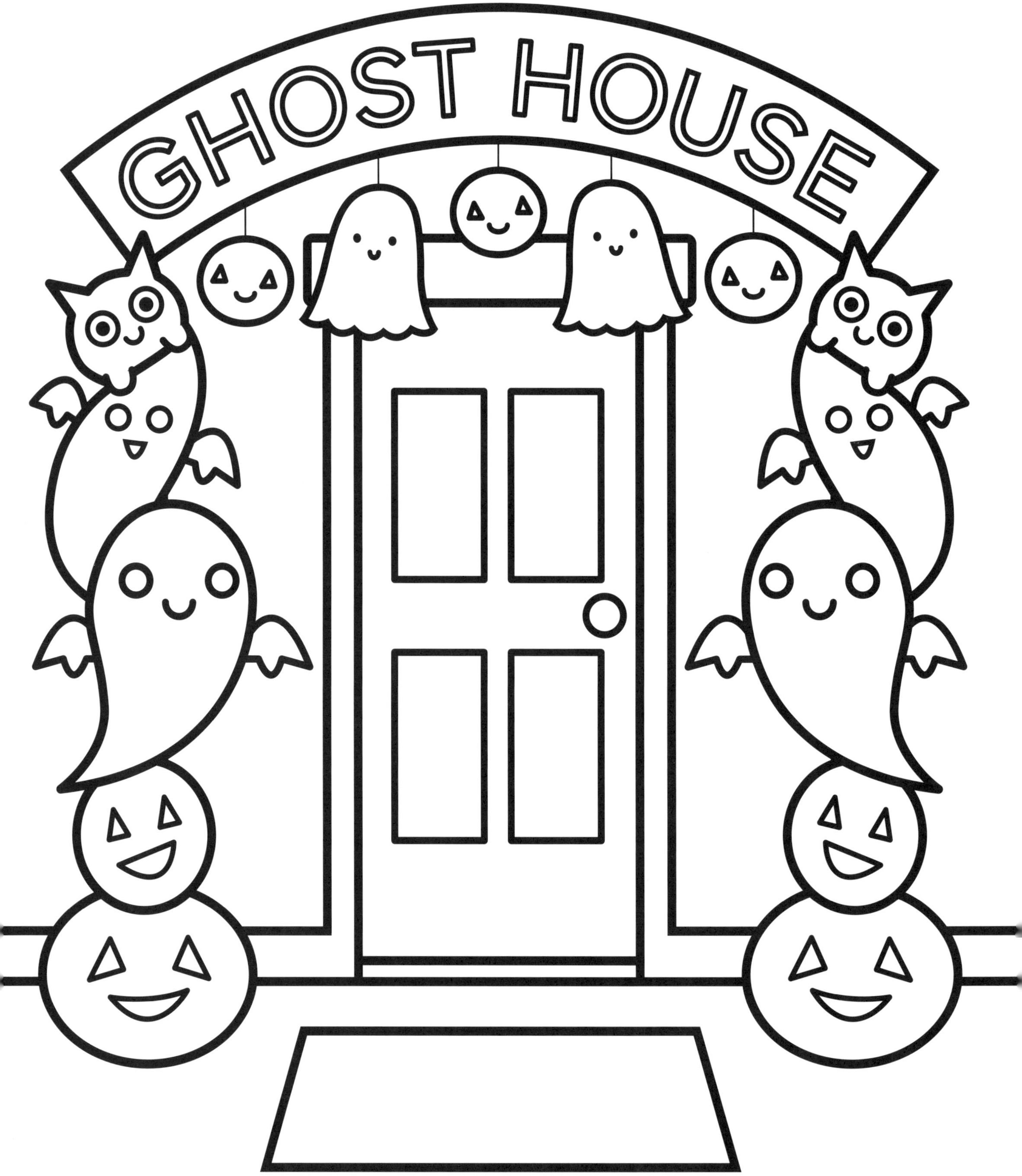
GHOST HOUSE

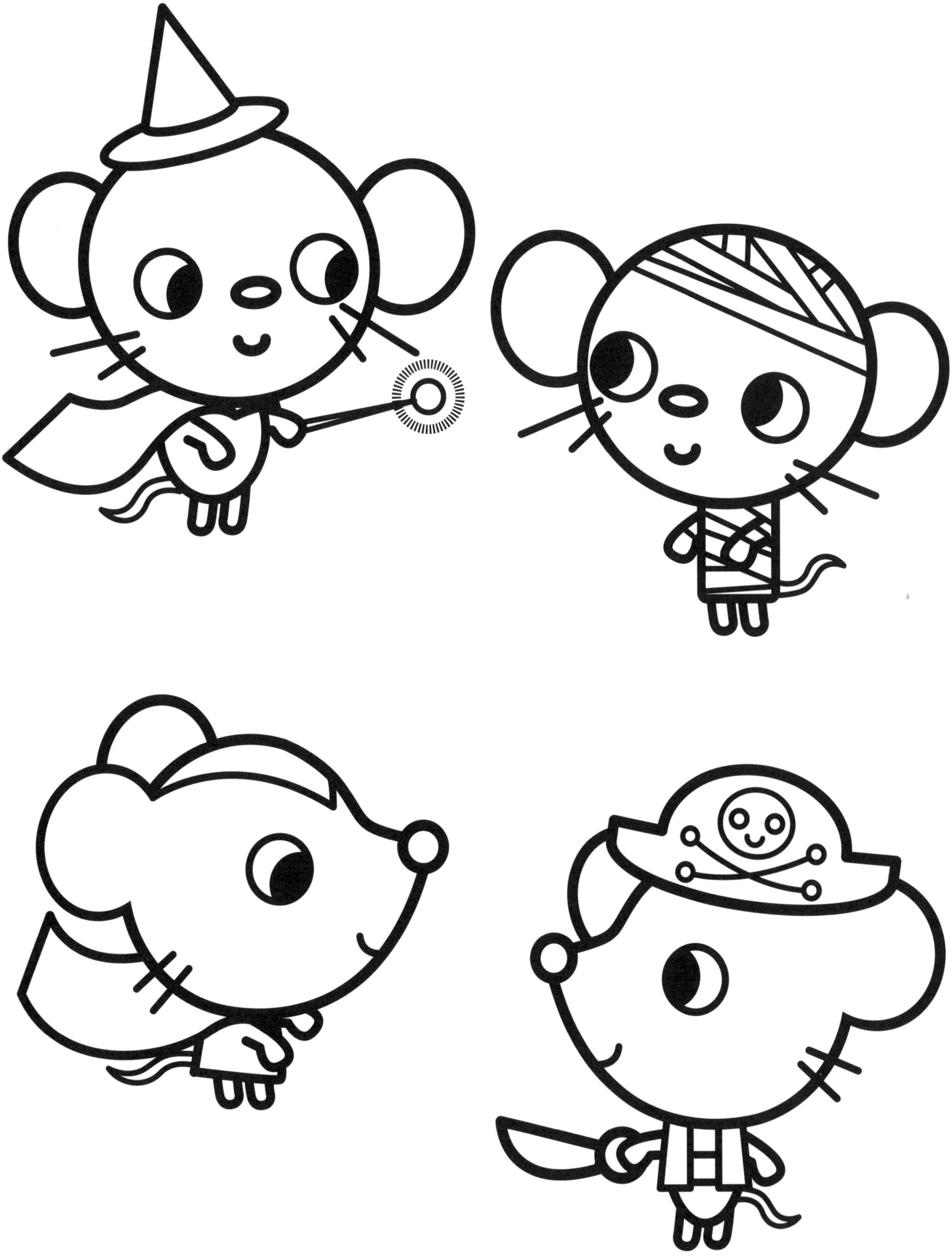

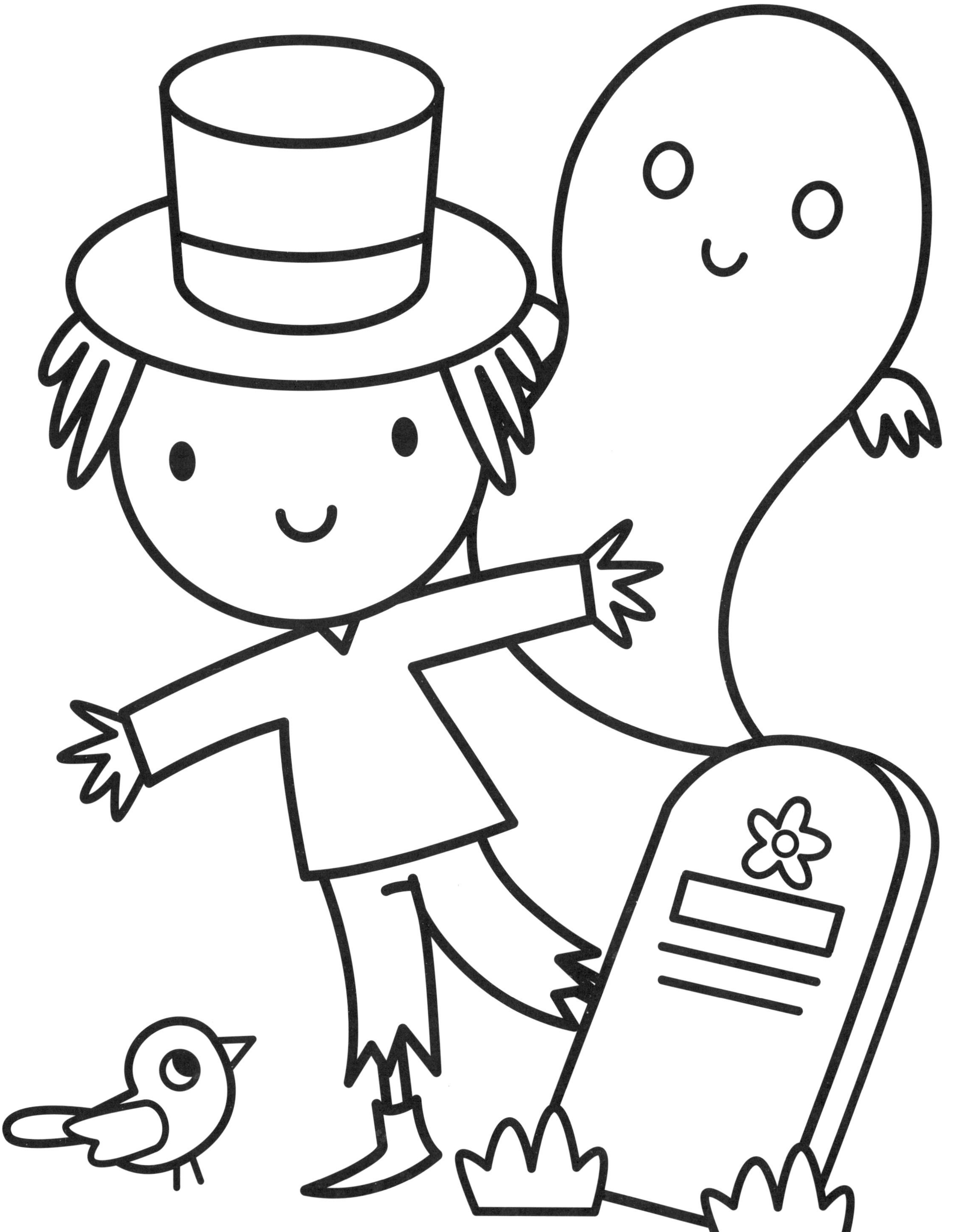

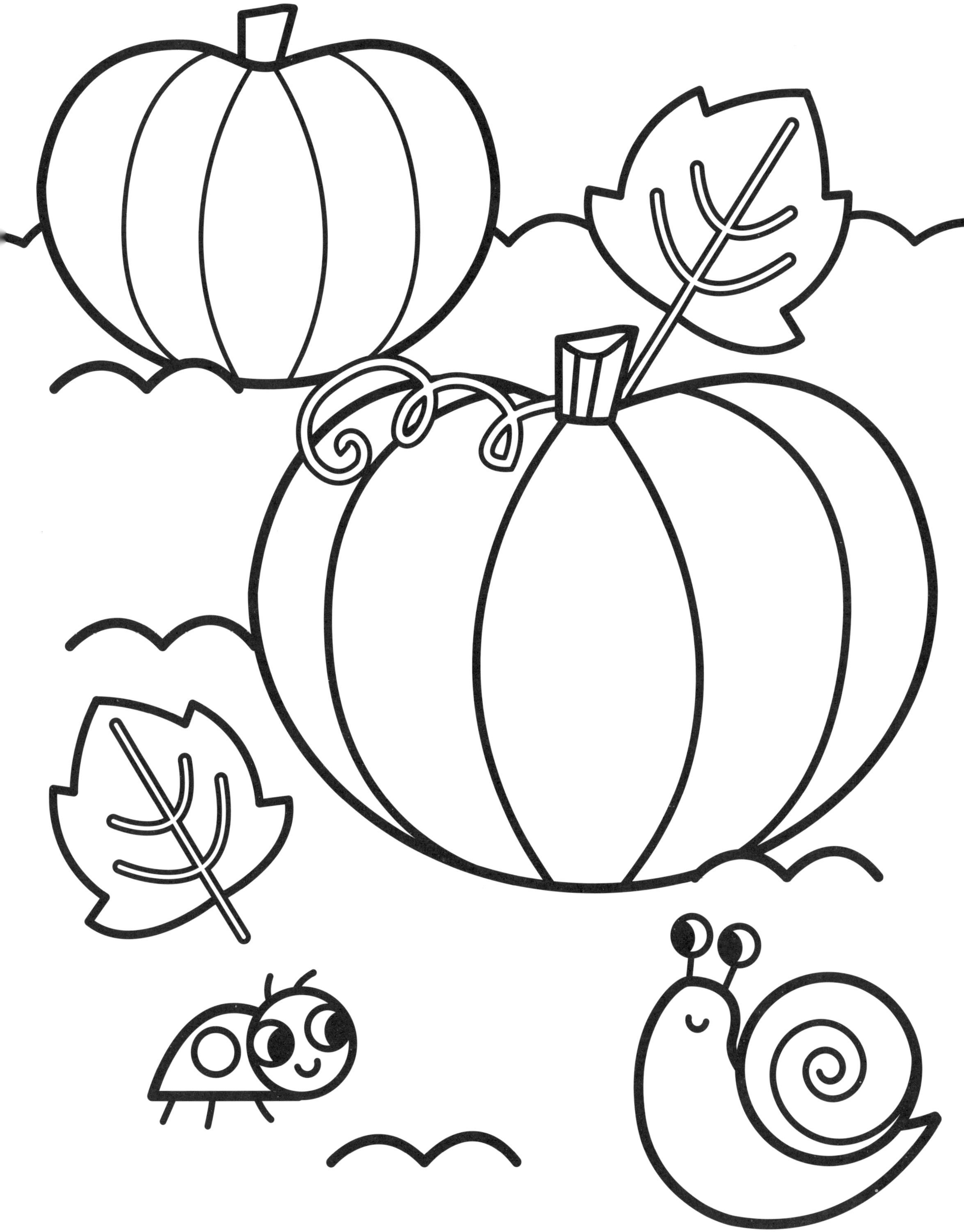

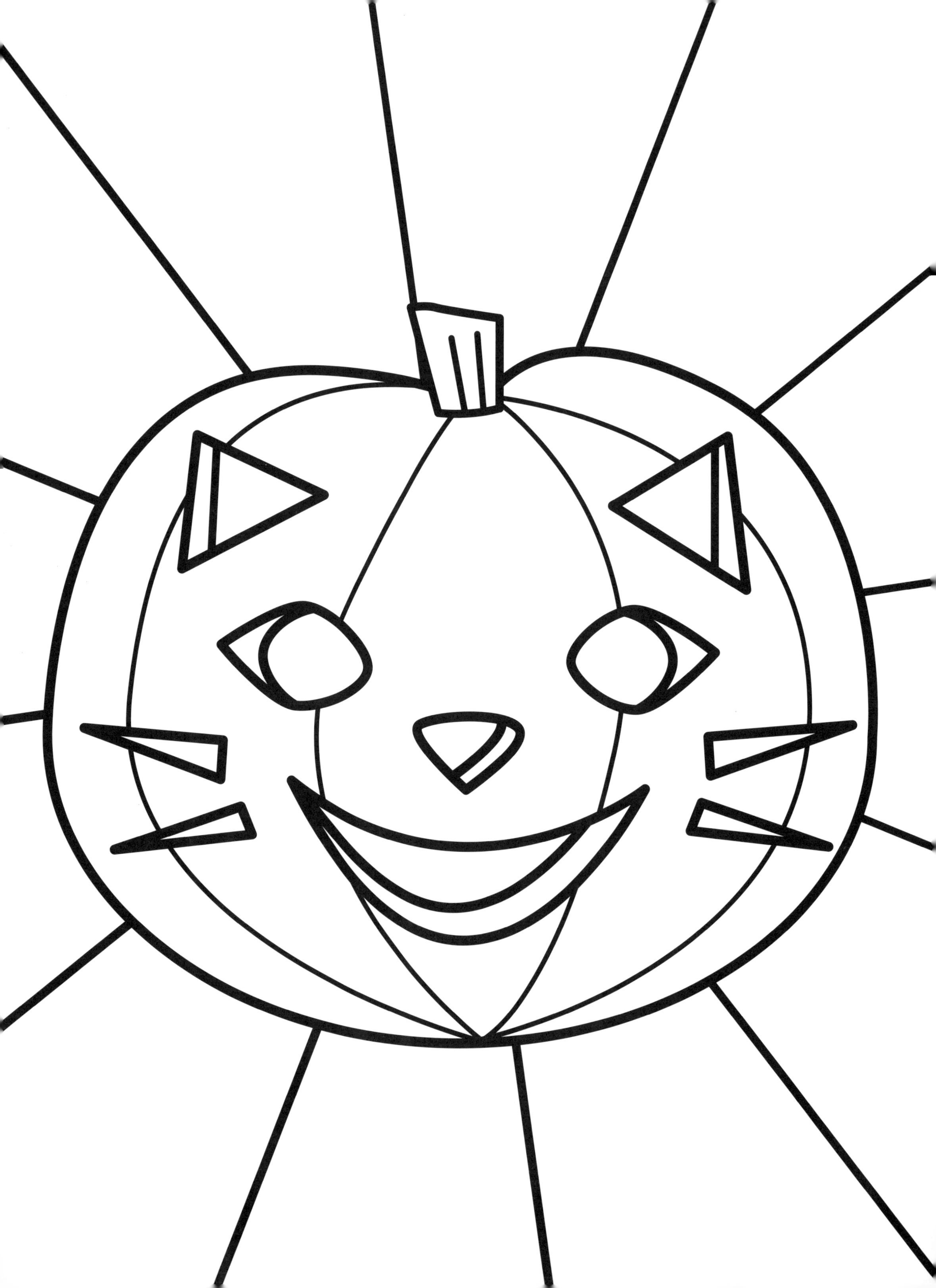

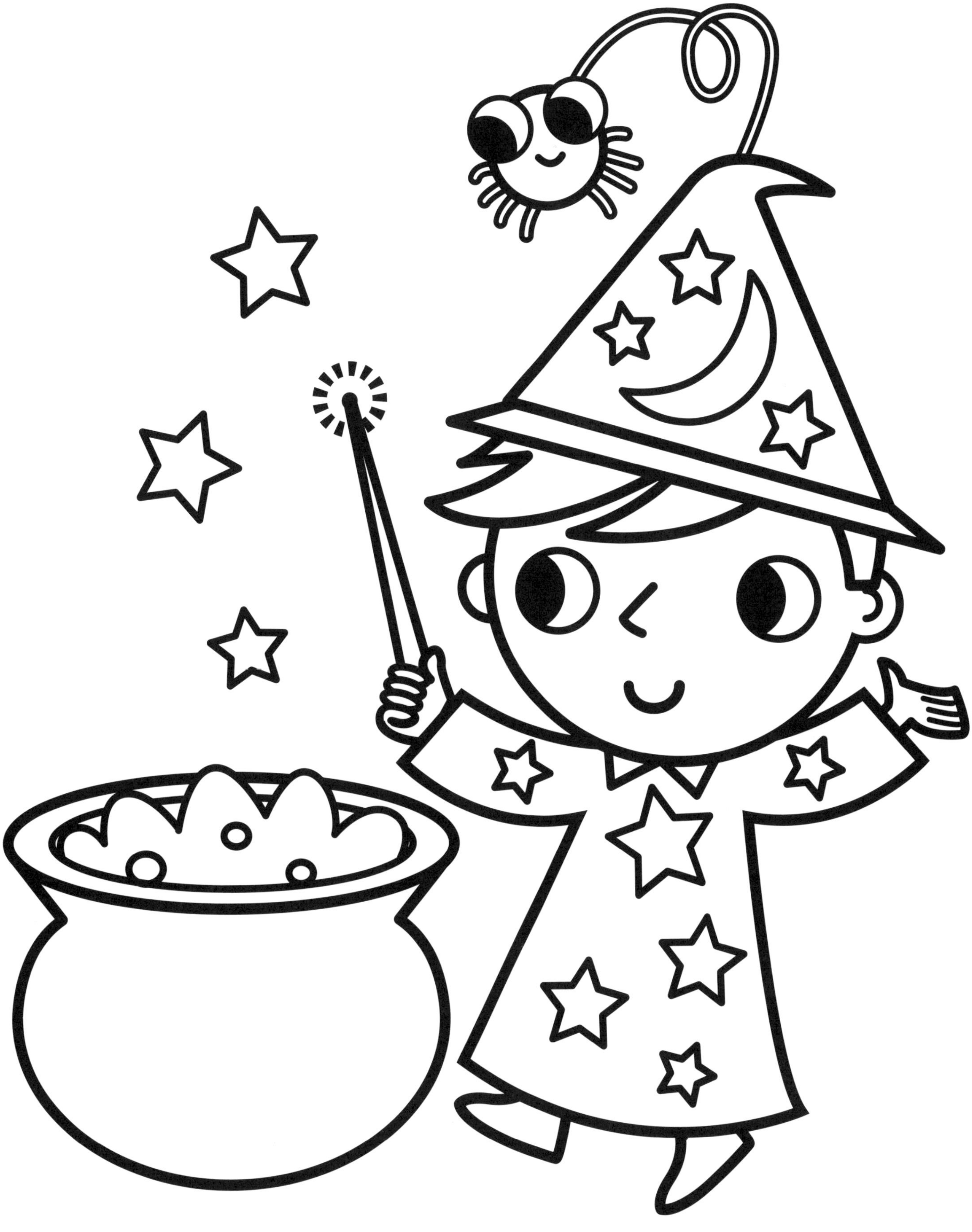

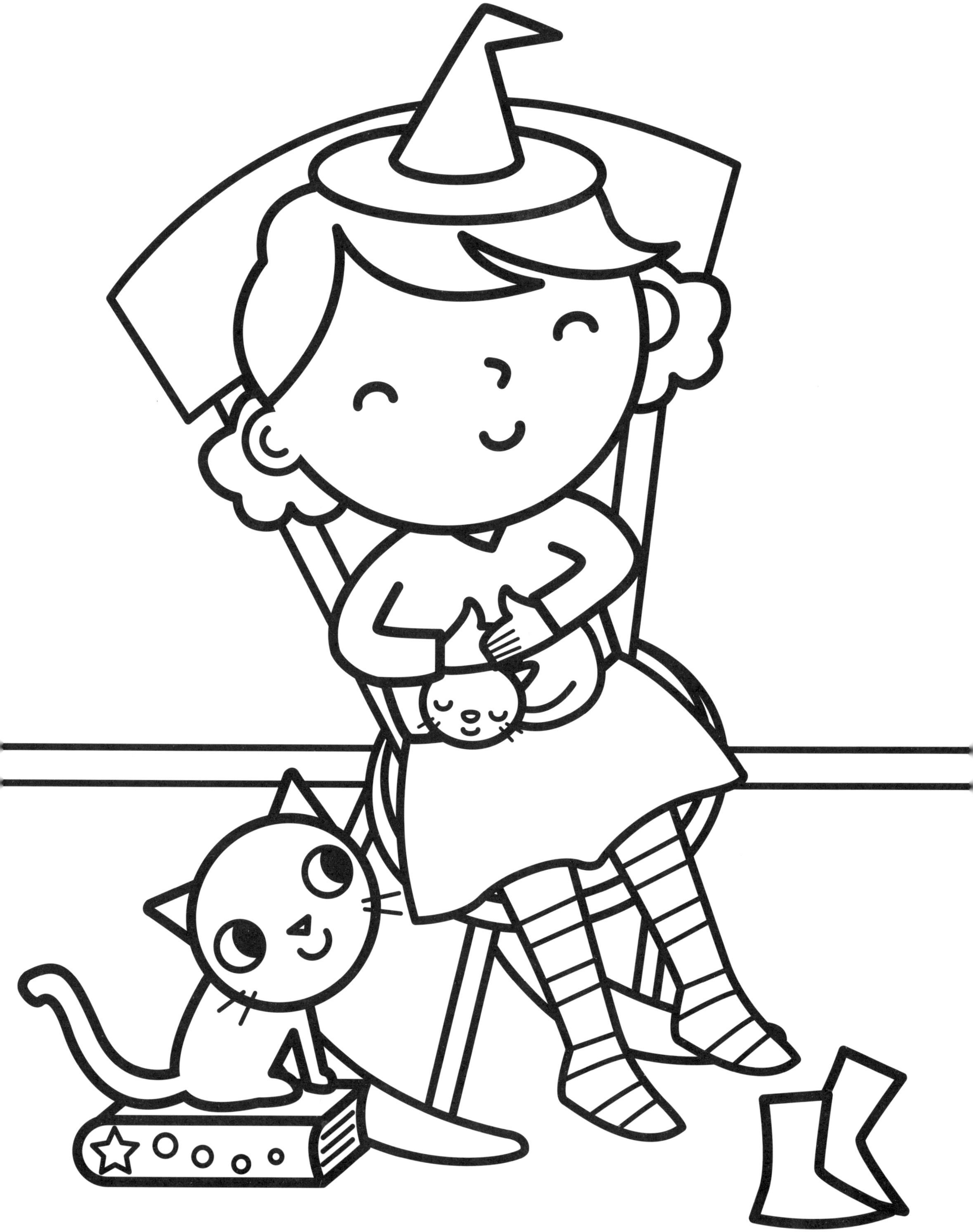

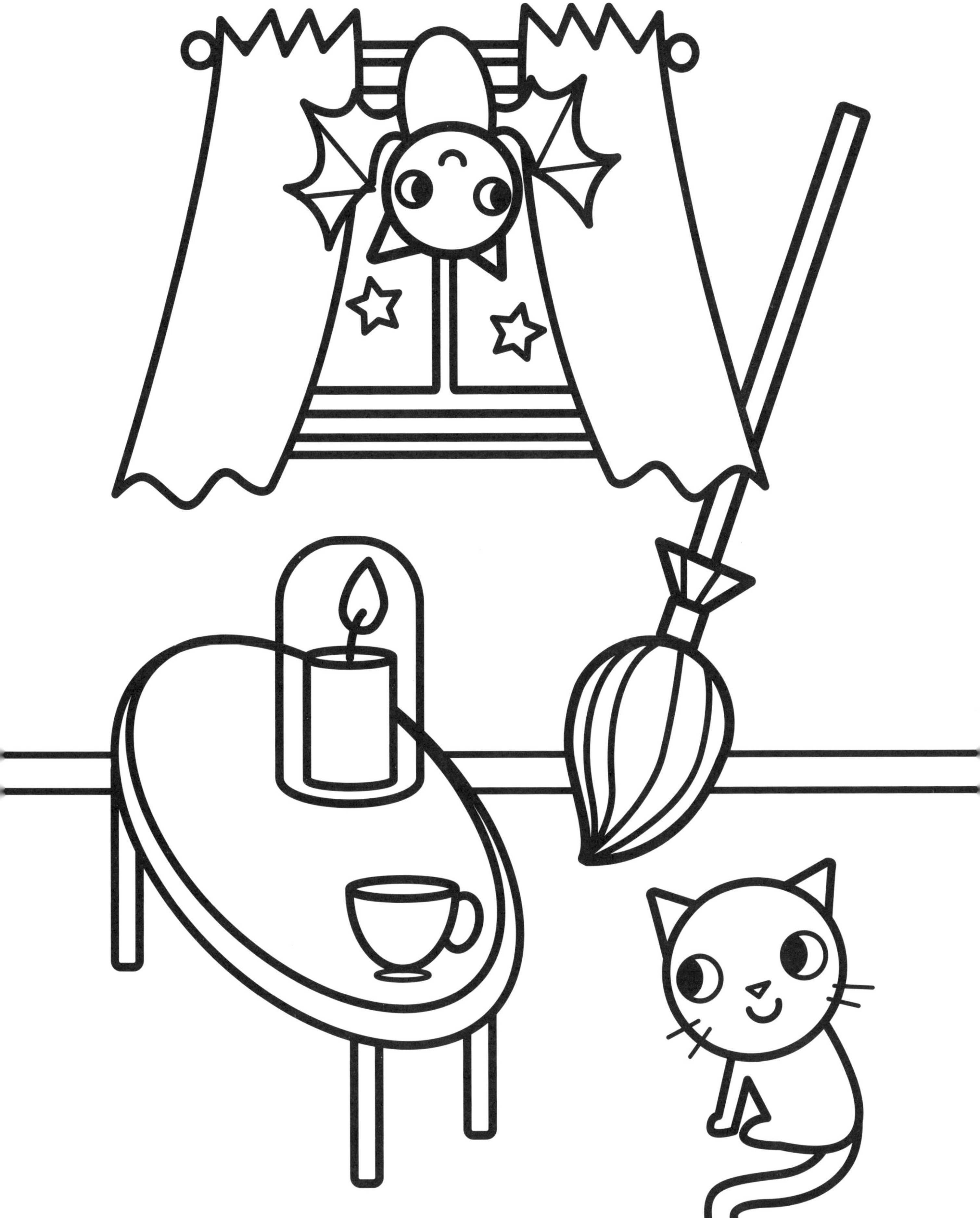

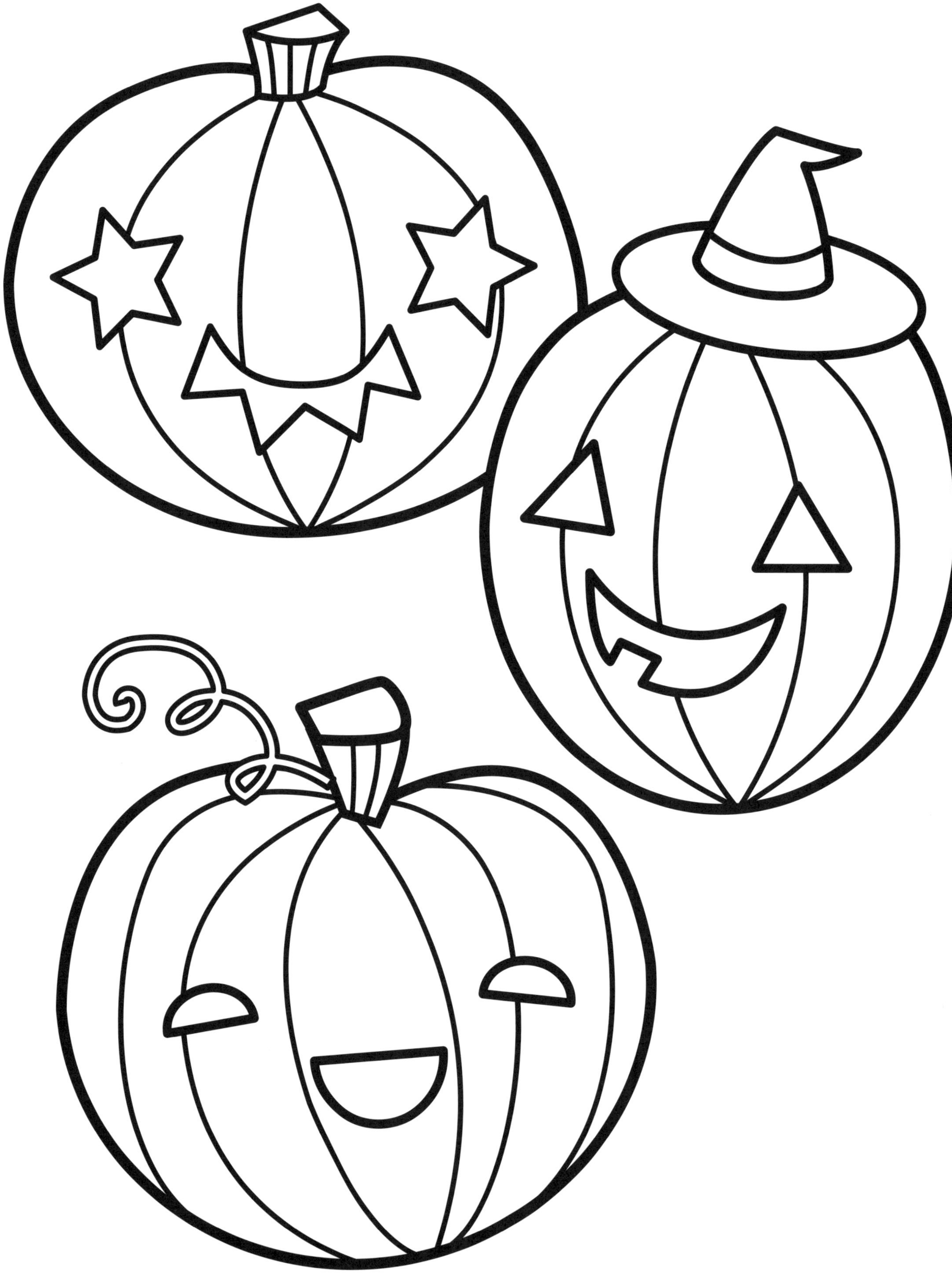

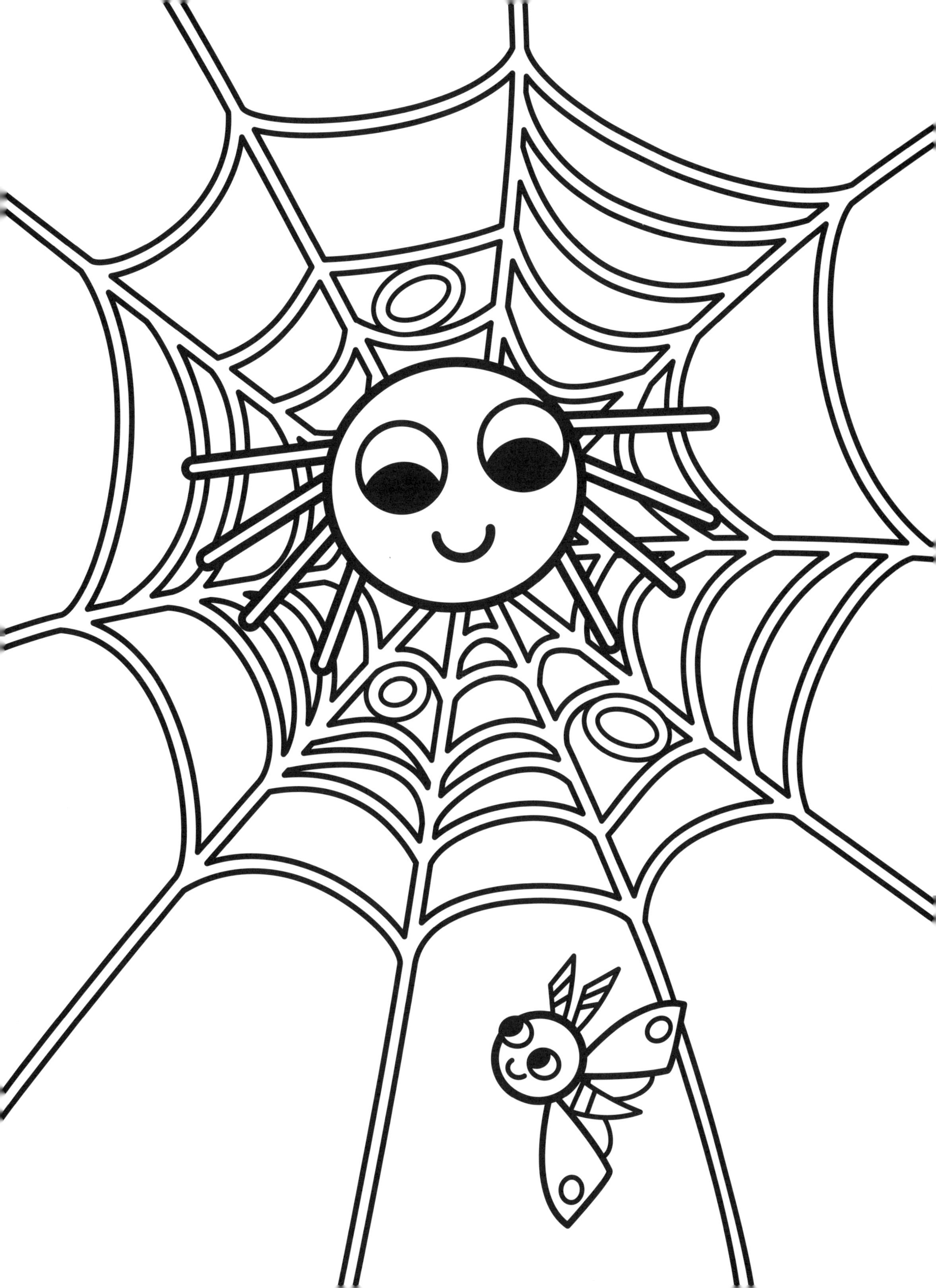

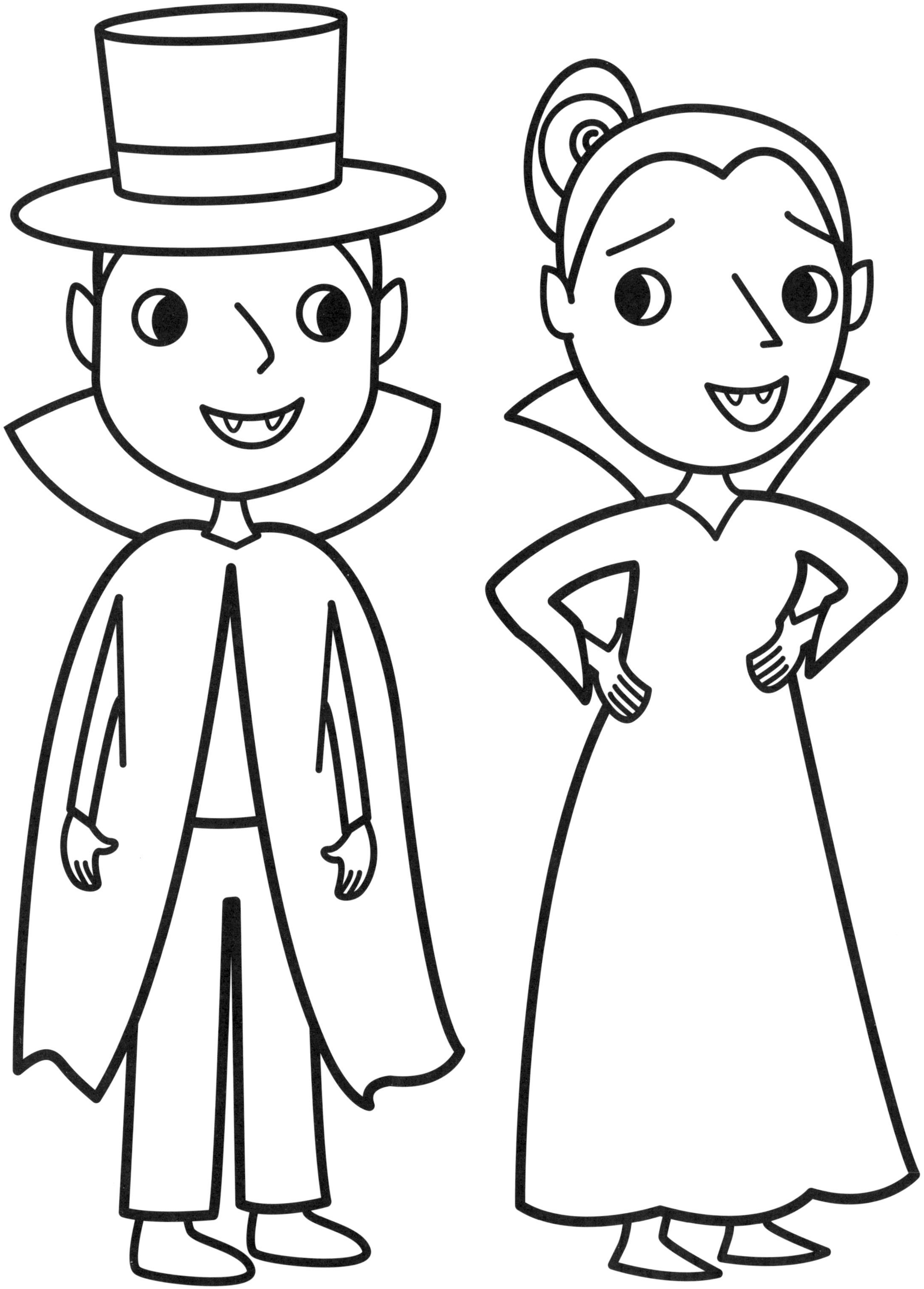

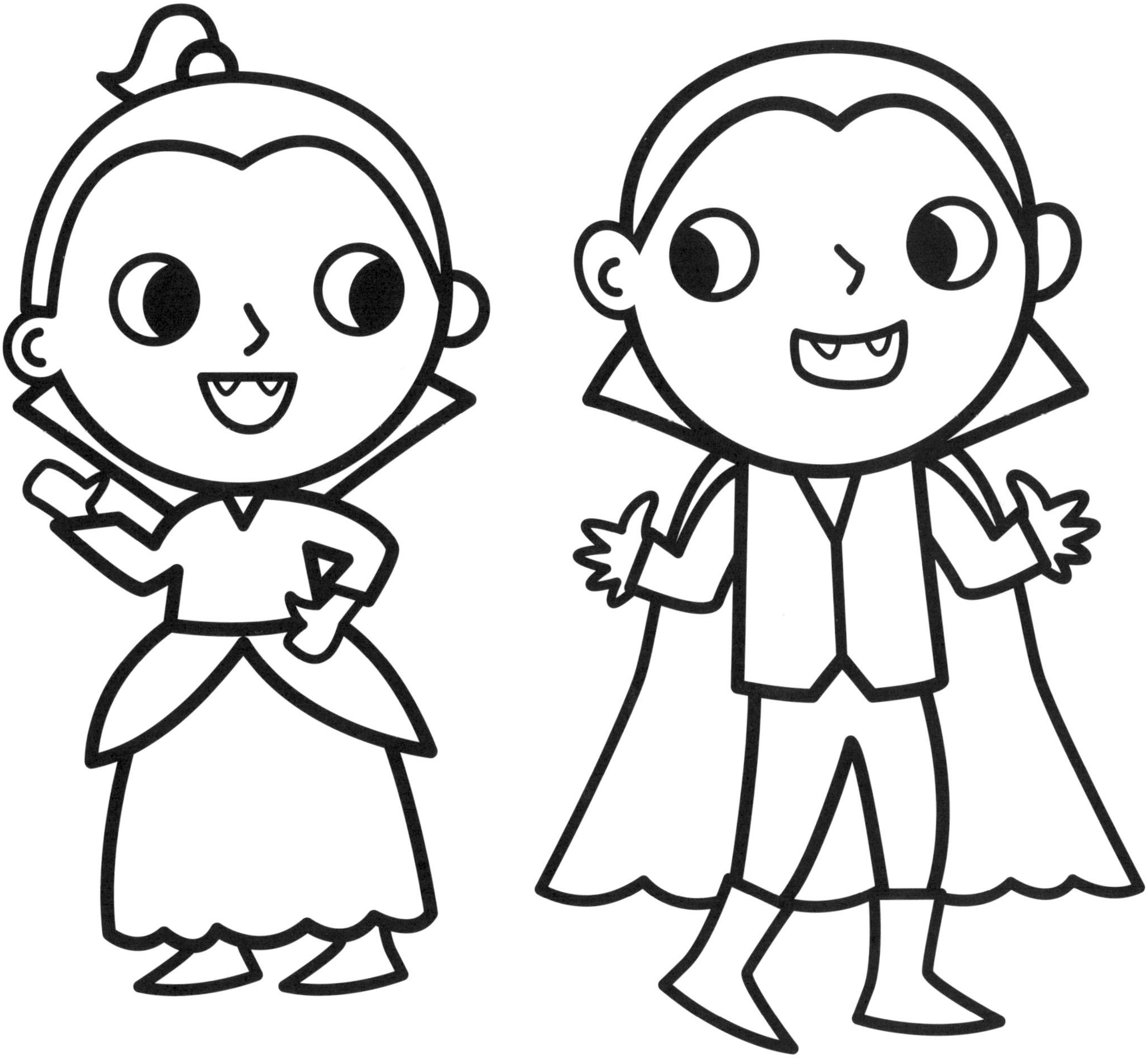

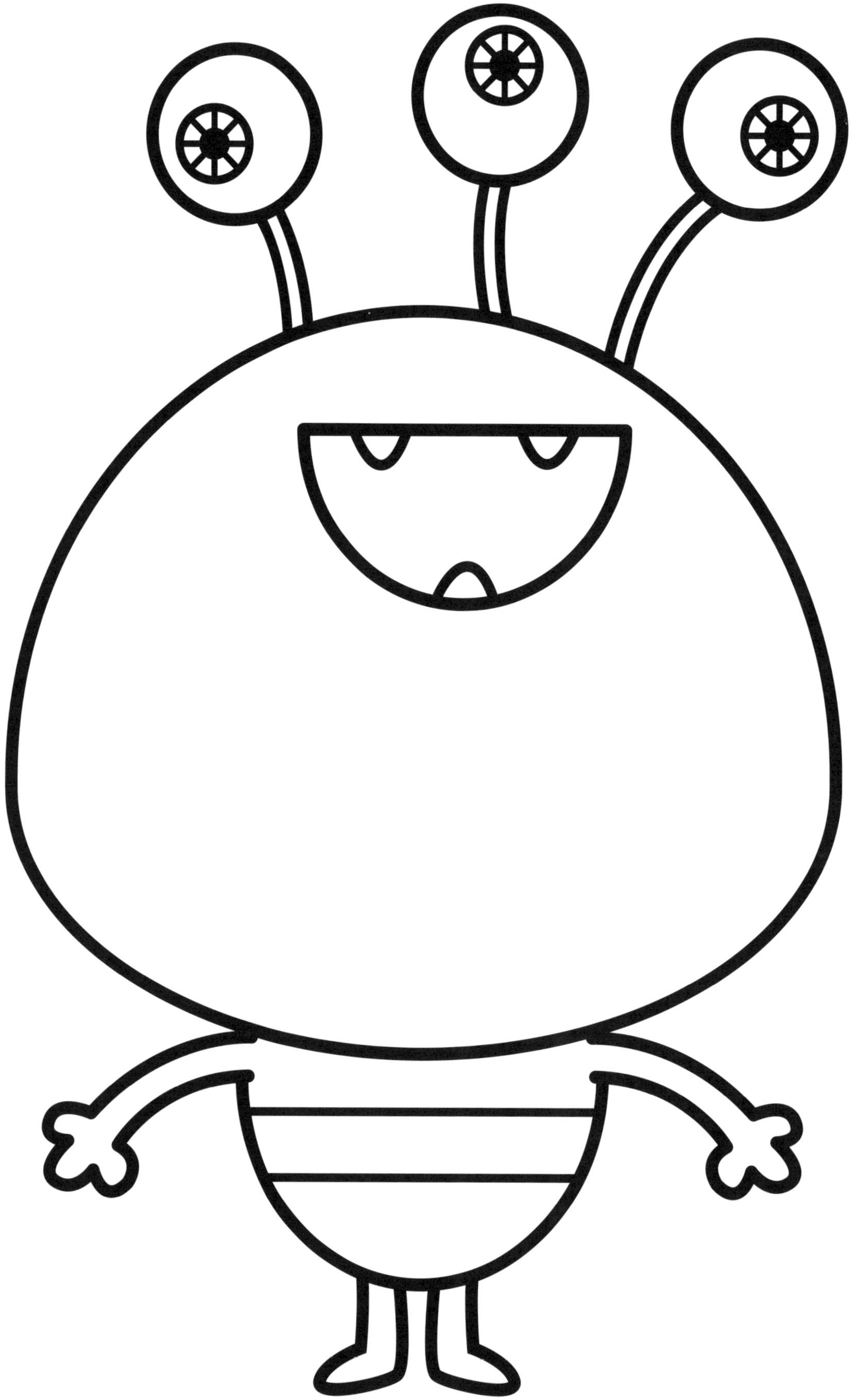

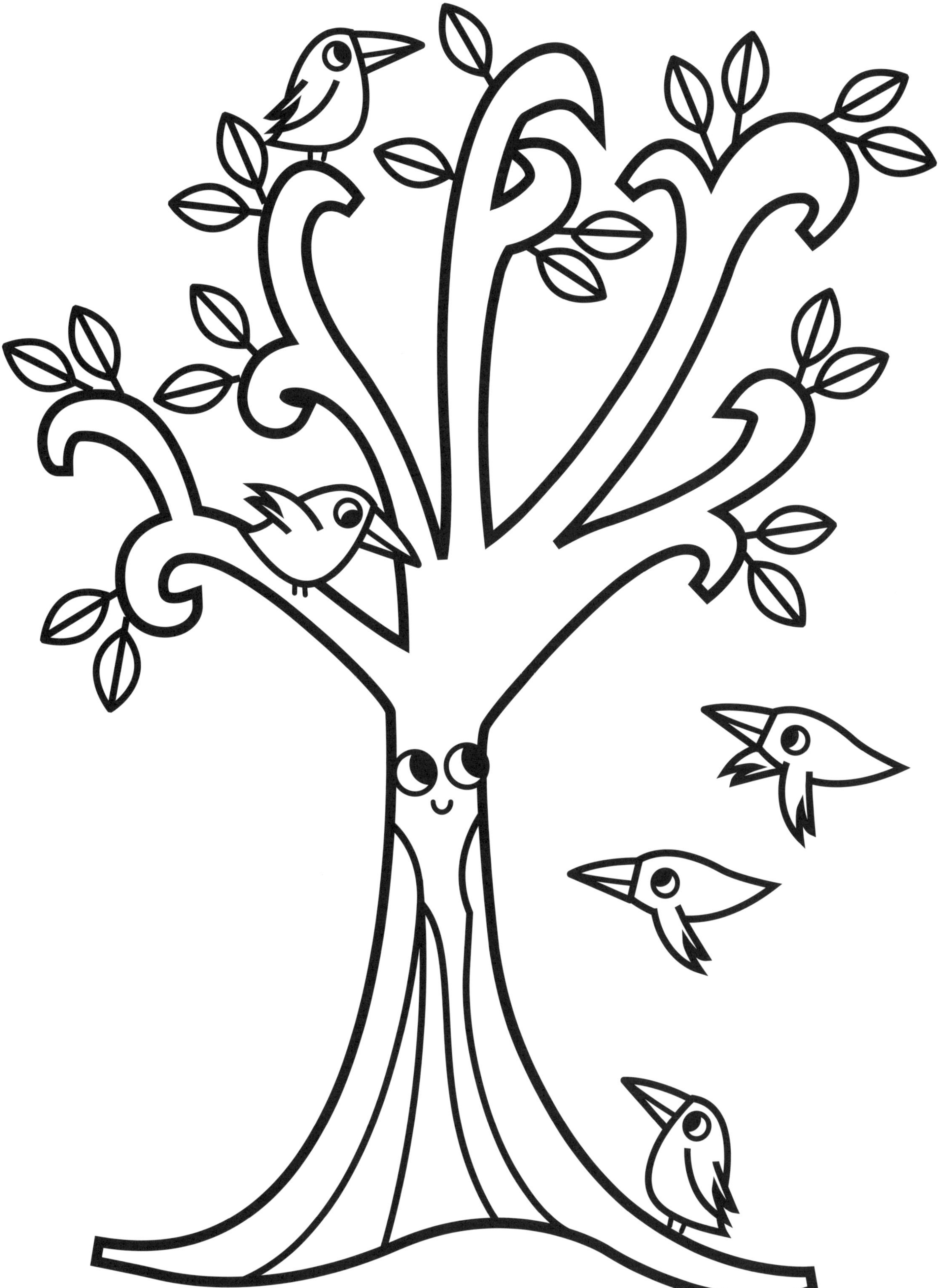

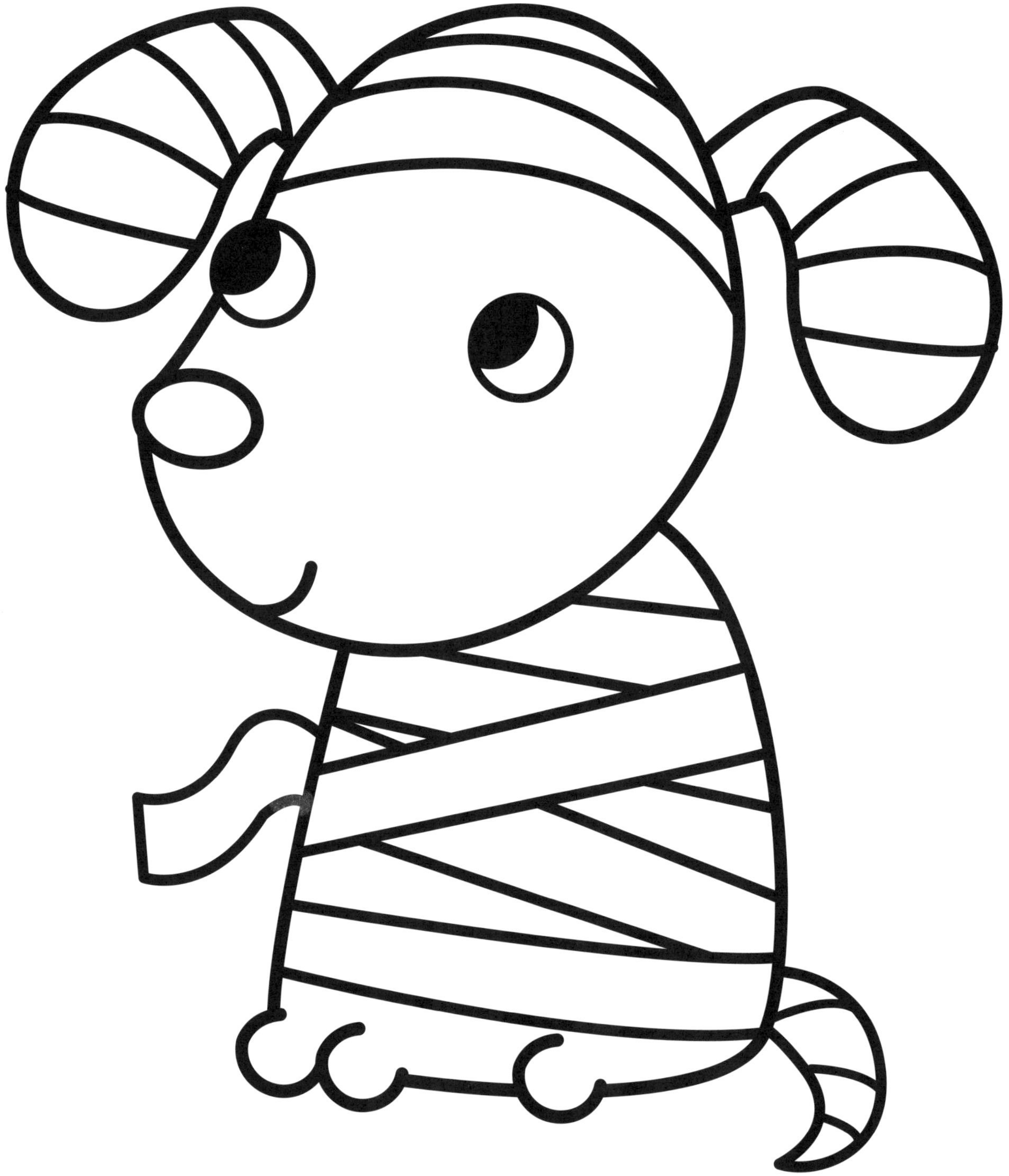

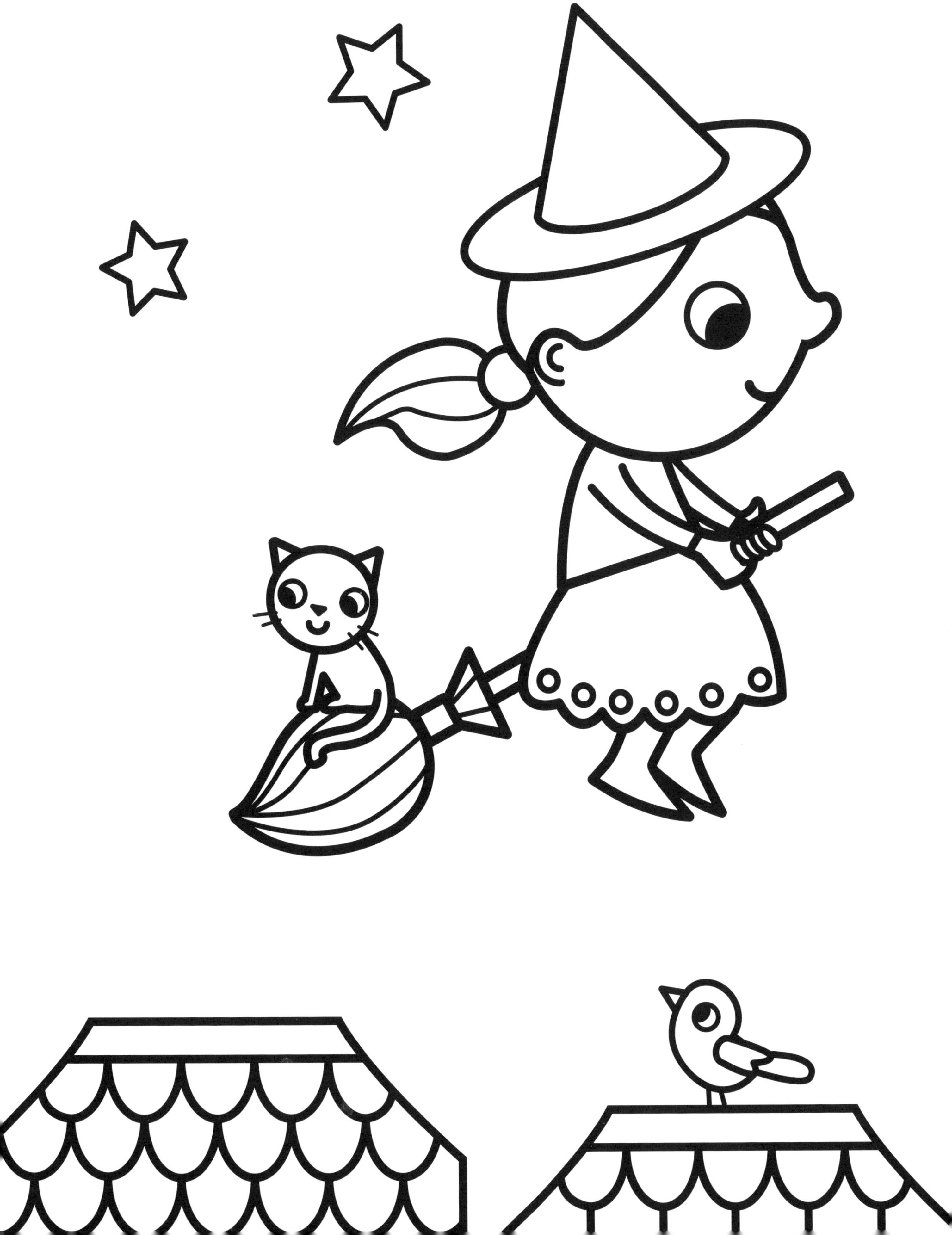

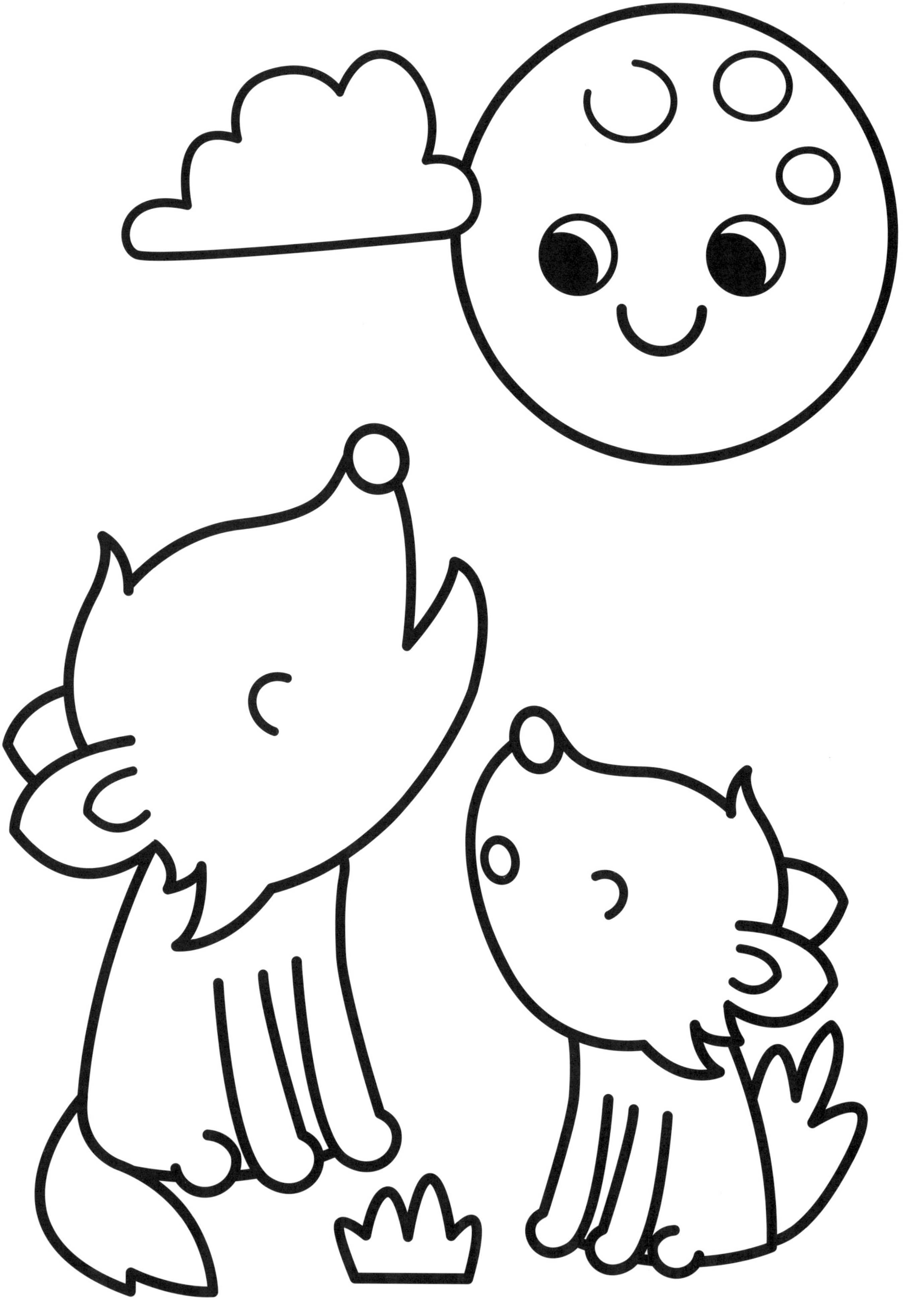

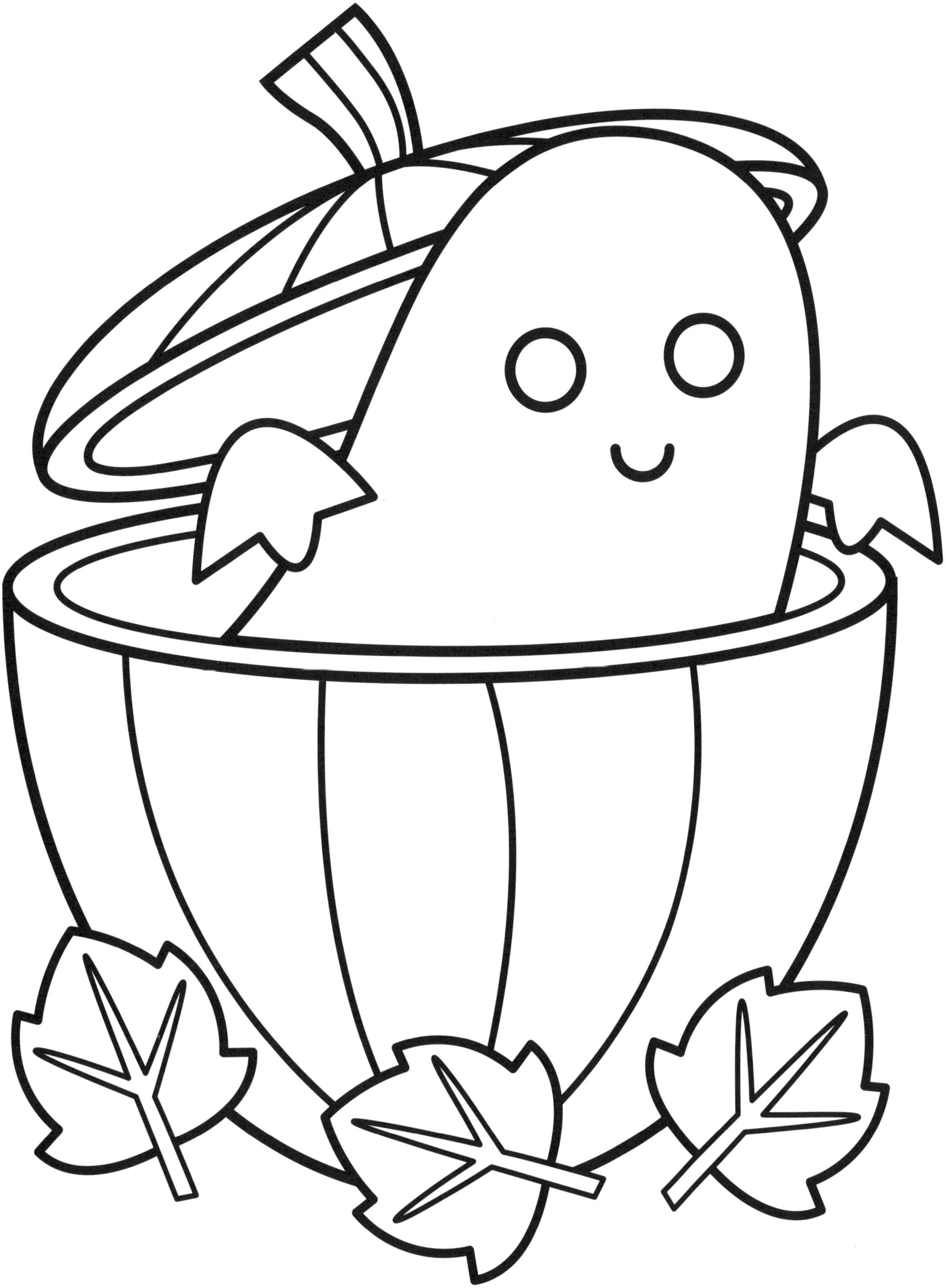

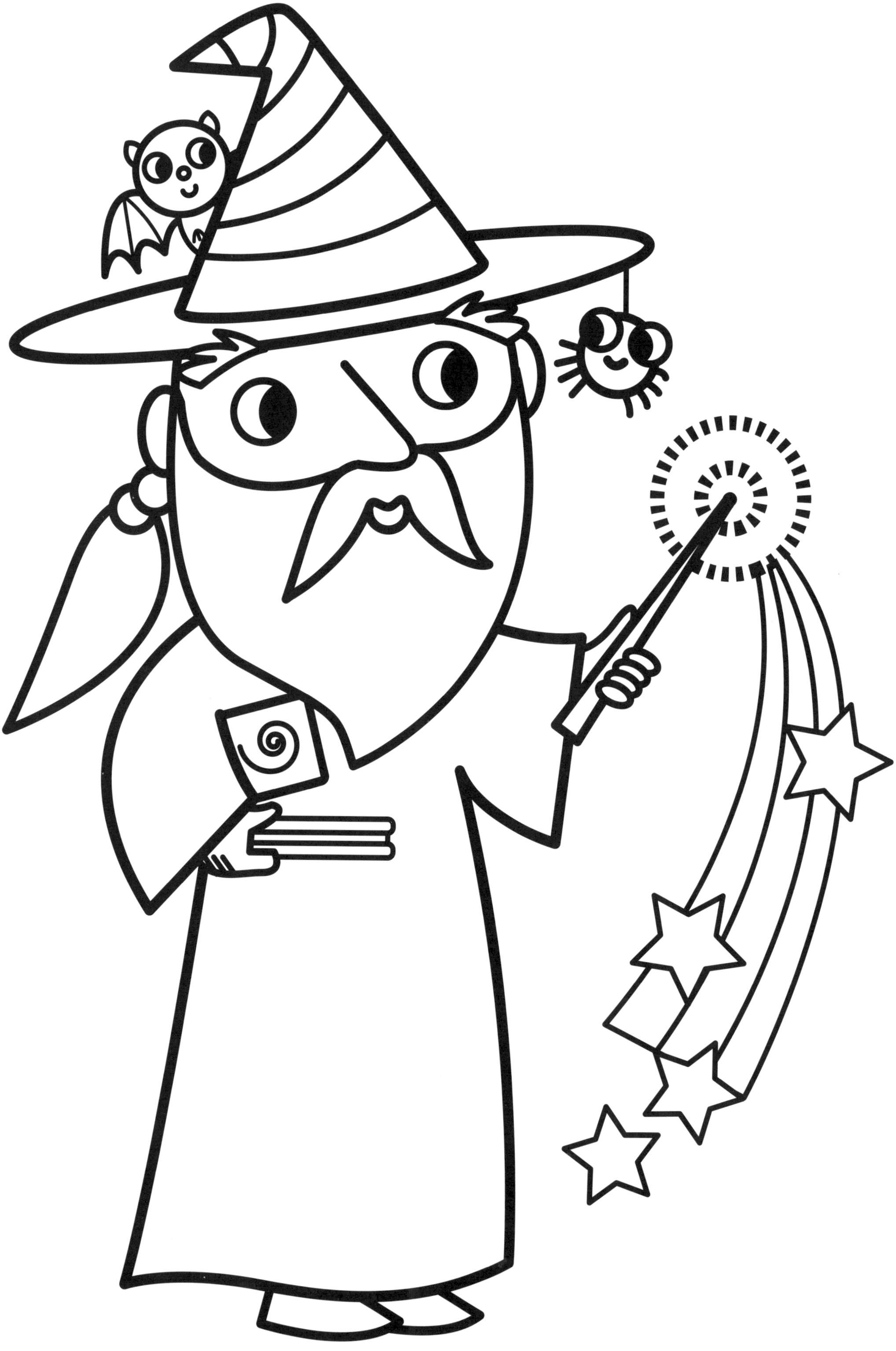

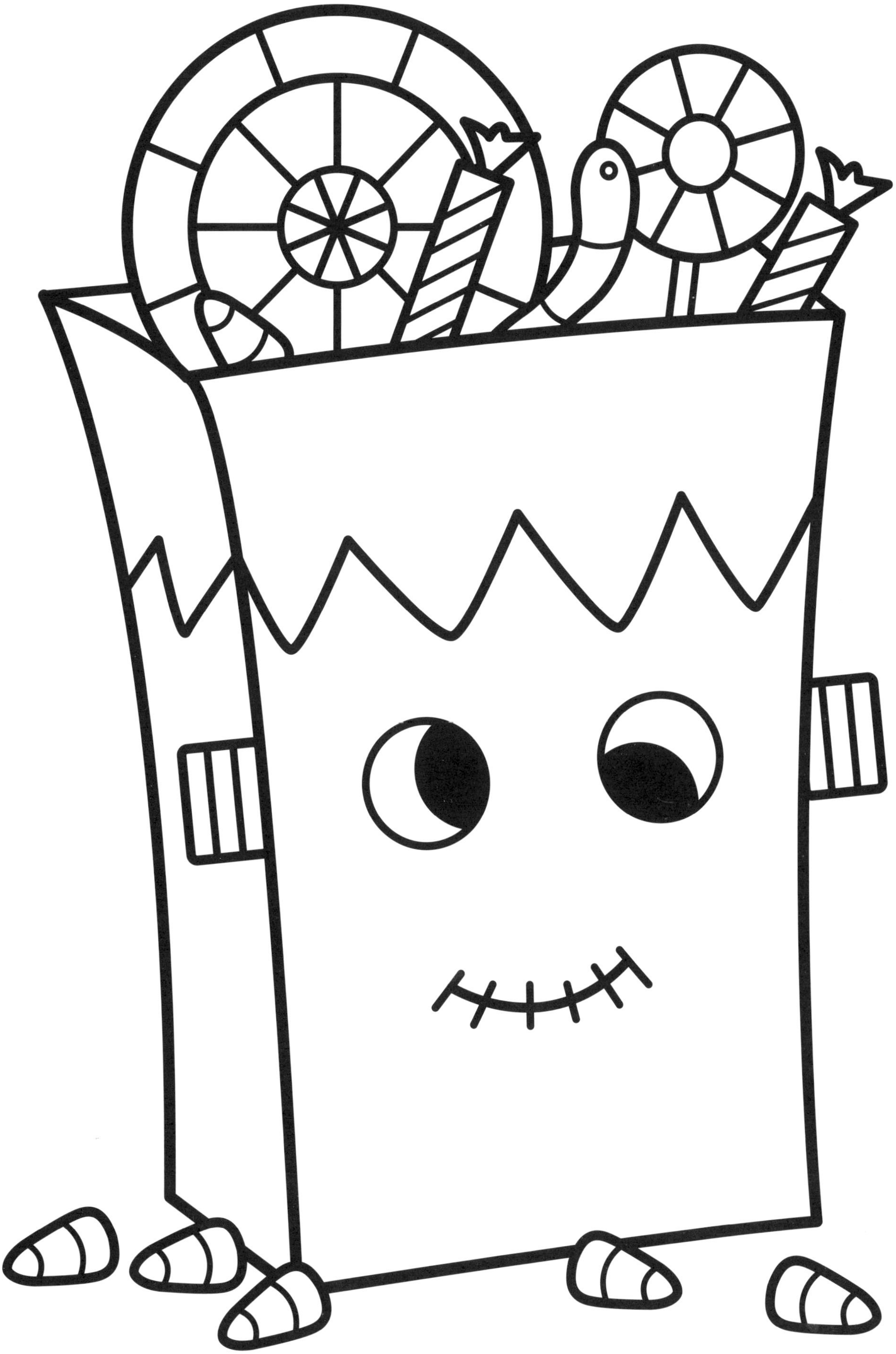

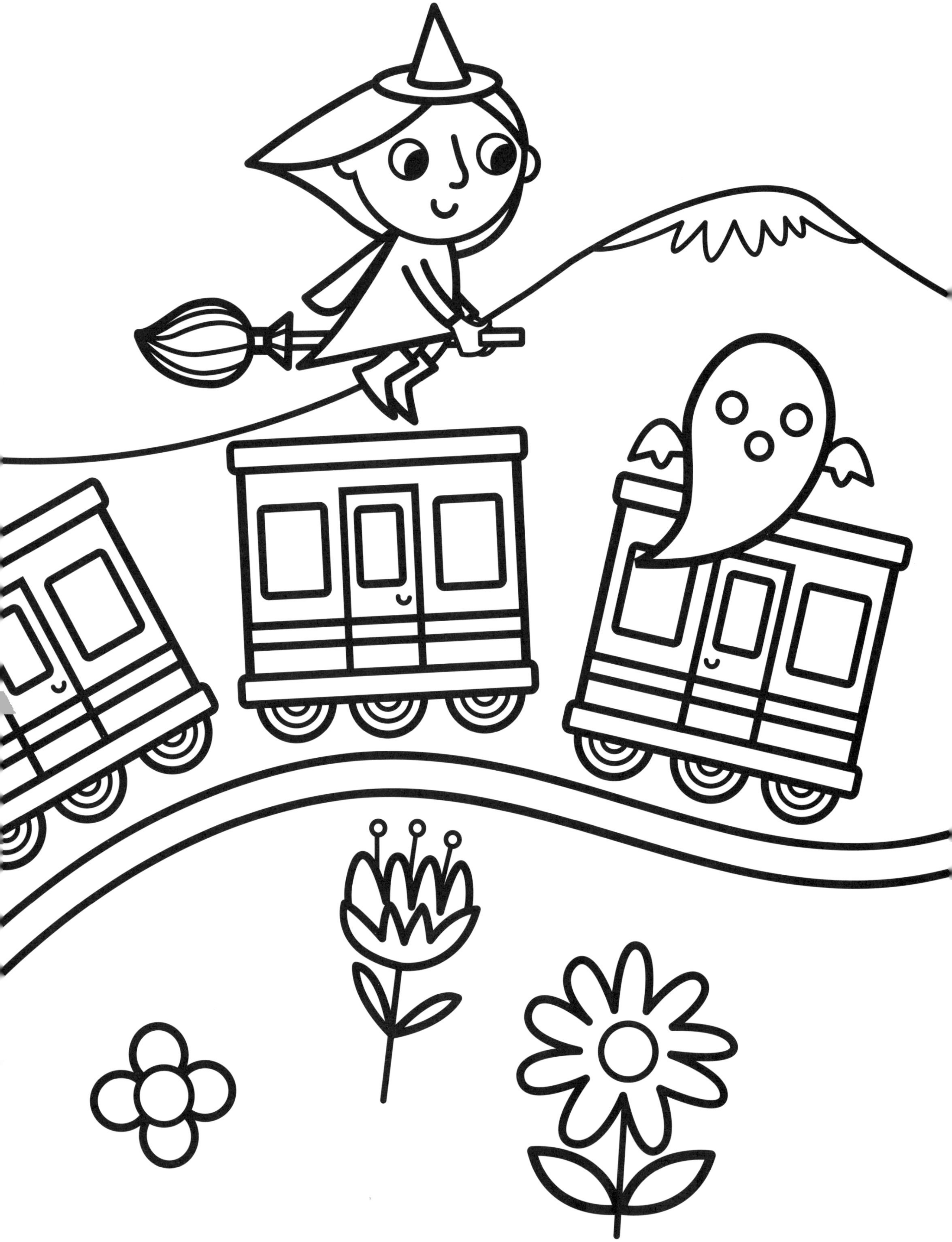

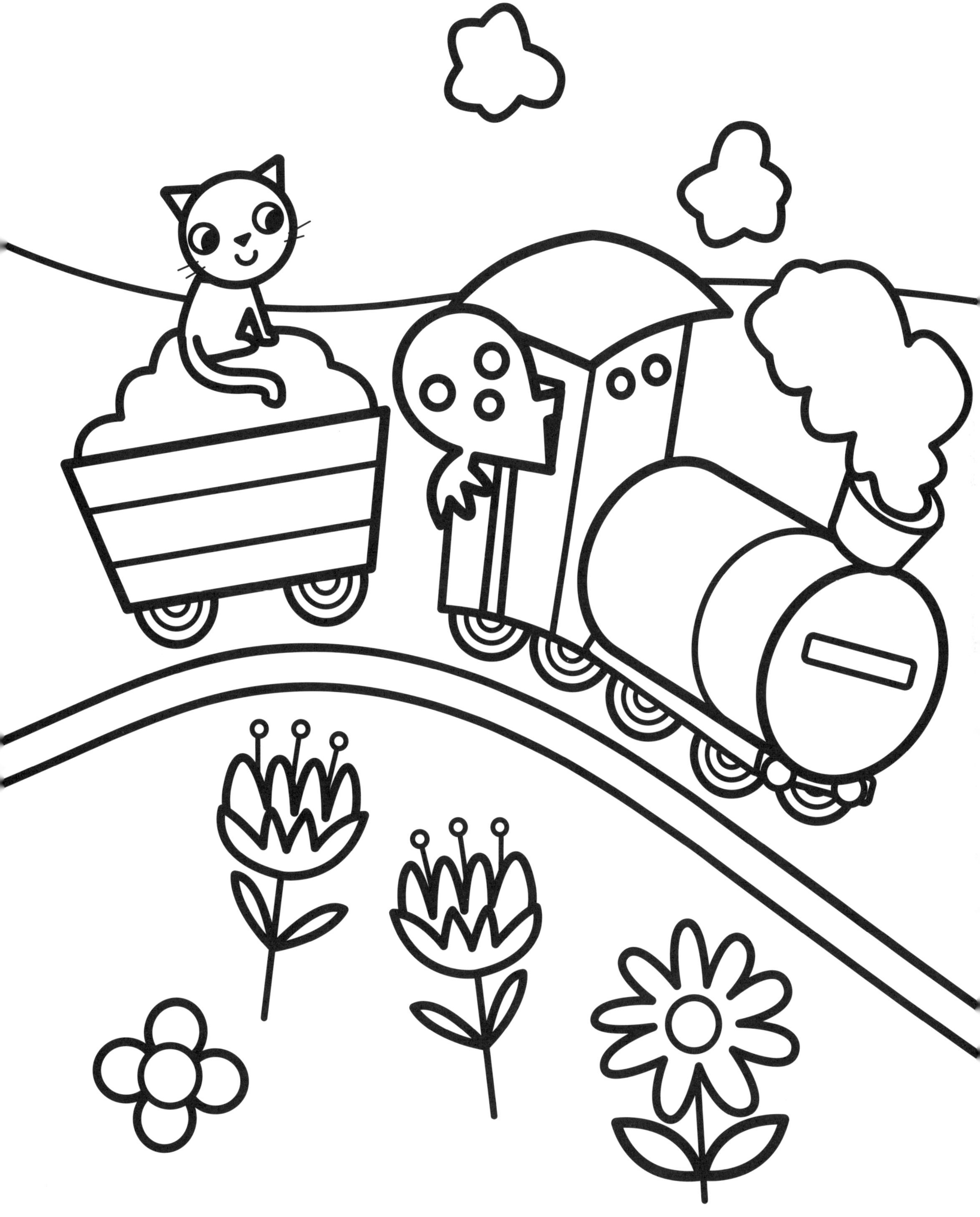

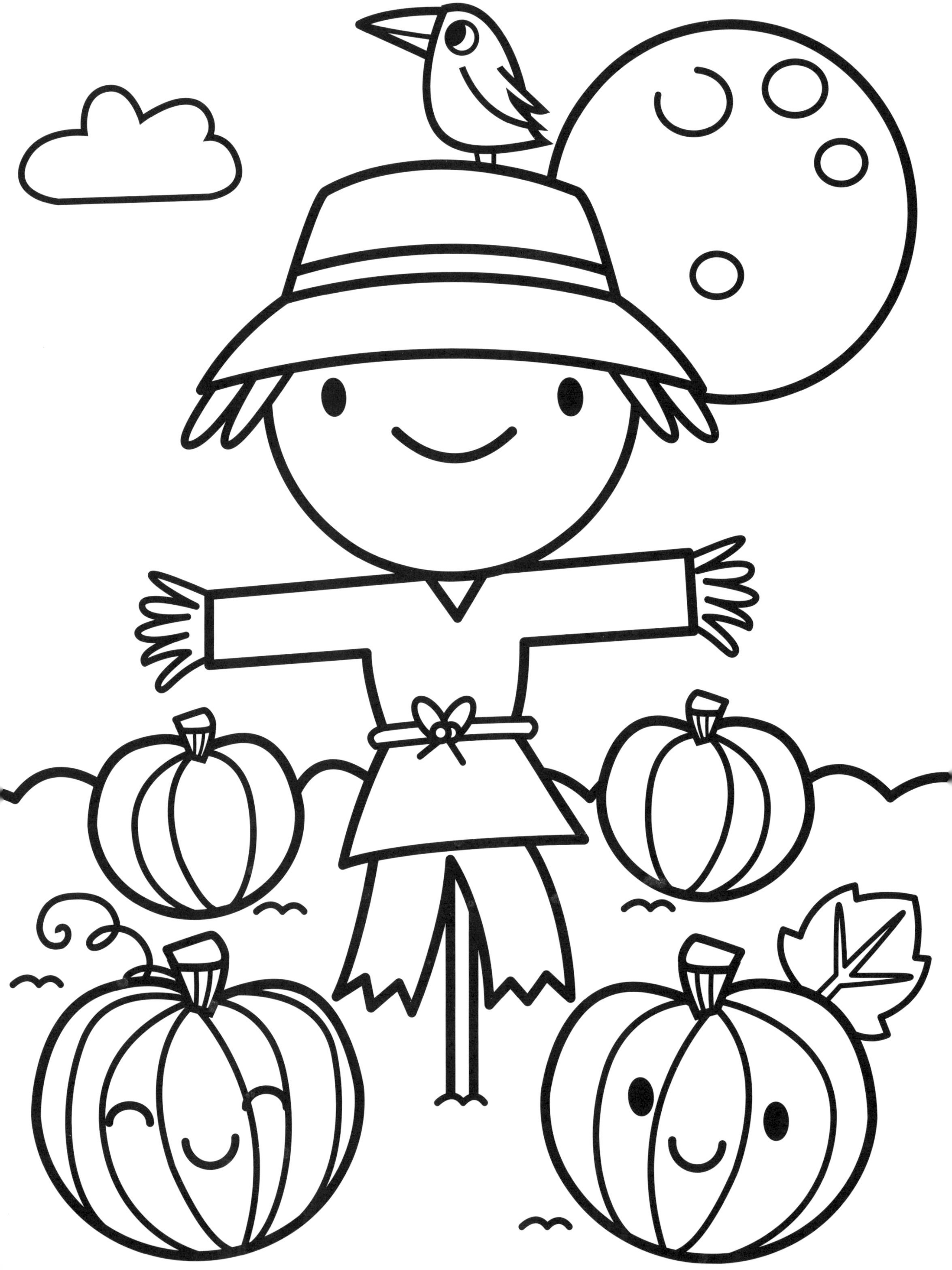

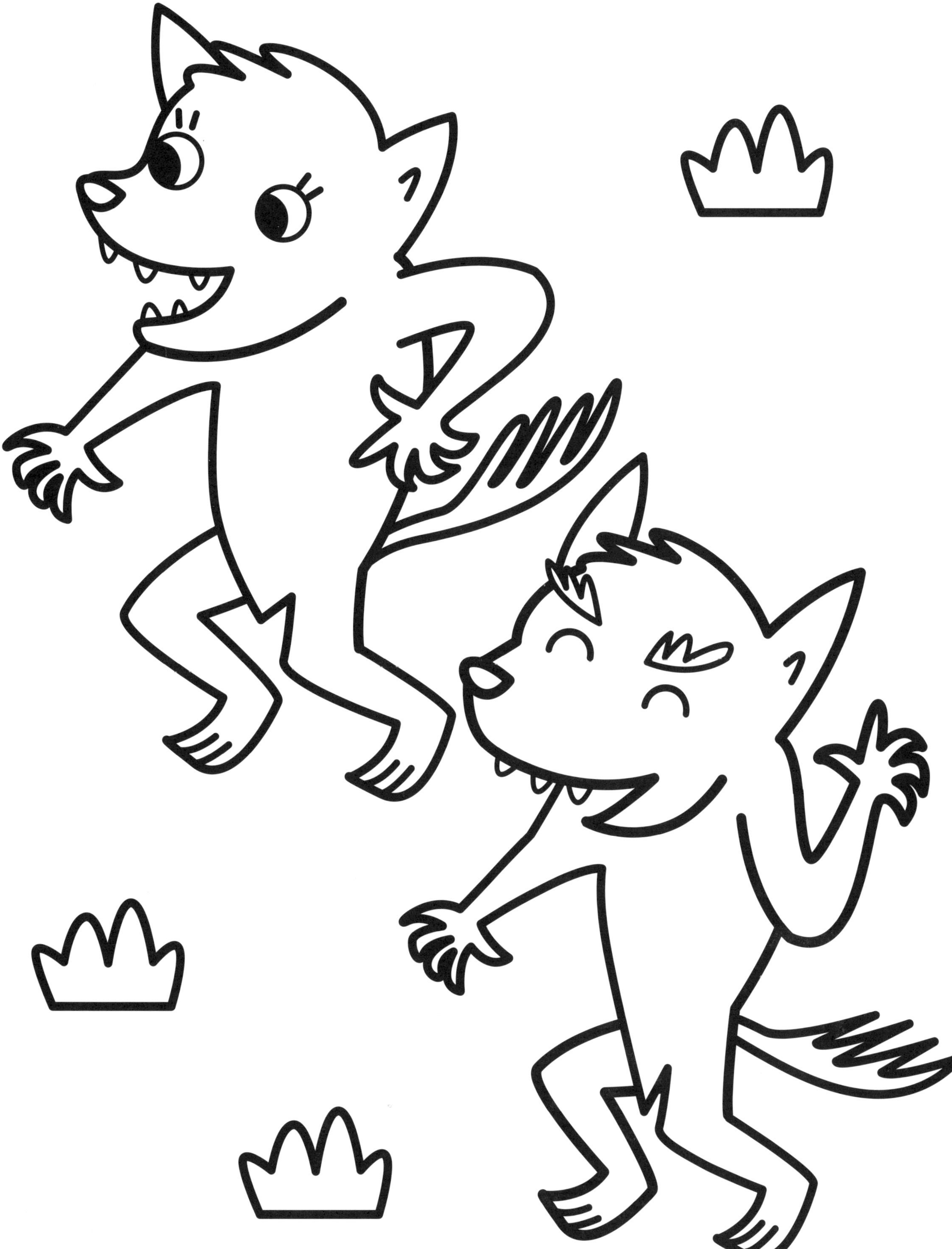

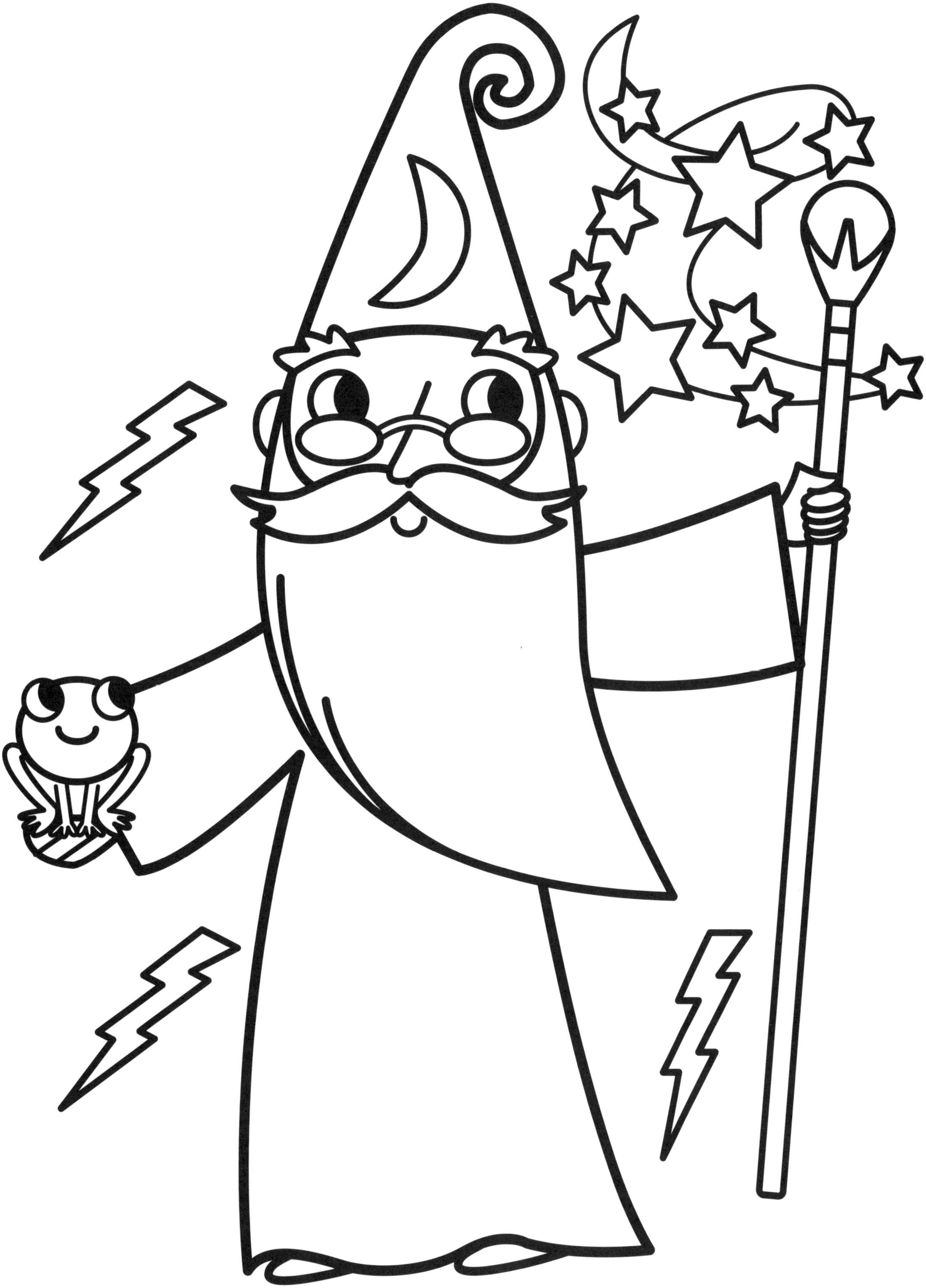

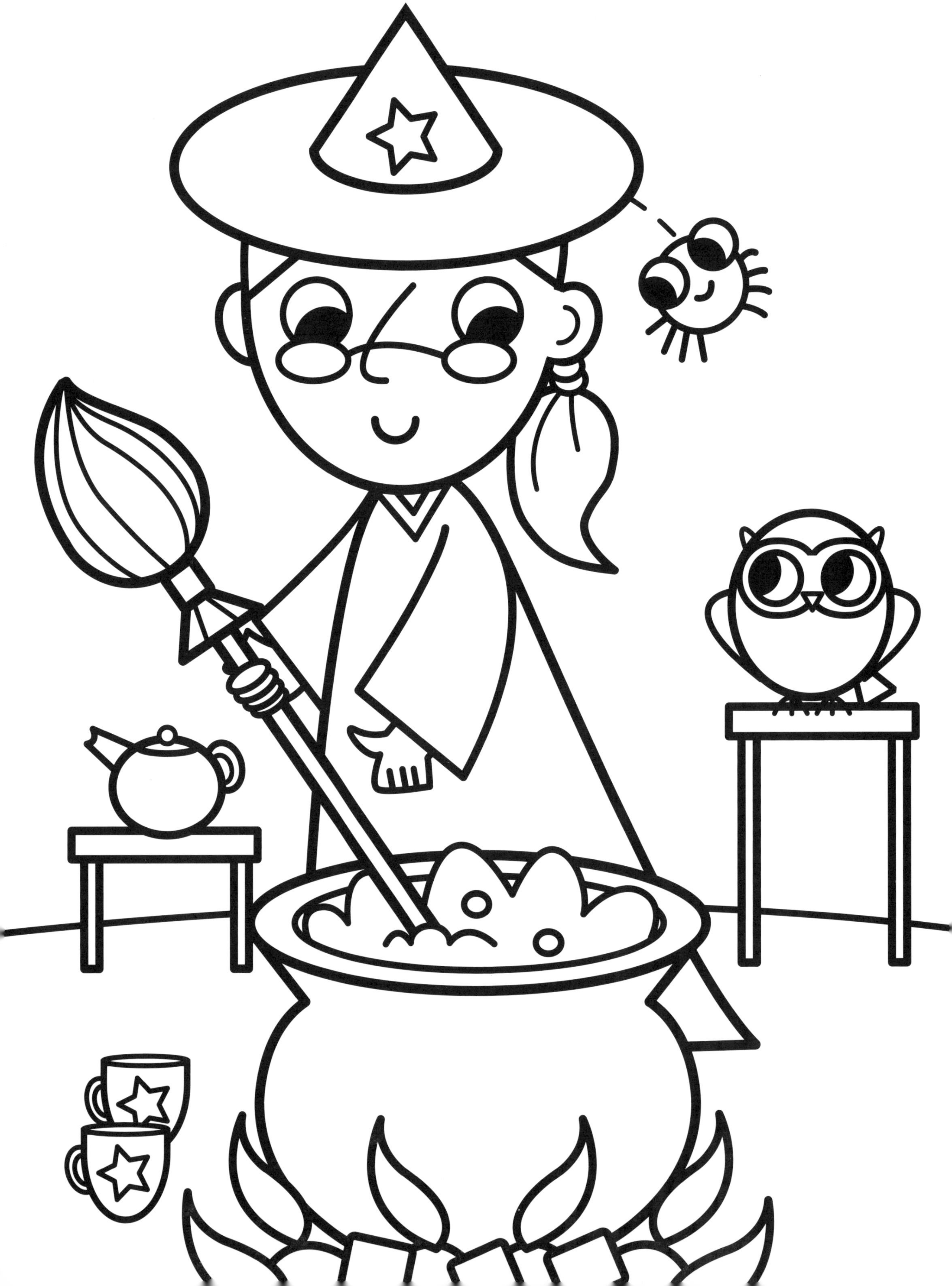

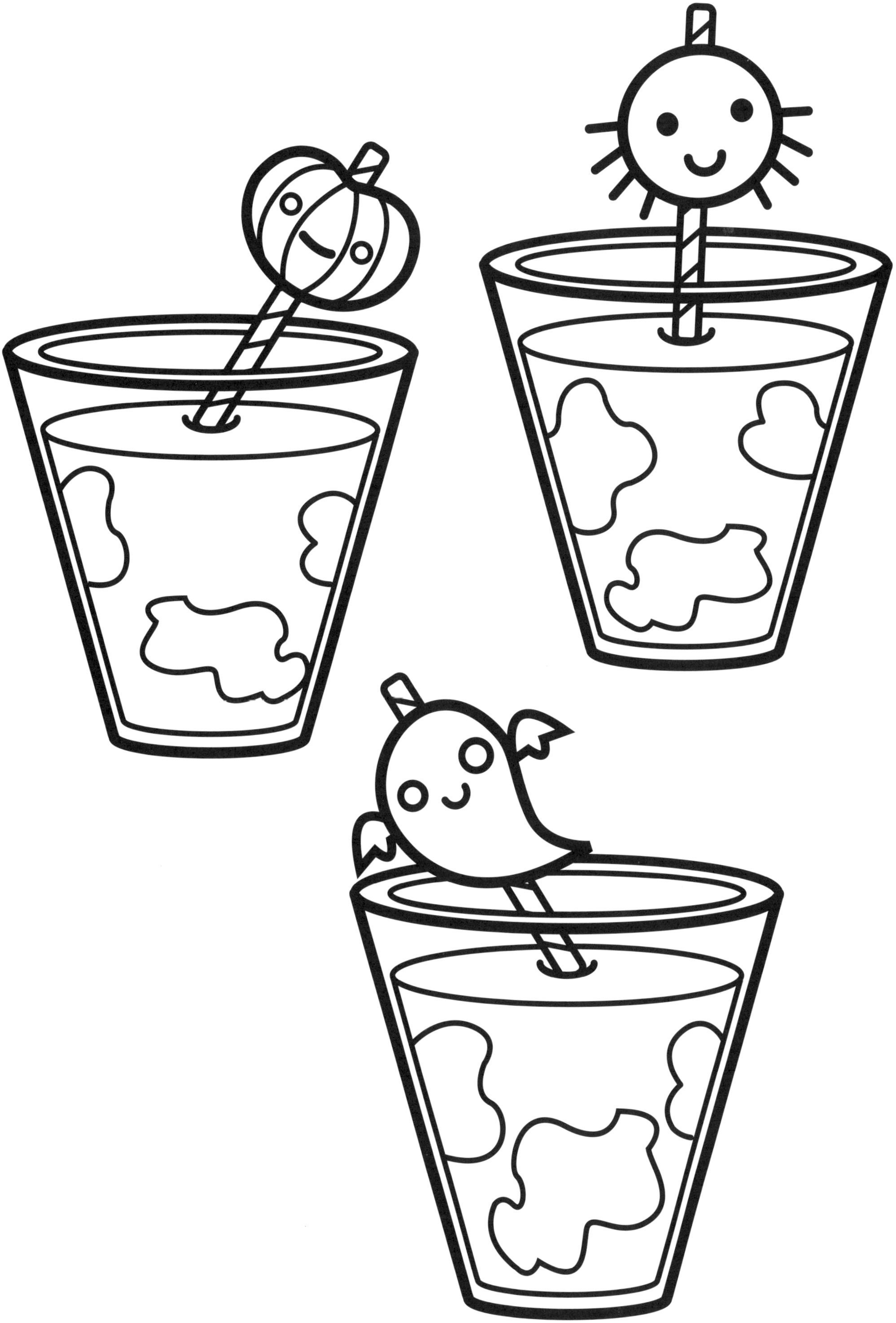

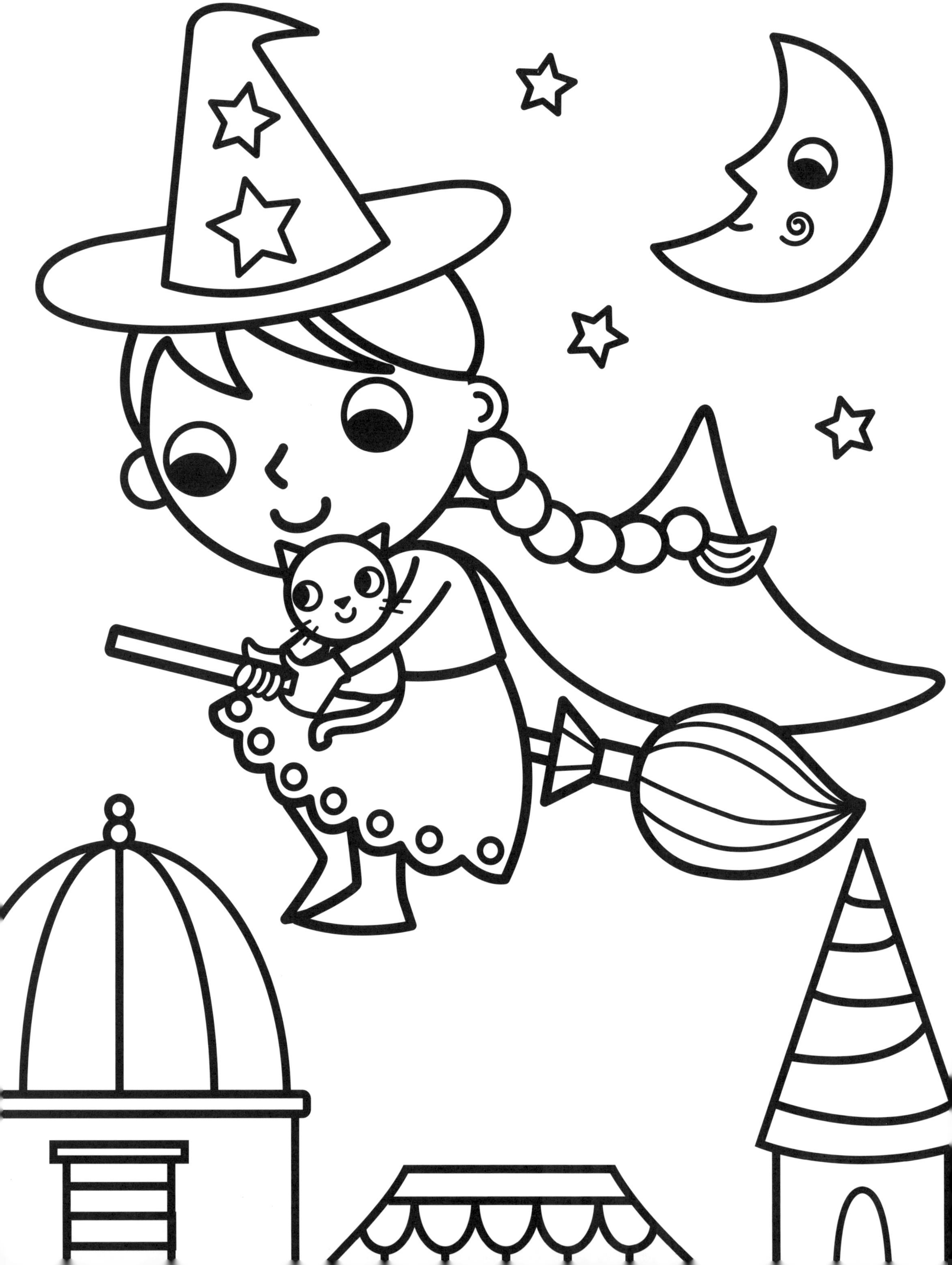

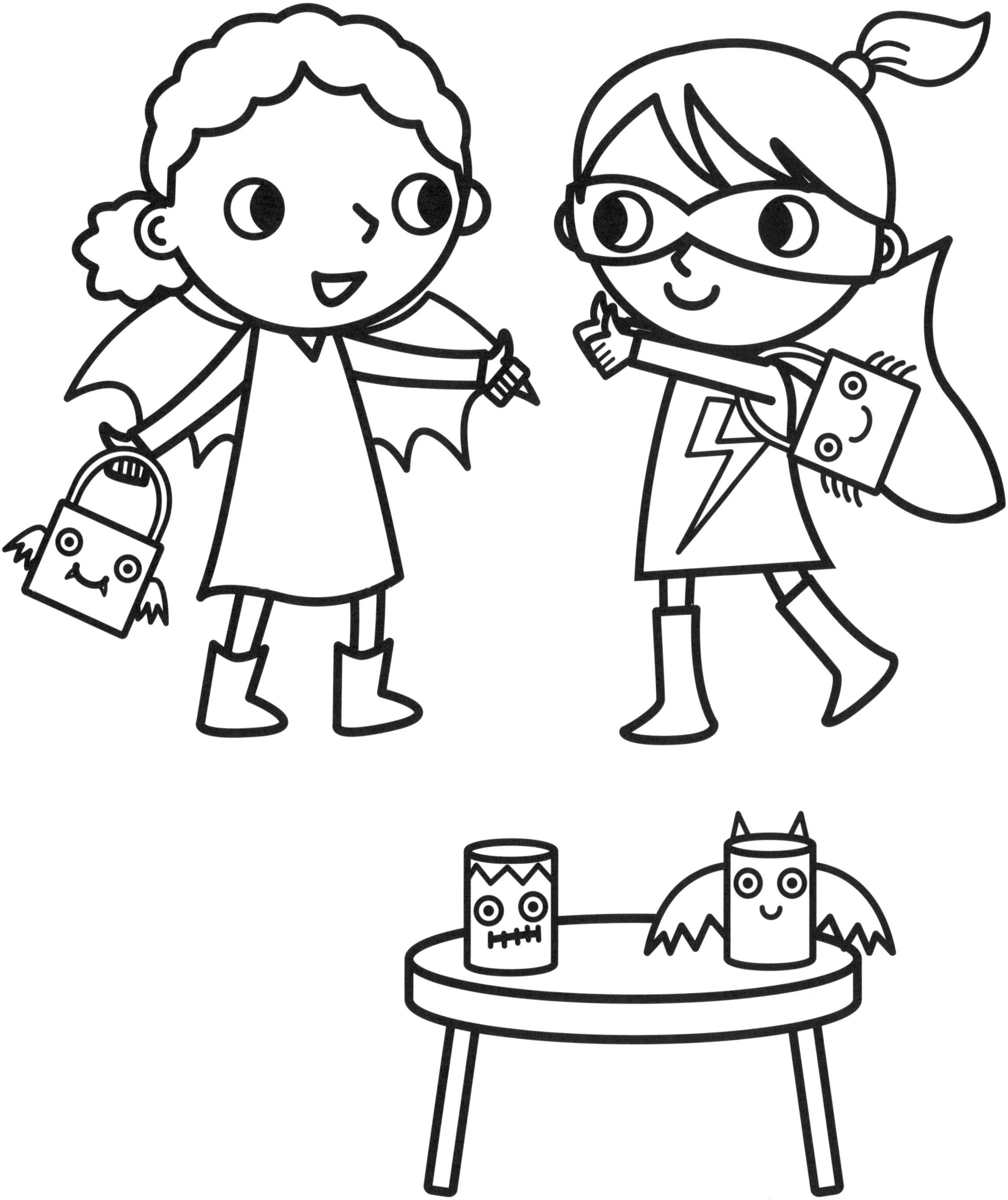

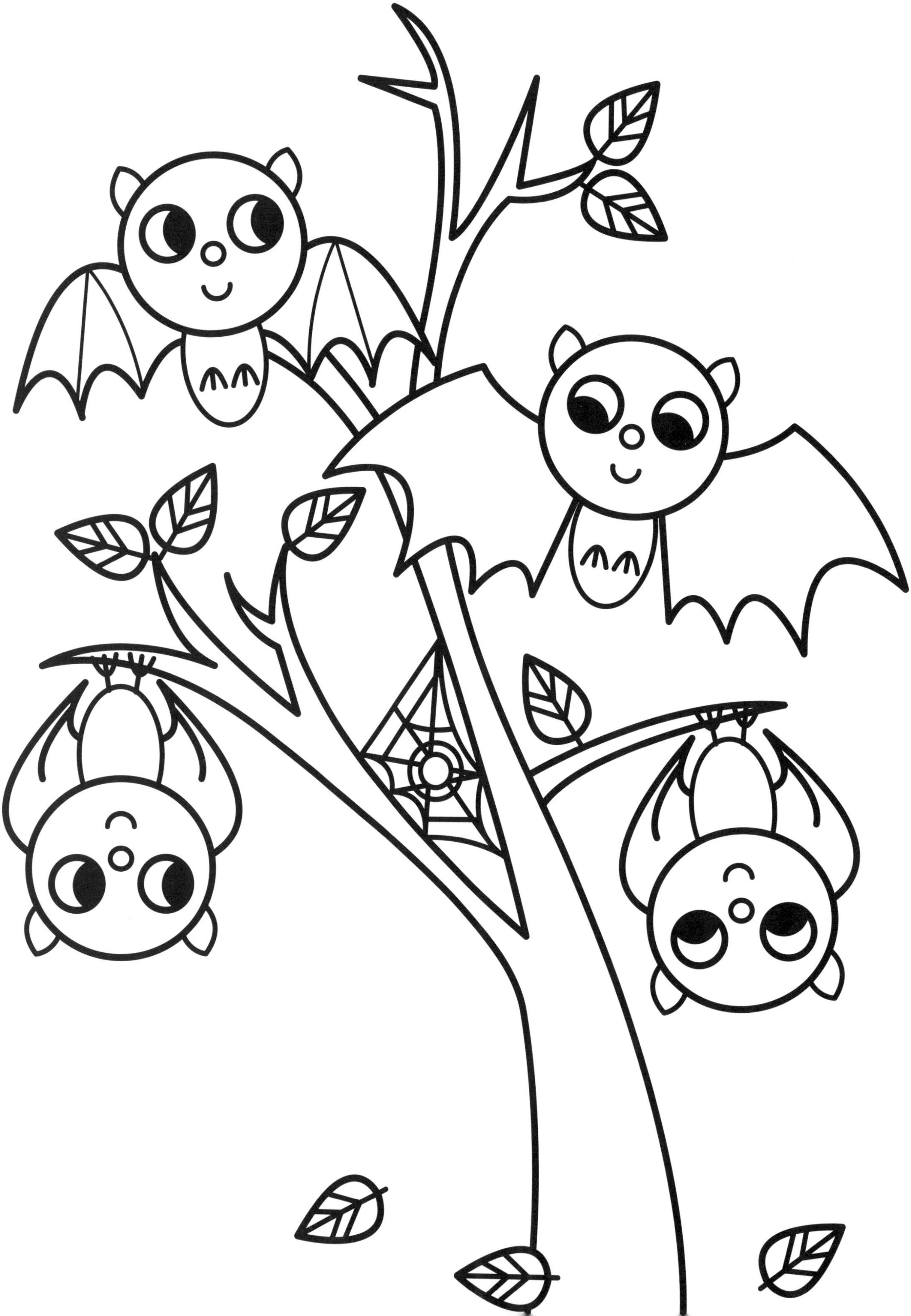

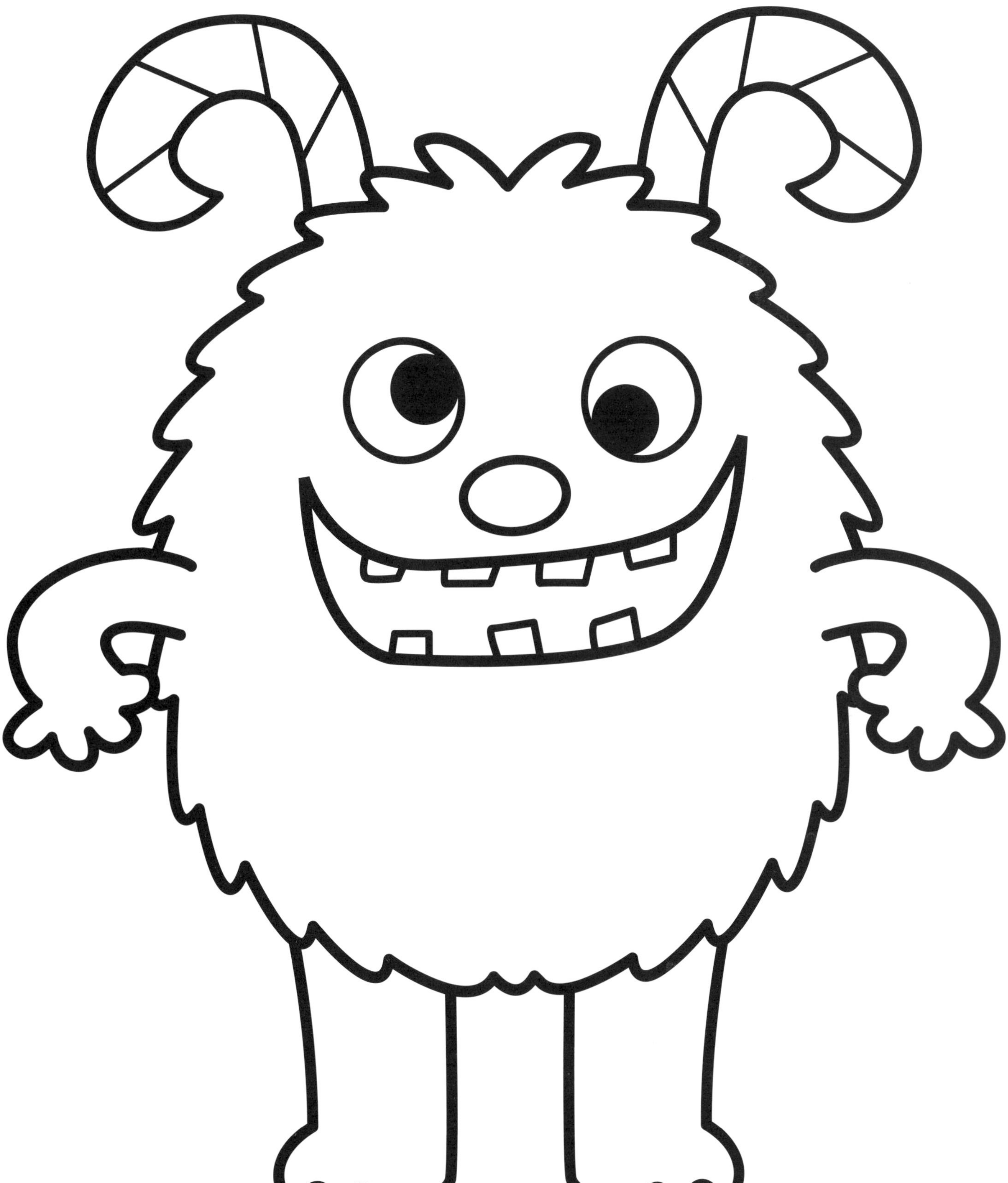

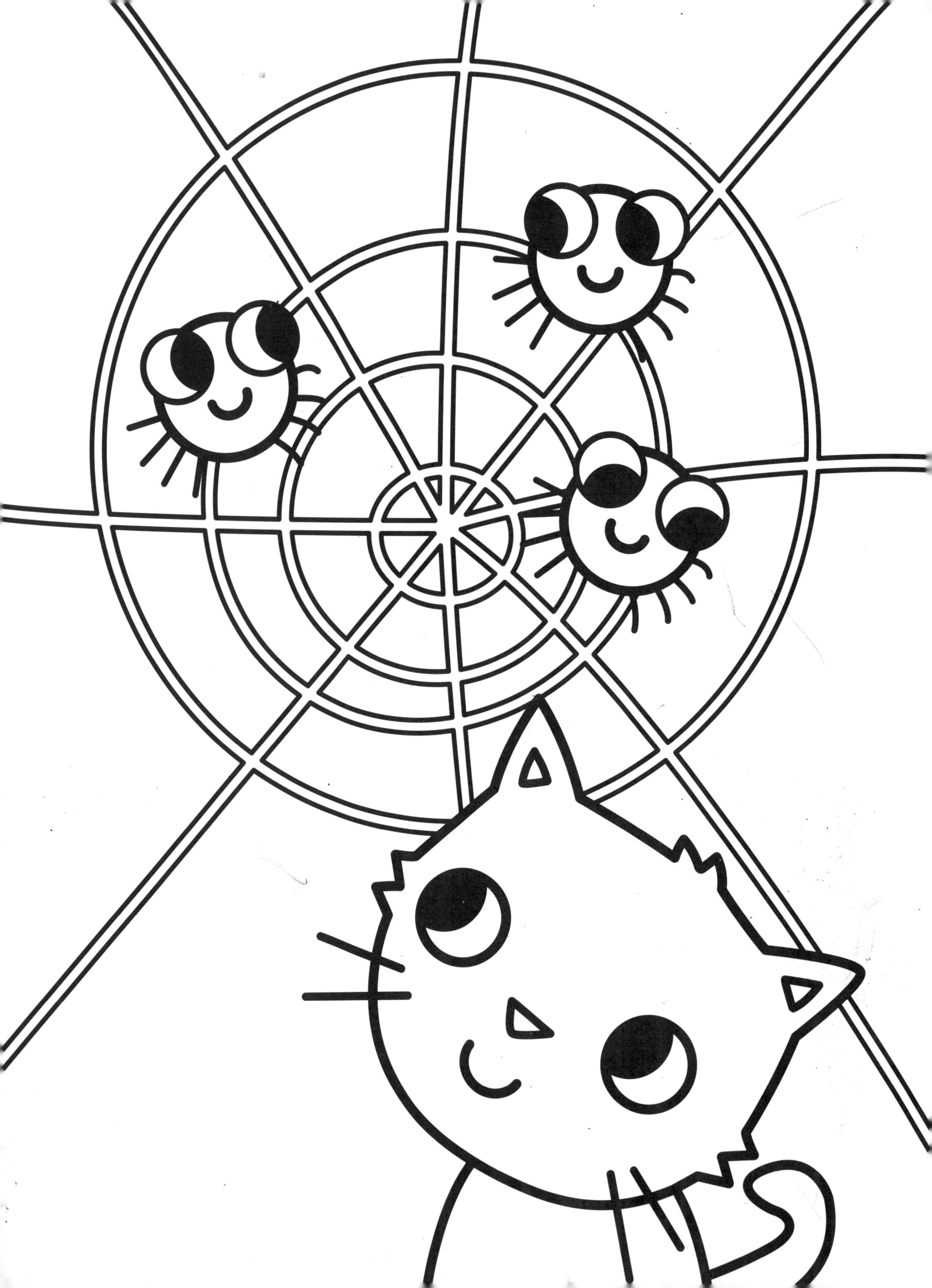

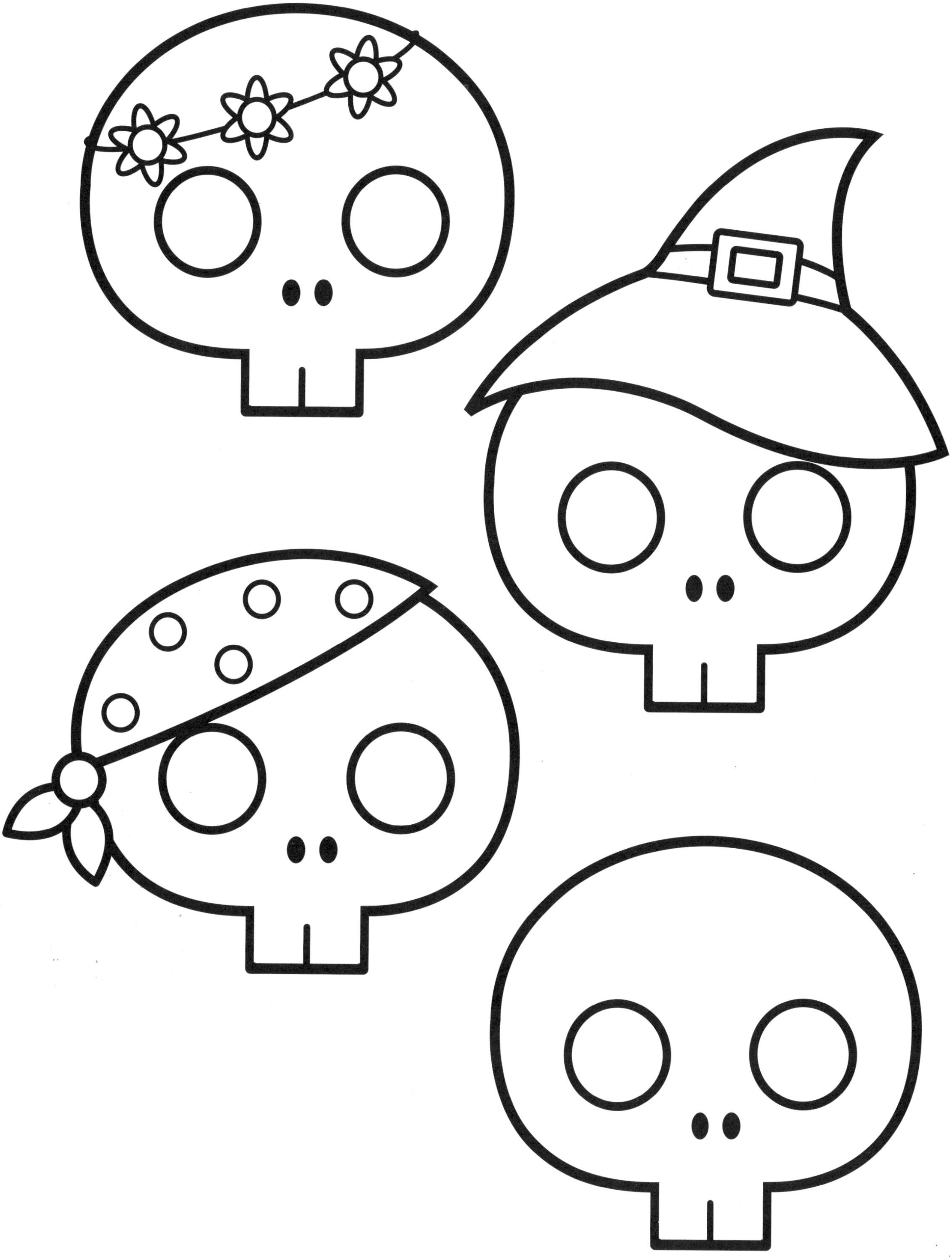

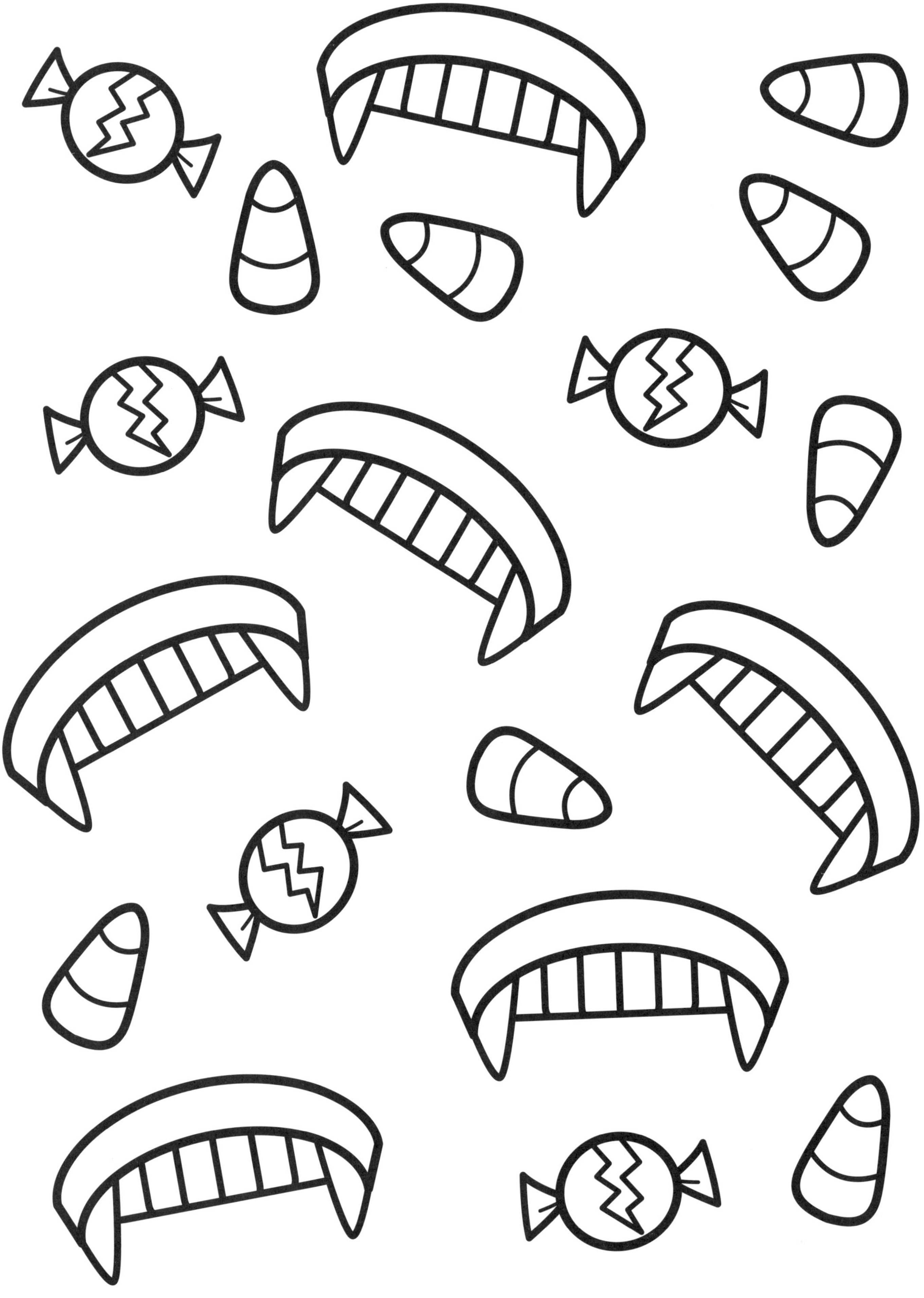

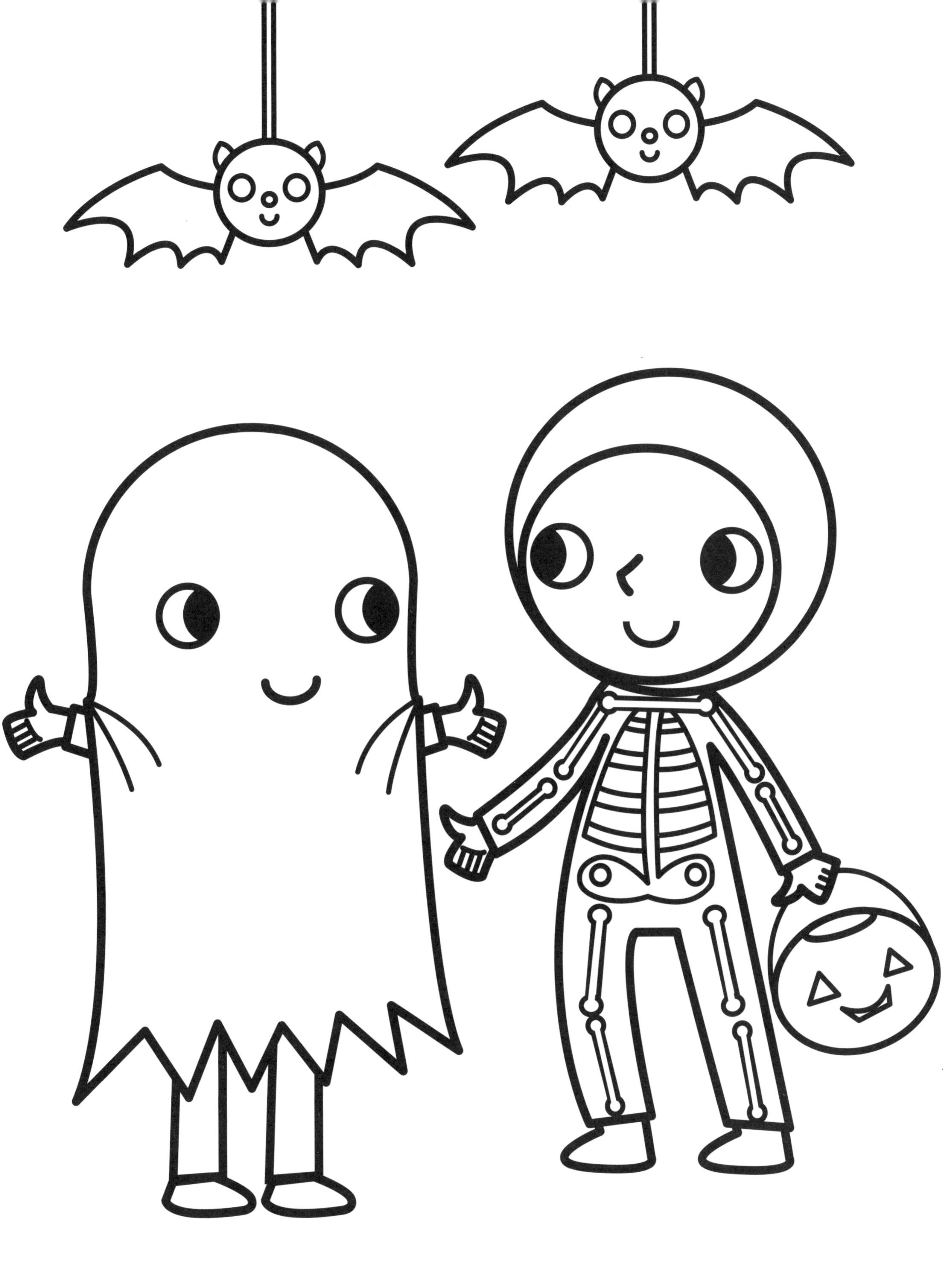

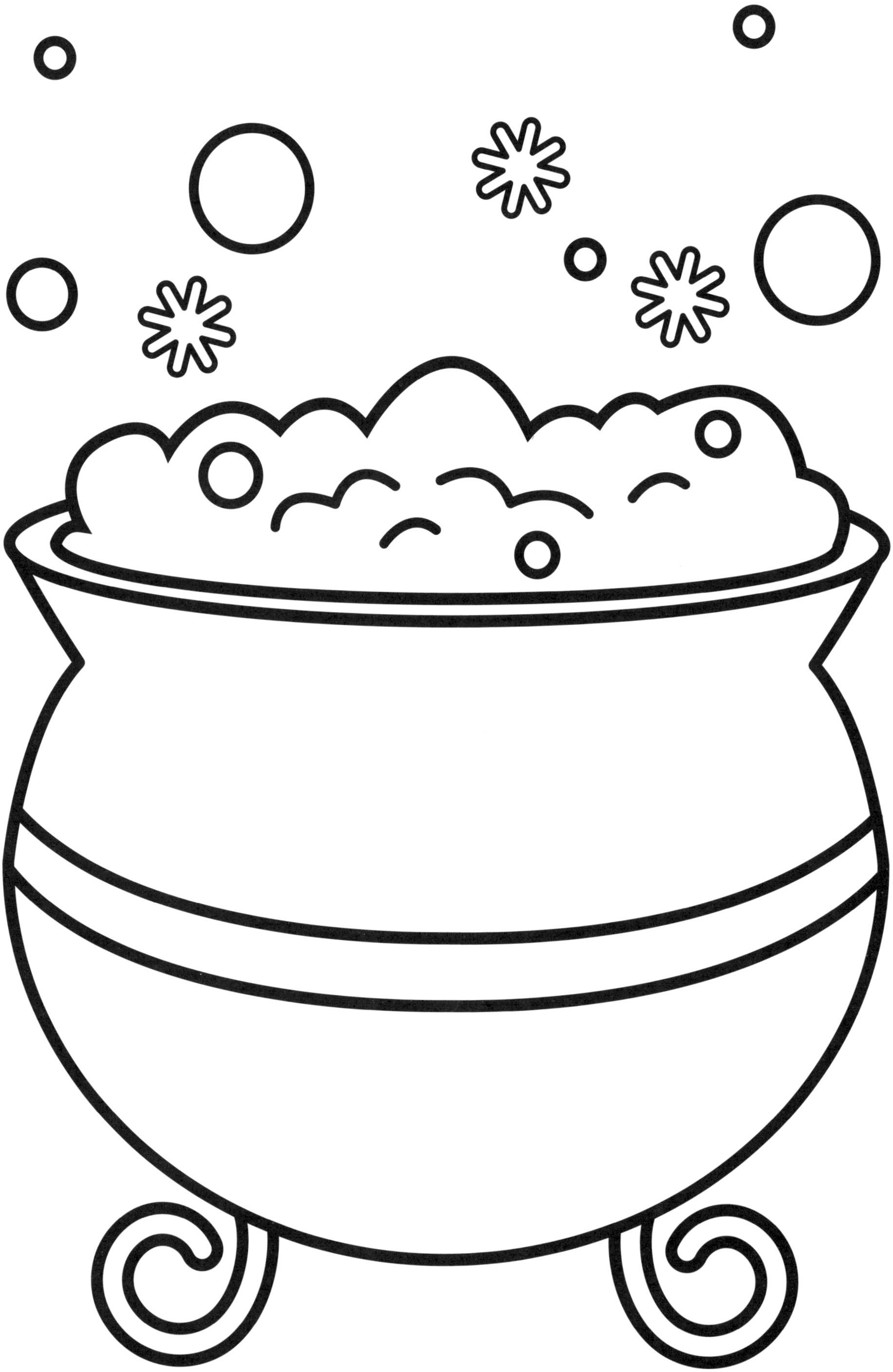

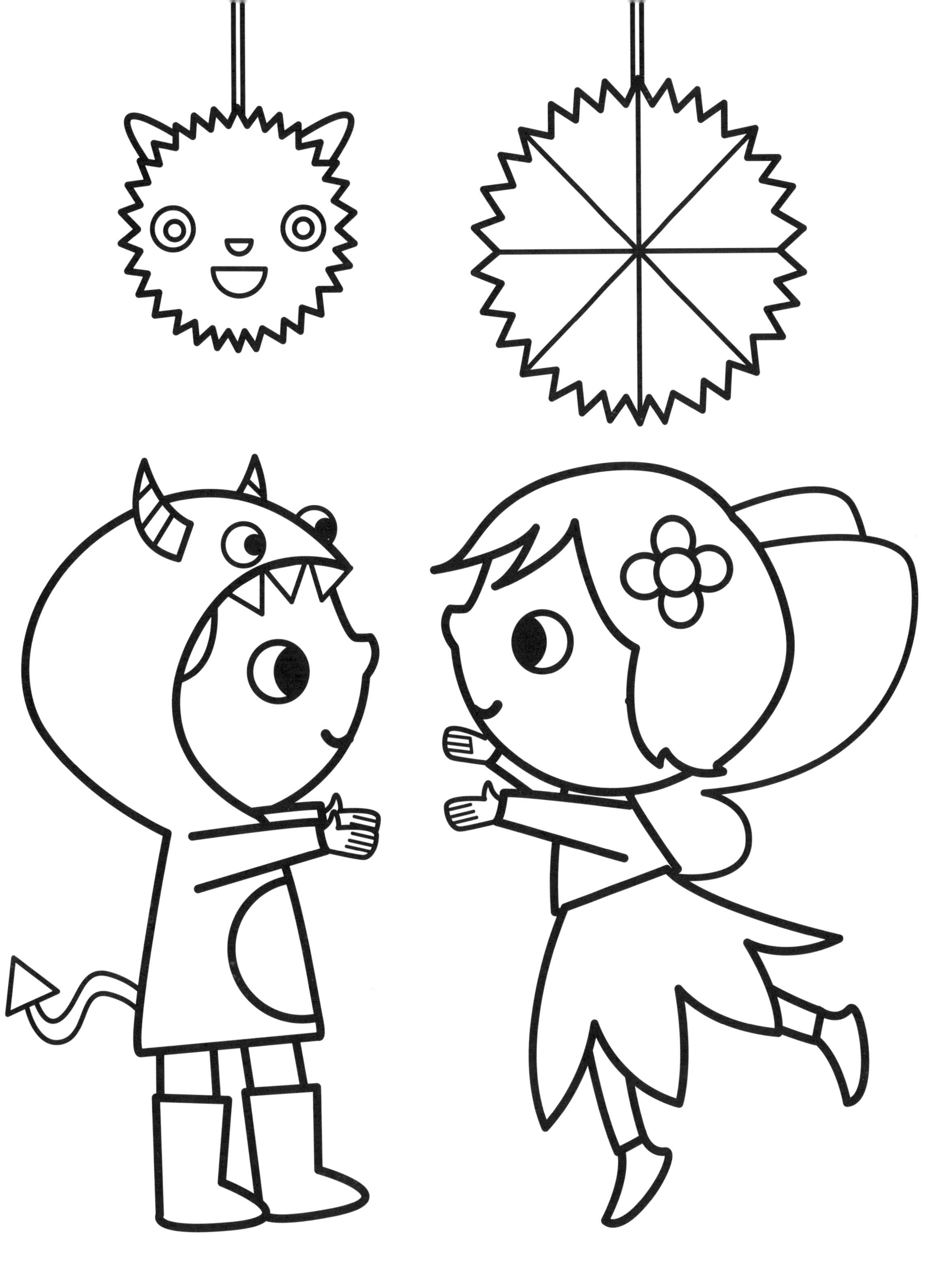

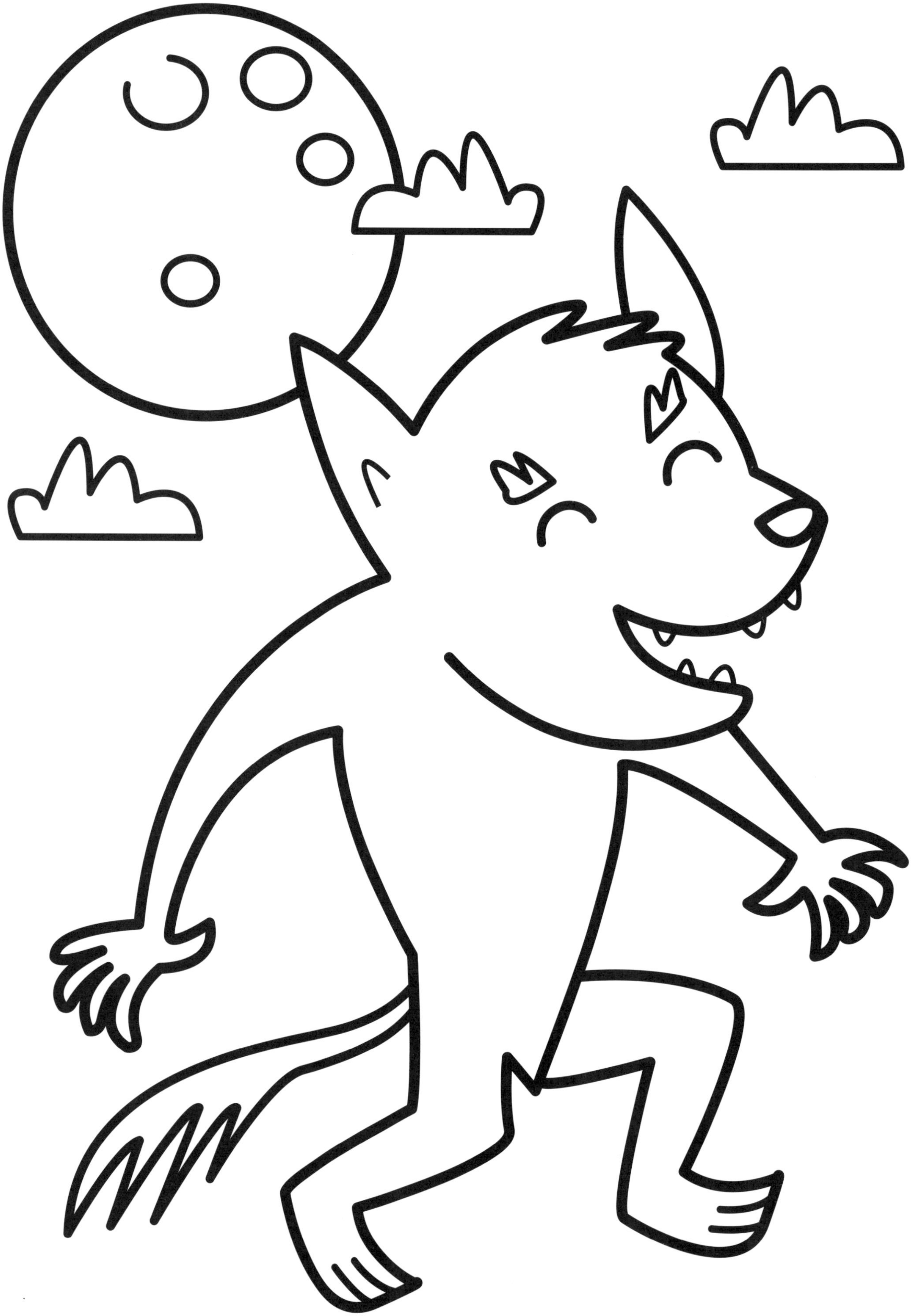

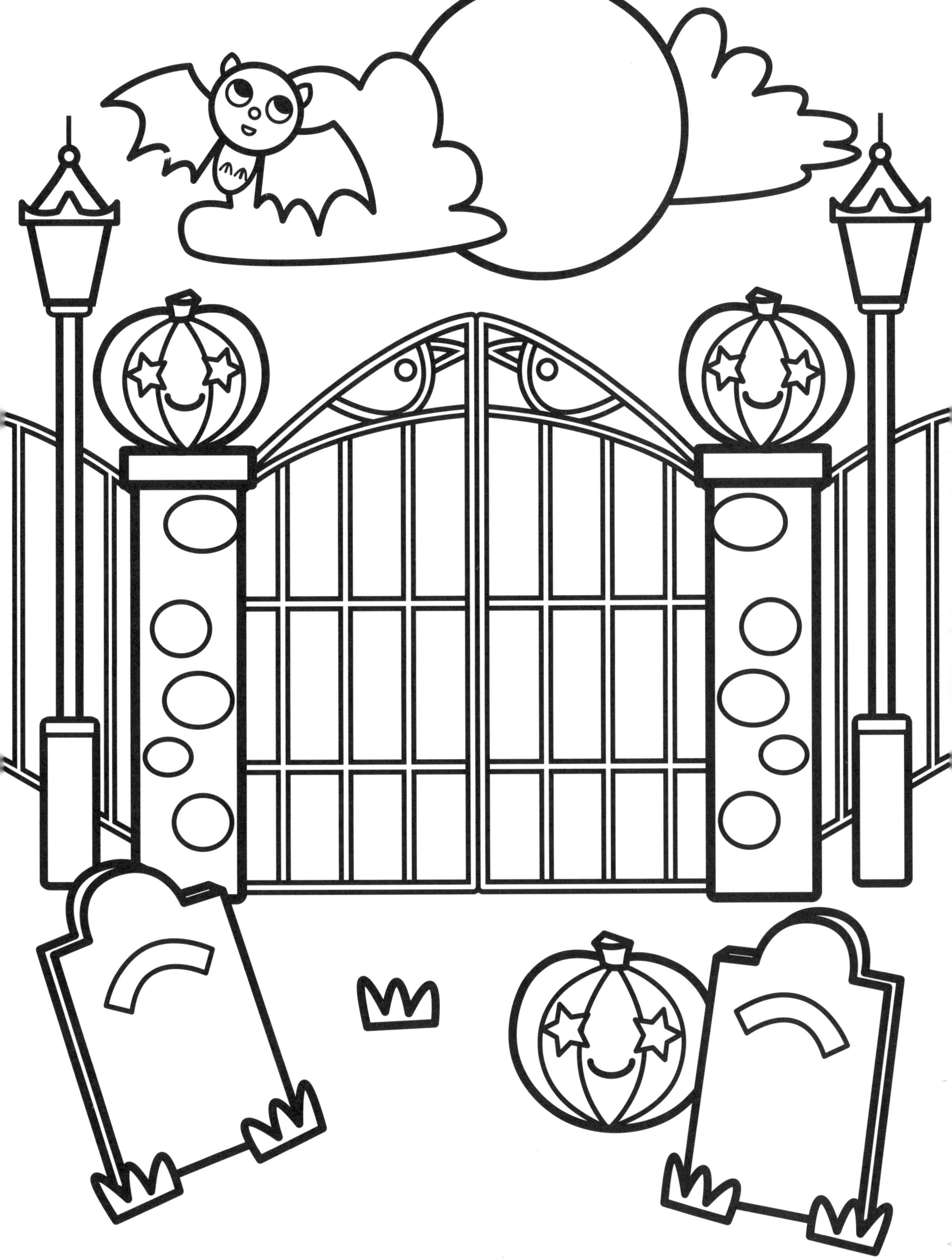

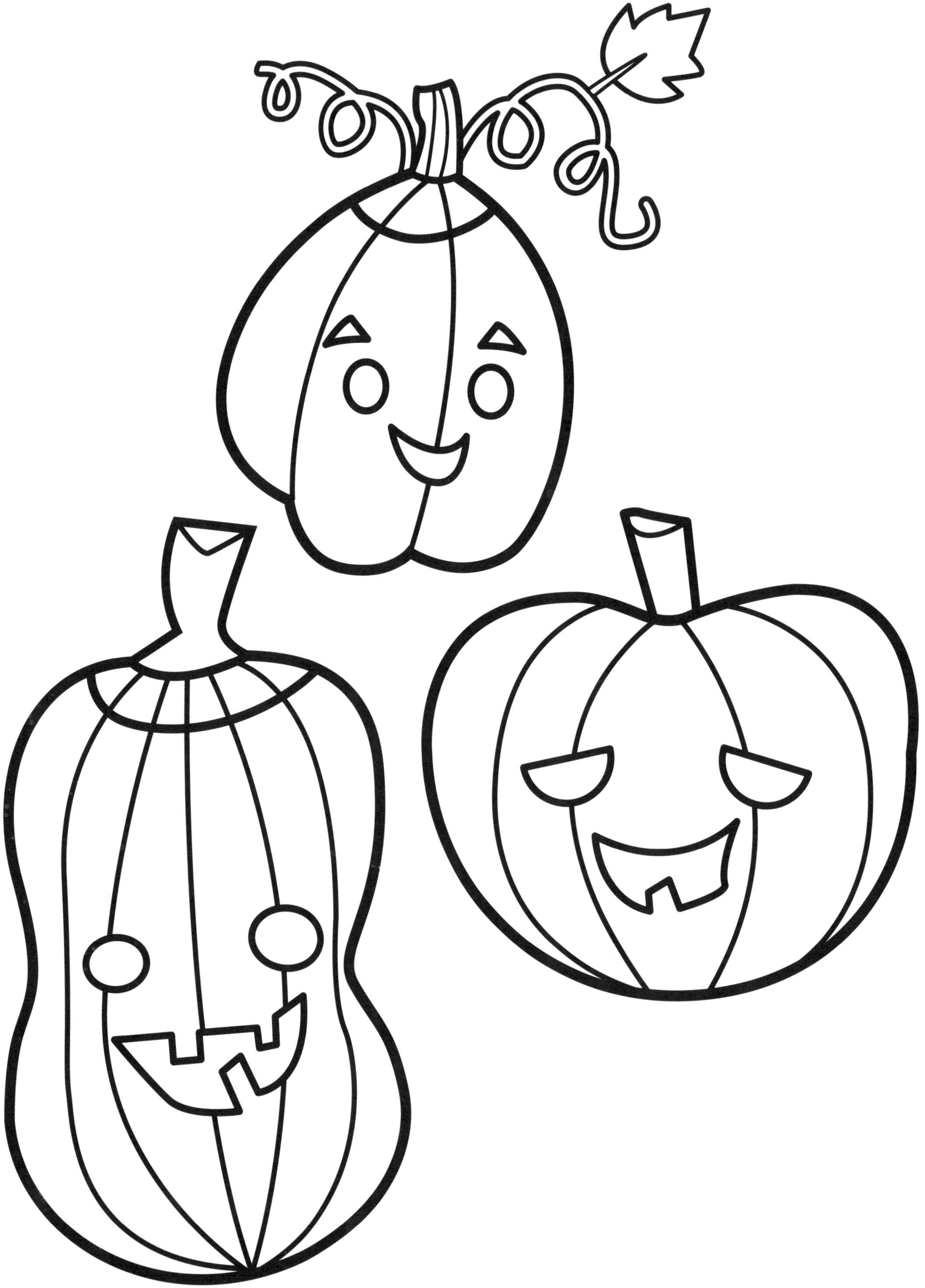

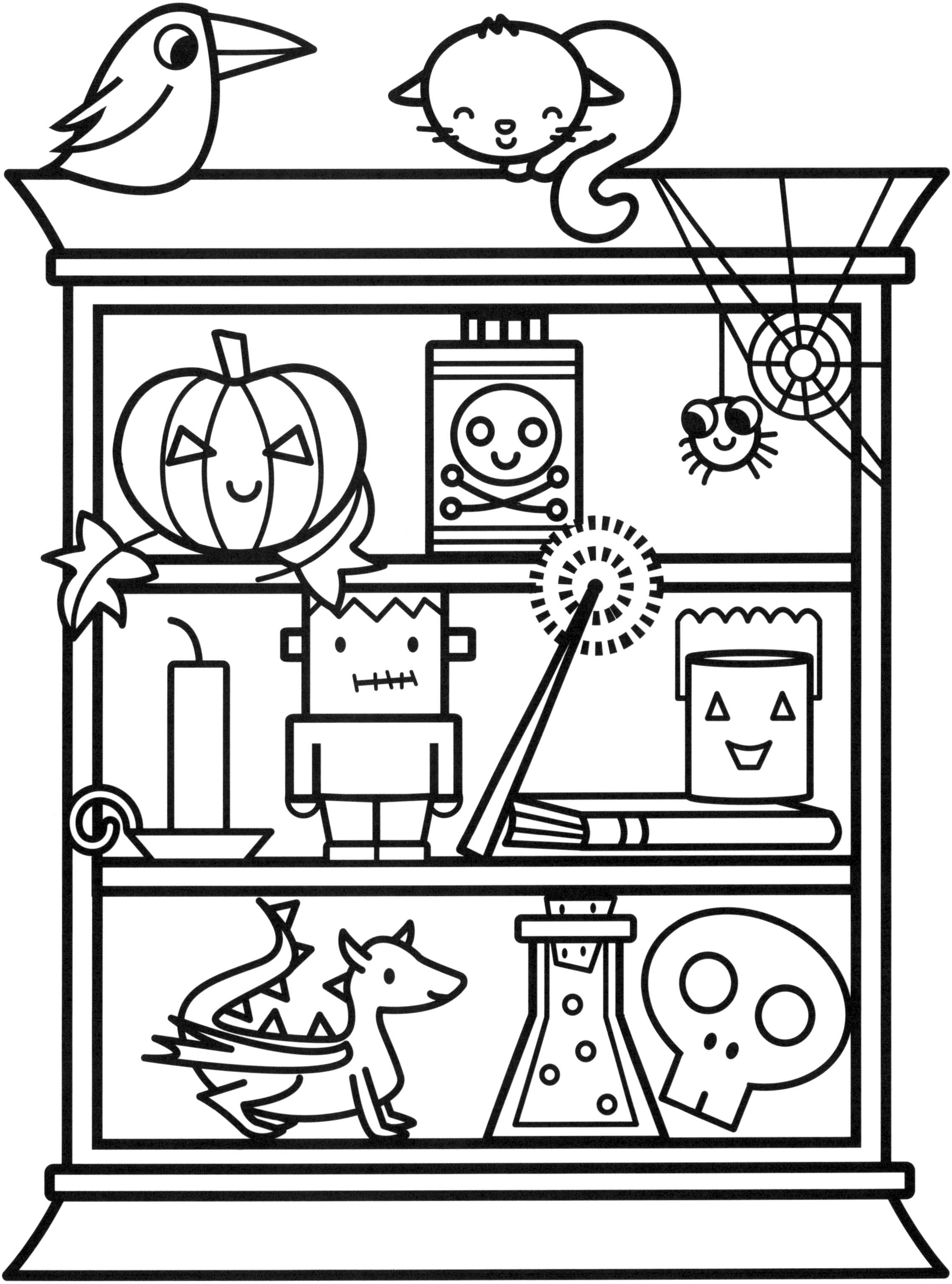

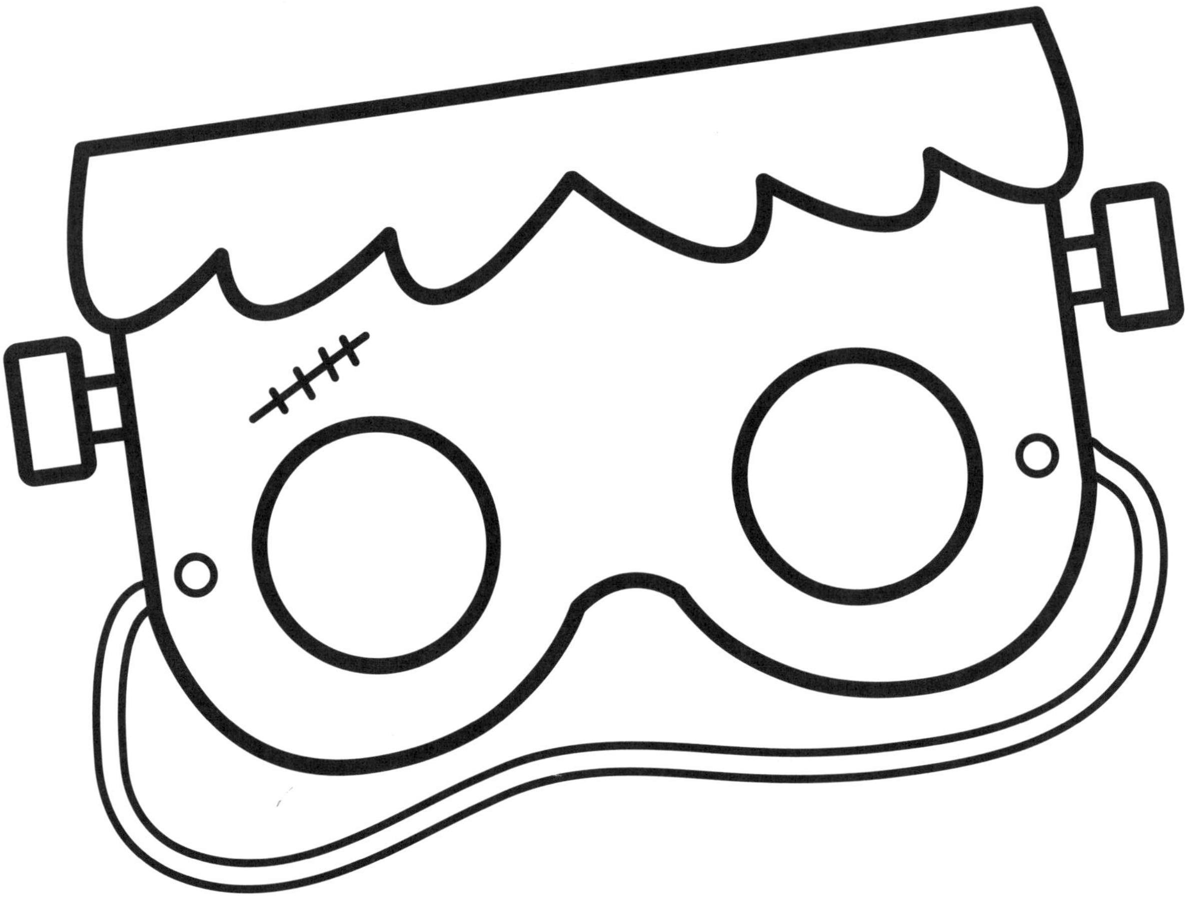

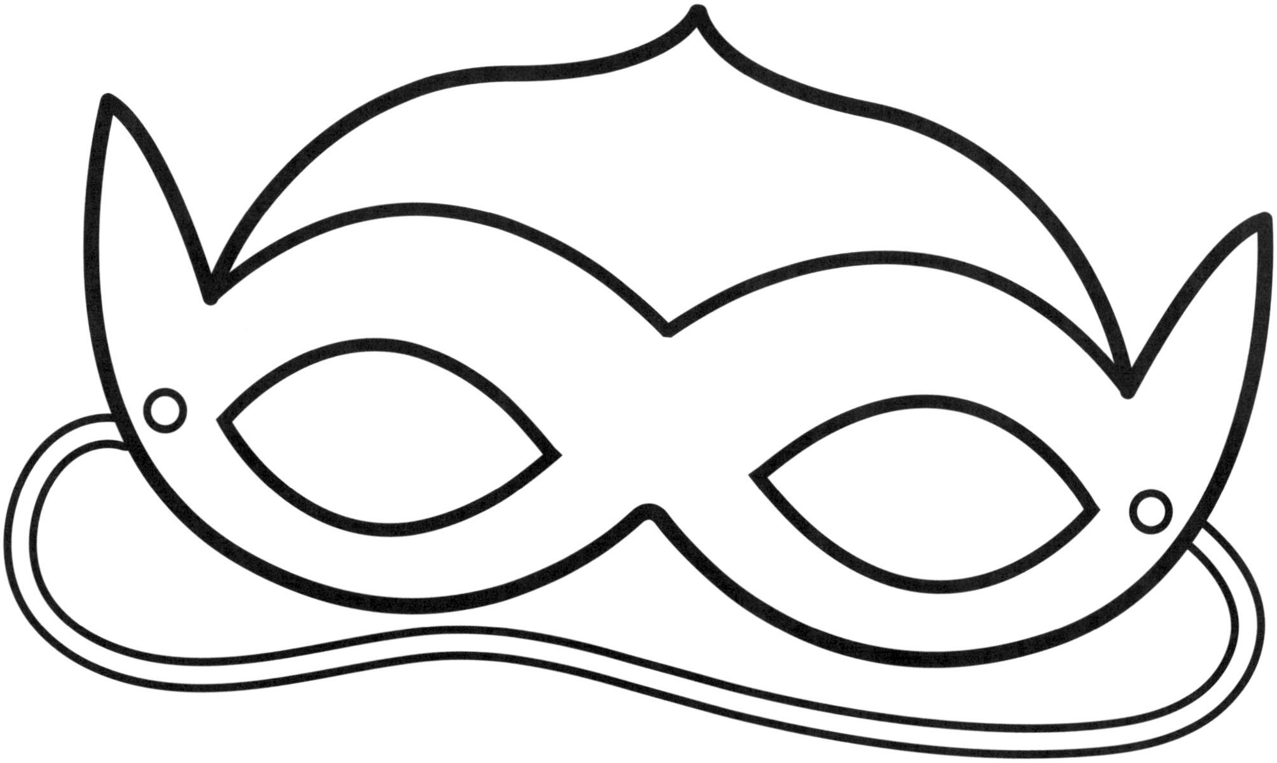

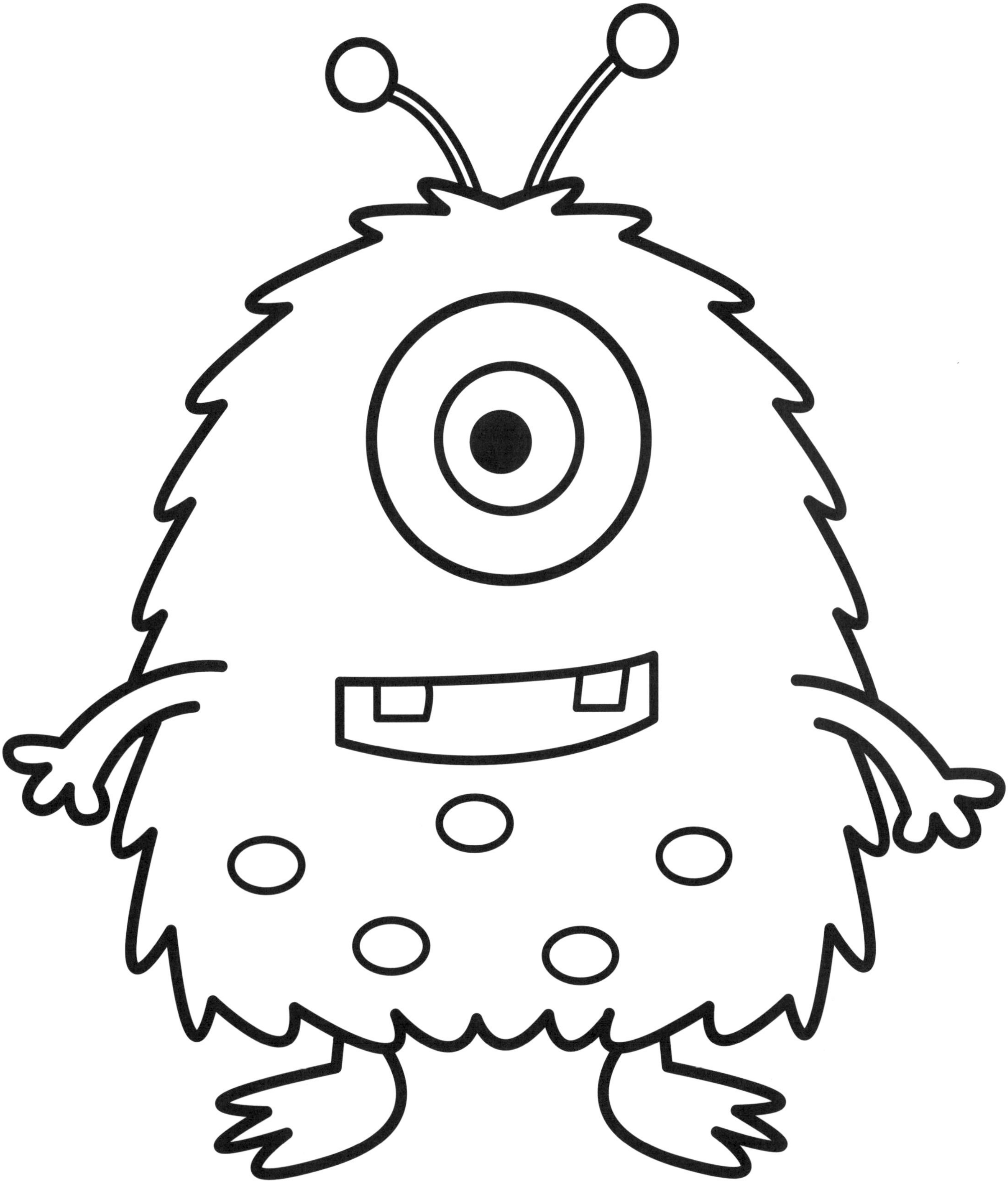

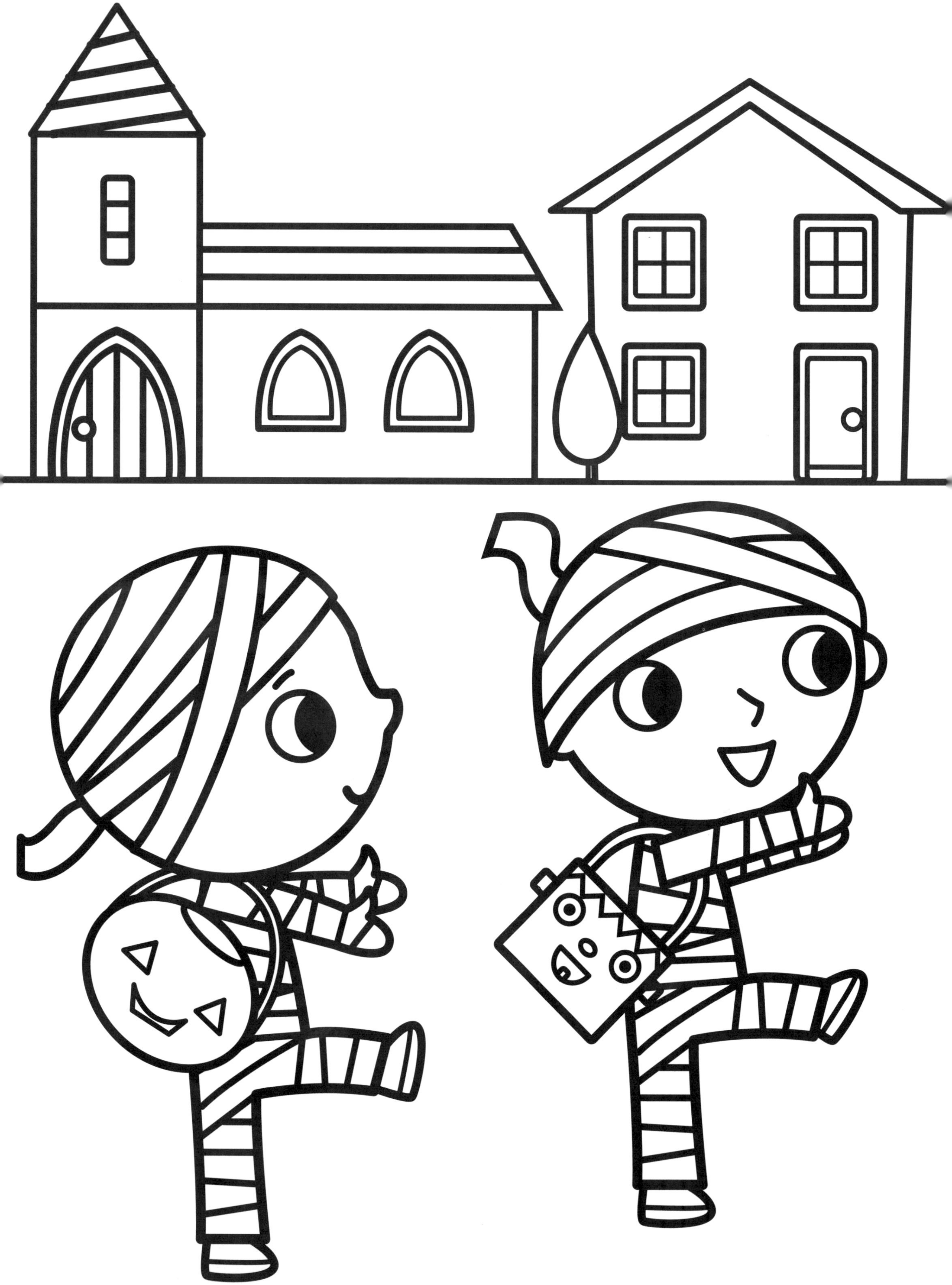

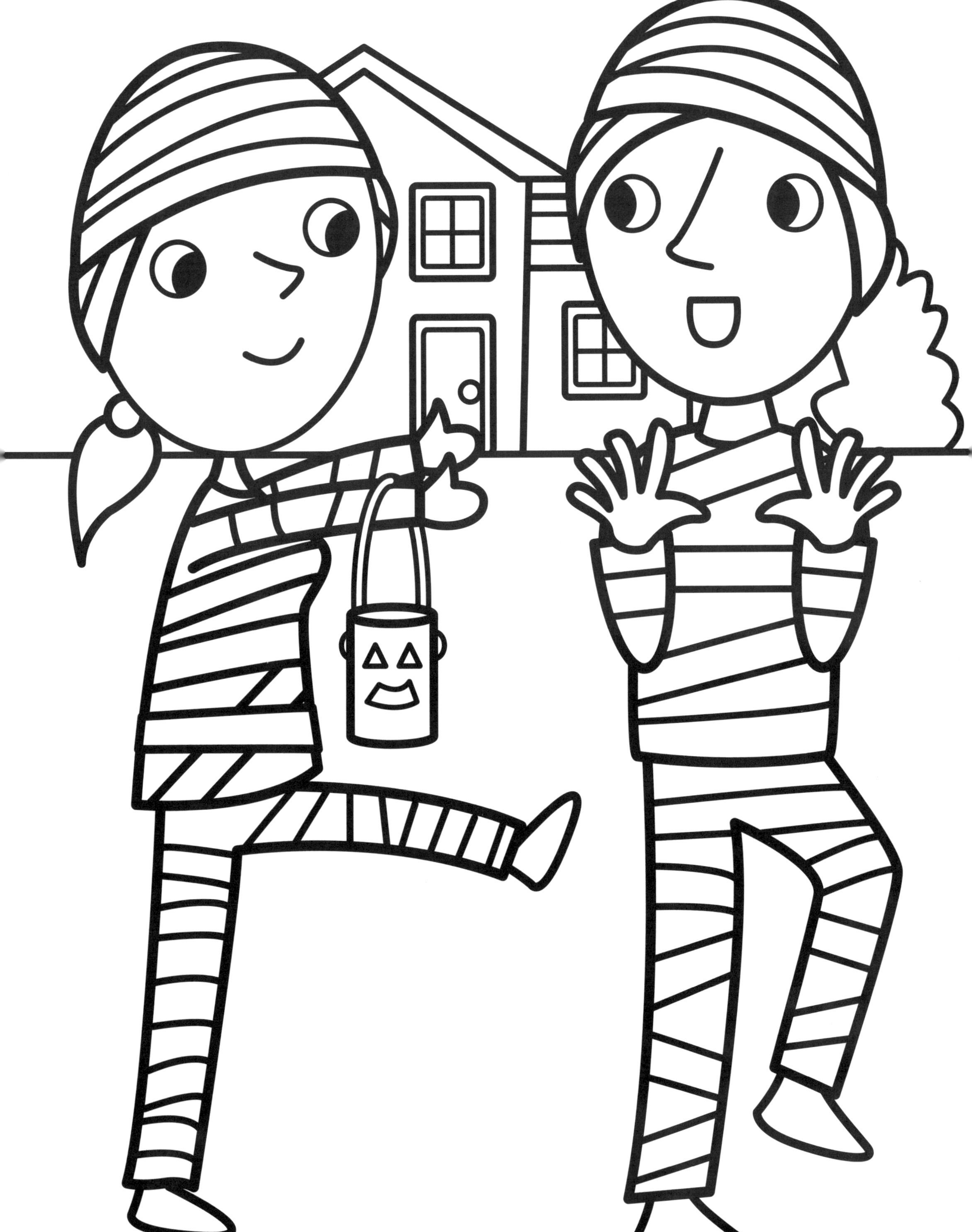

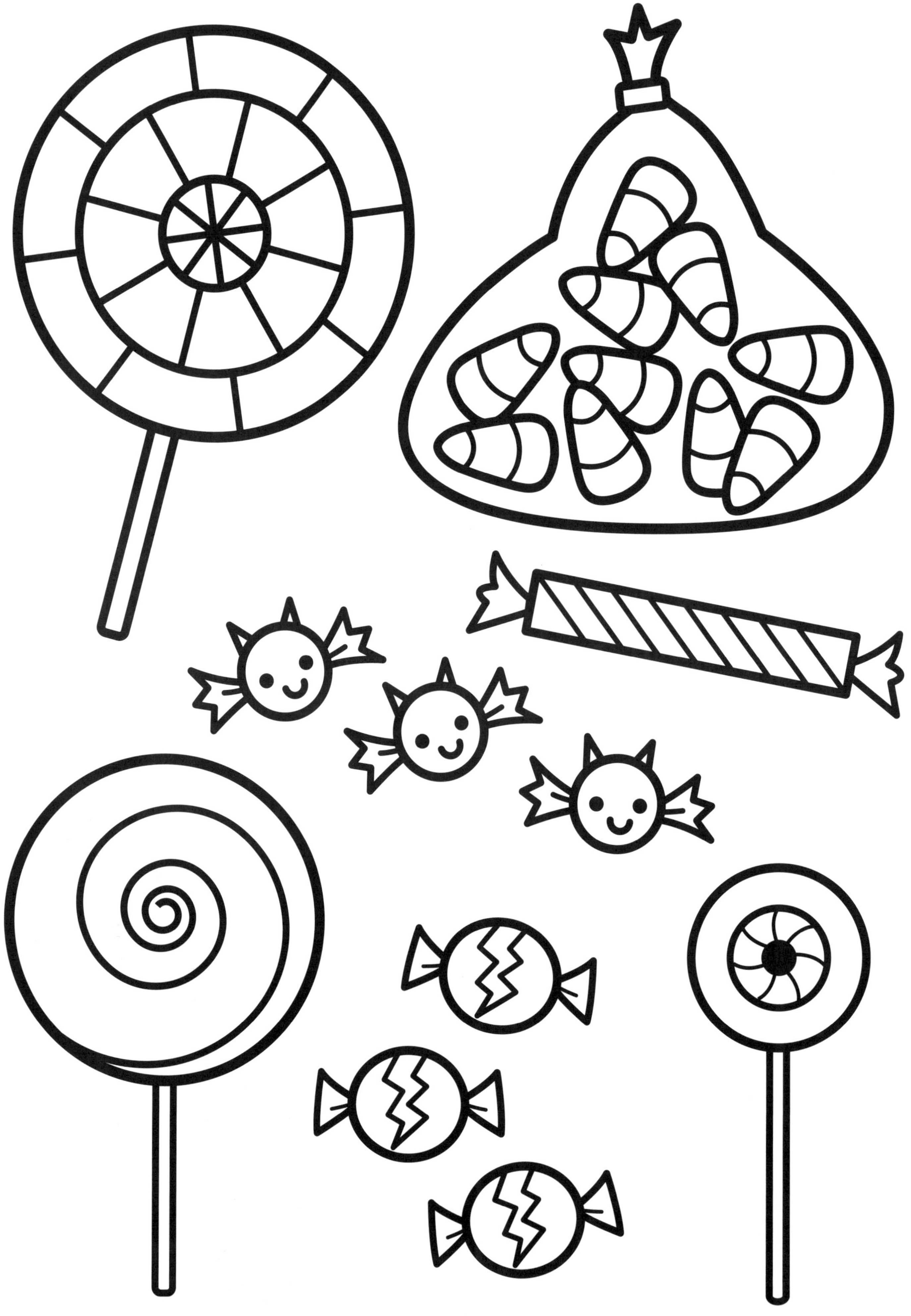

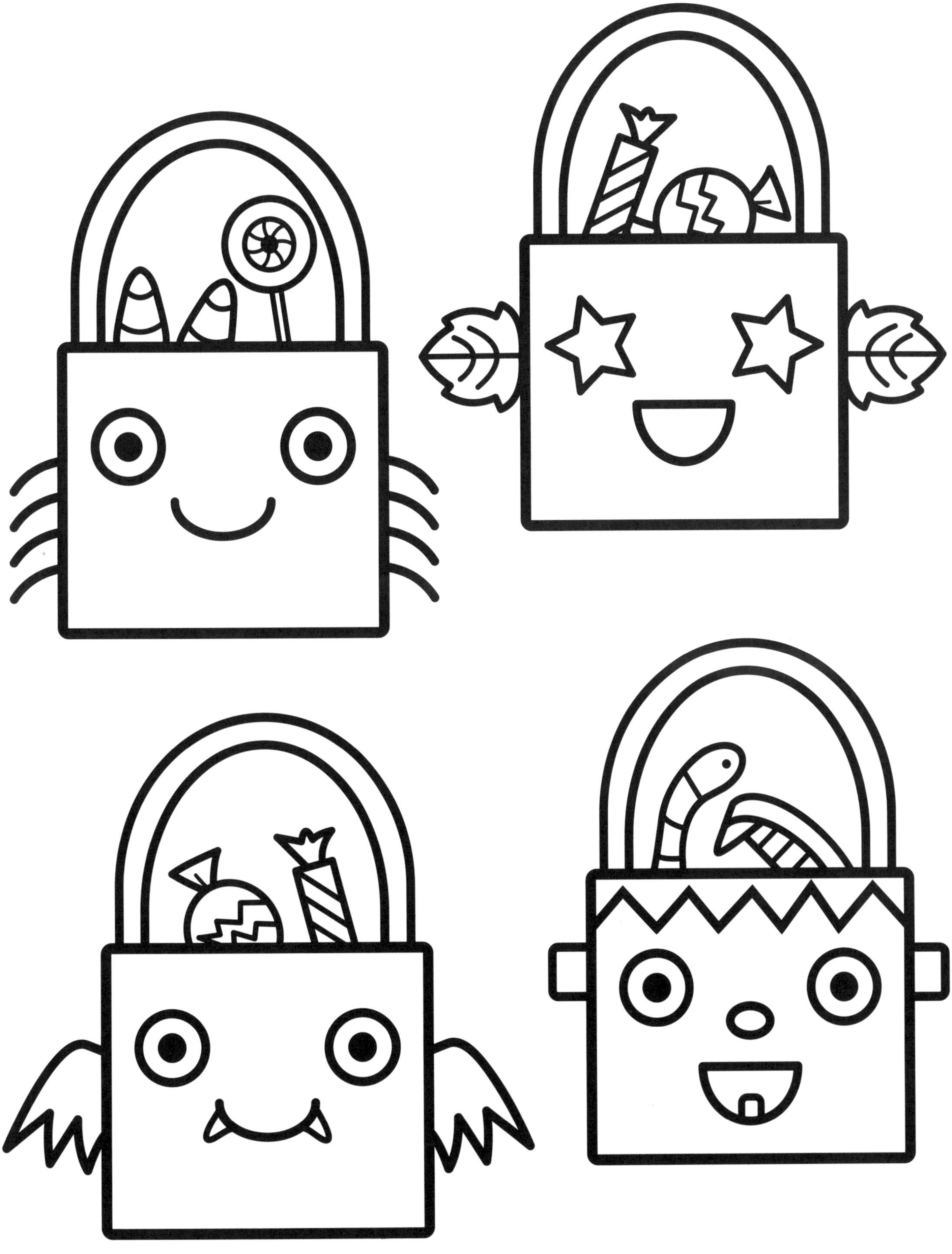

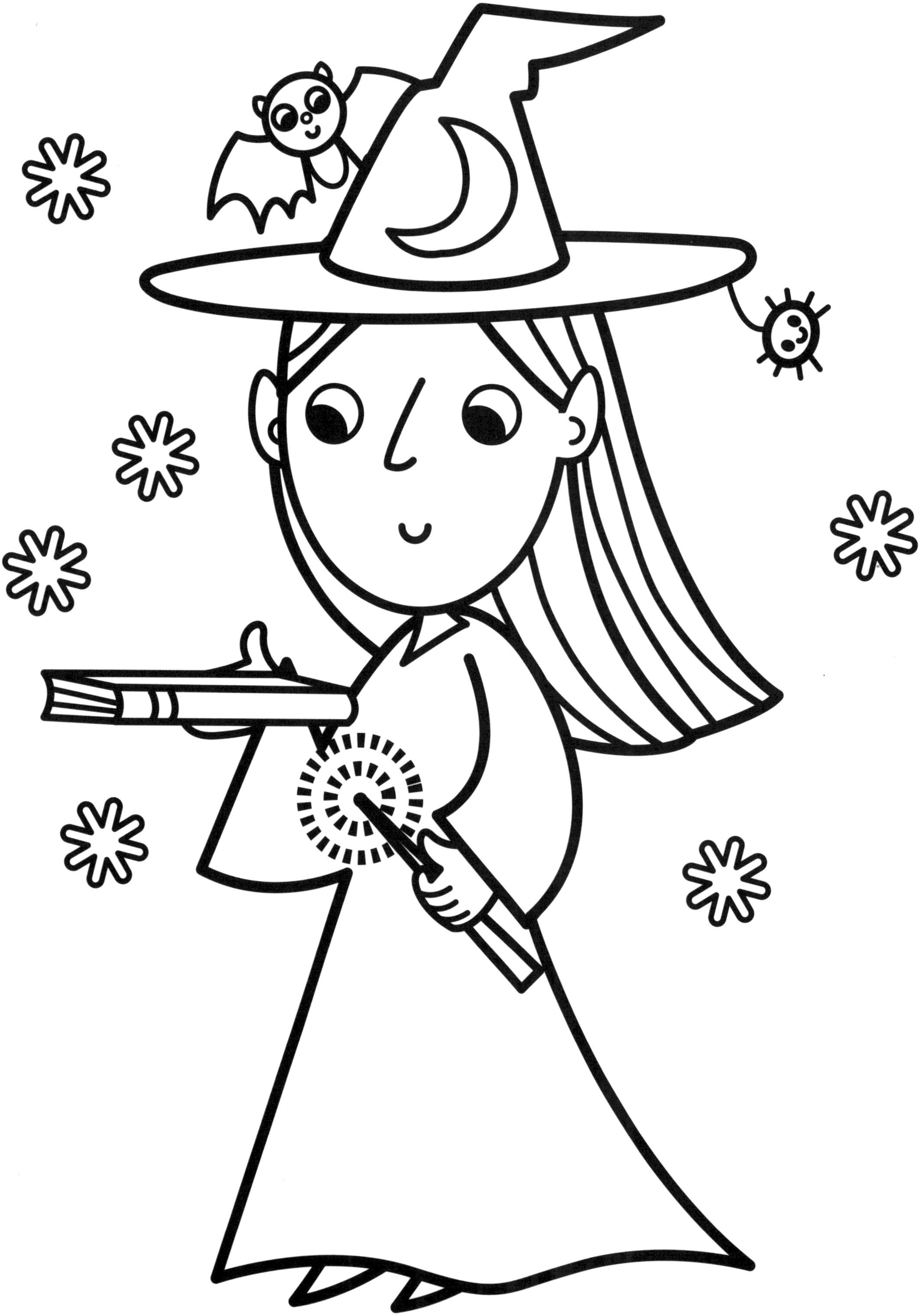

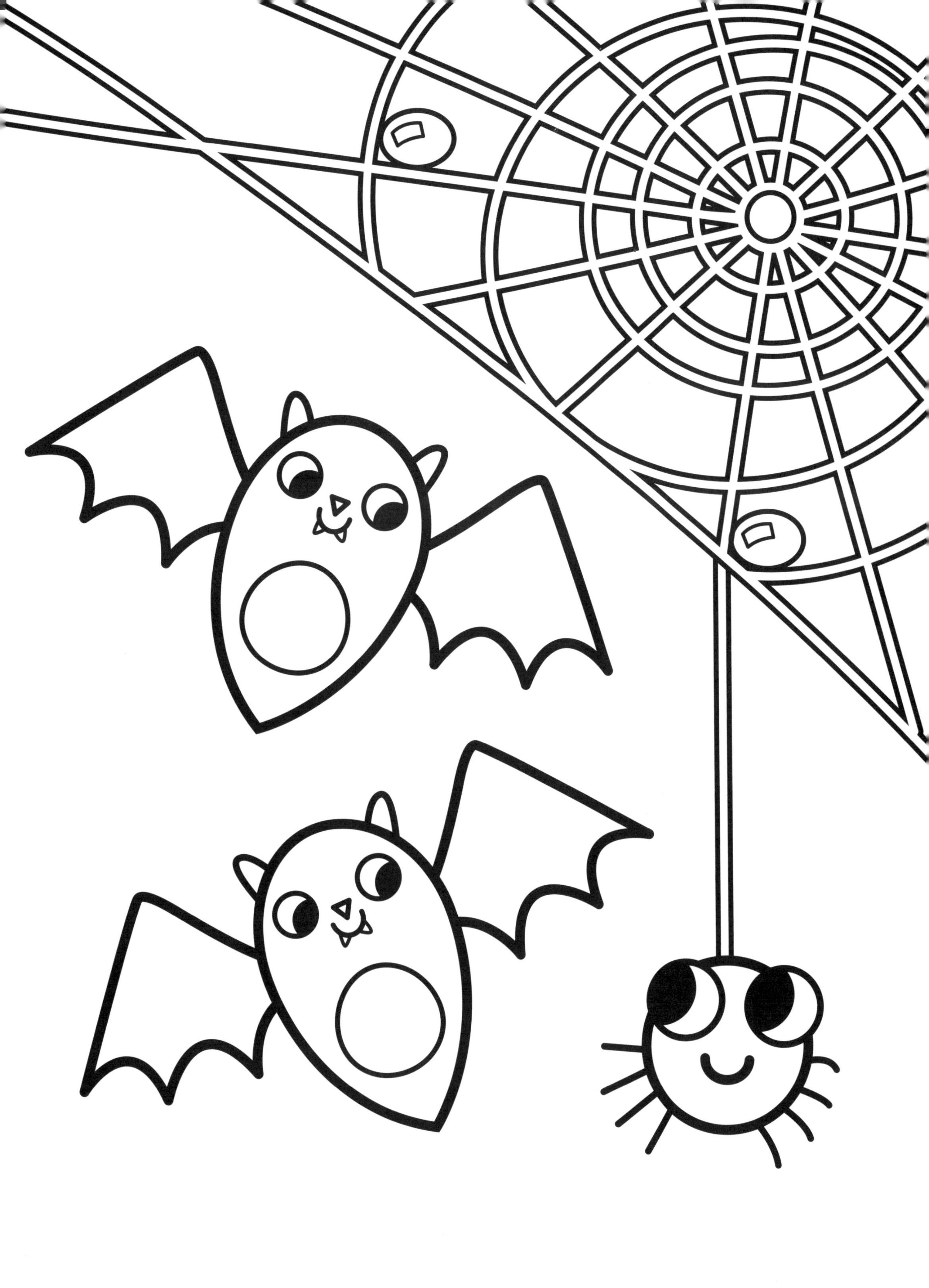

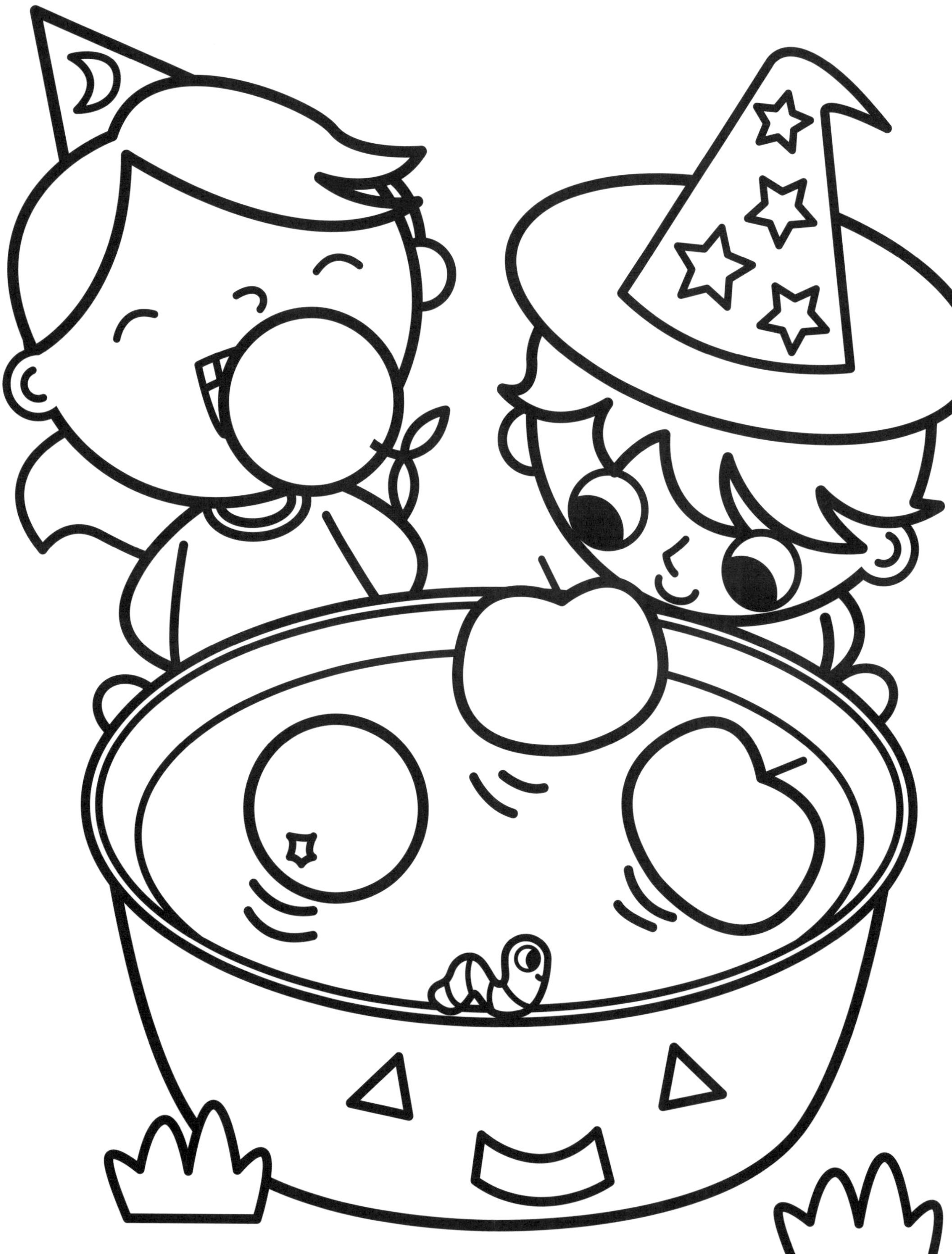

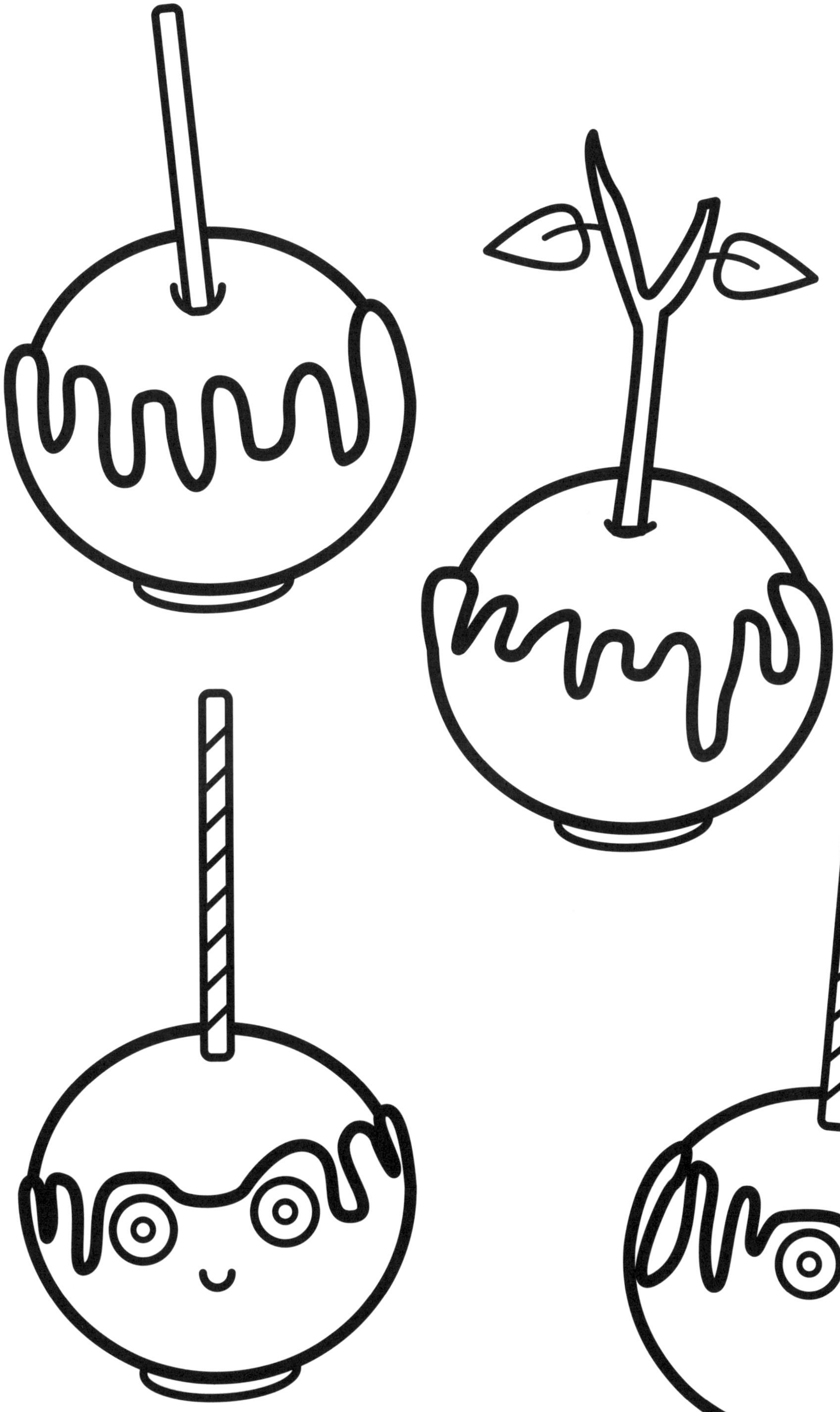

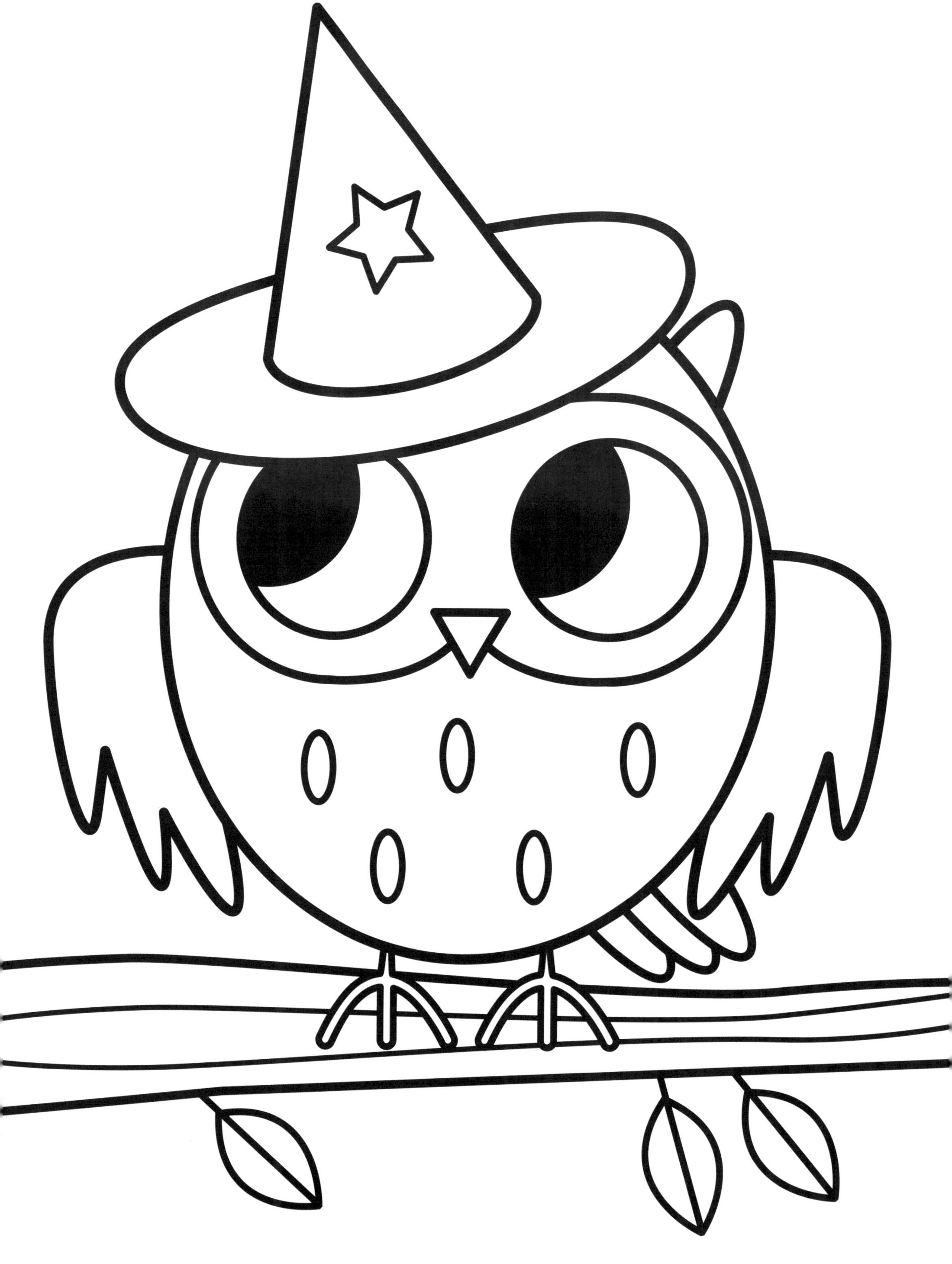

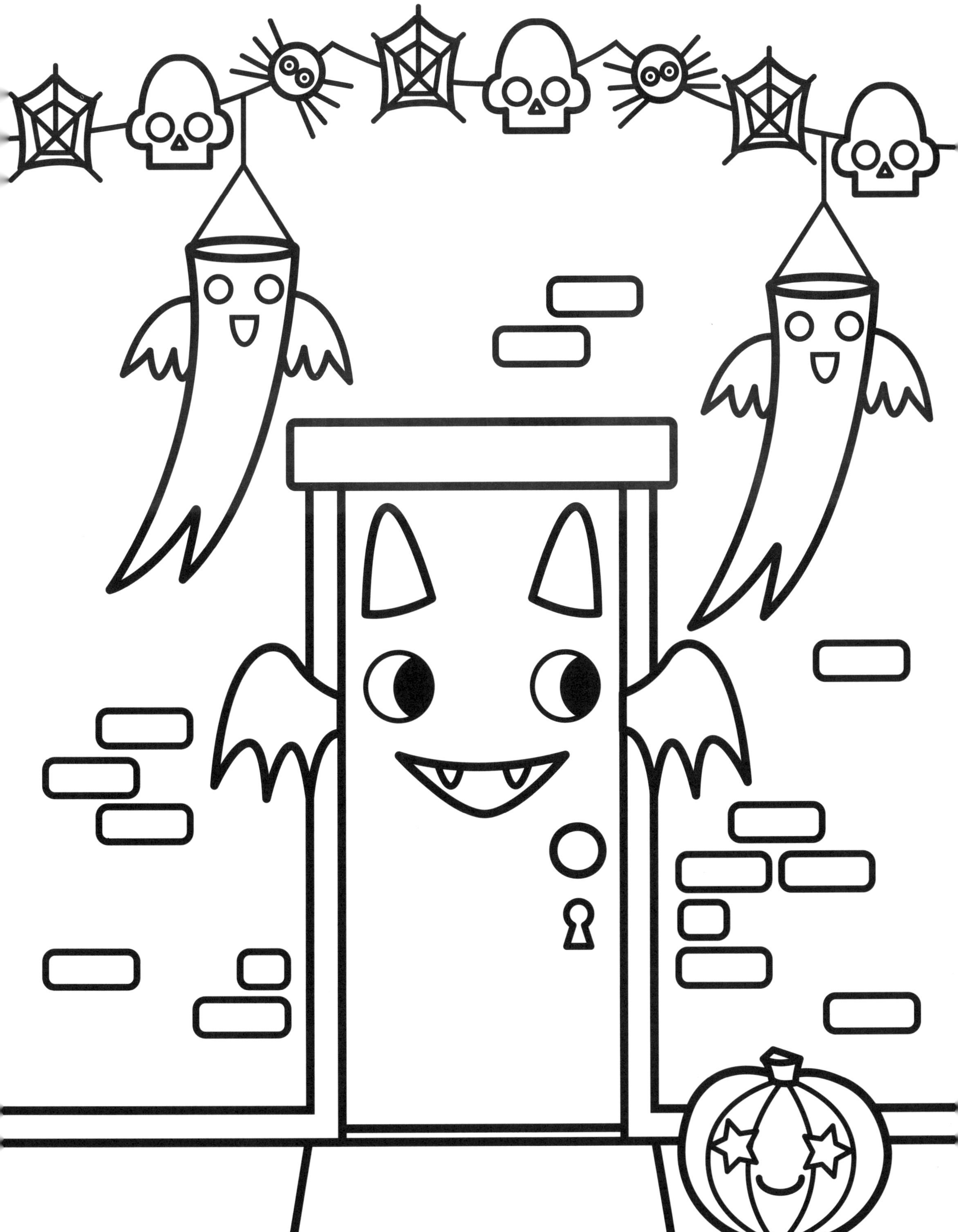

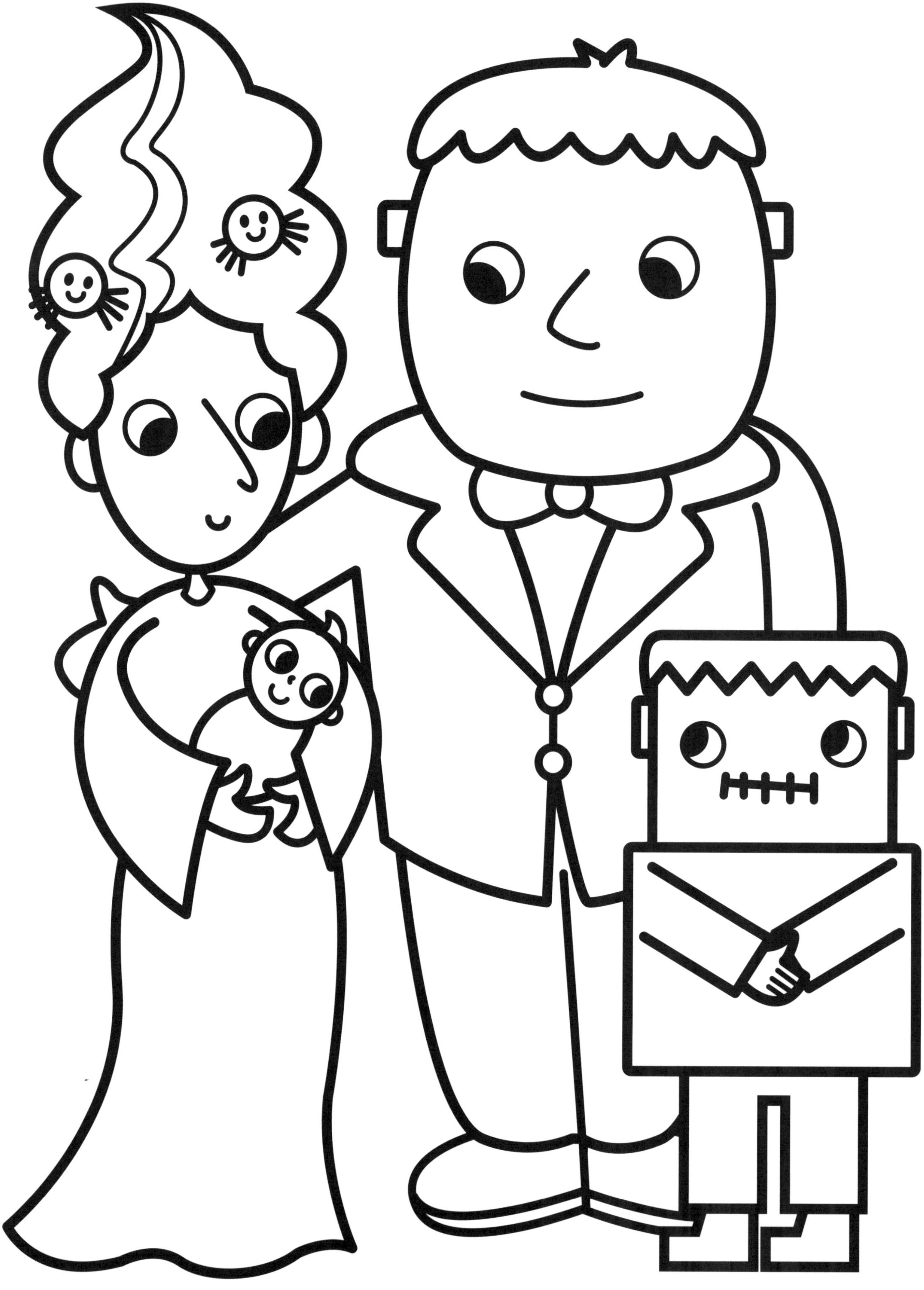

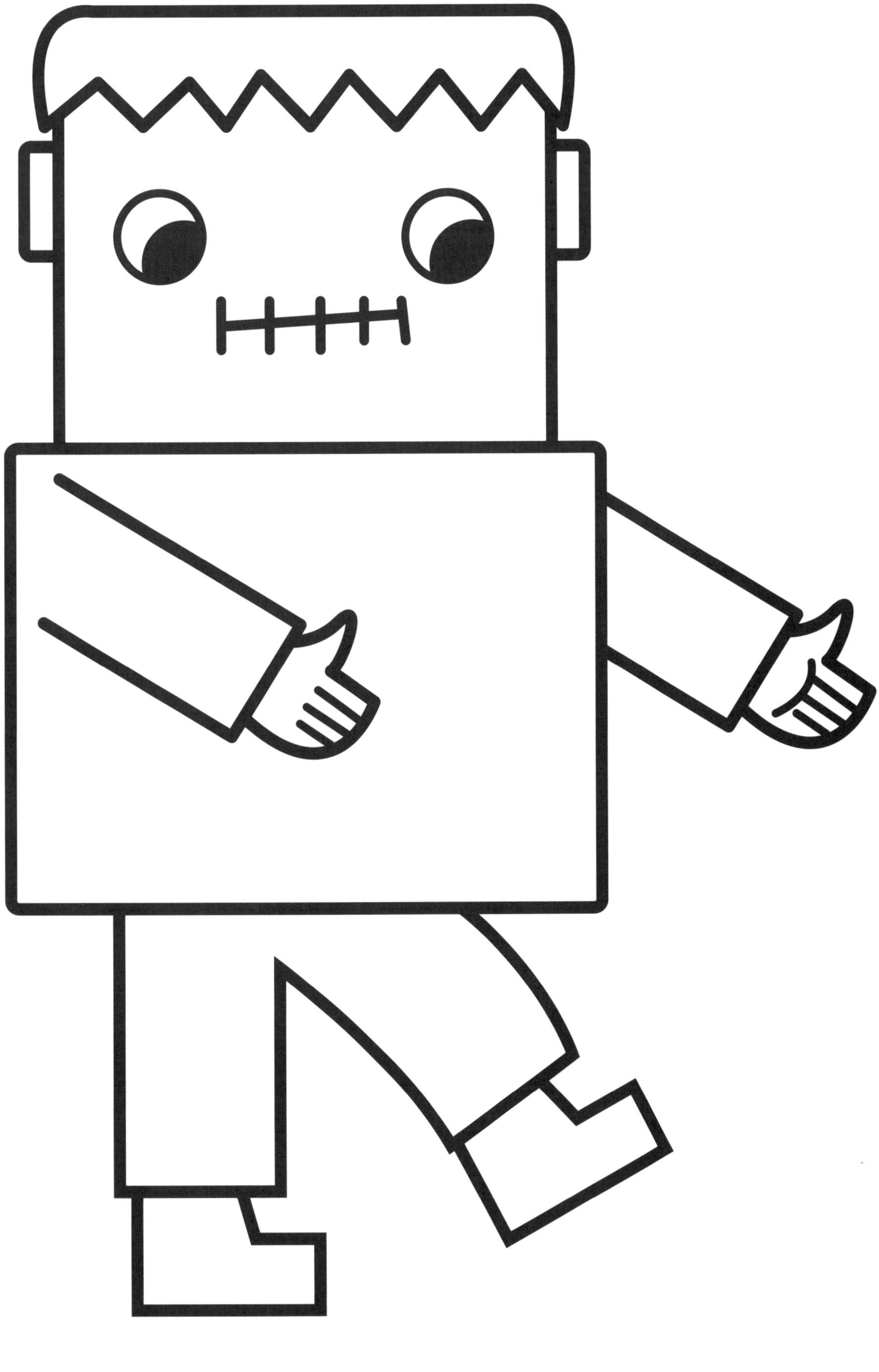

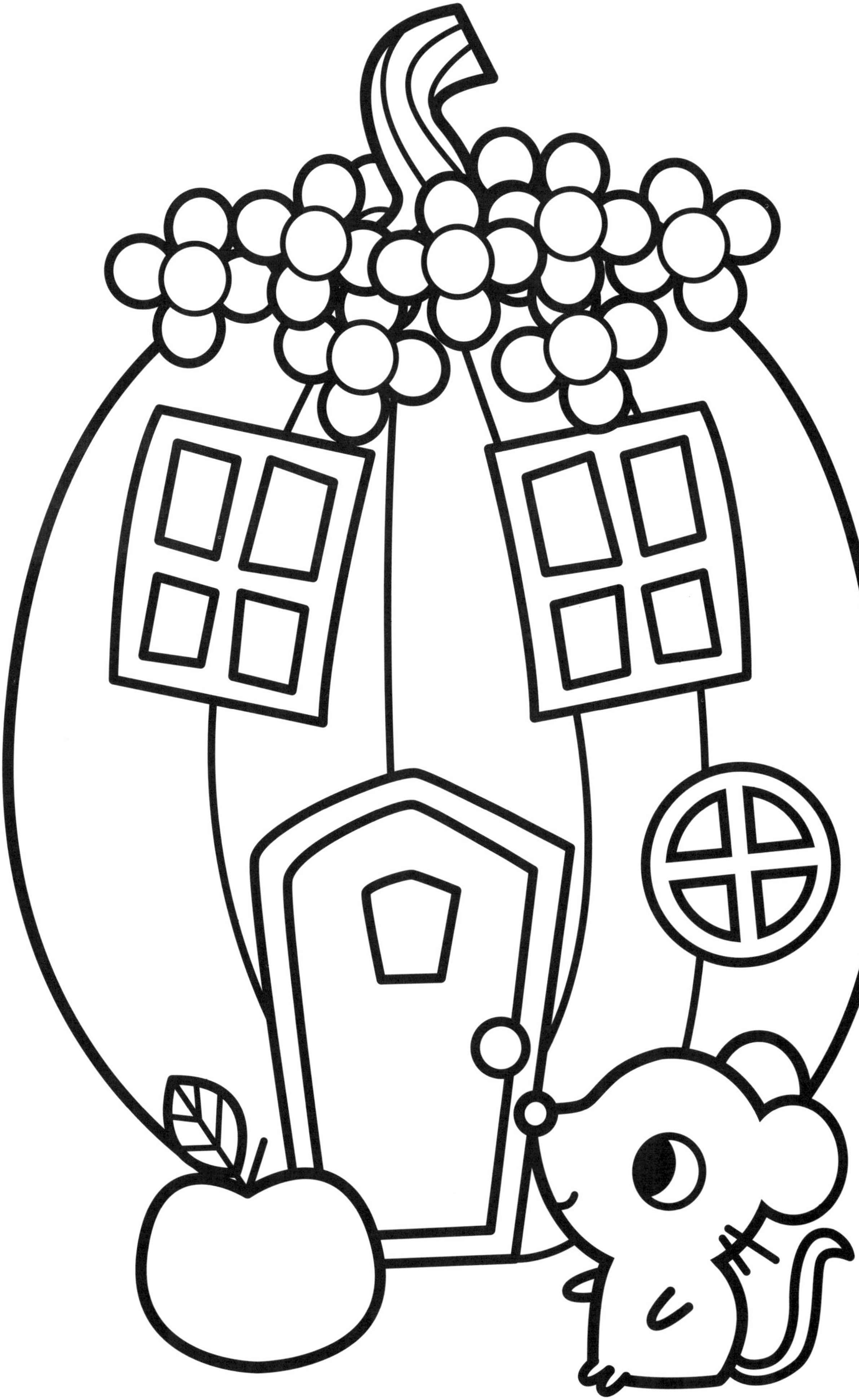

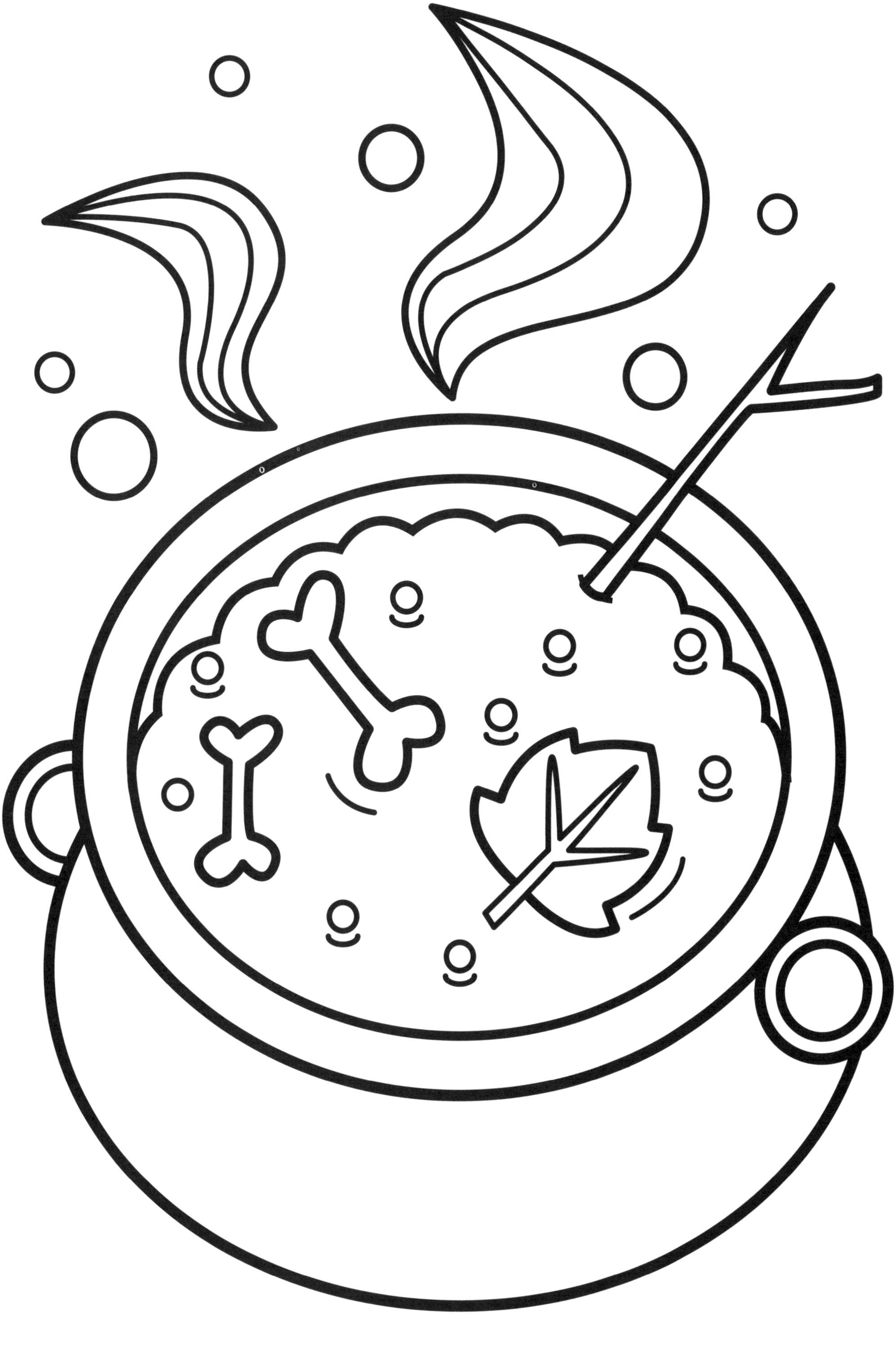

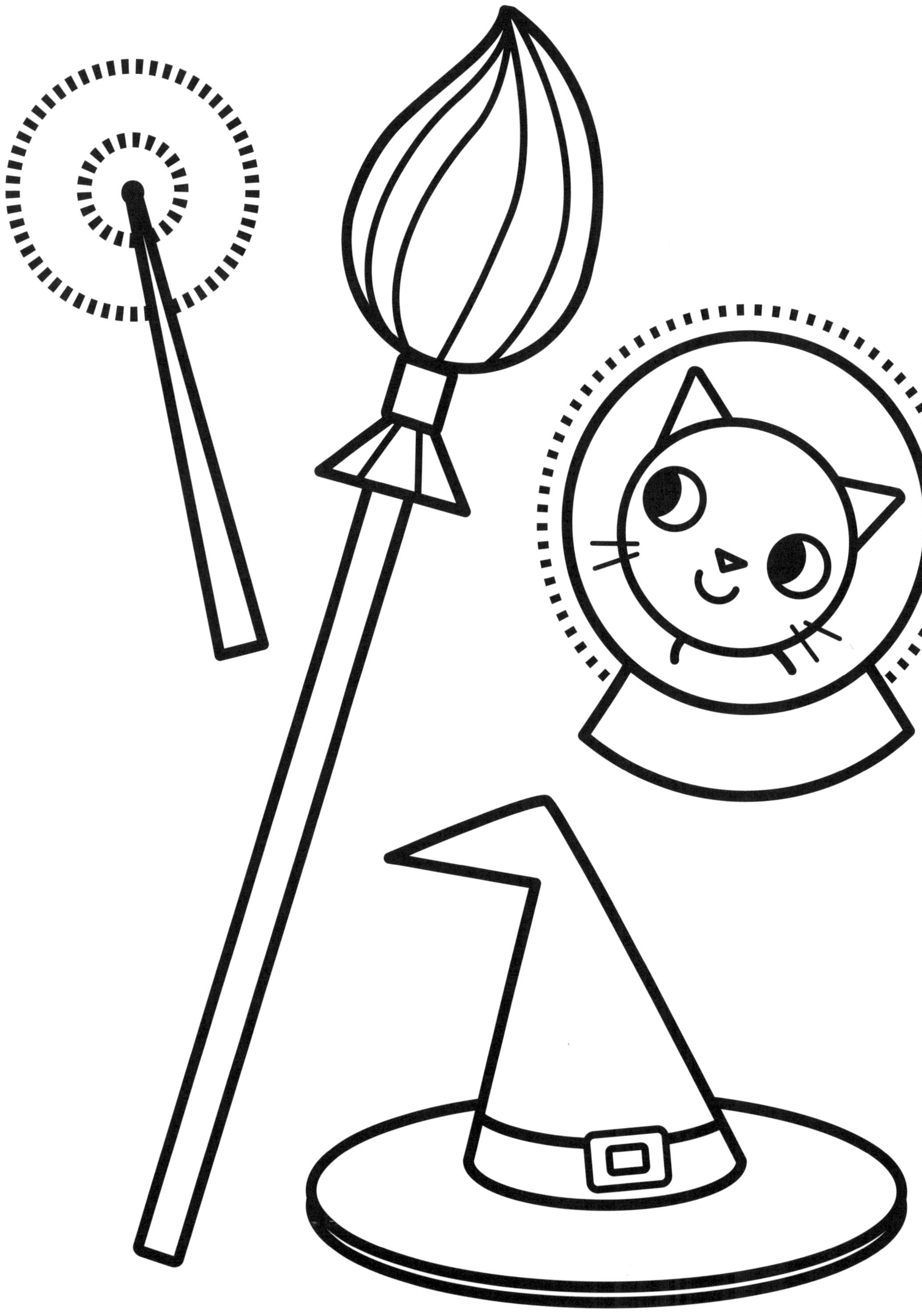

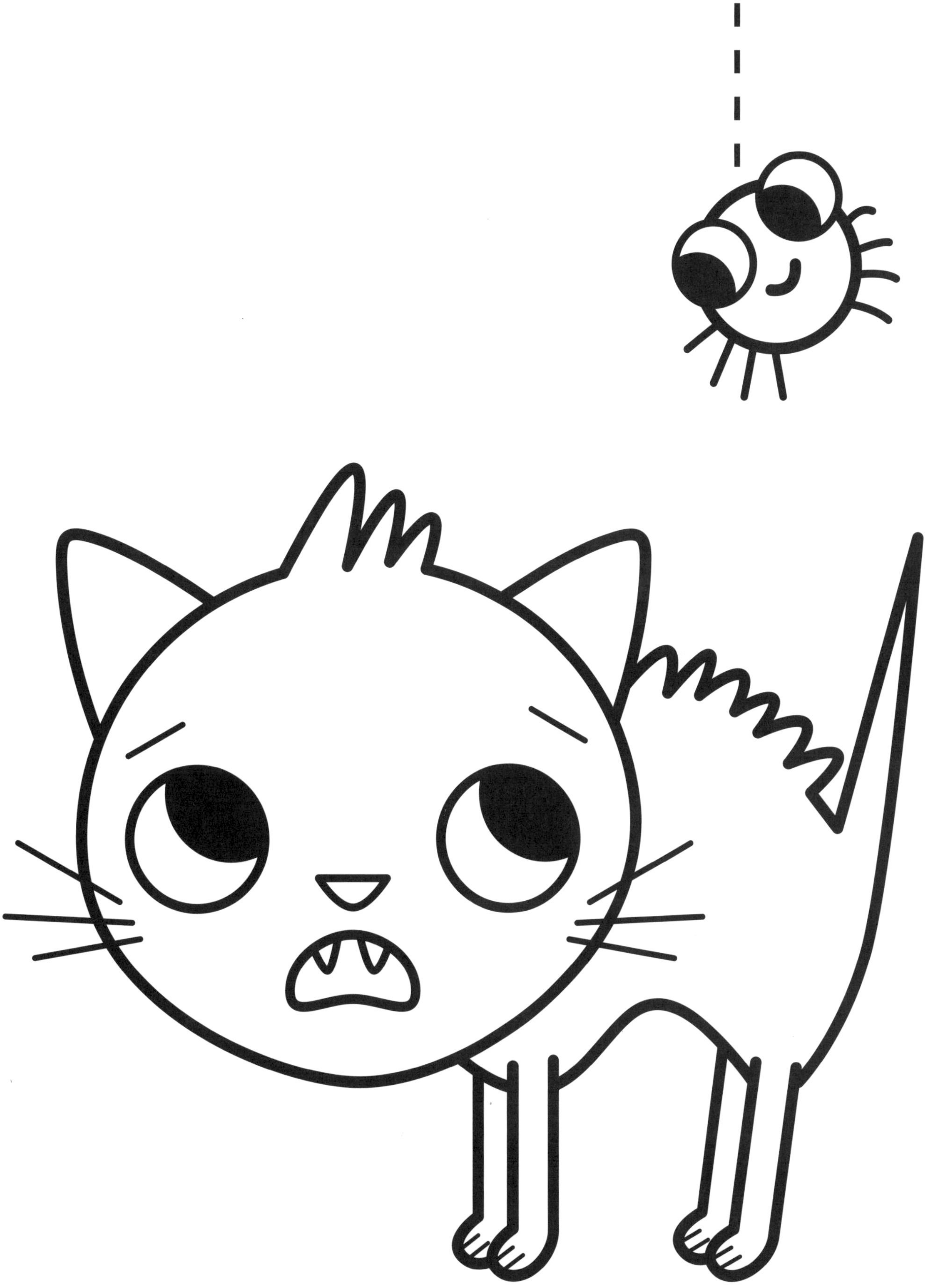

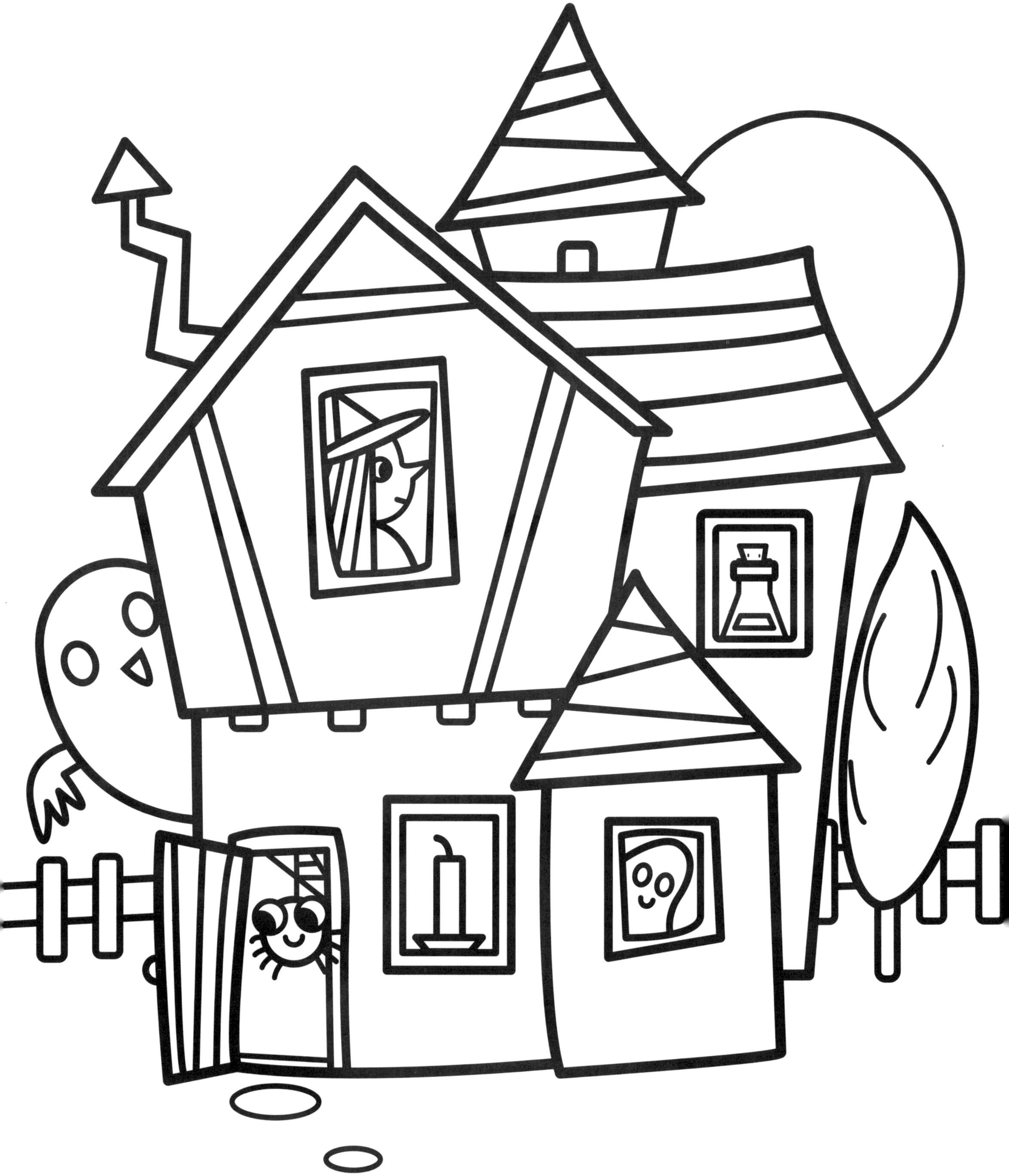

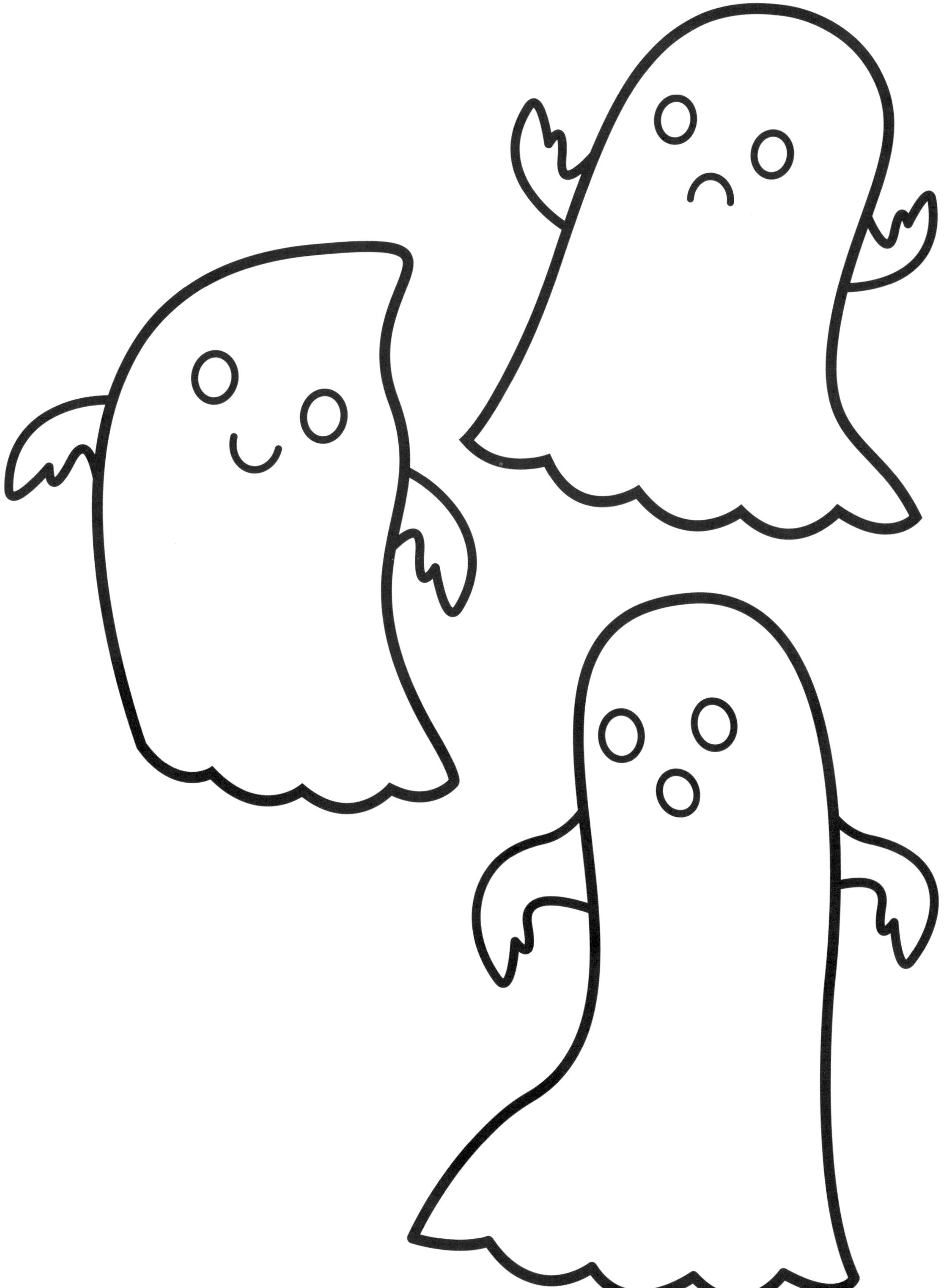

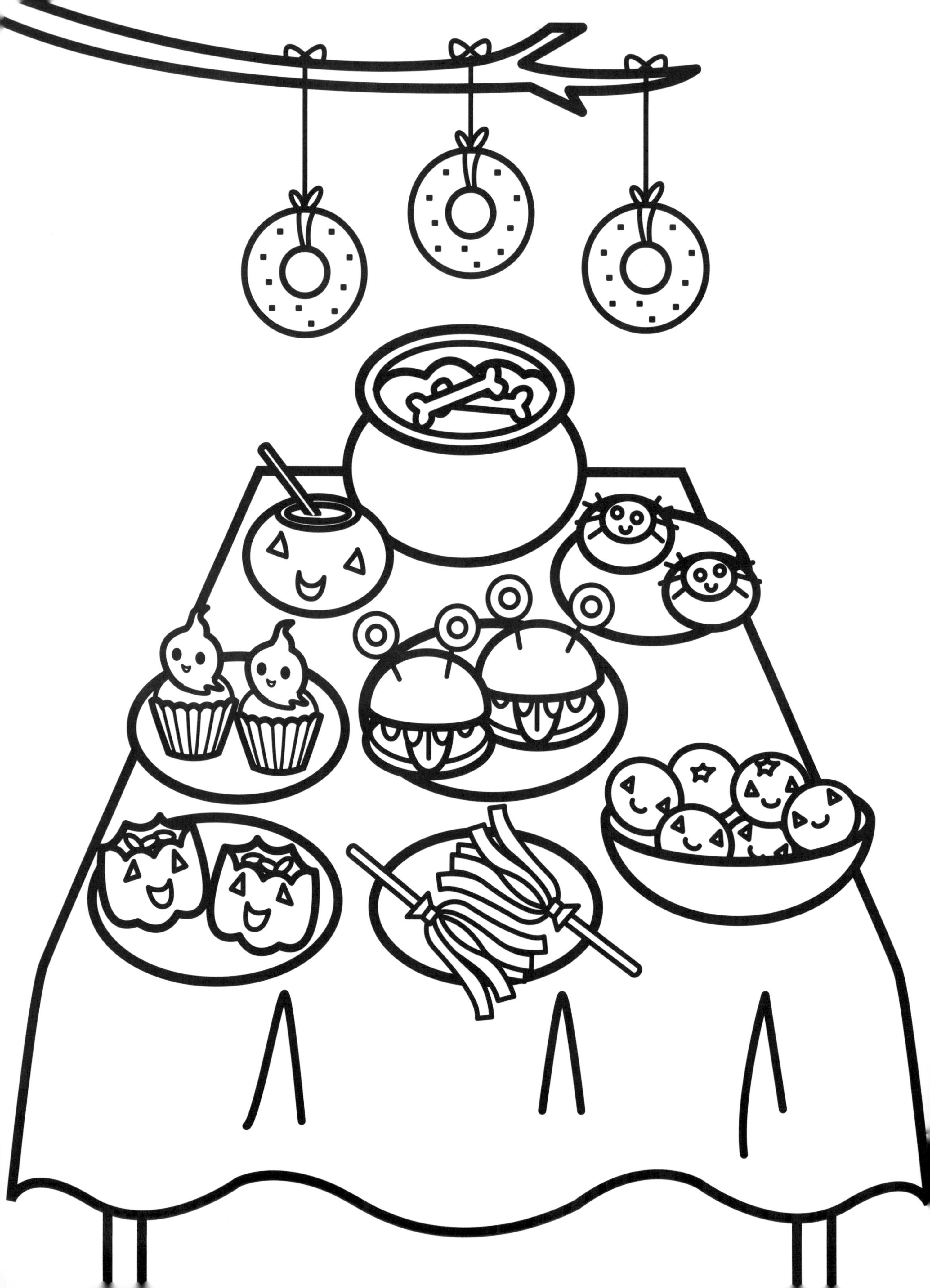

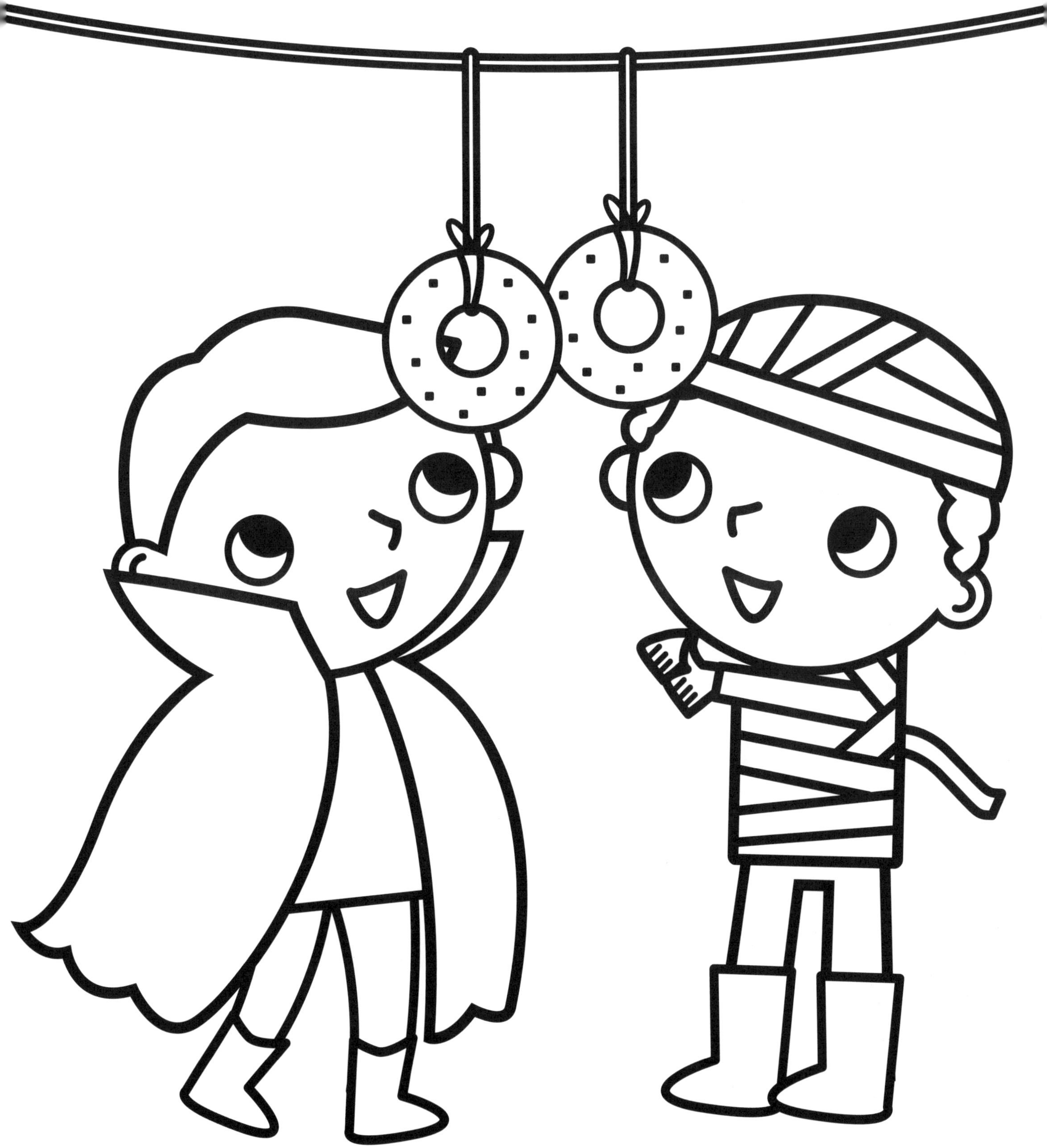

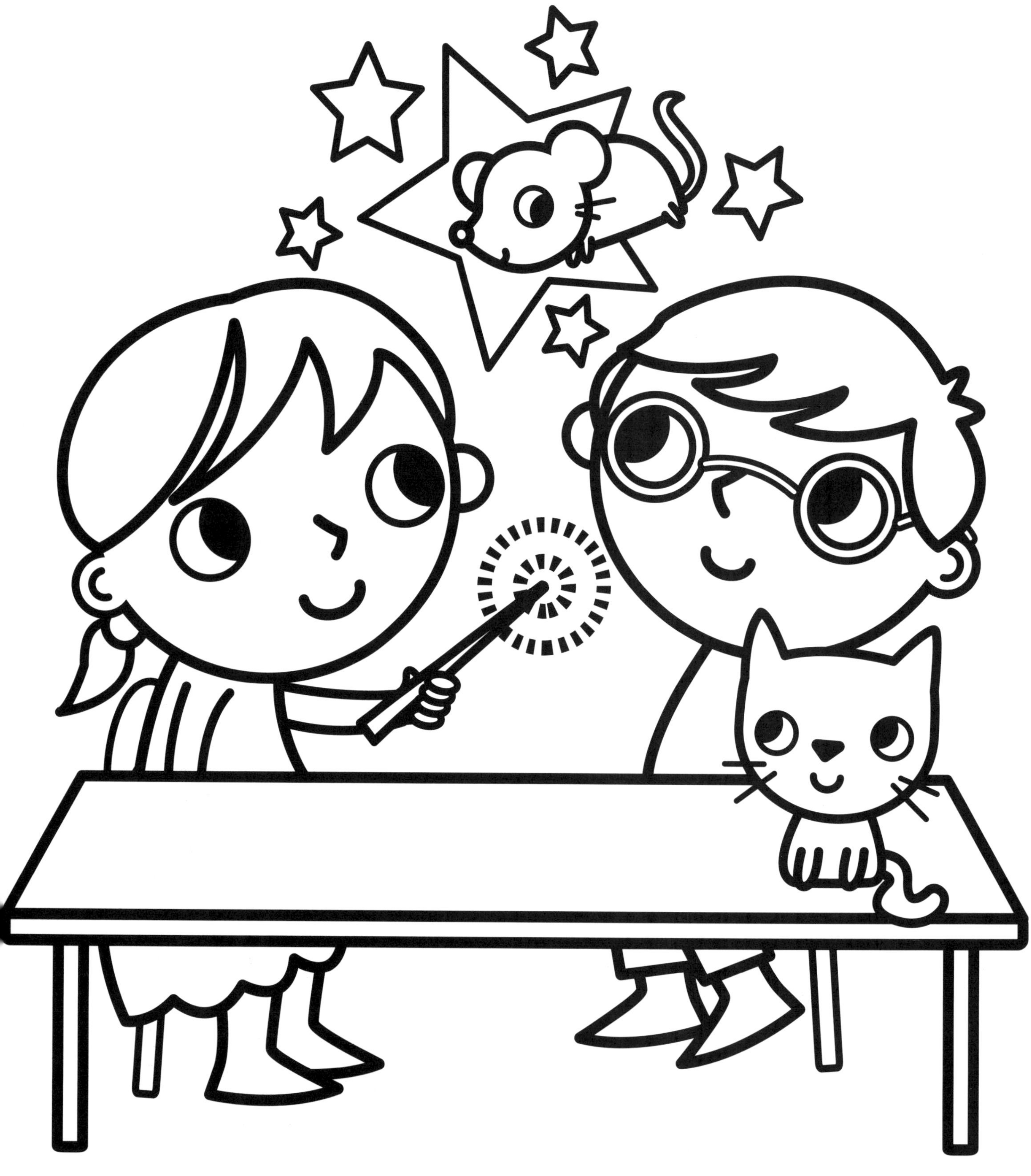

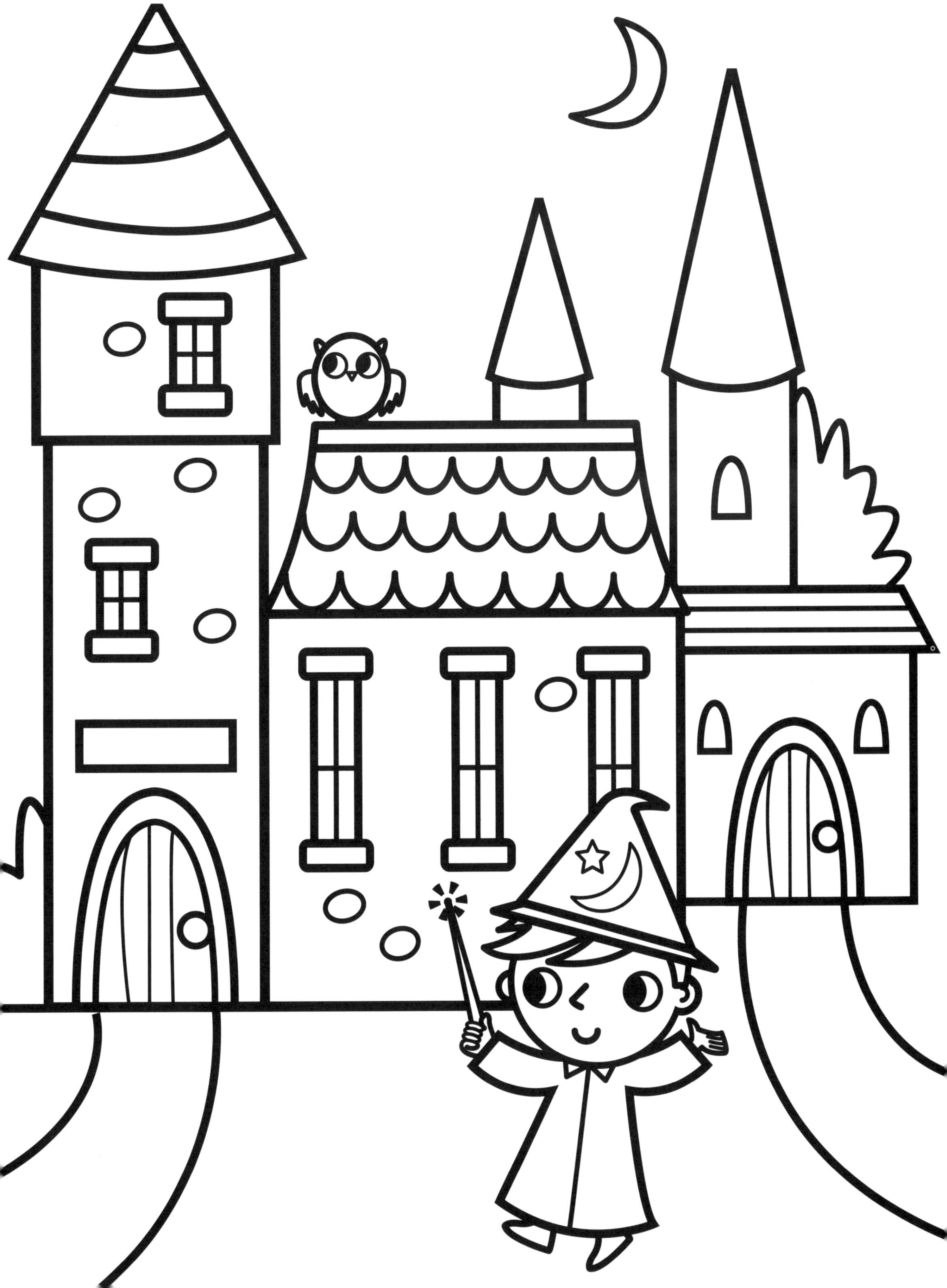

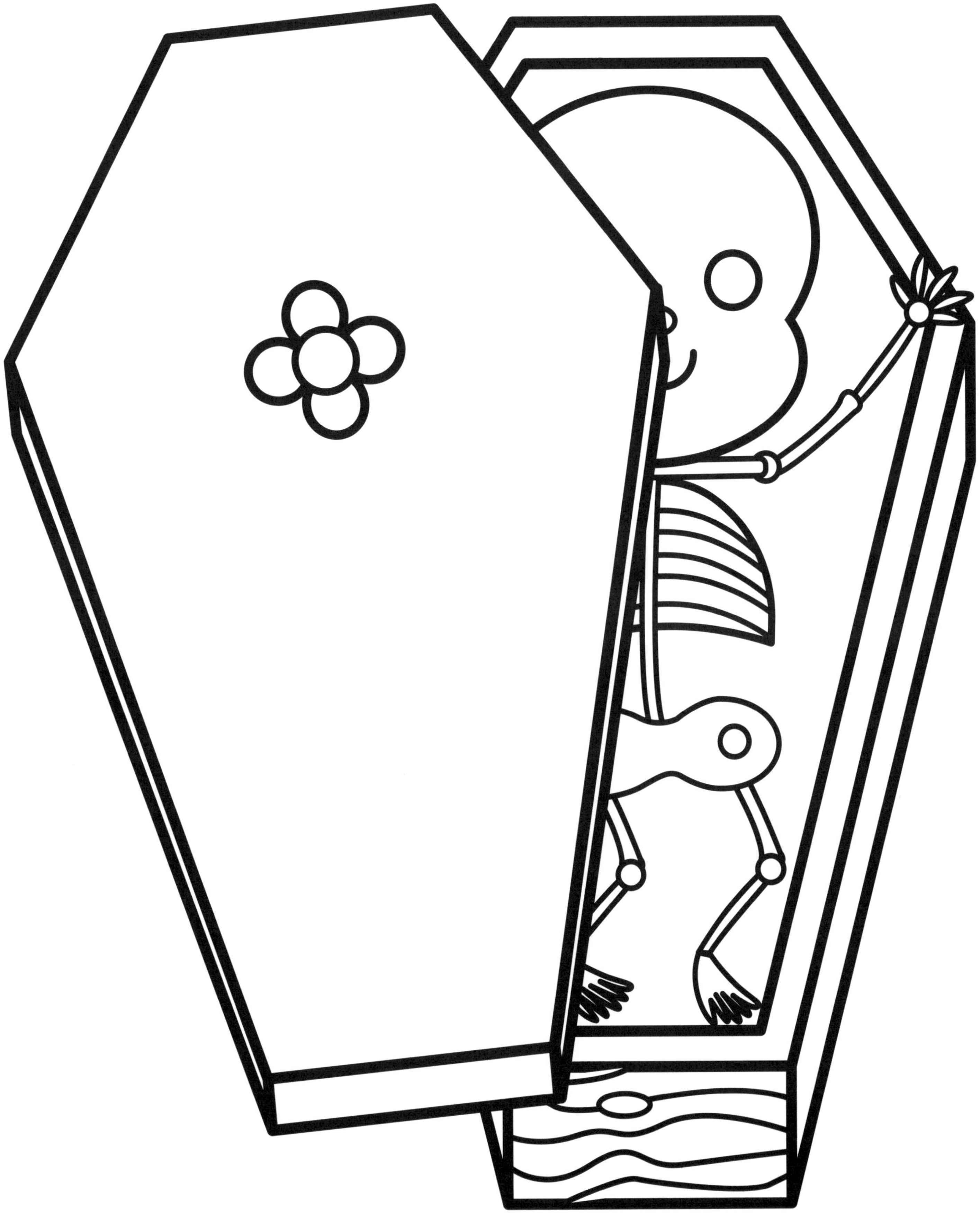

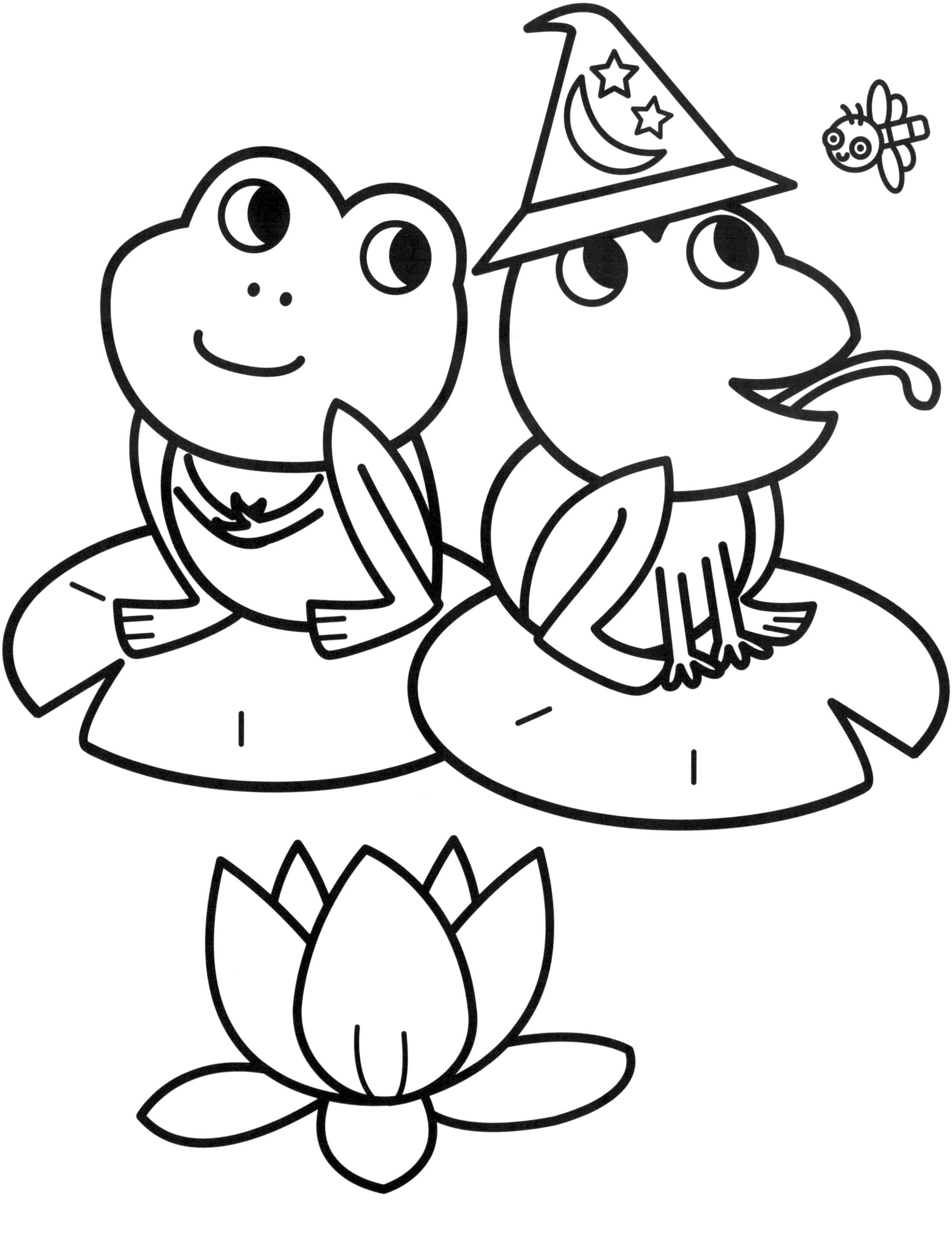

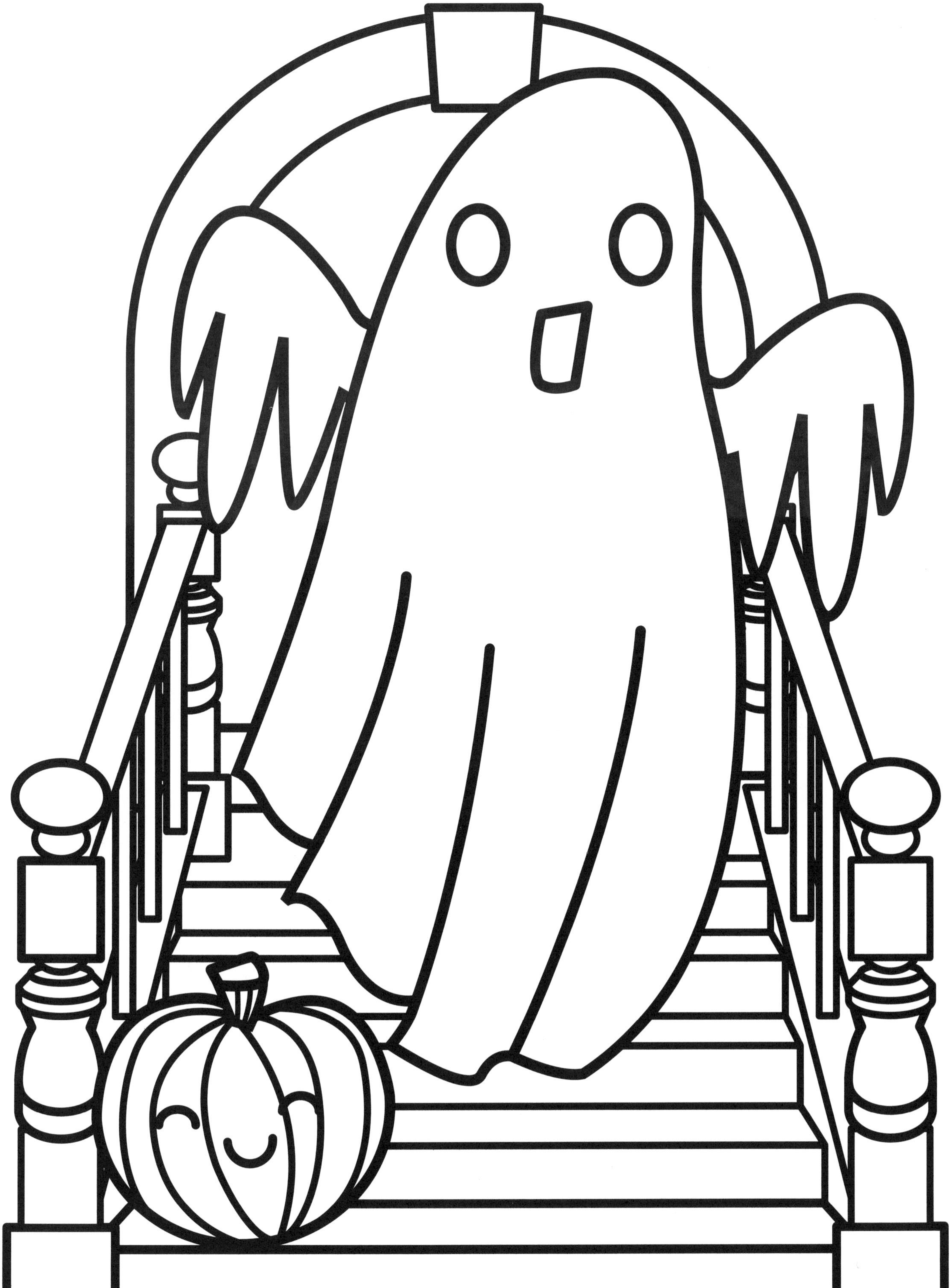

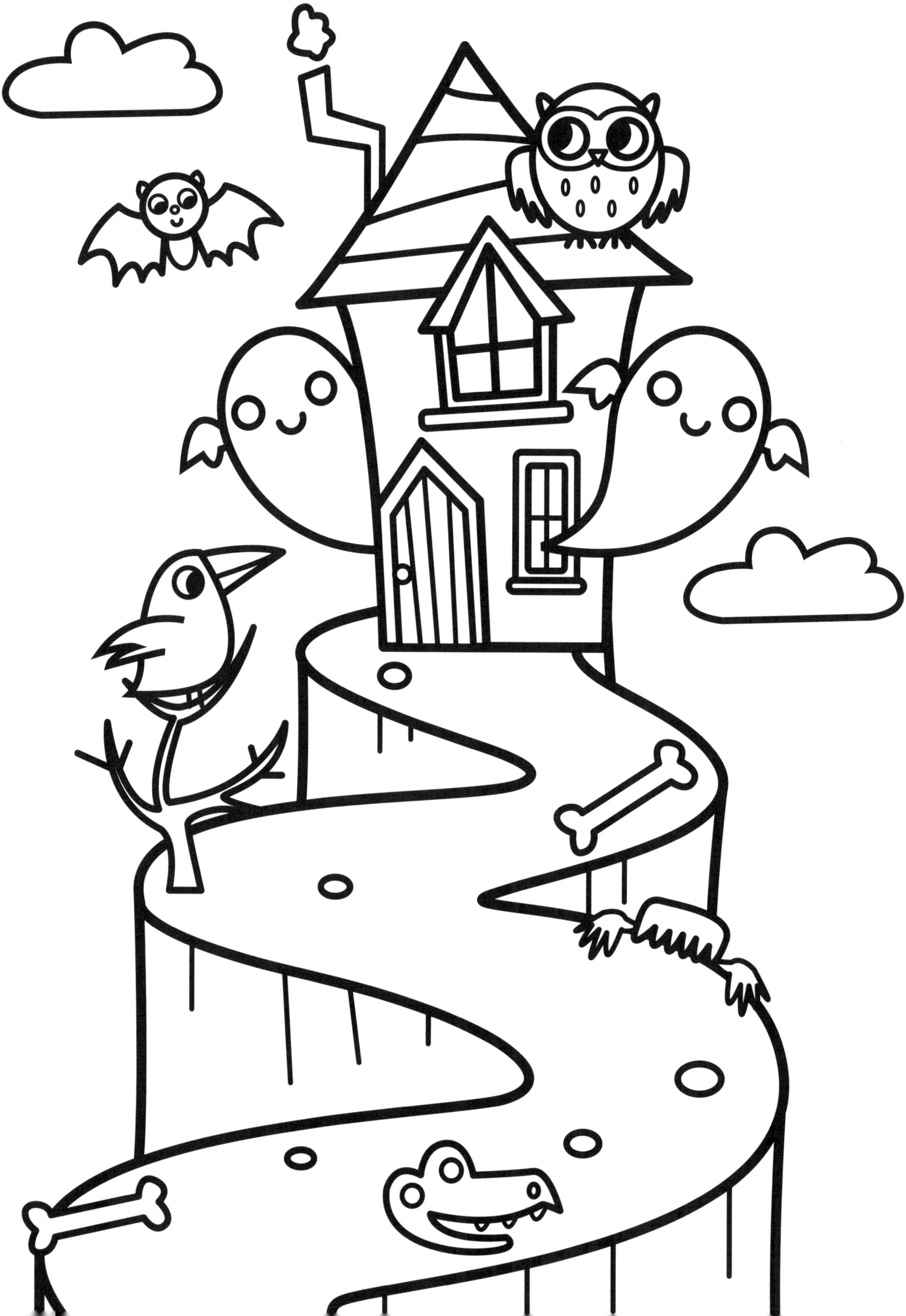

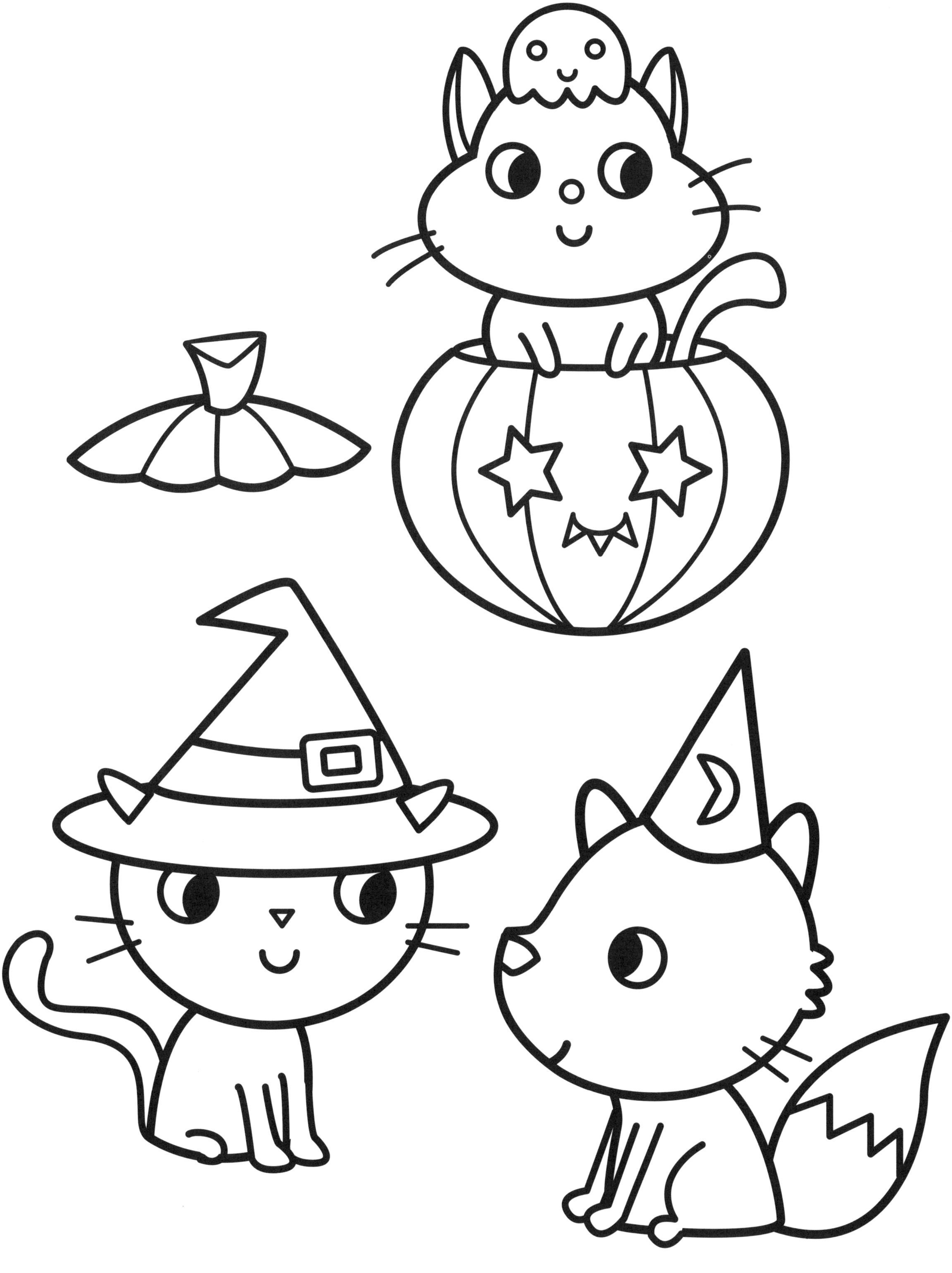

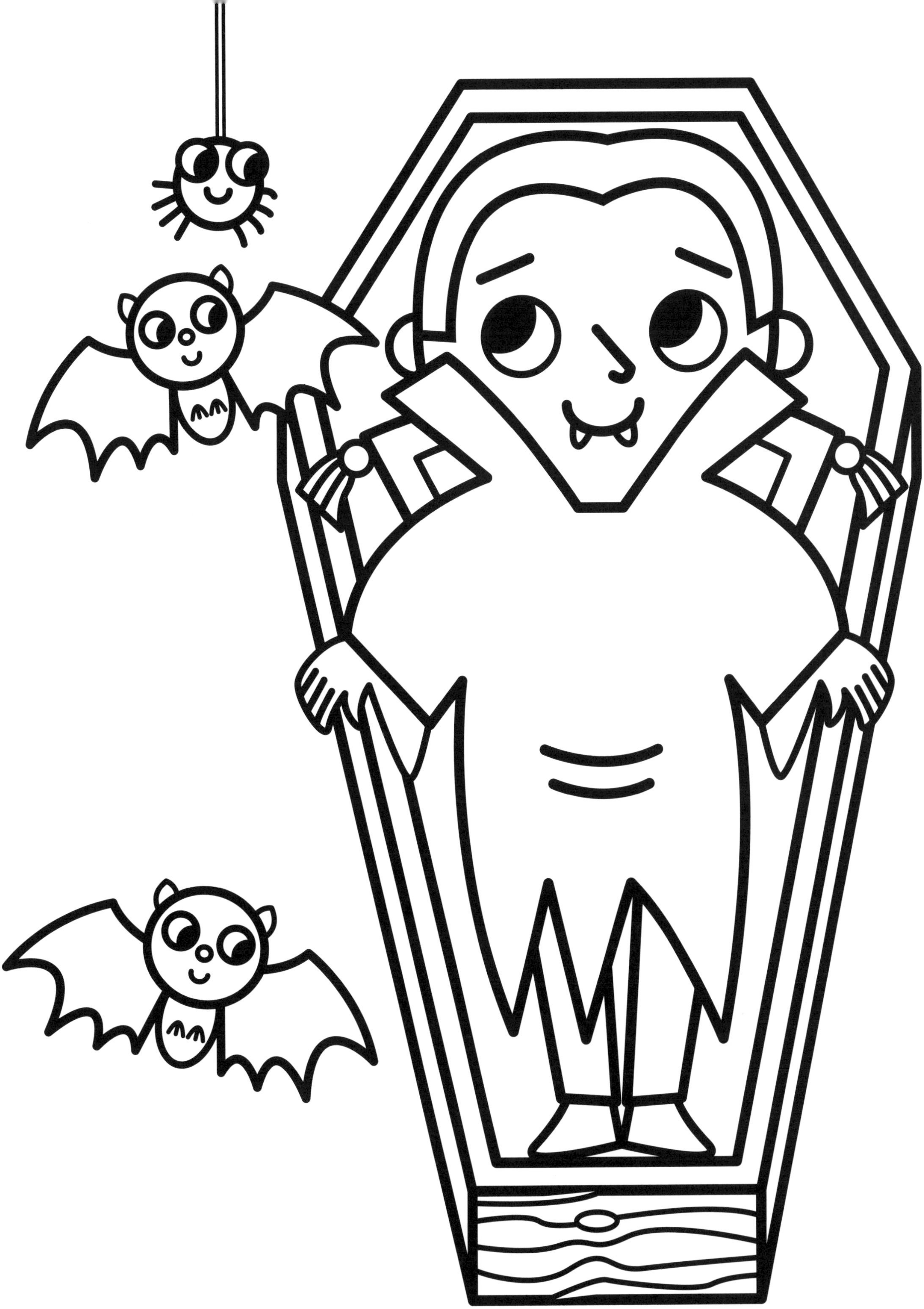

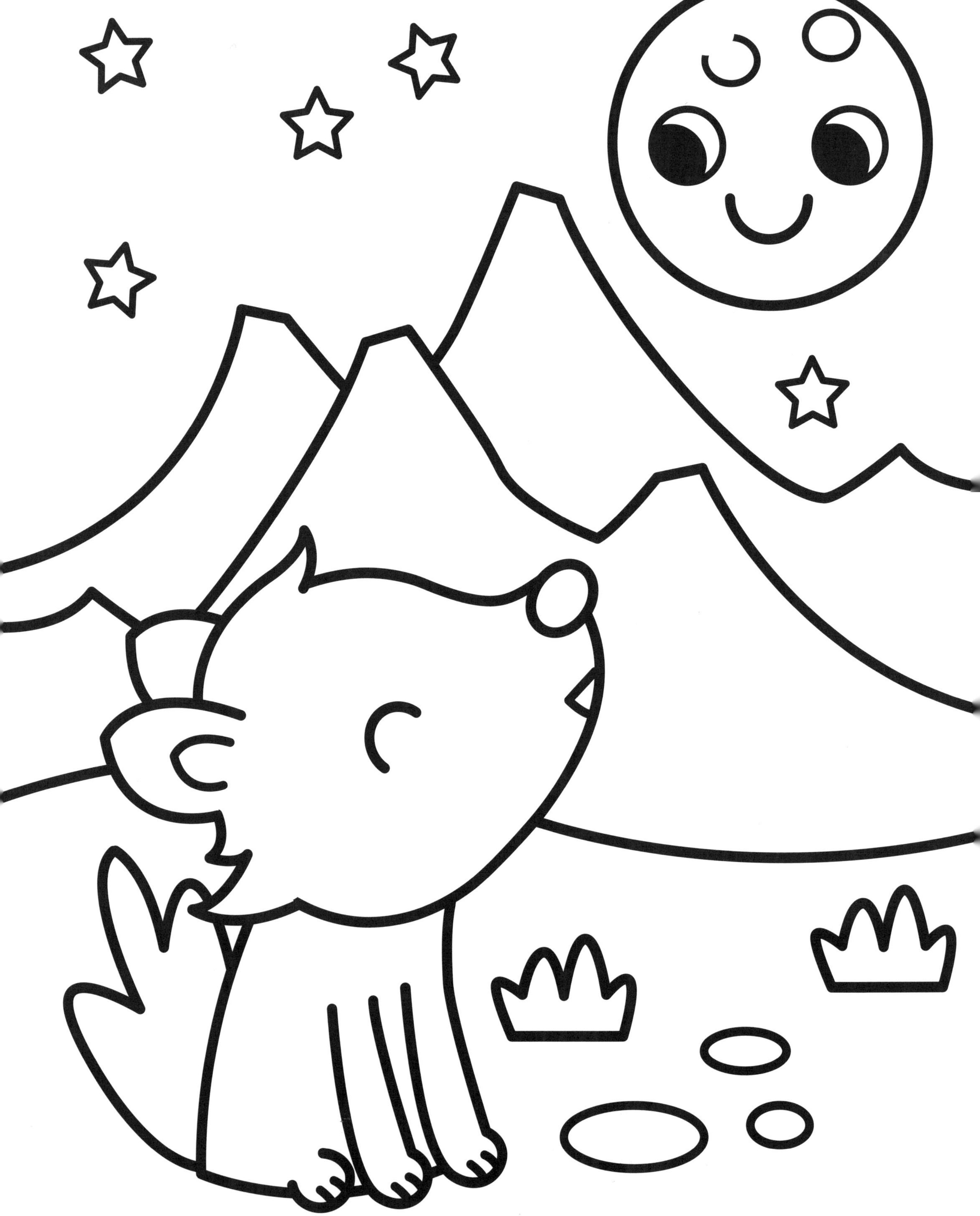

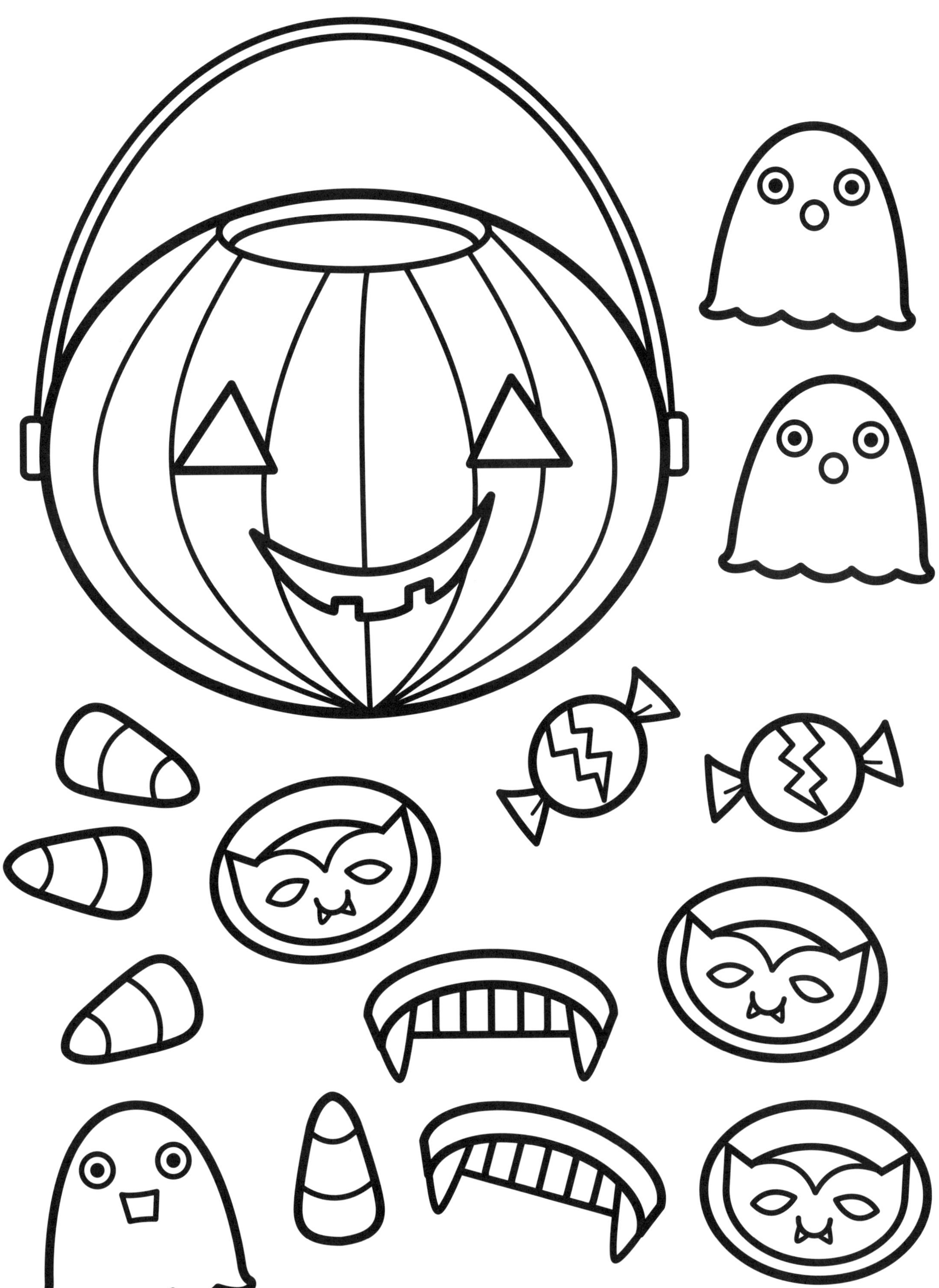

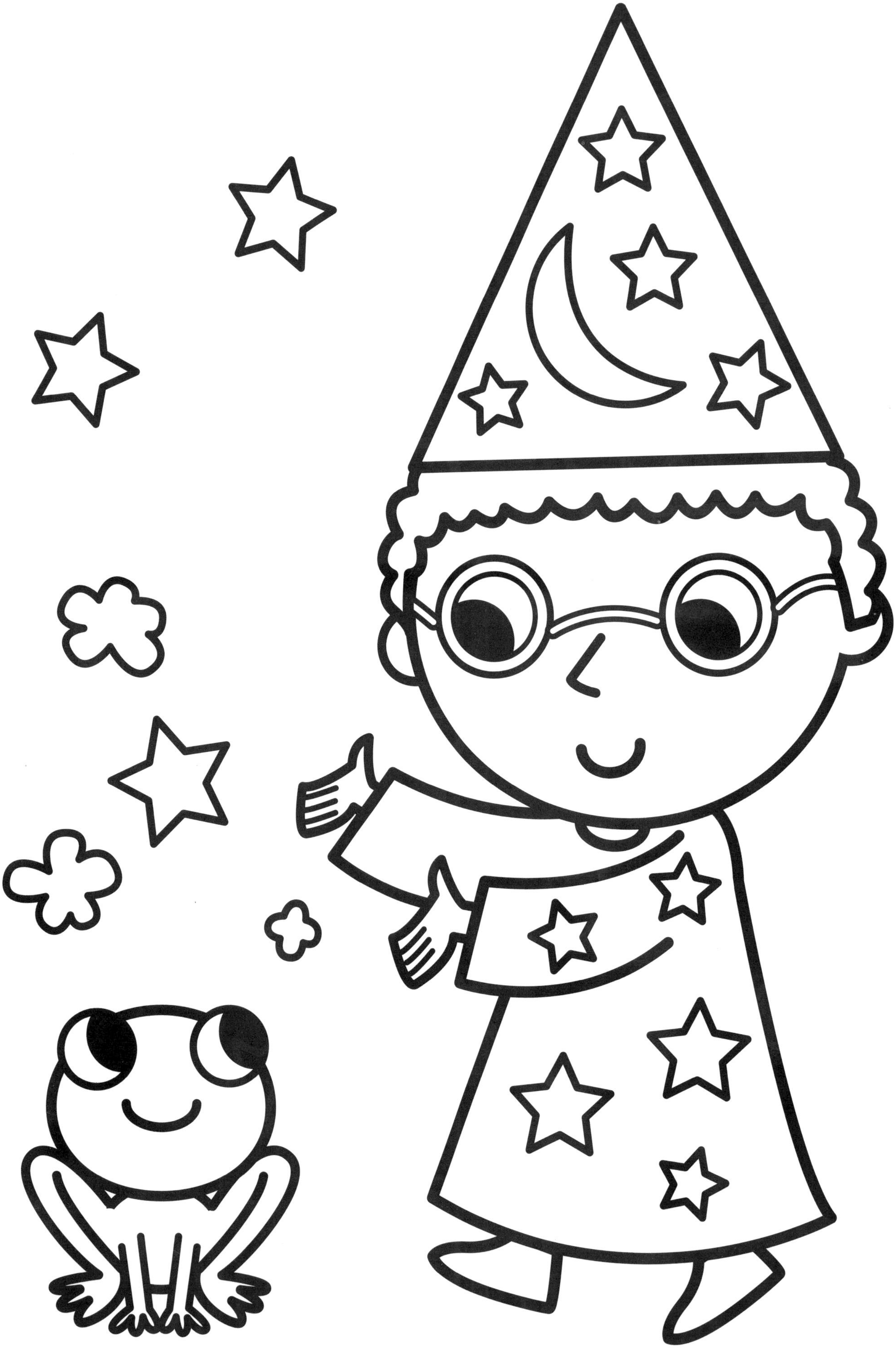

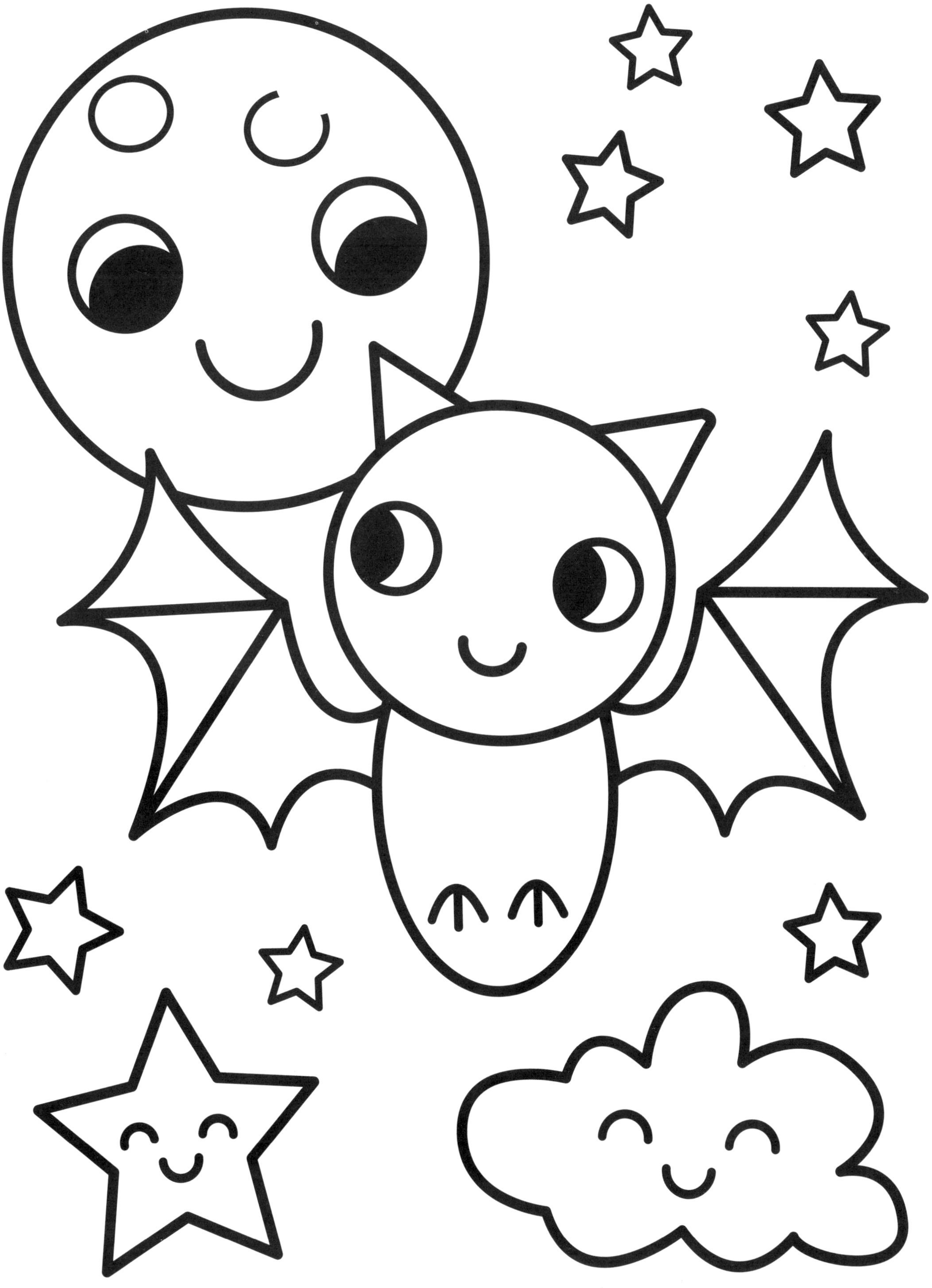

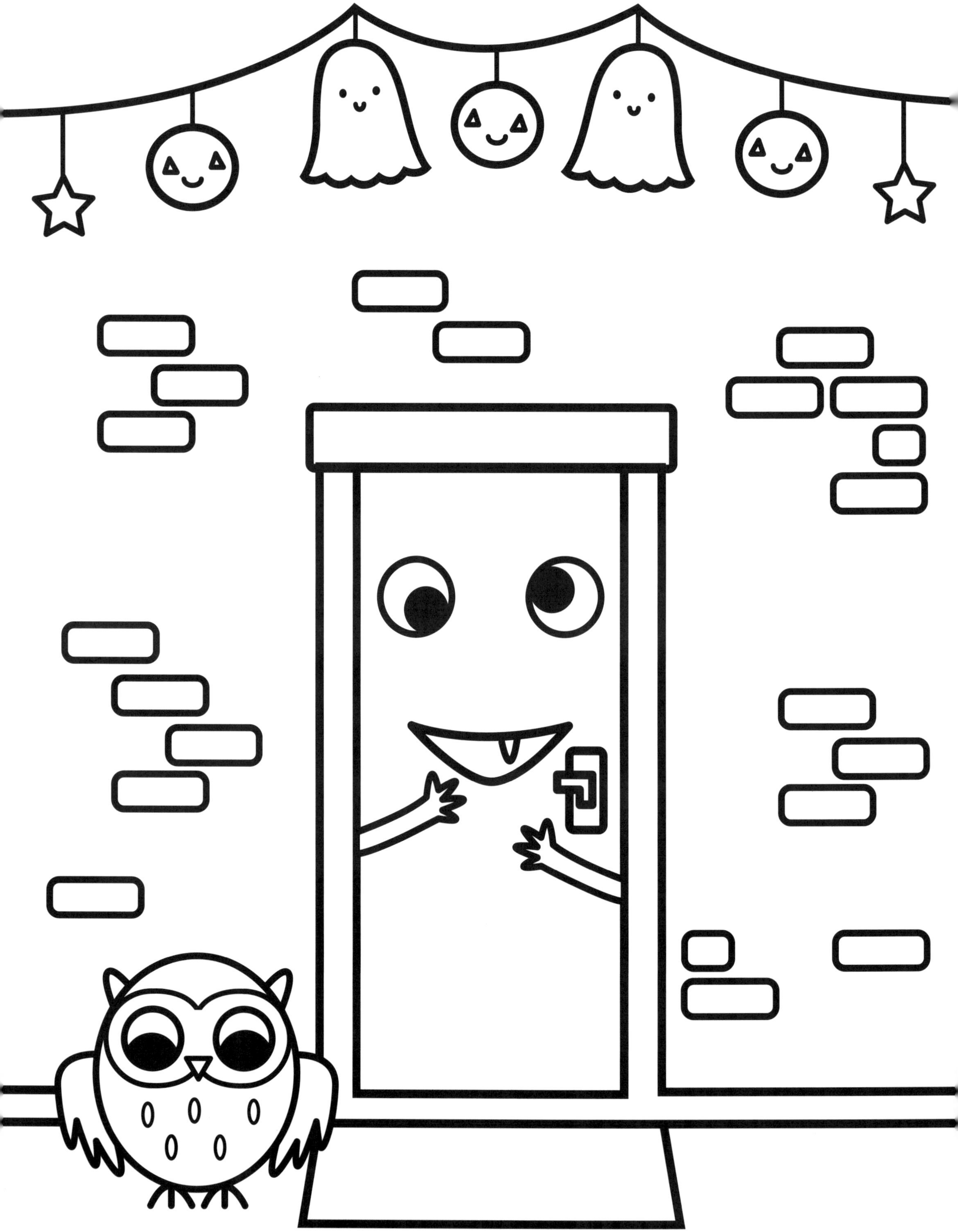

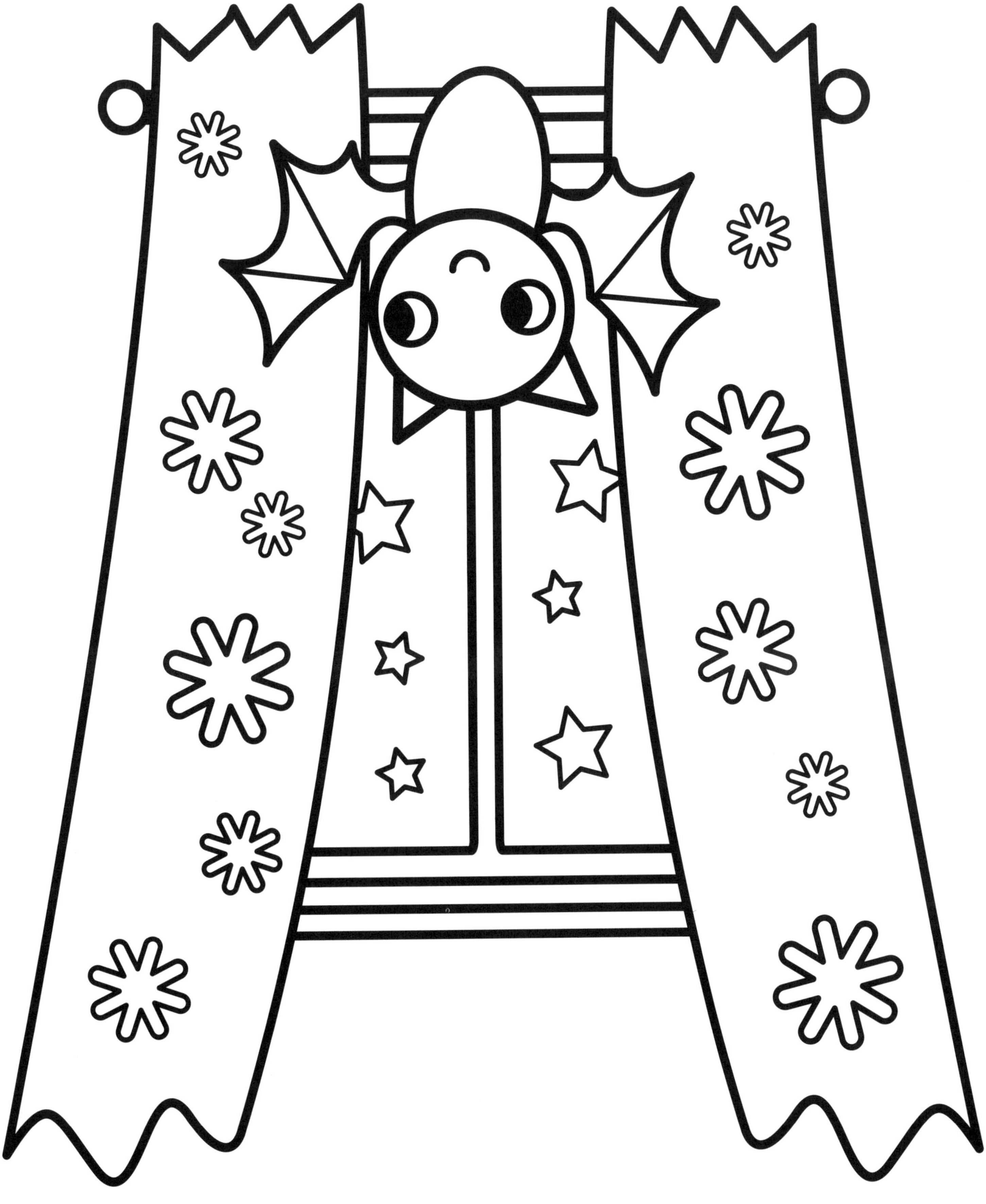

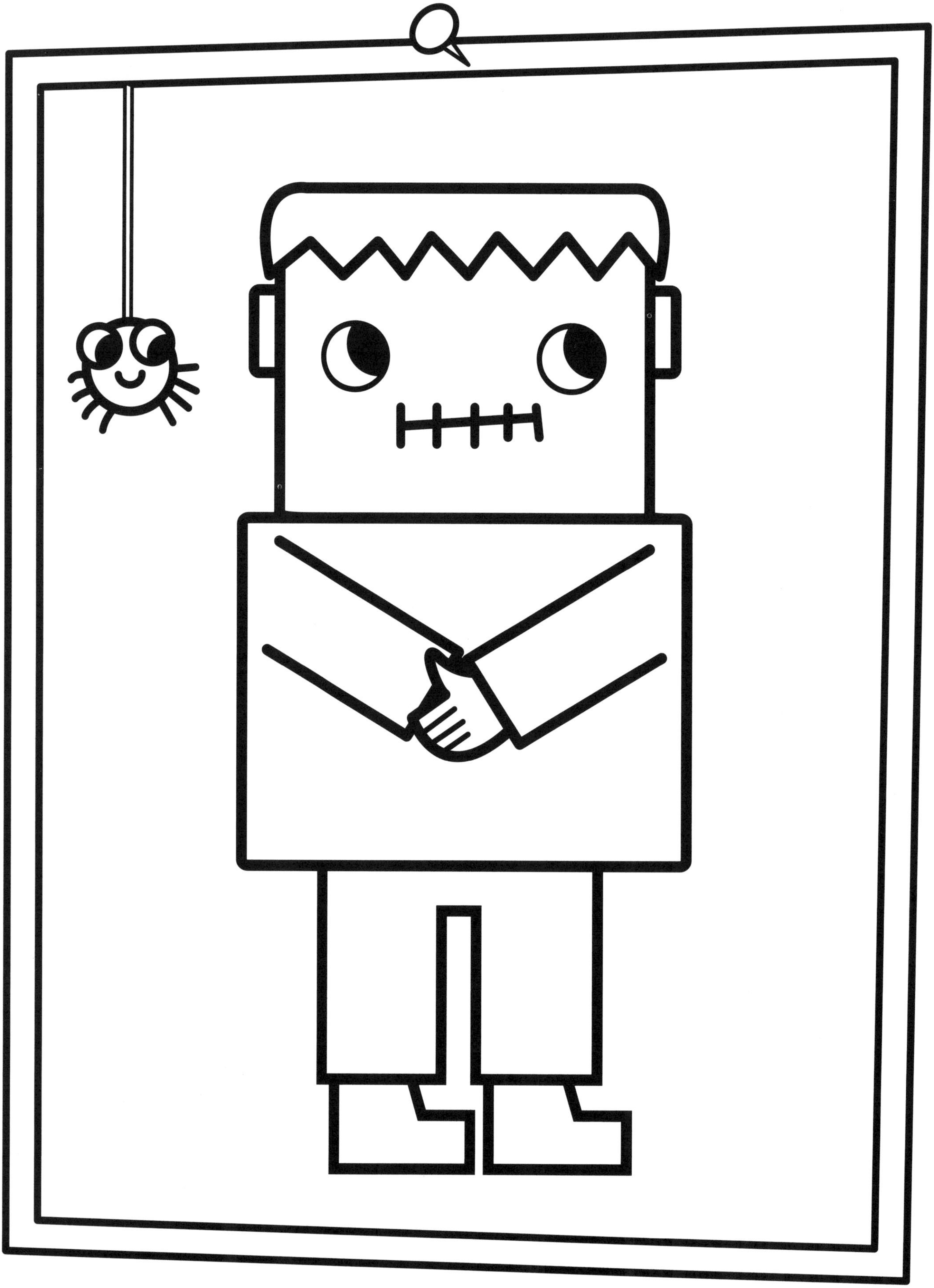

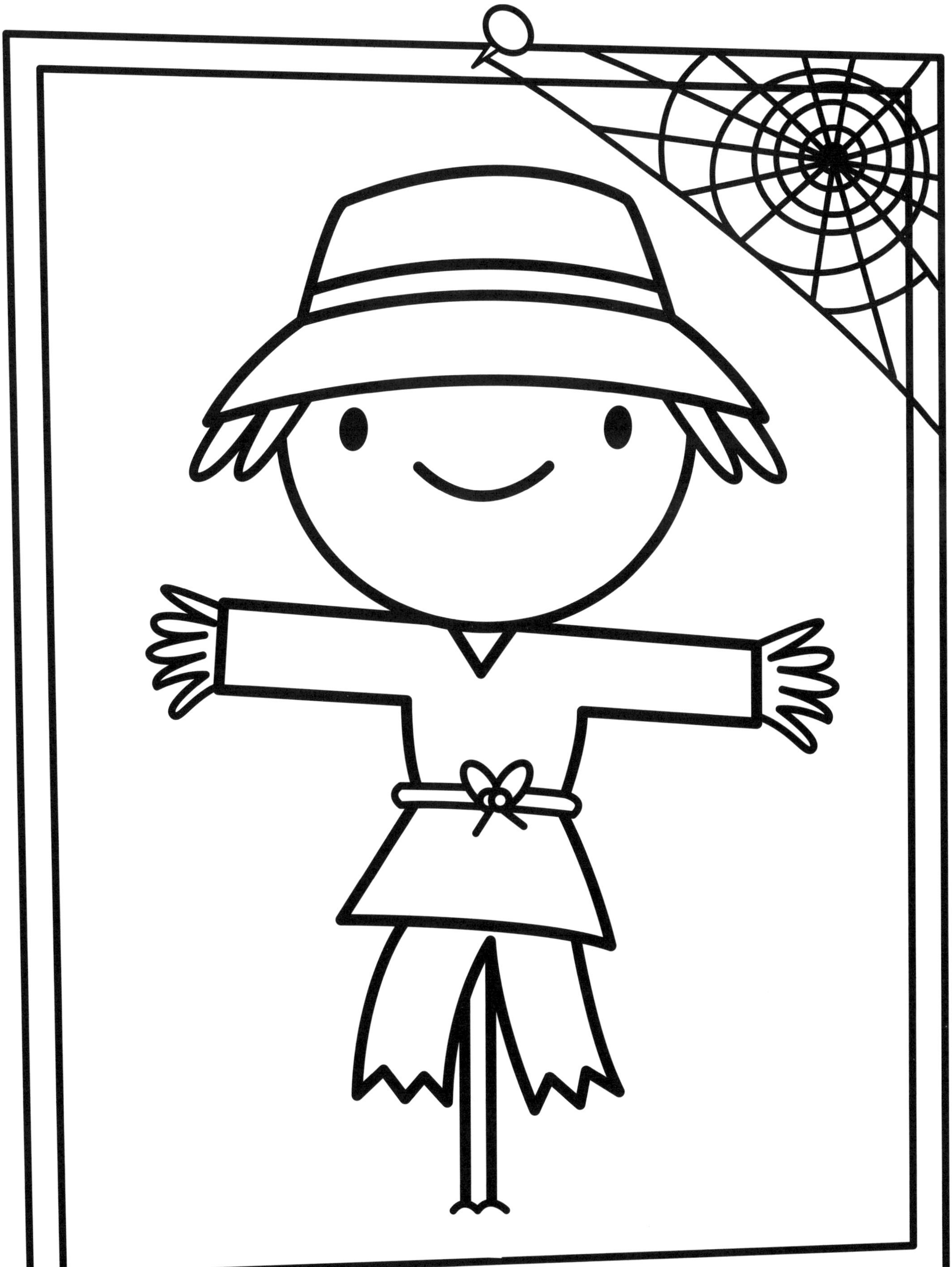

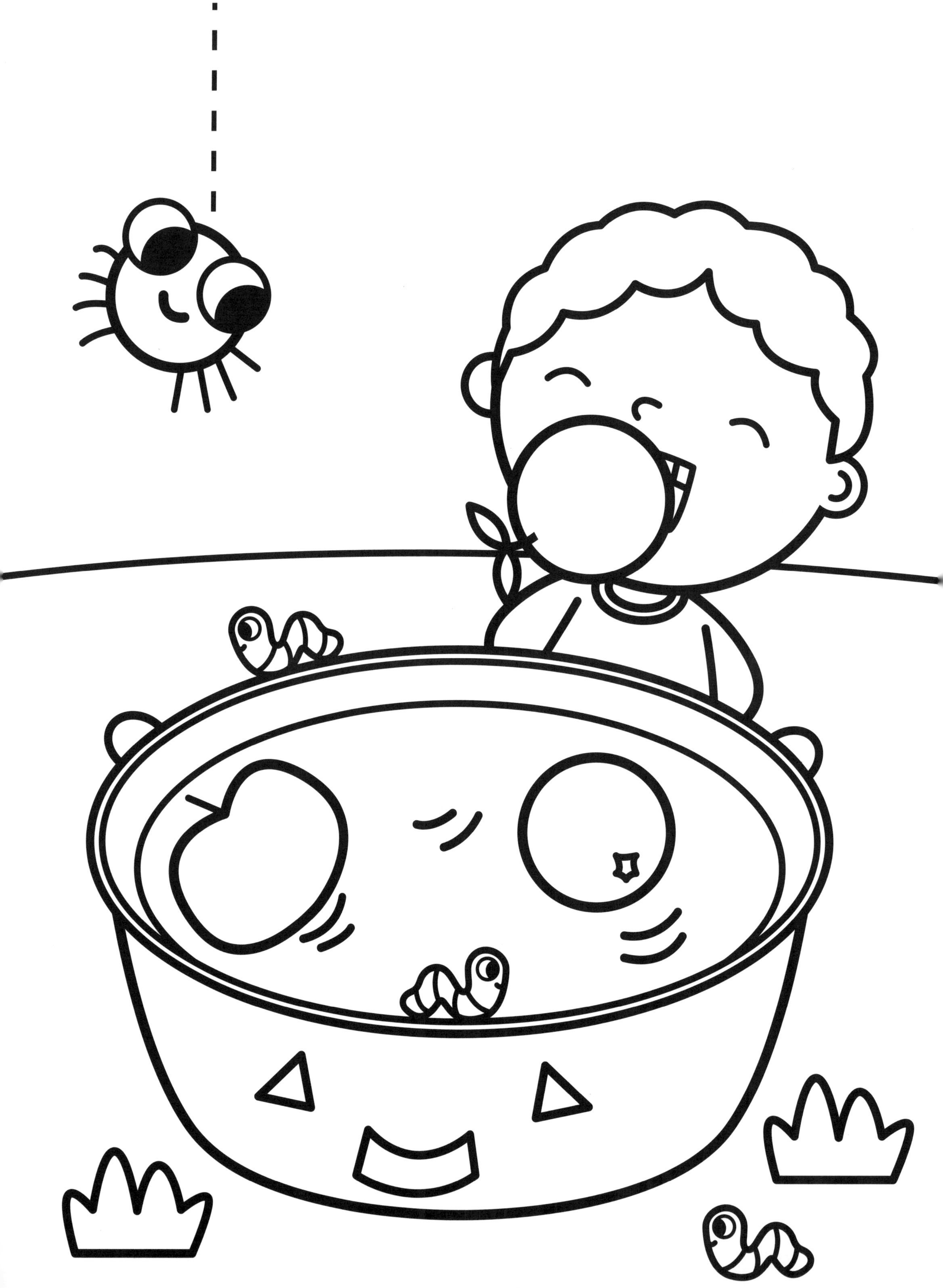

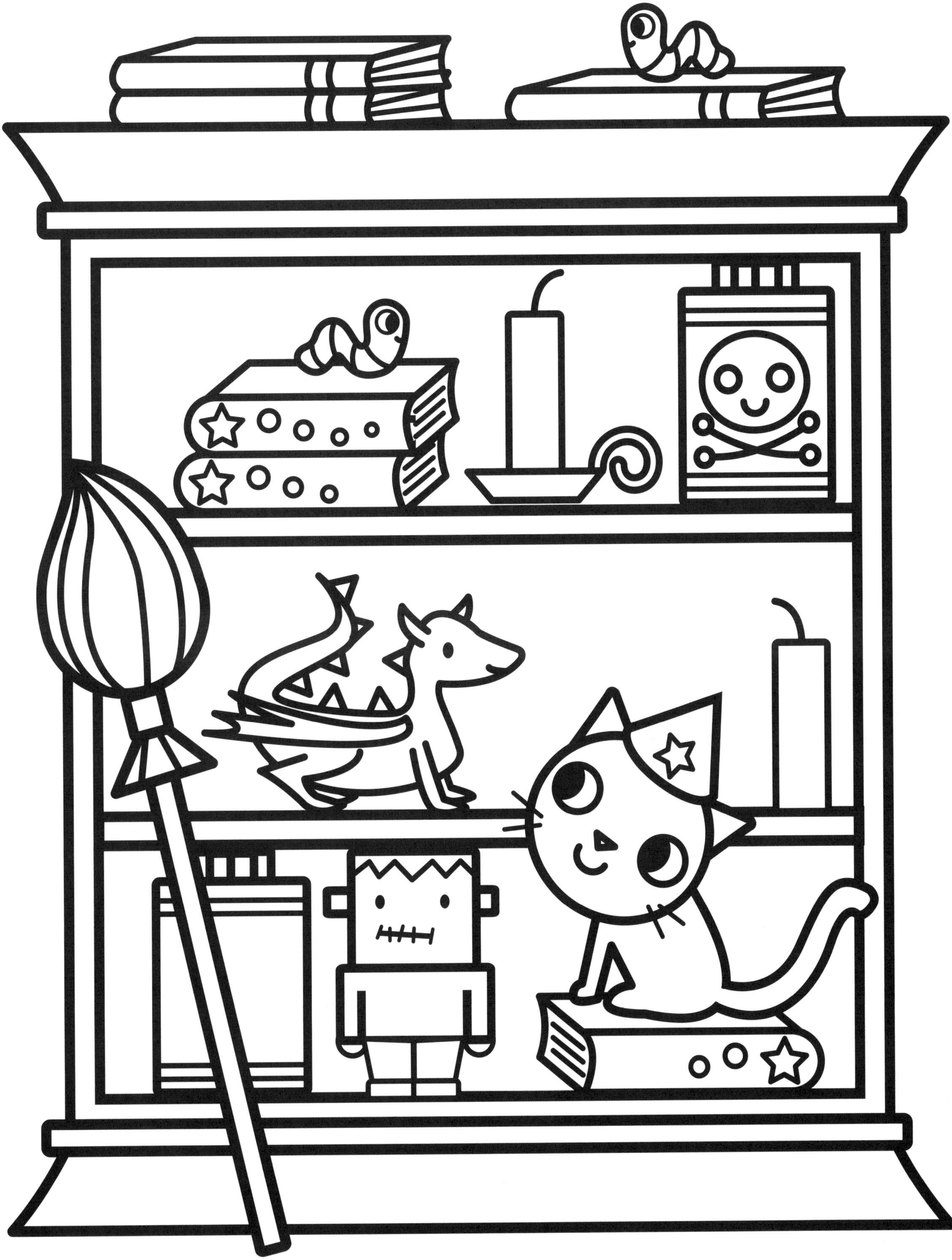

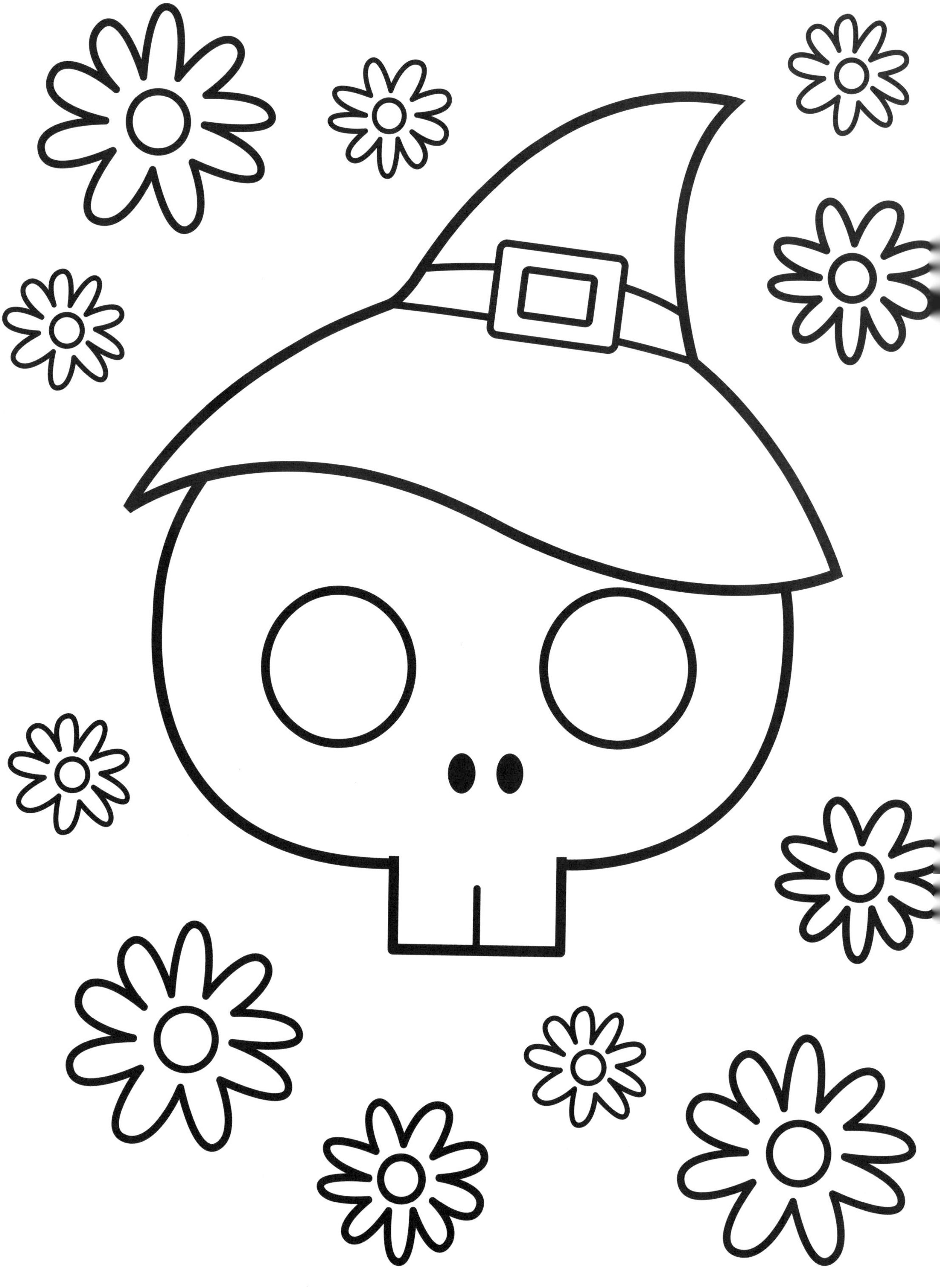

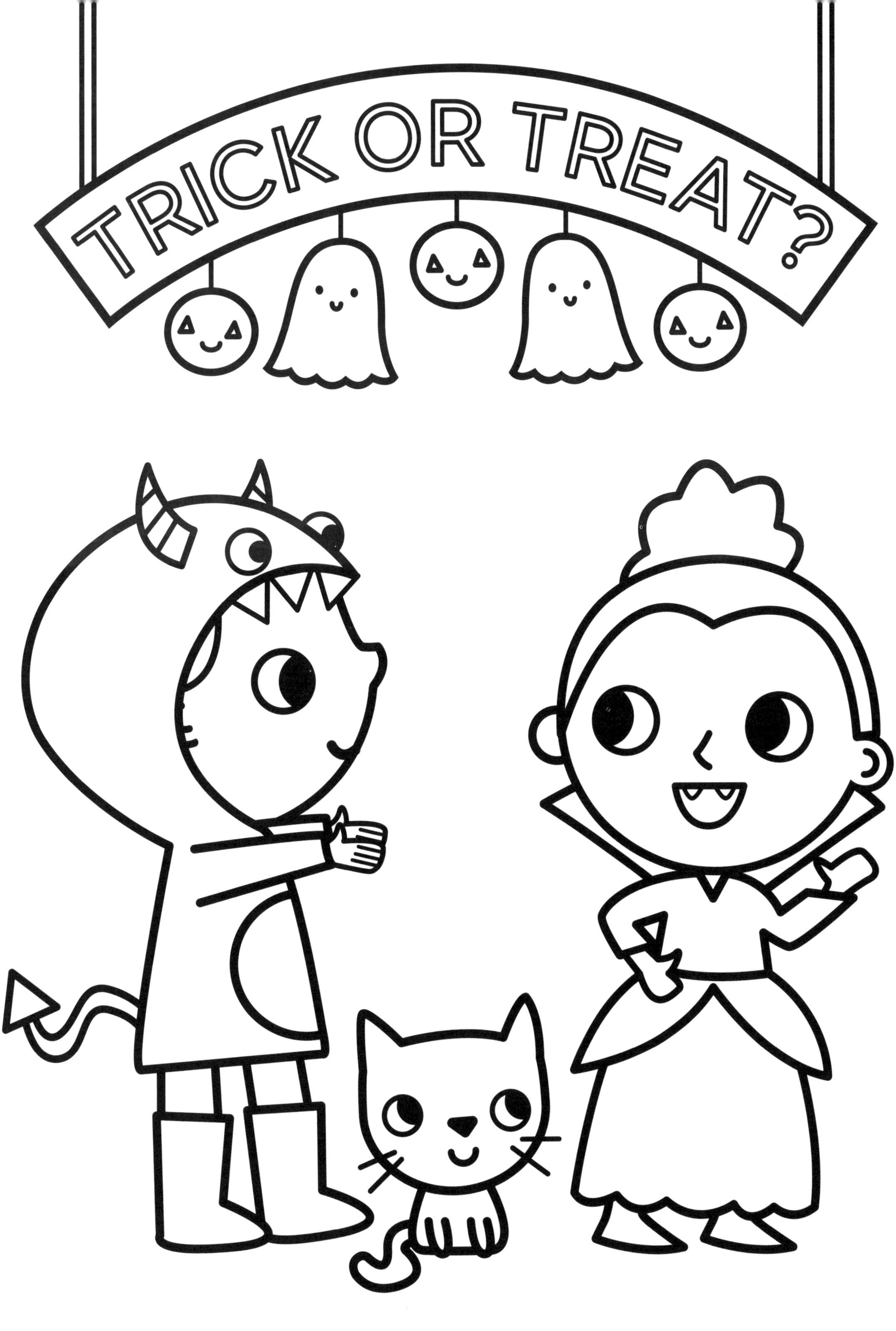
TRICK OR TREAT?

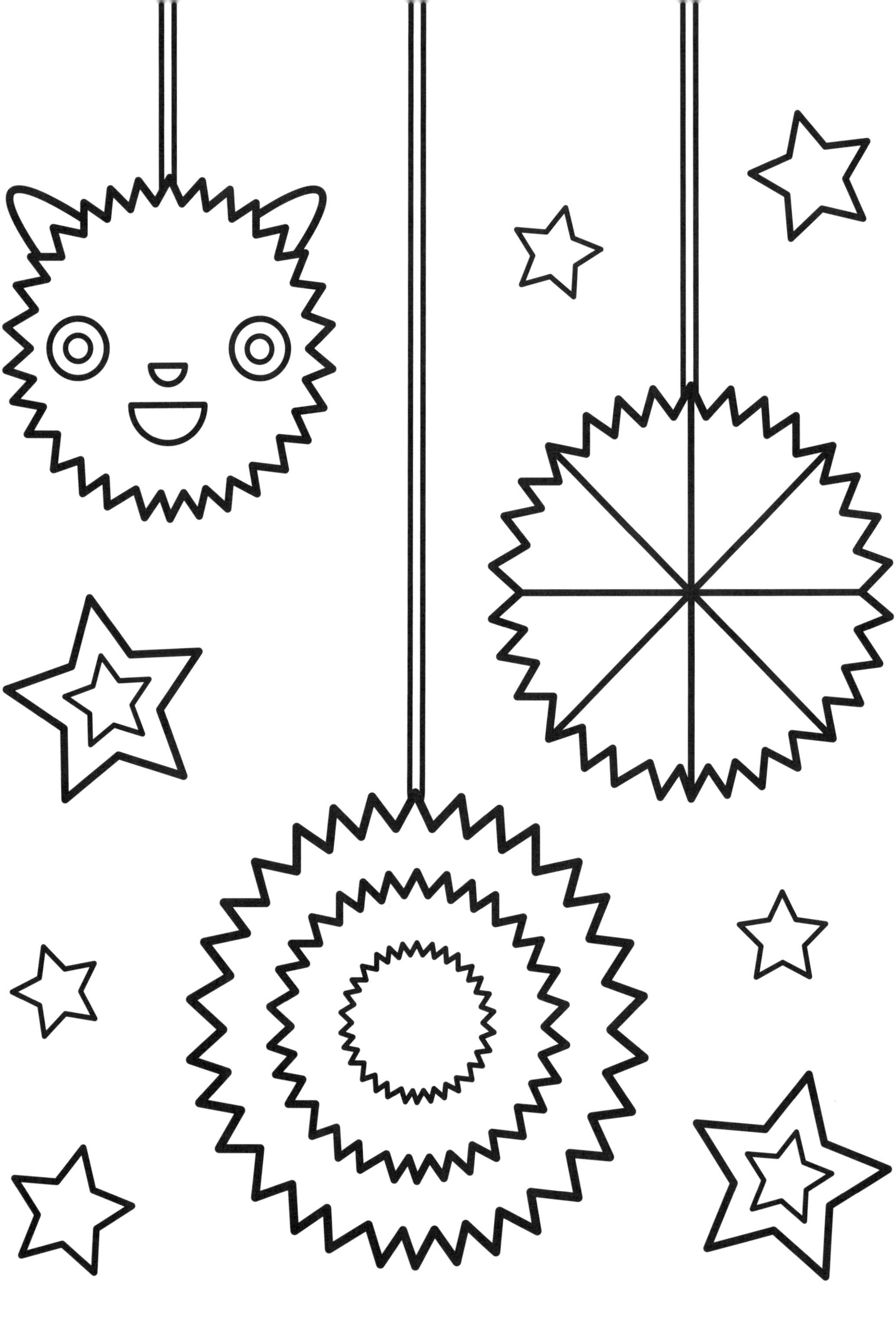

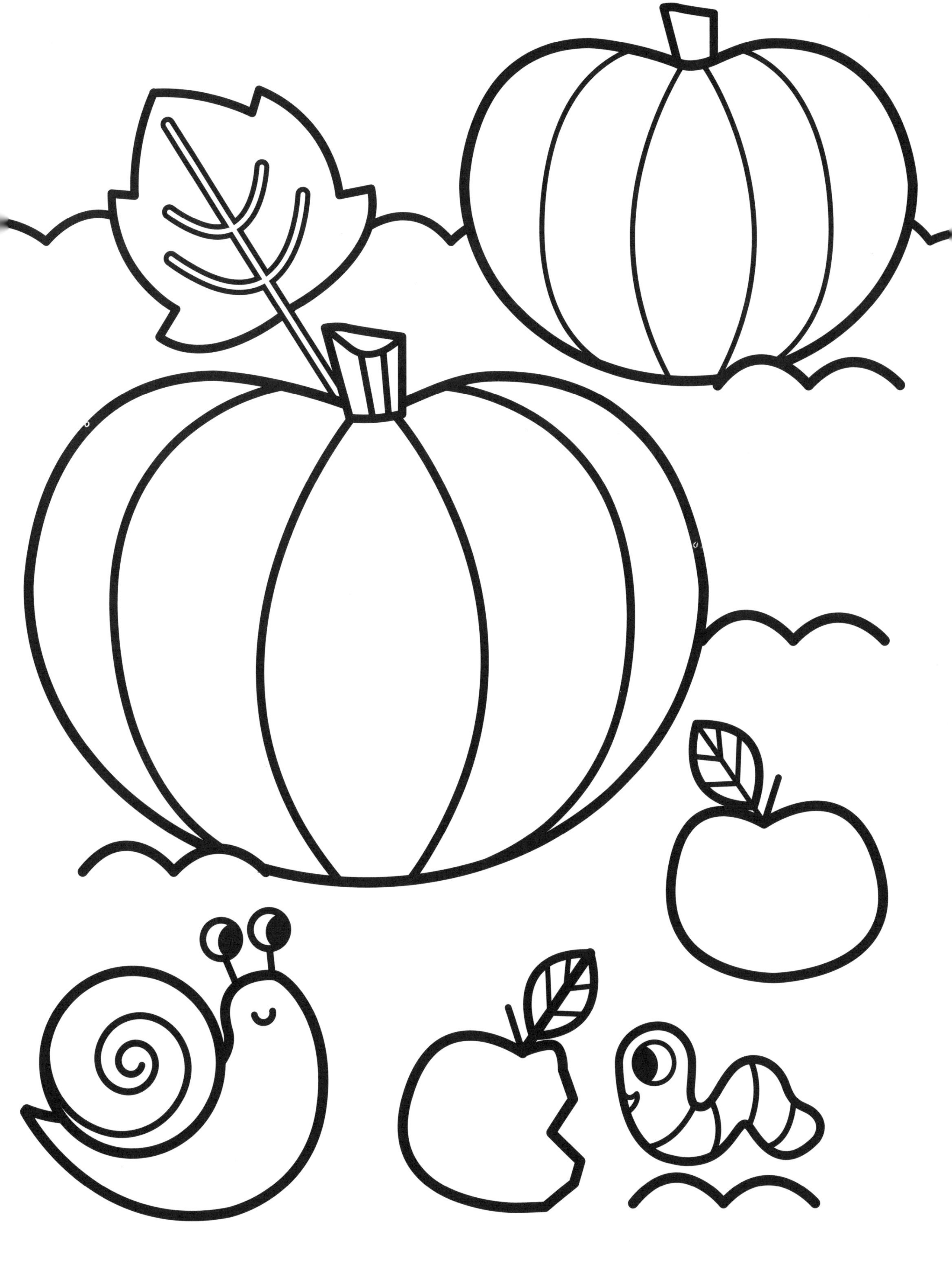

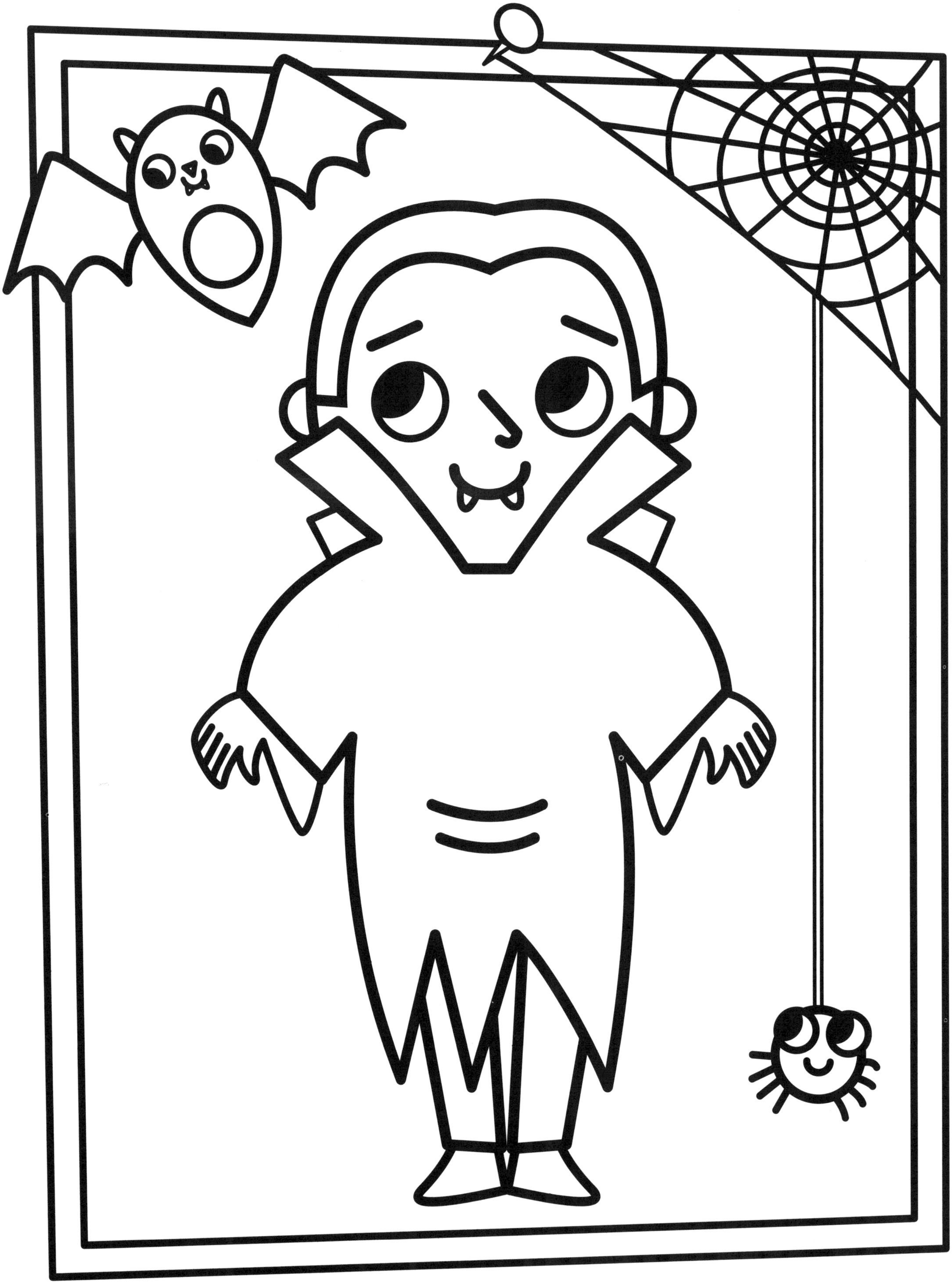

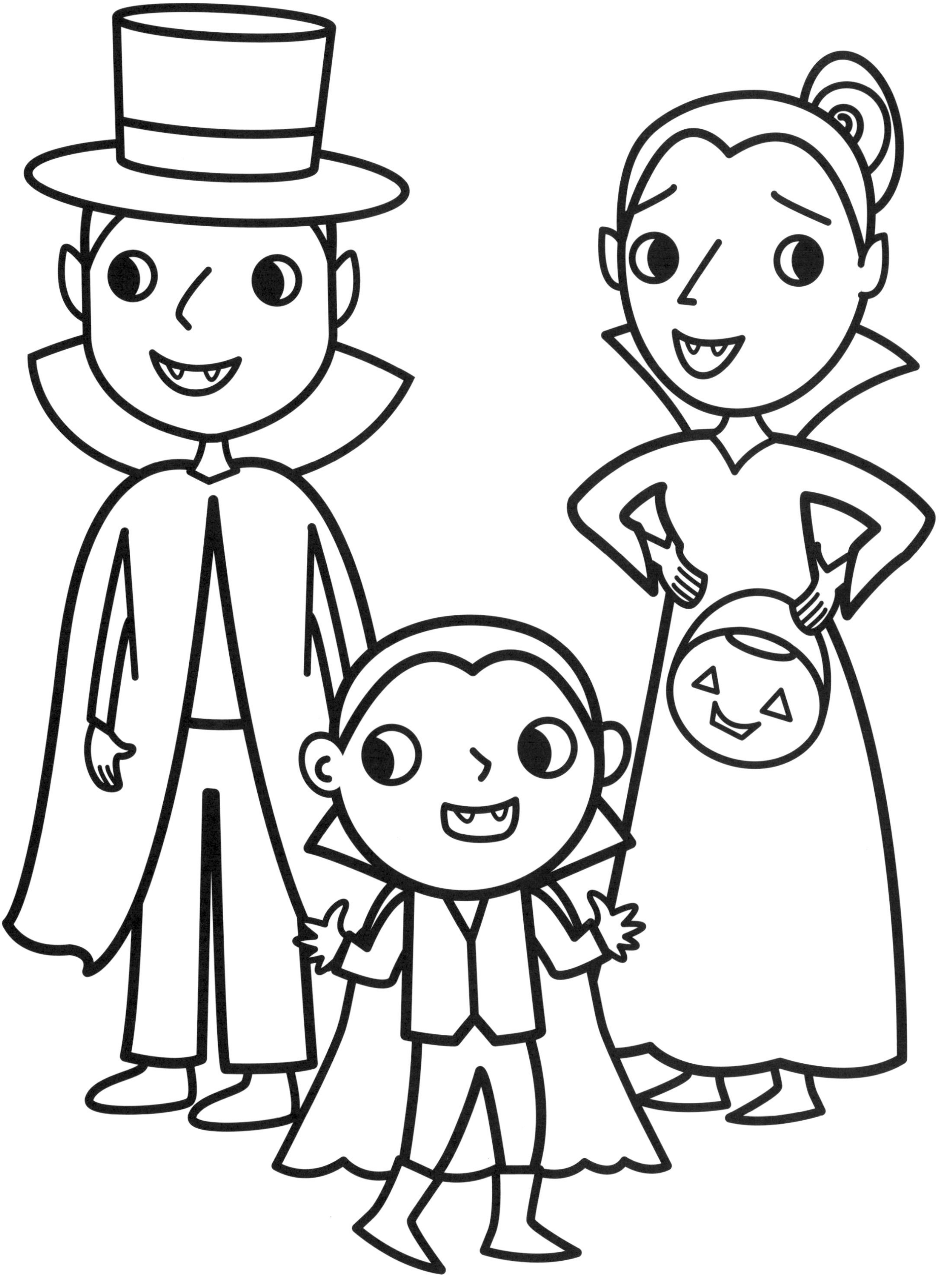

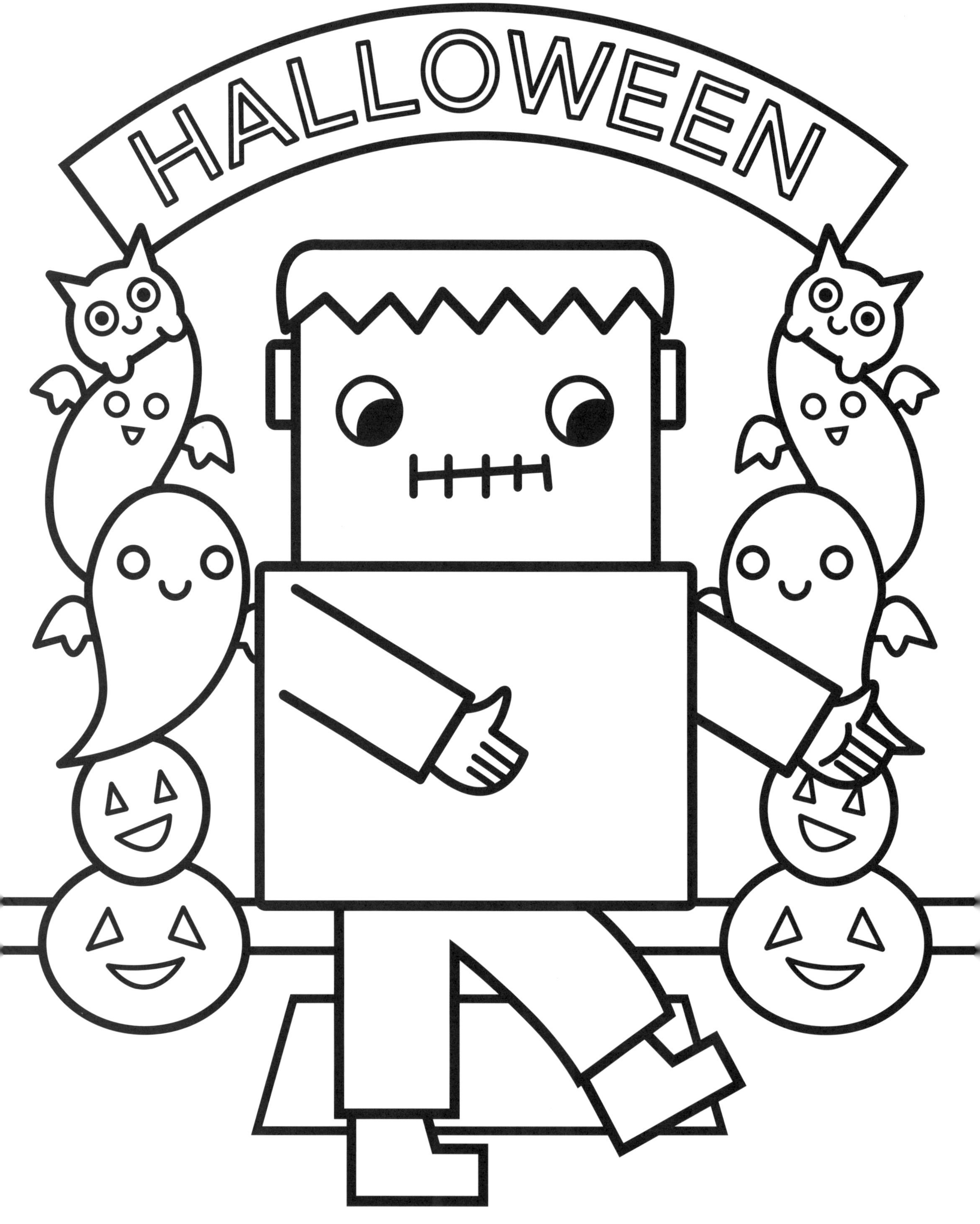
HALLOWEEN

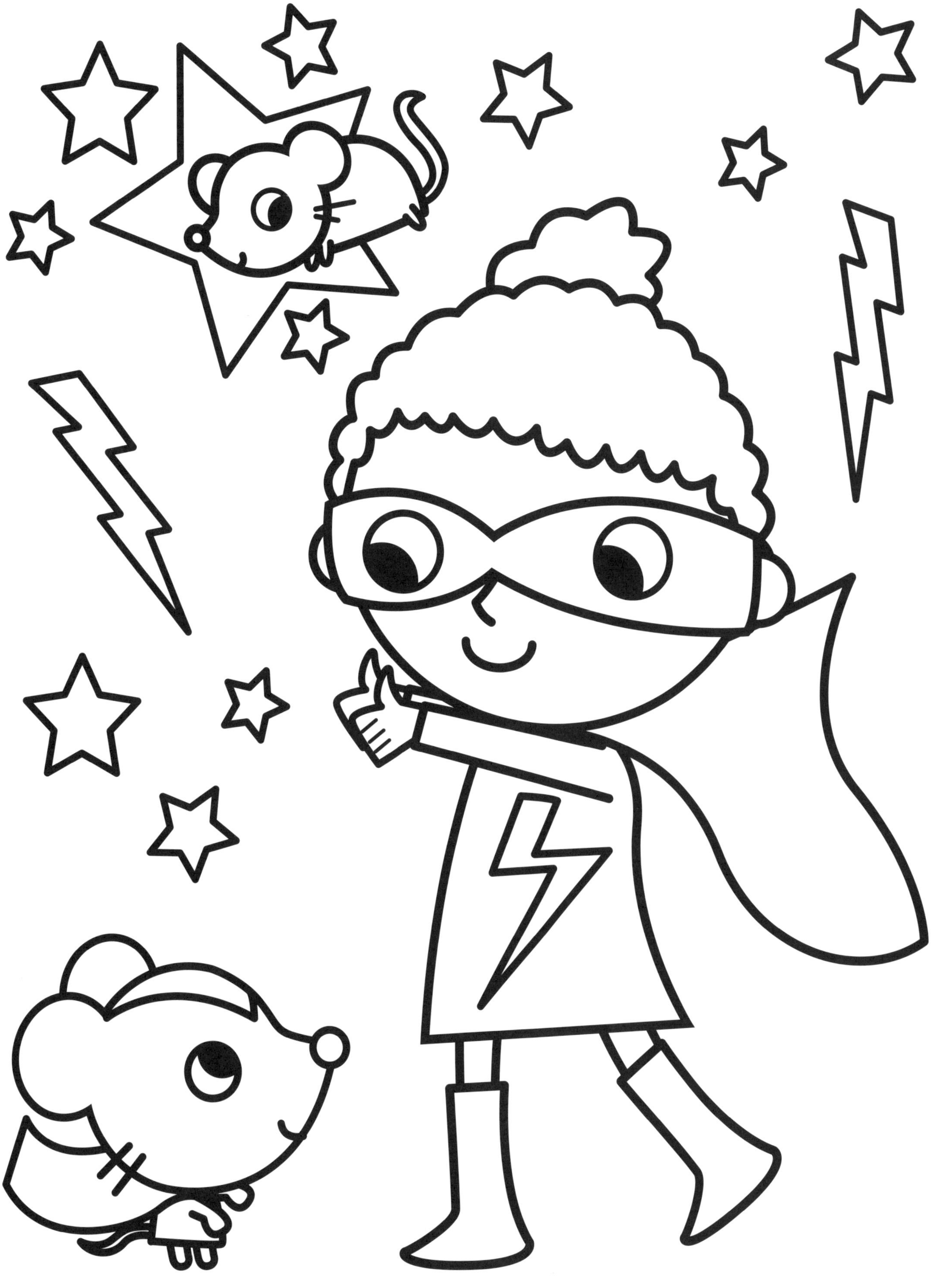

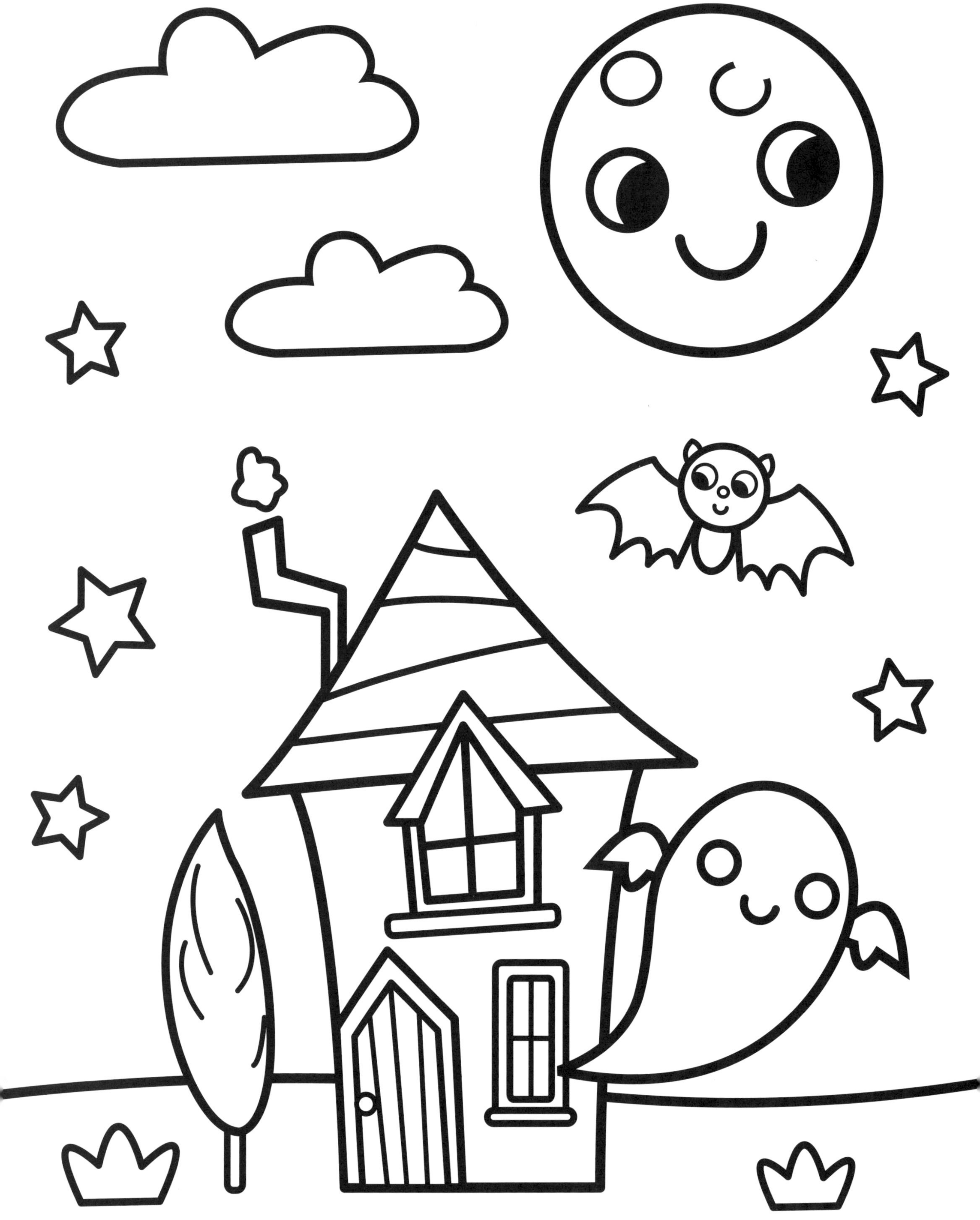

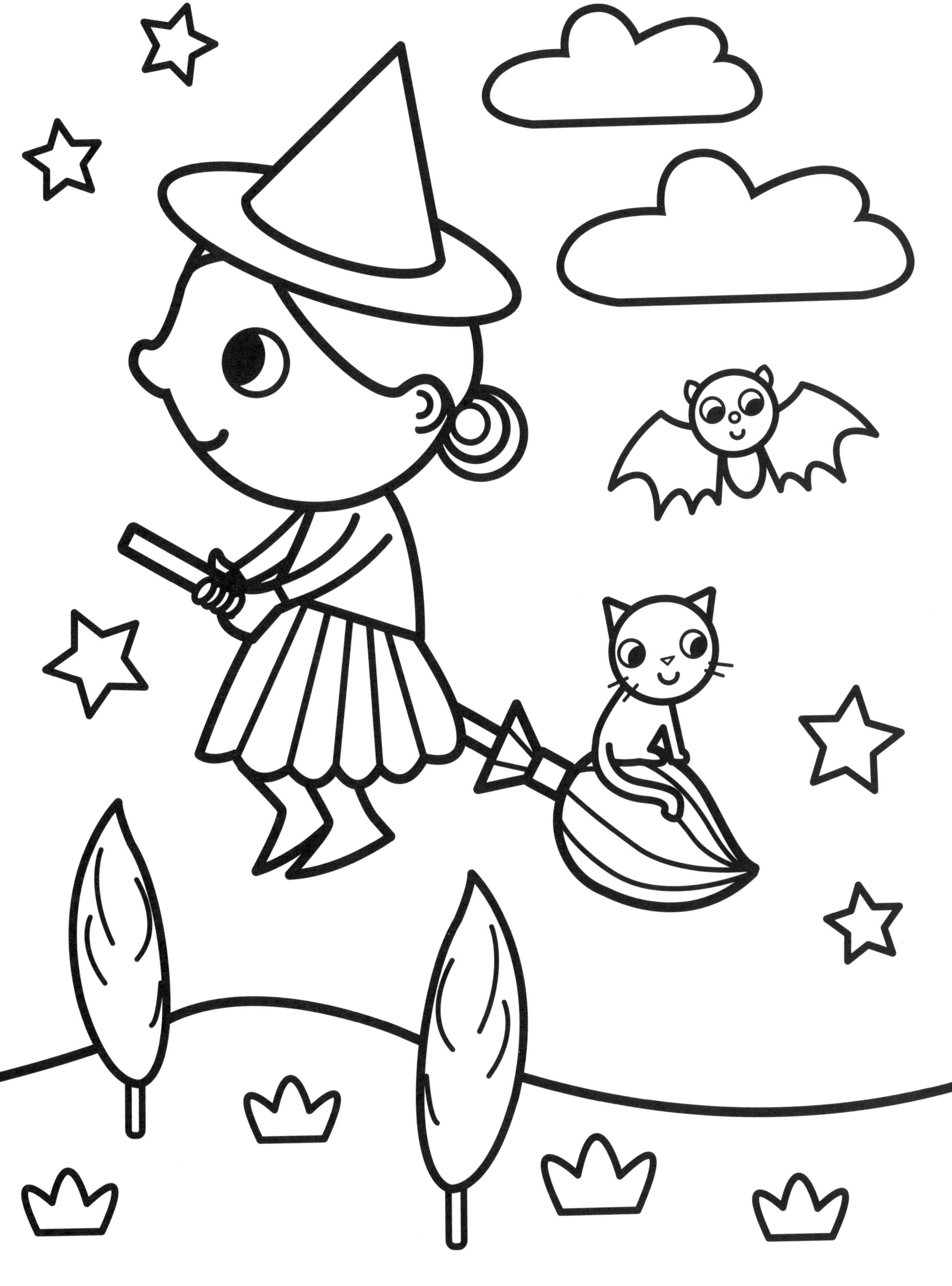

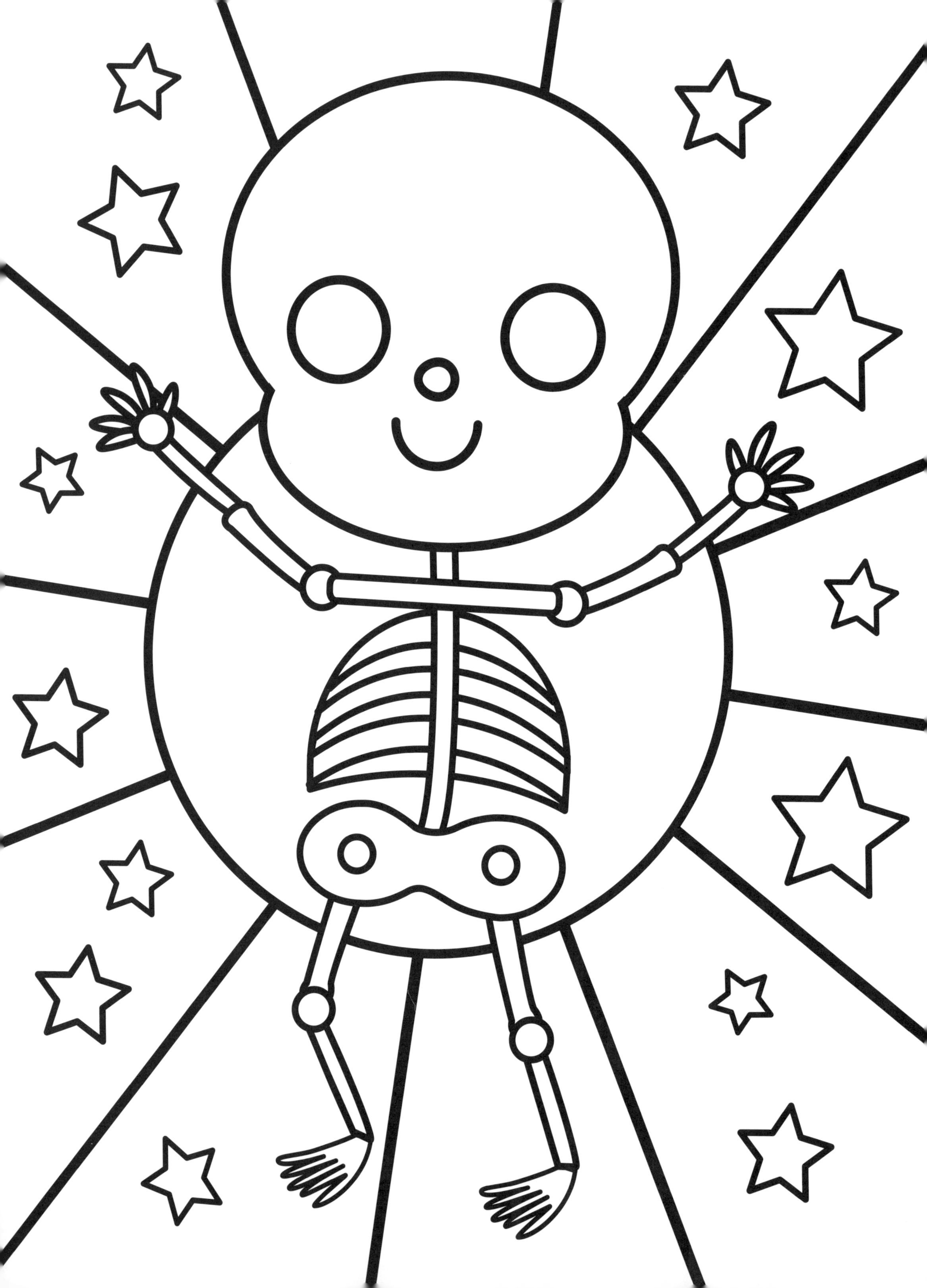

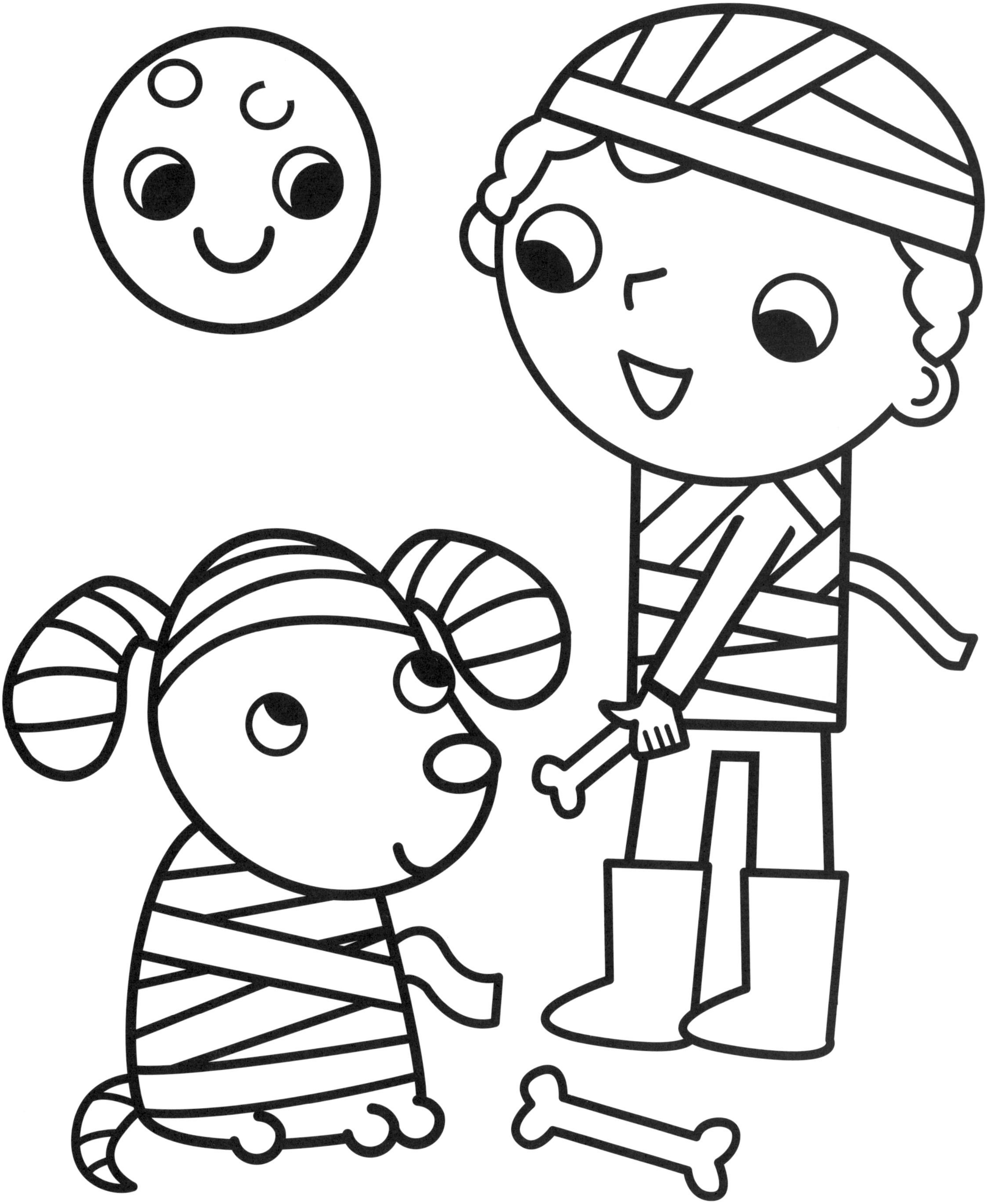

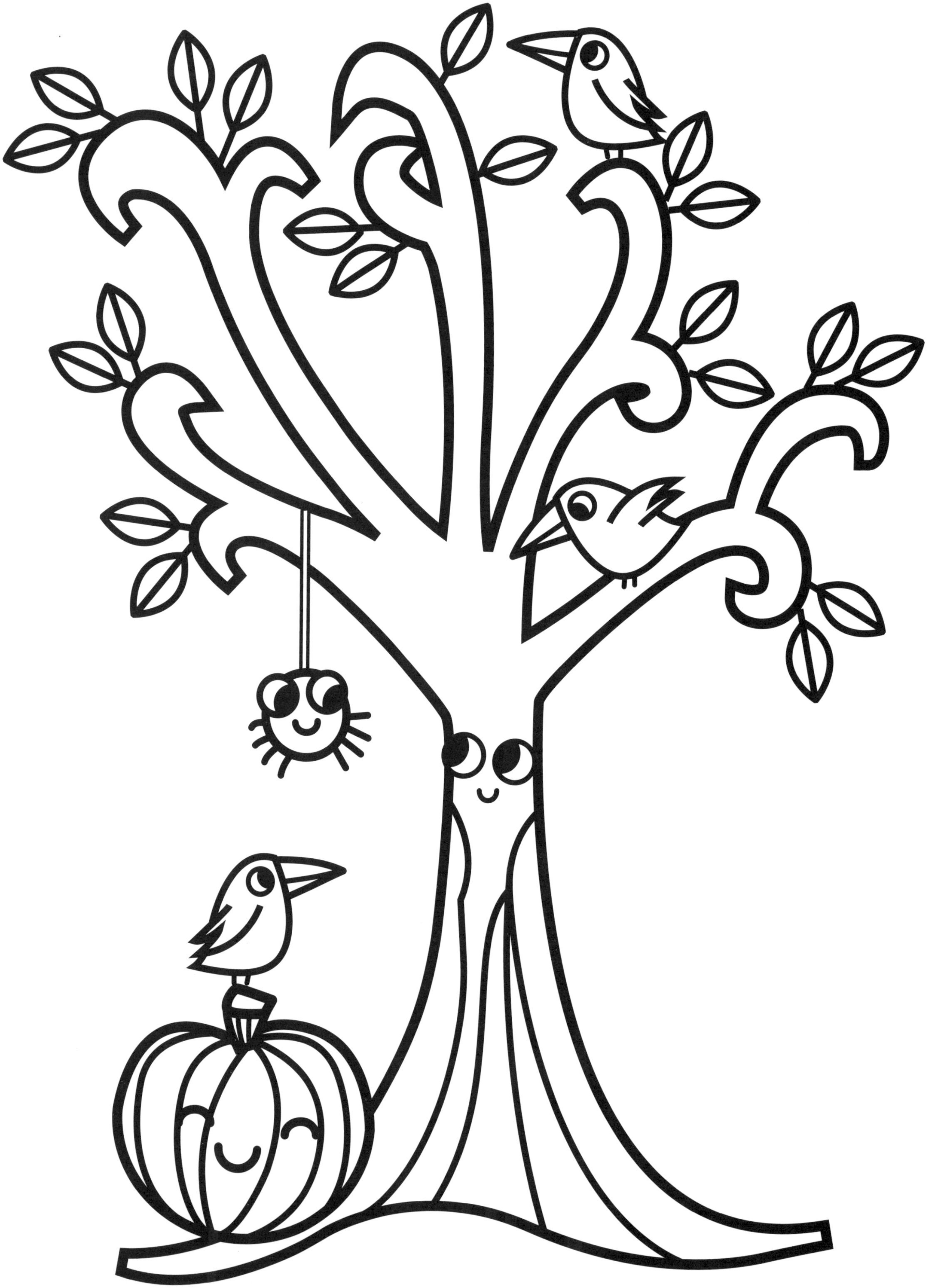

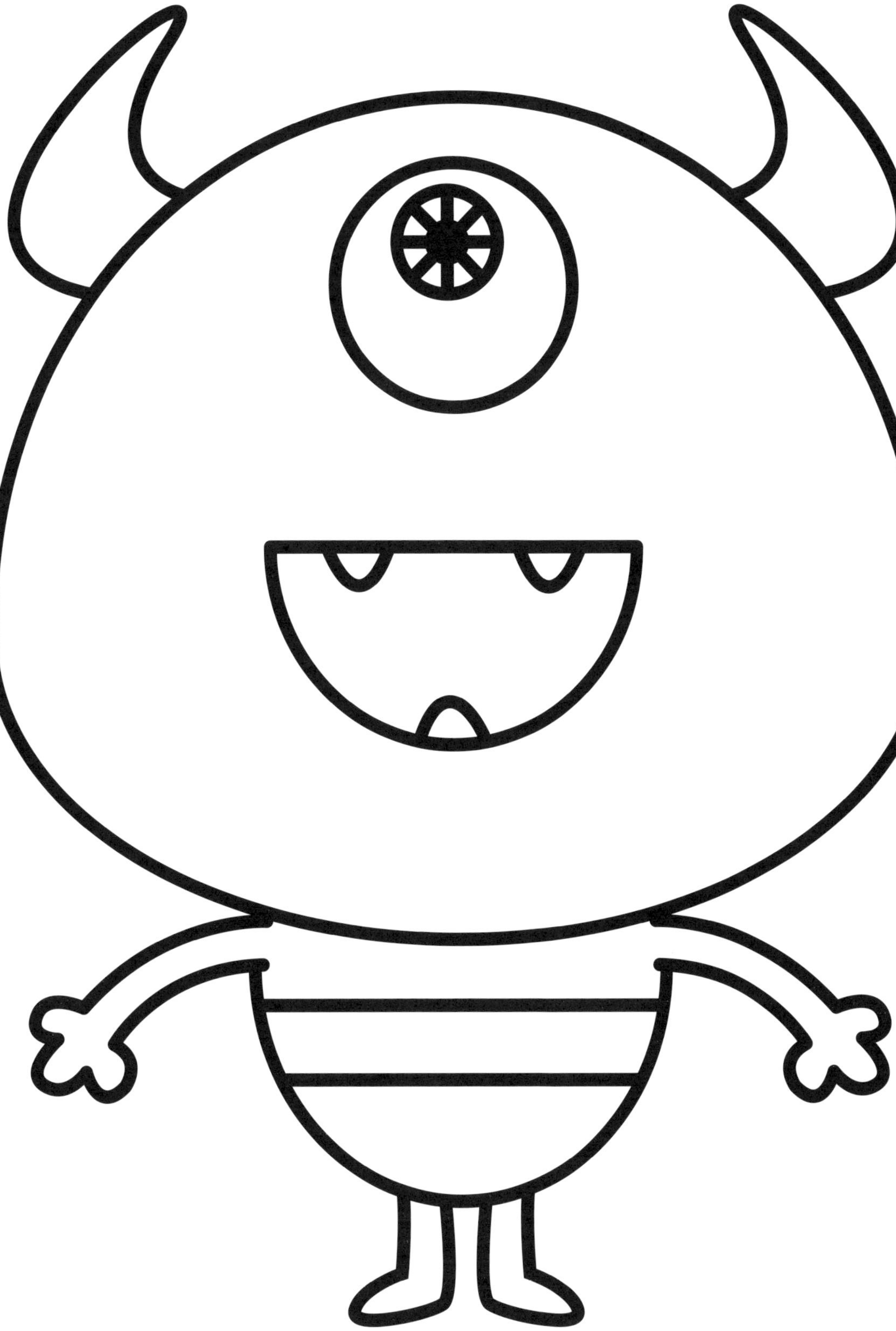

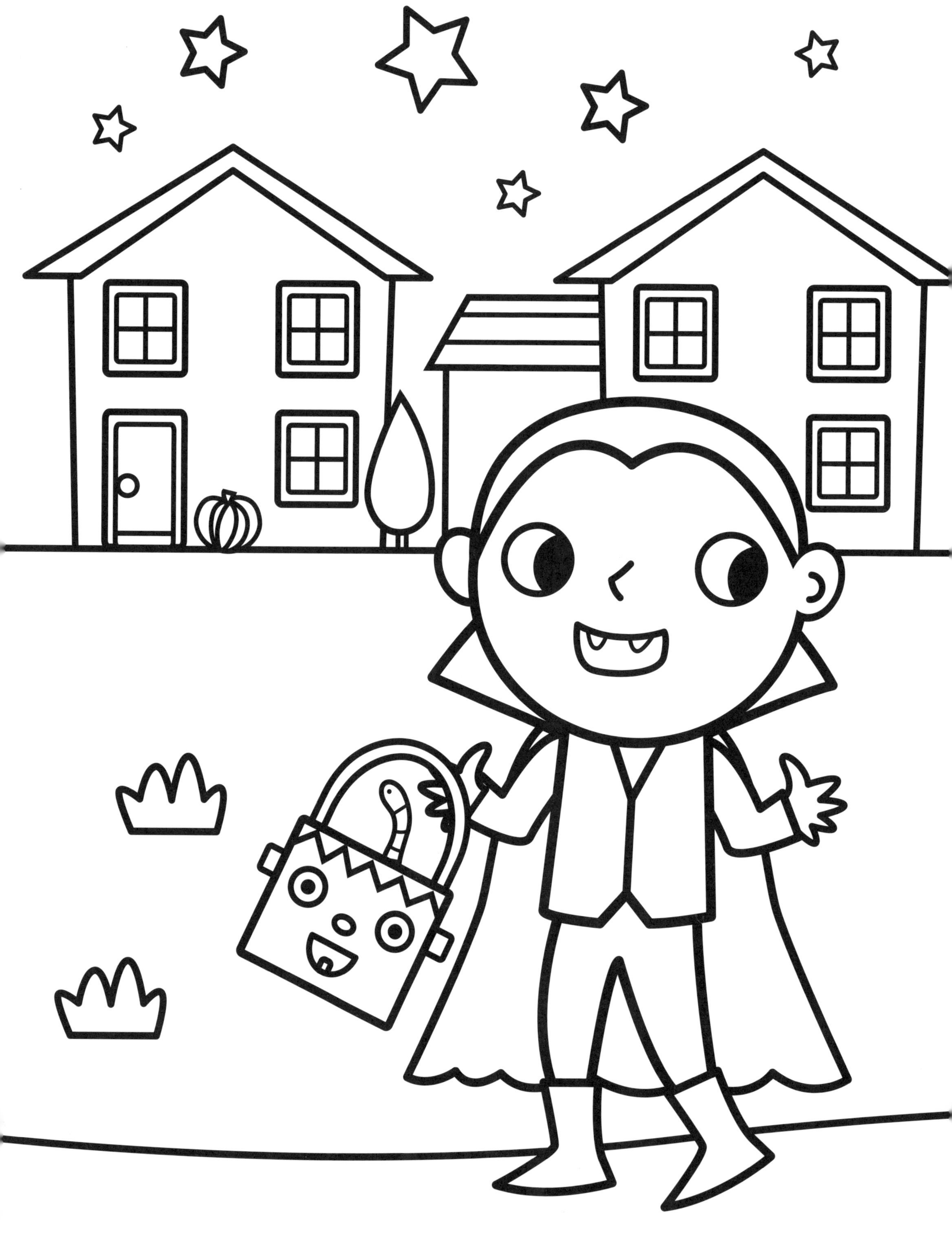

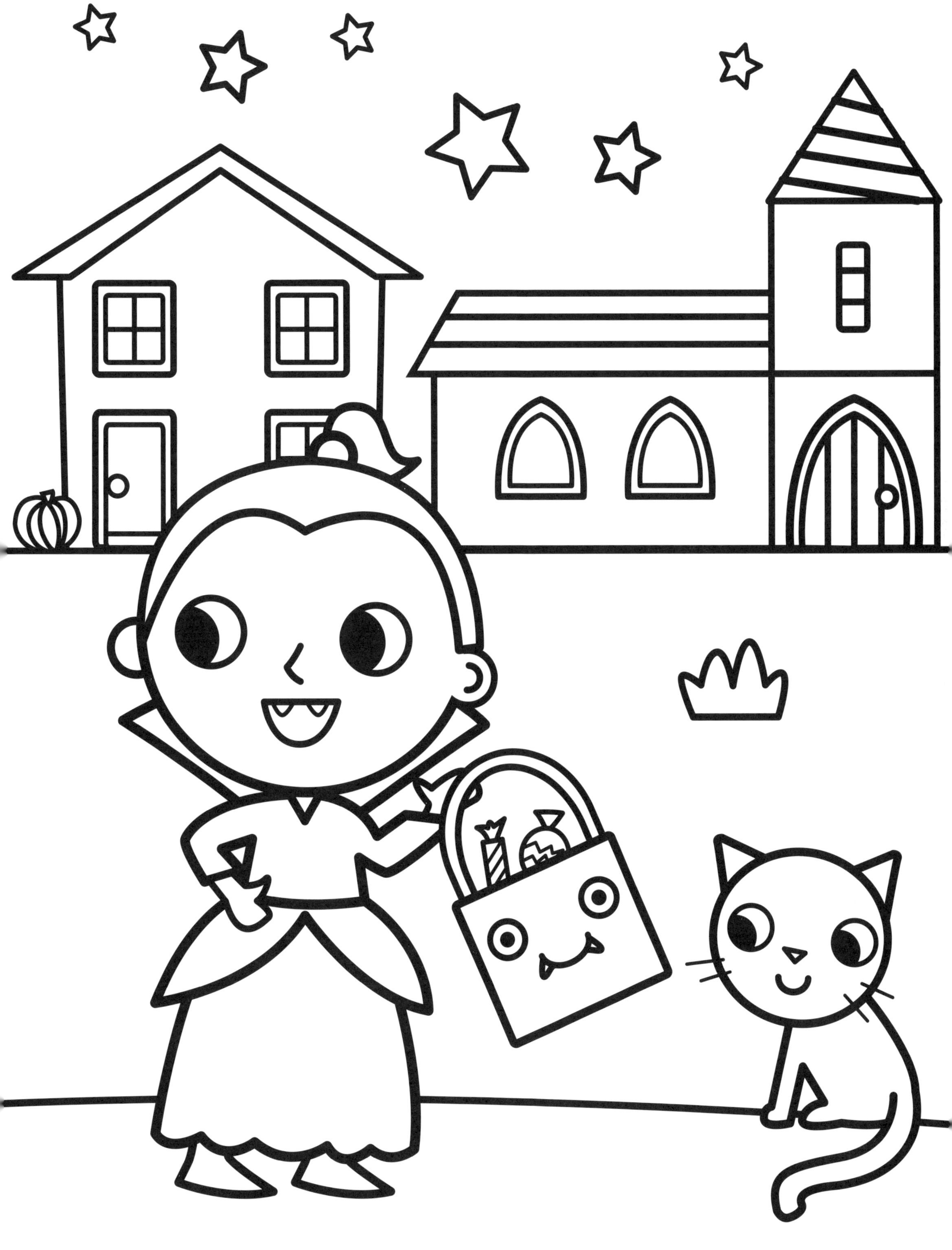

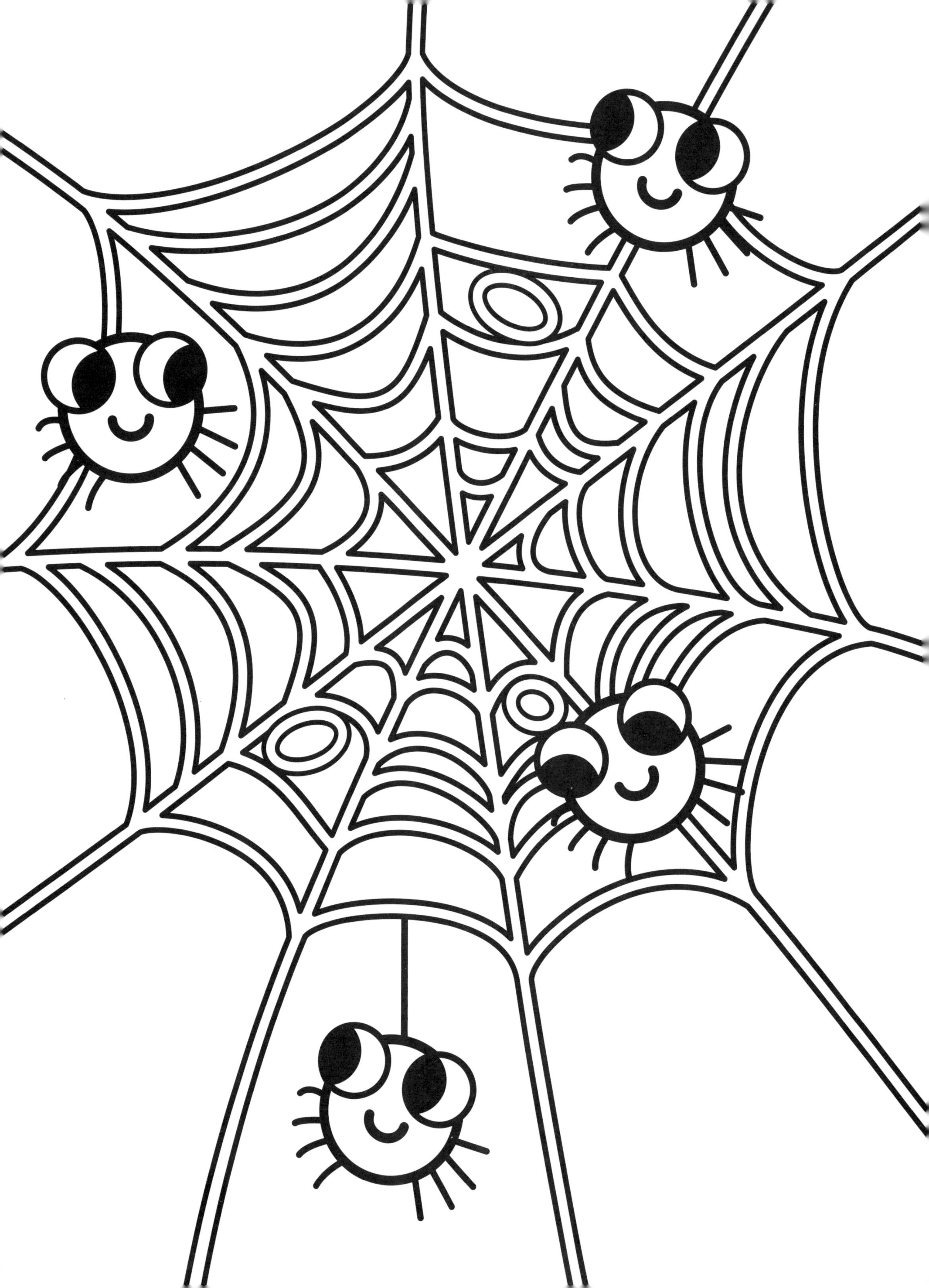

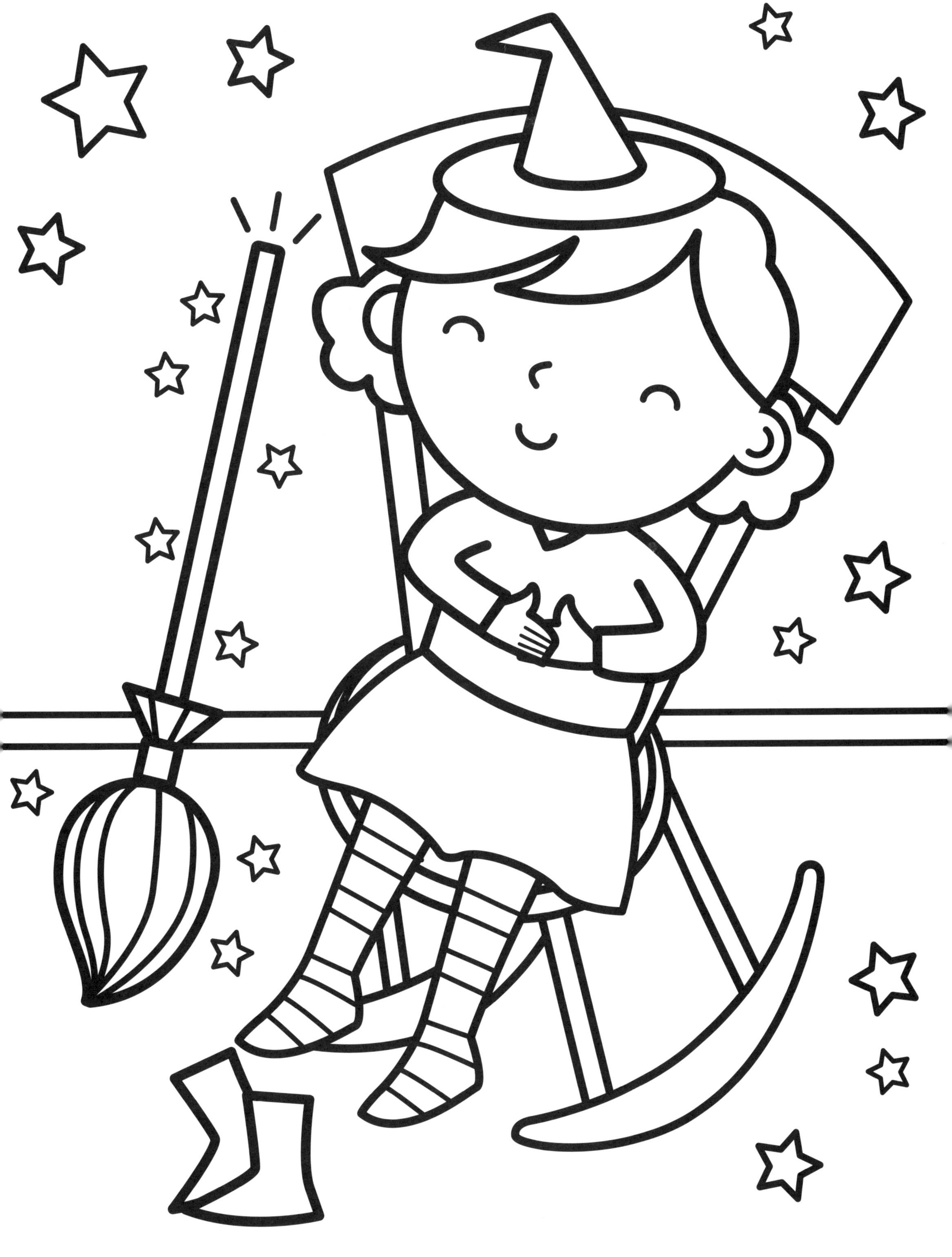

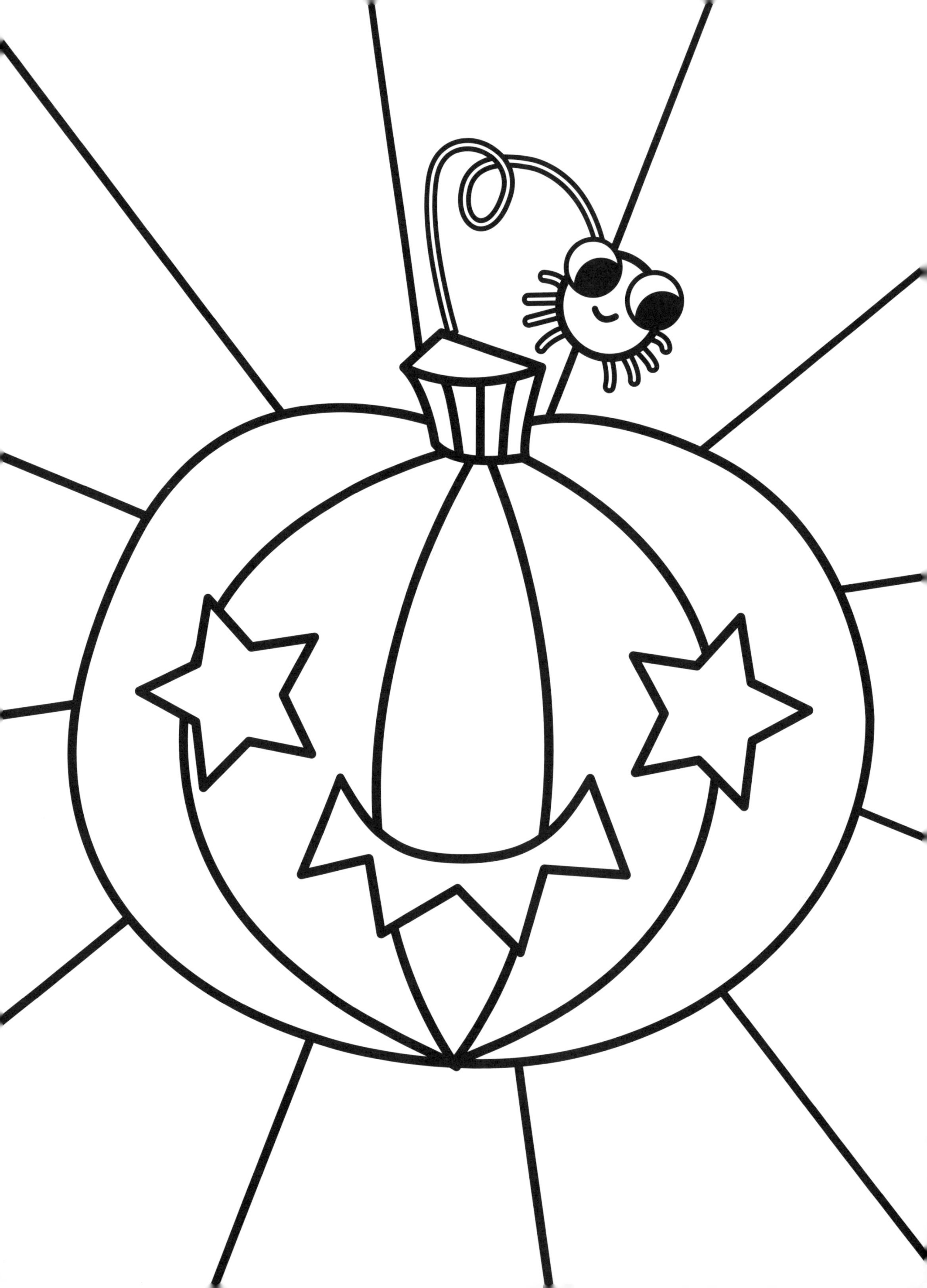

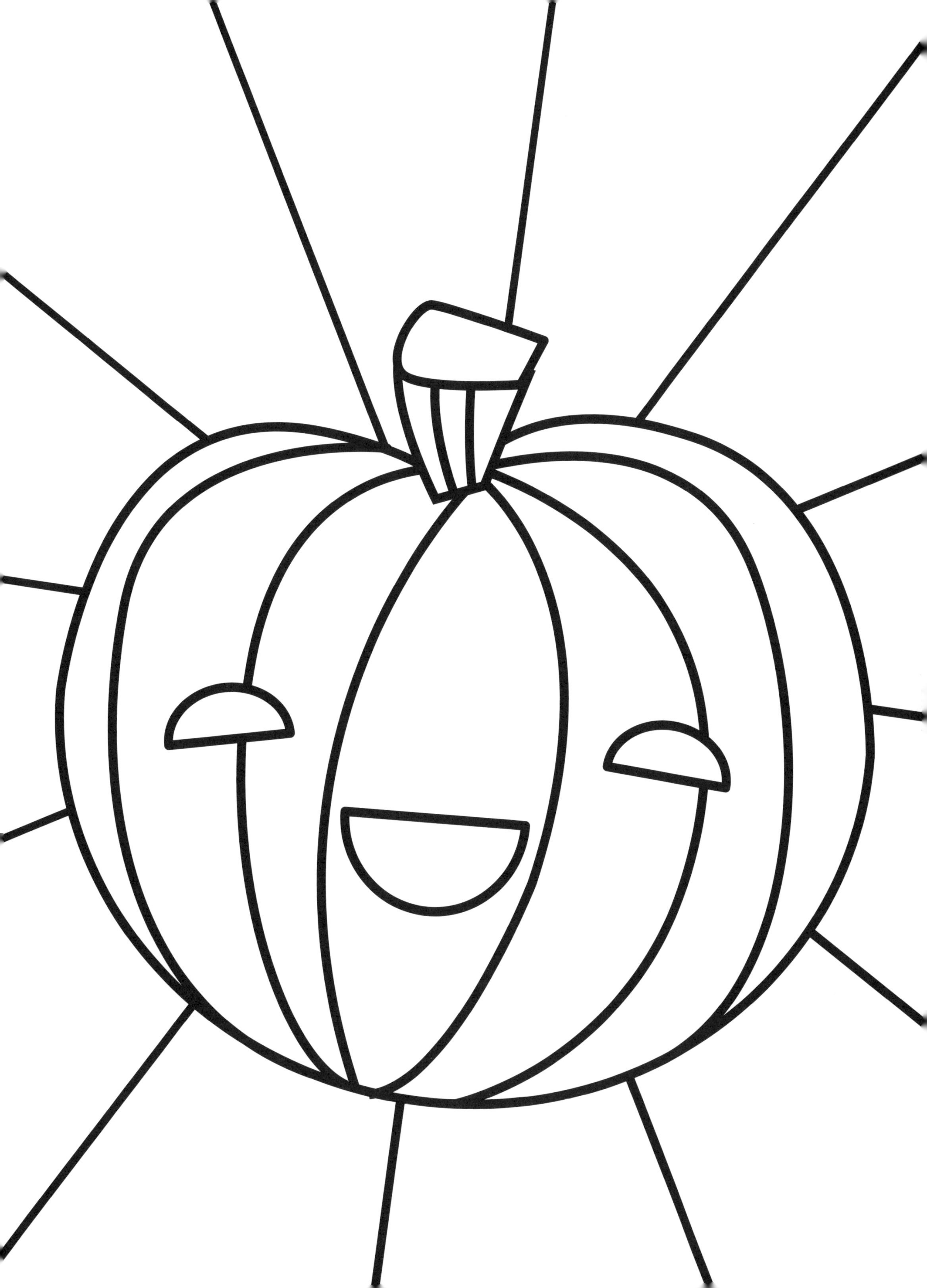

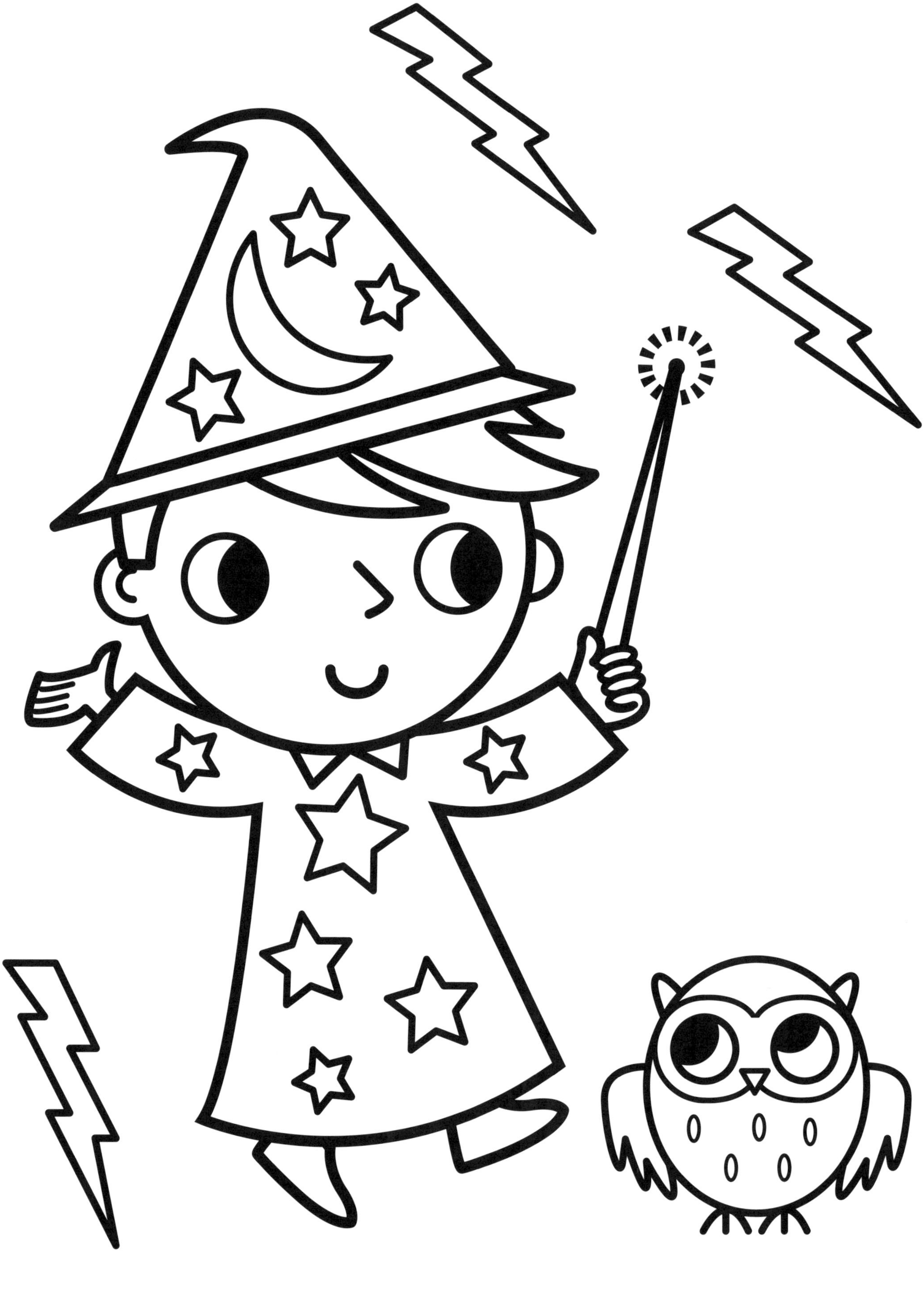

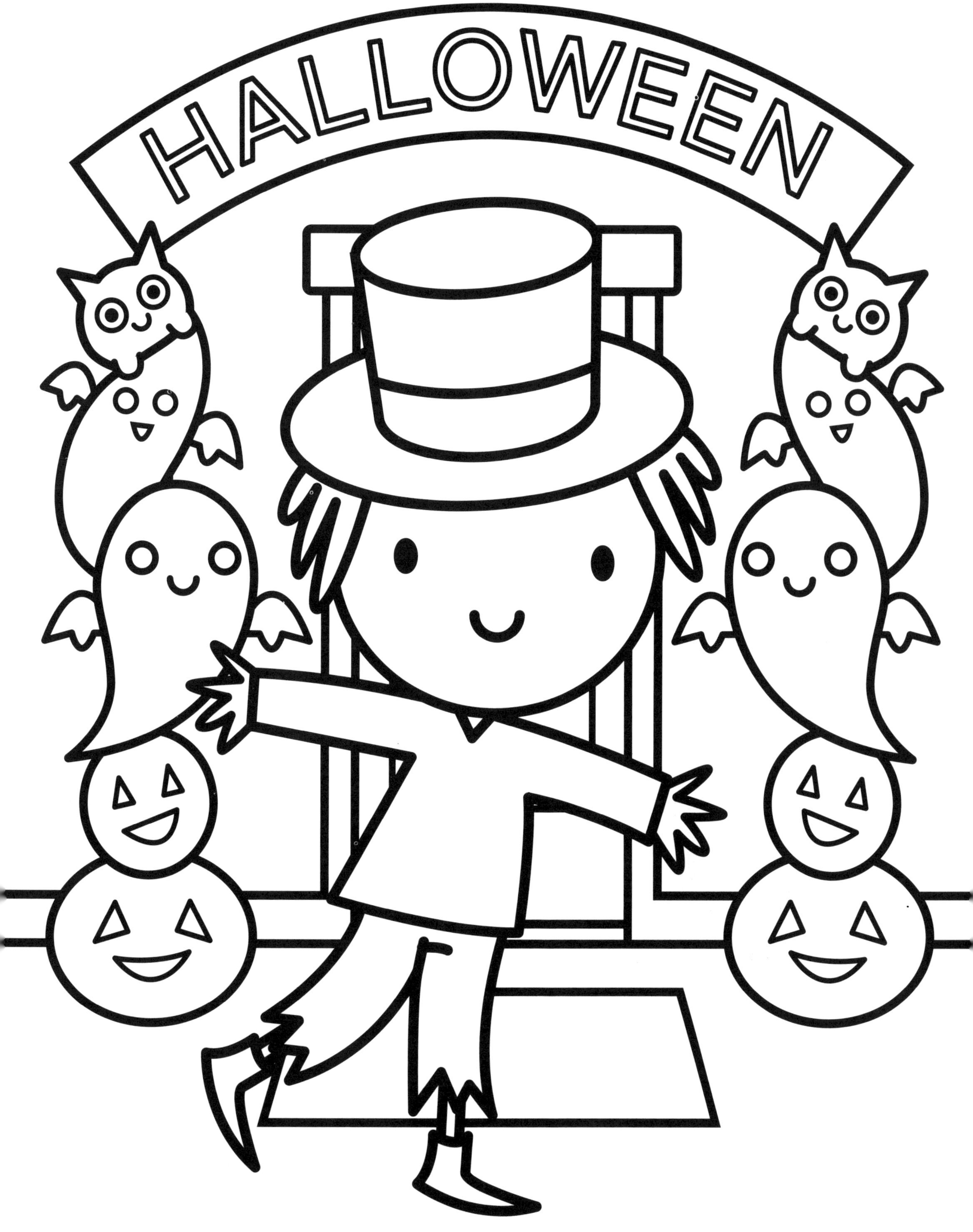
HALLOWEEN

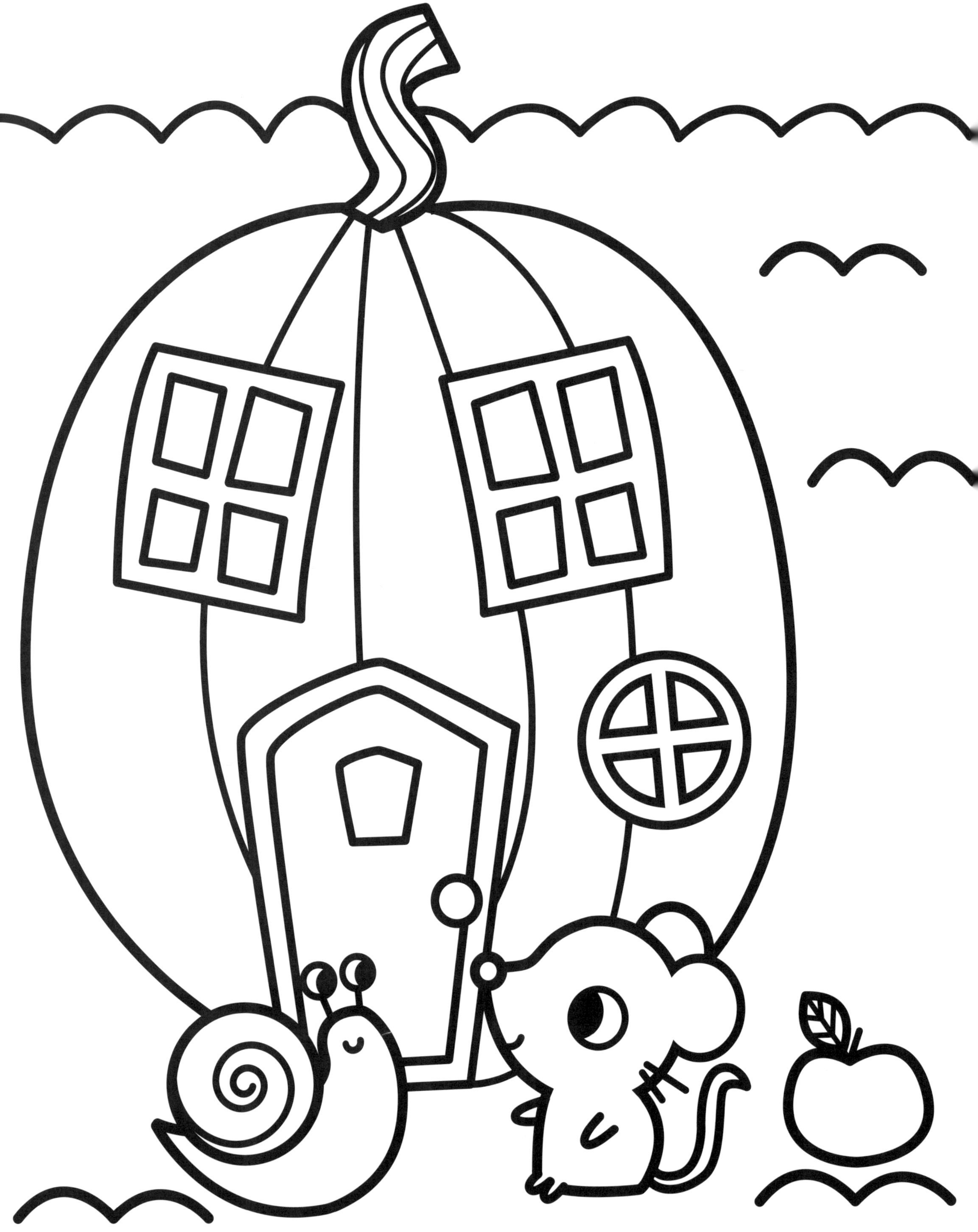

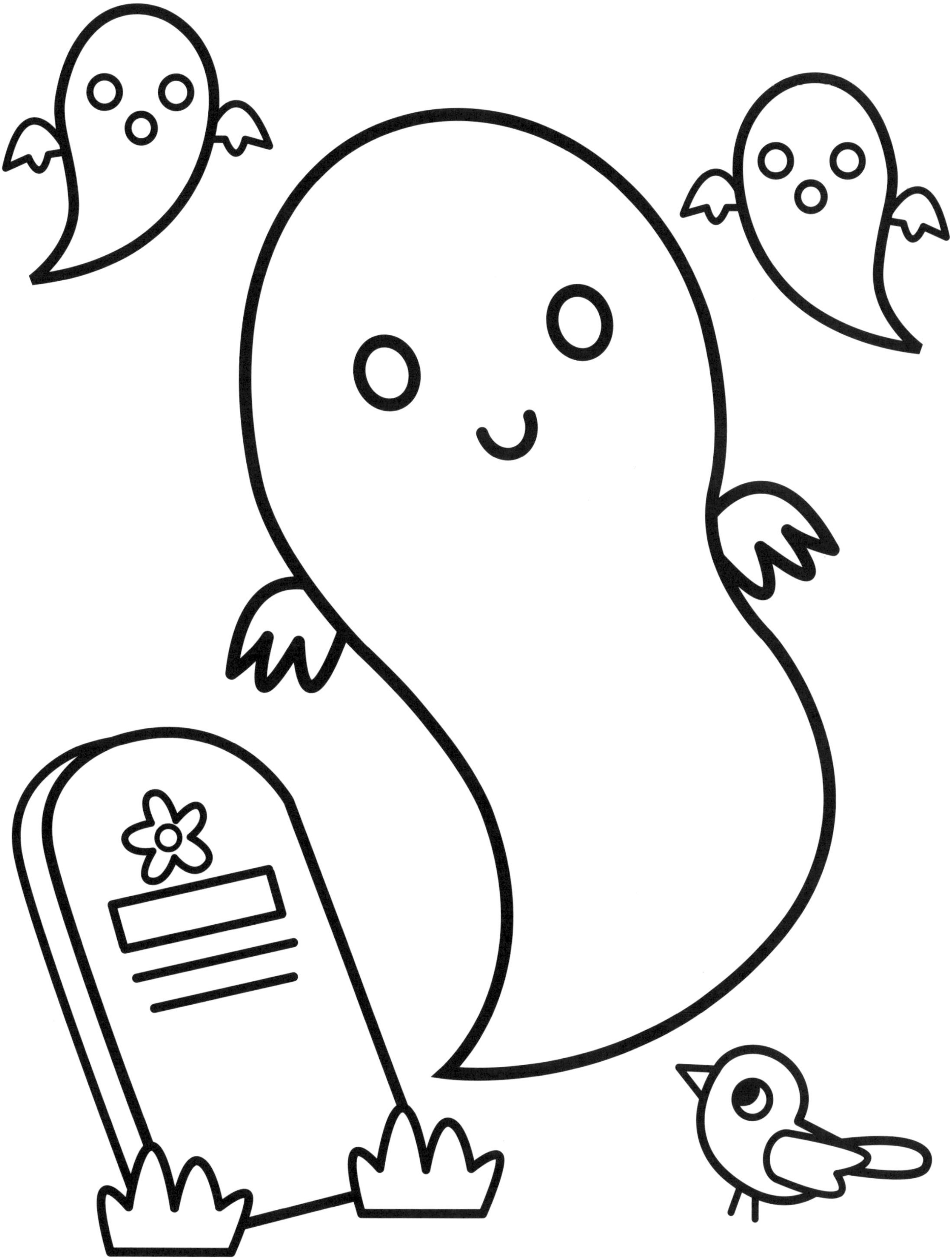

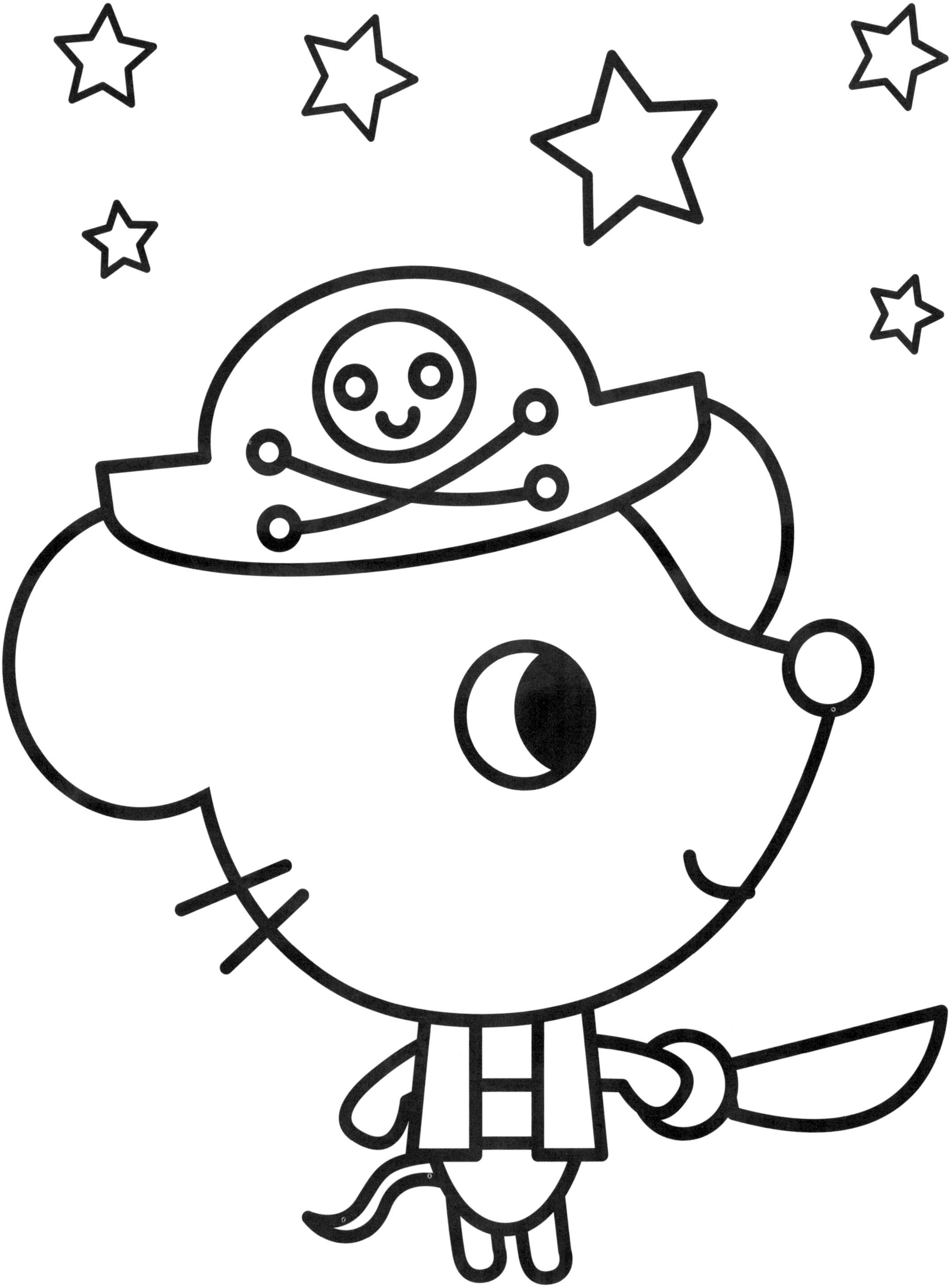

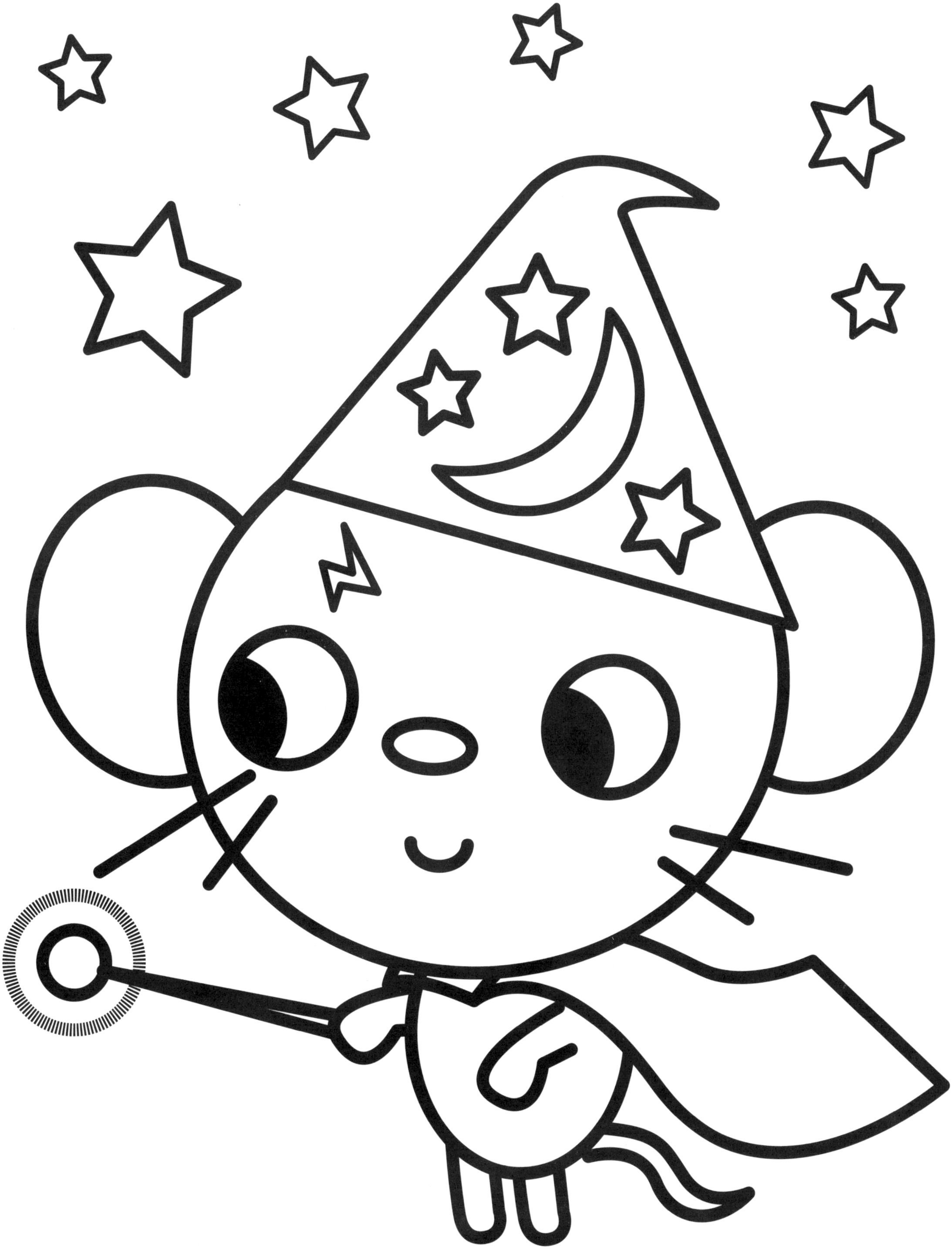

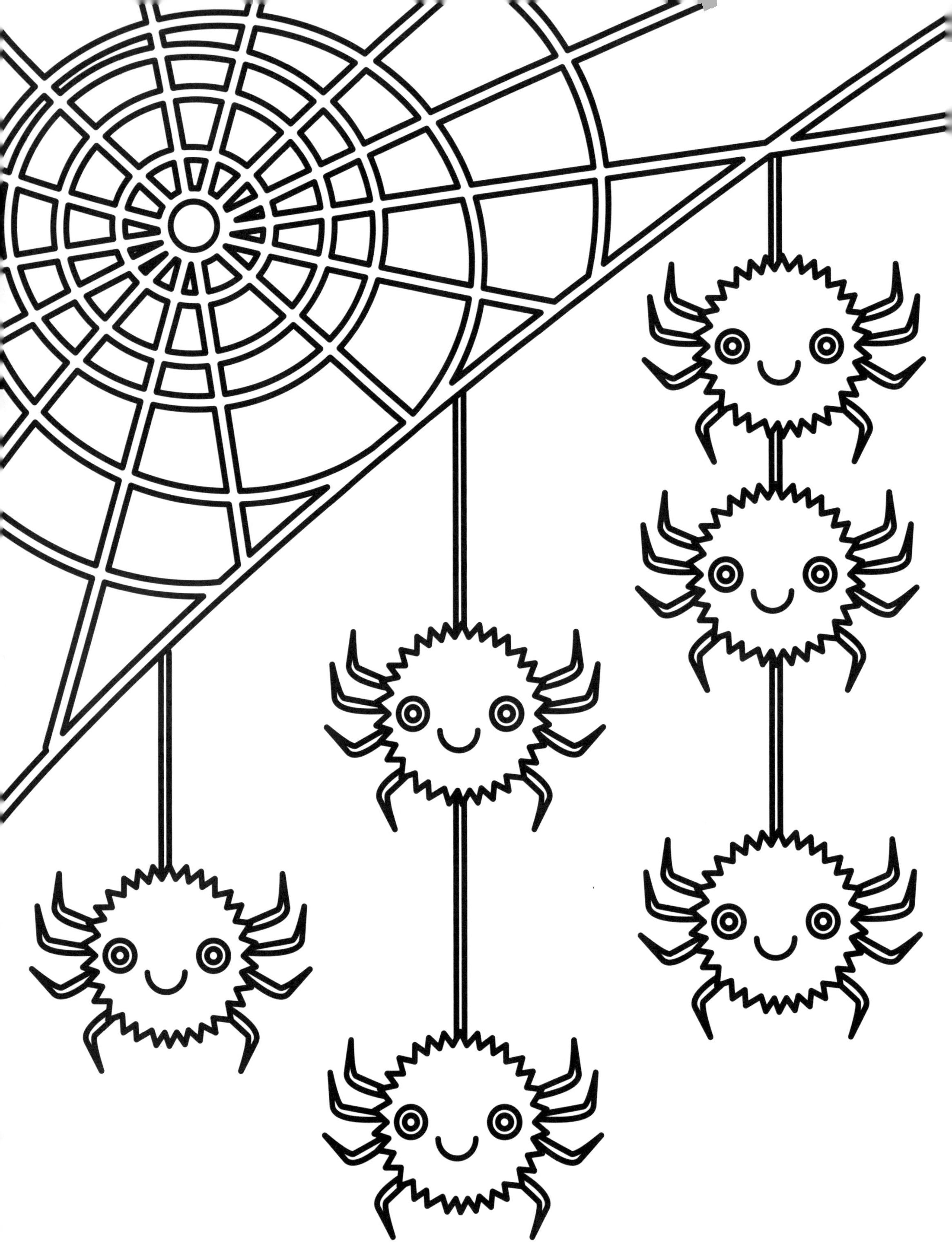

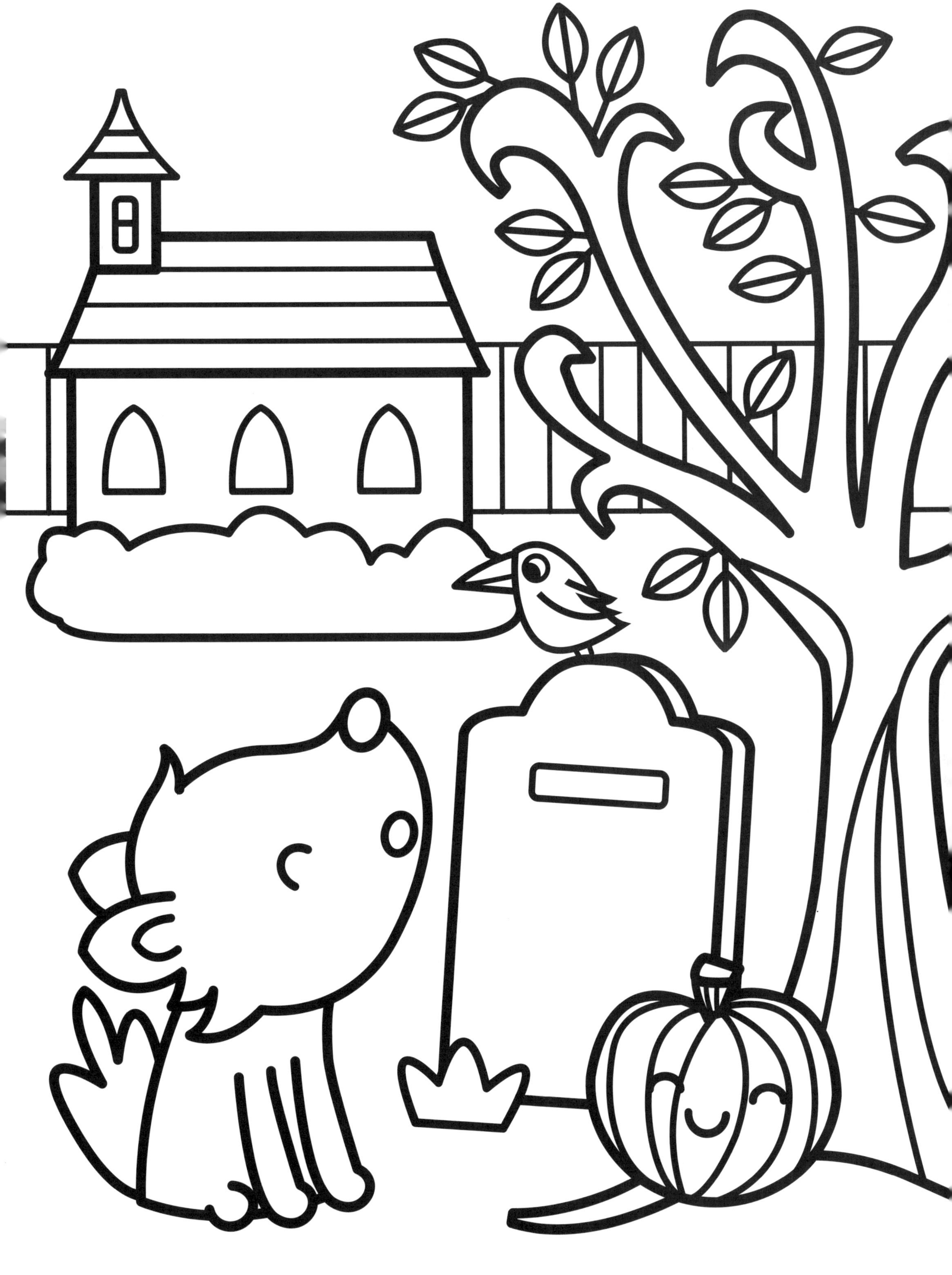

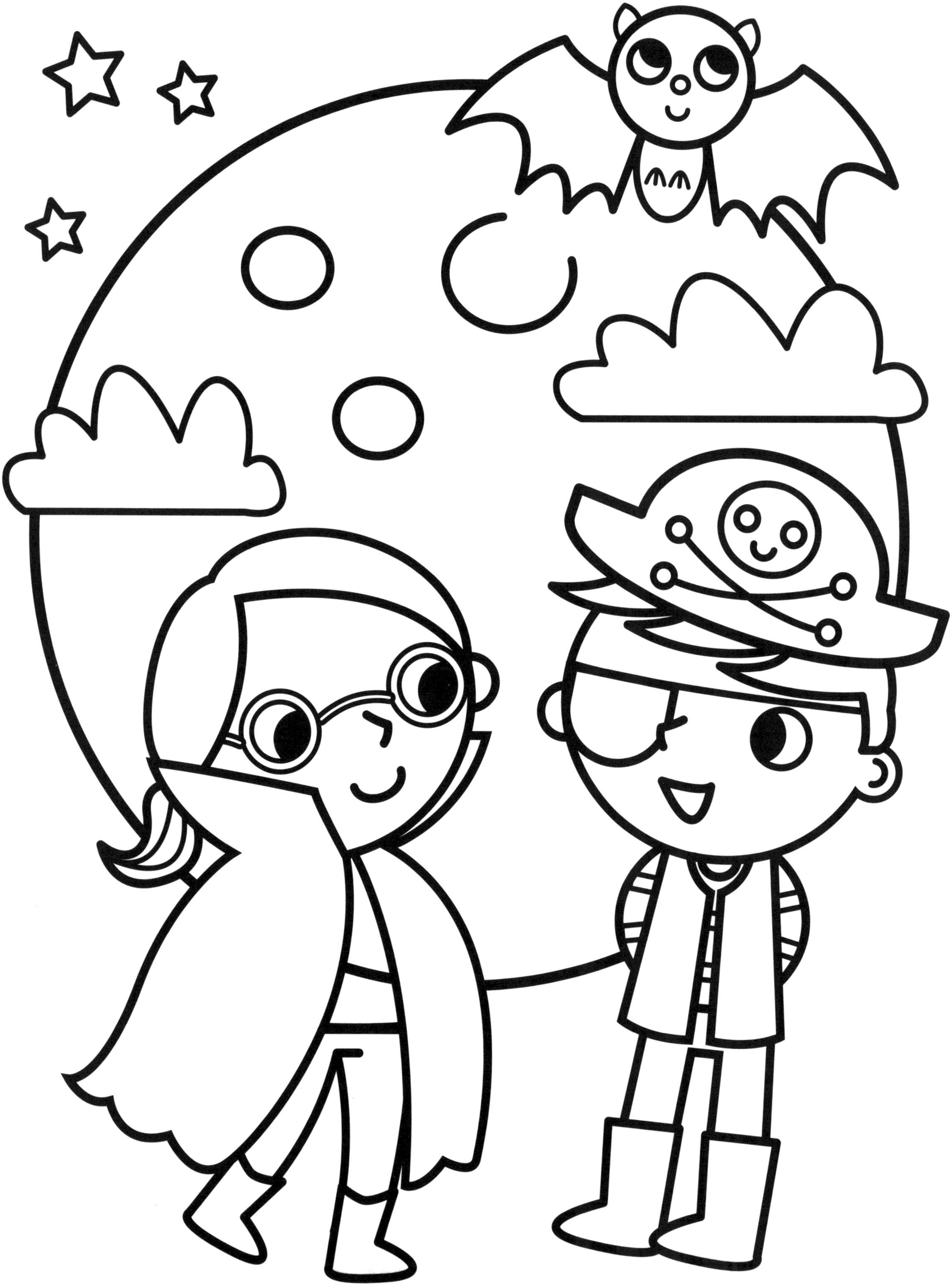

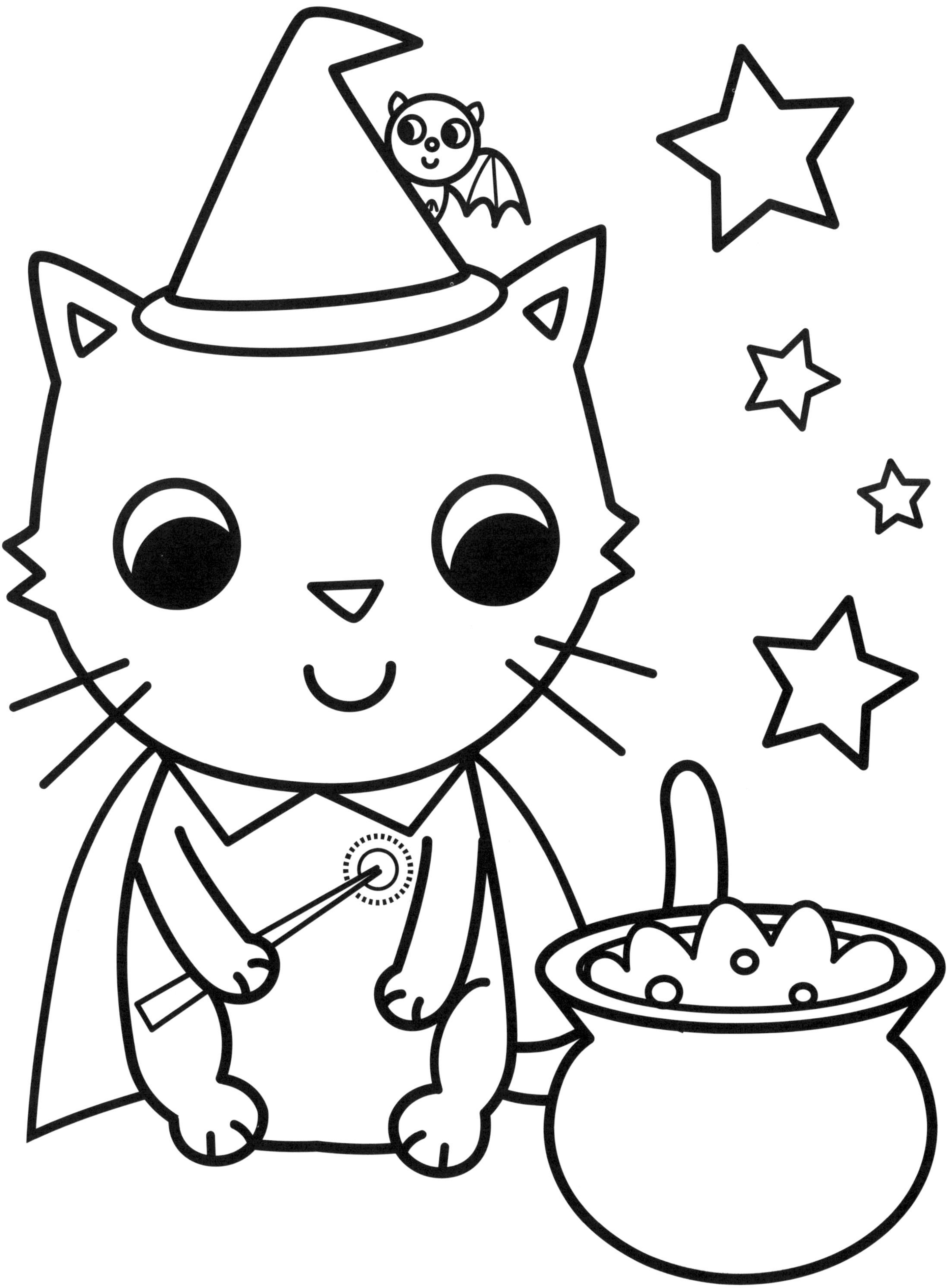

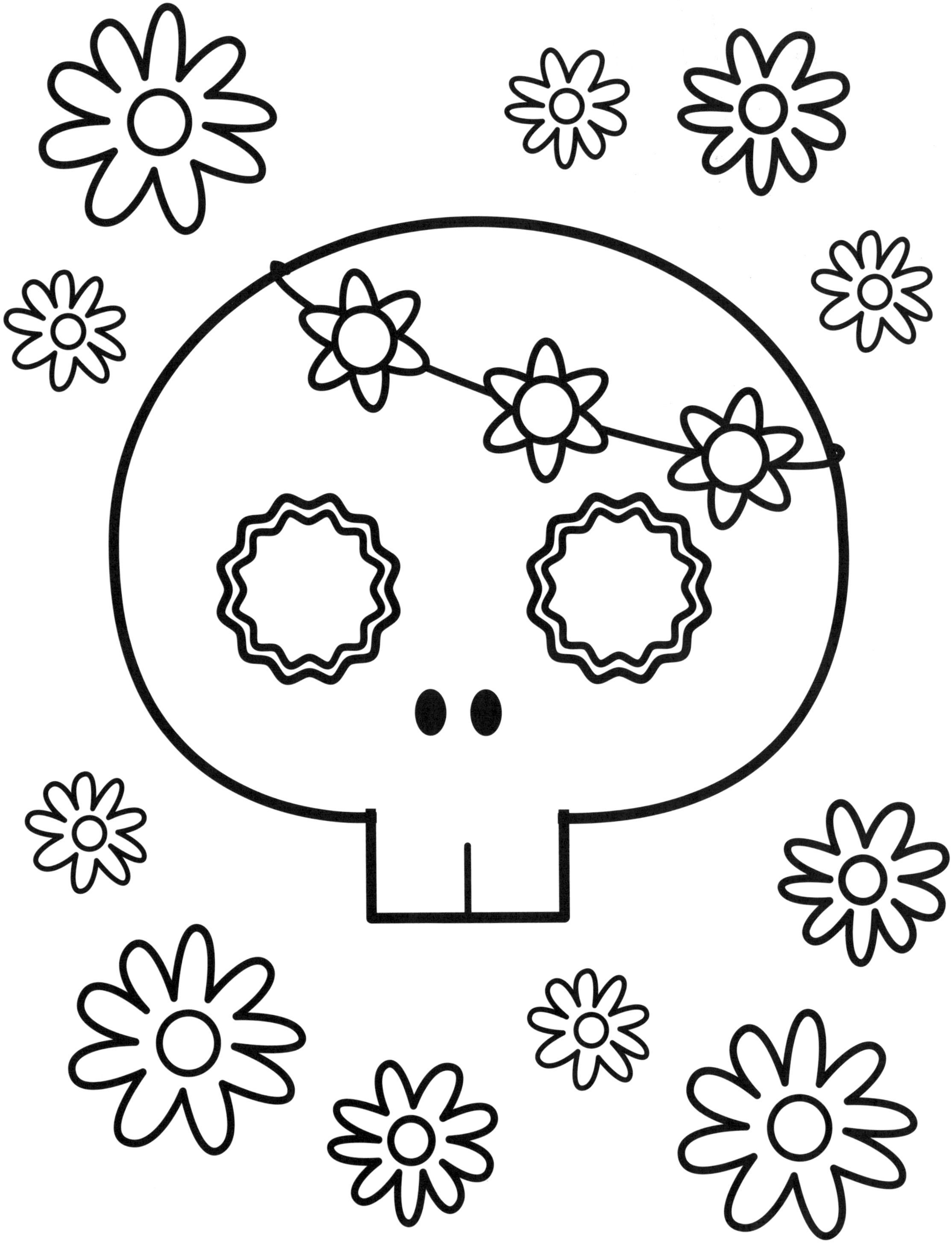

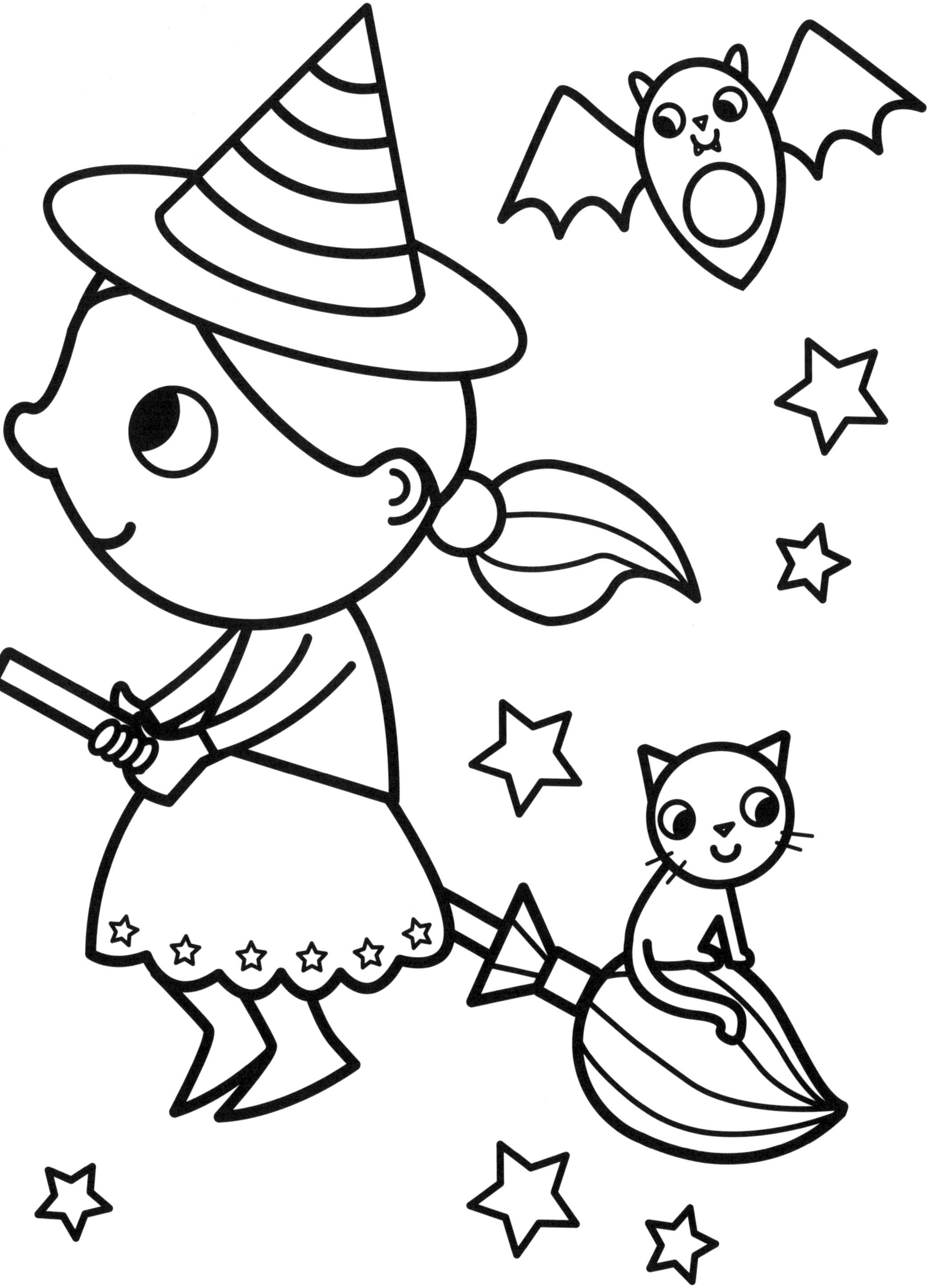

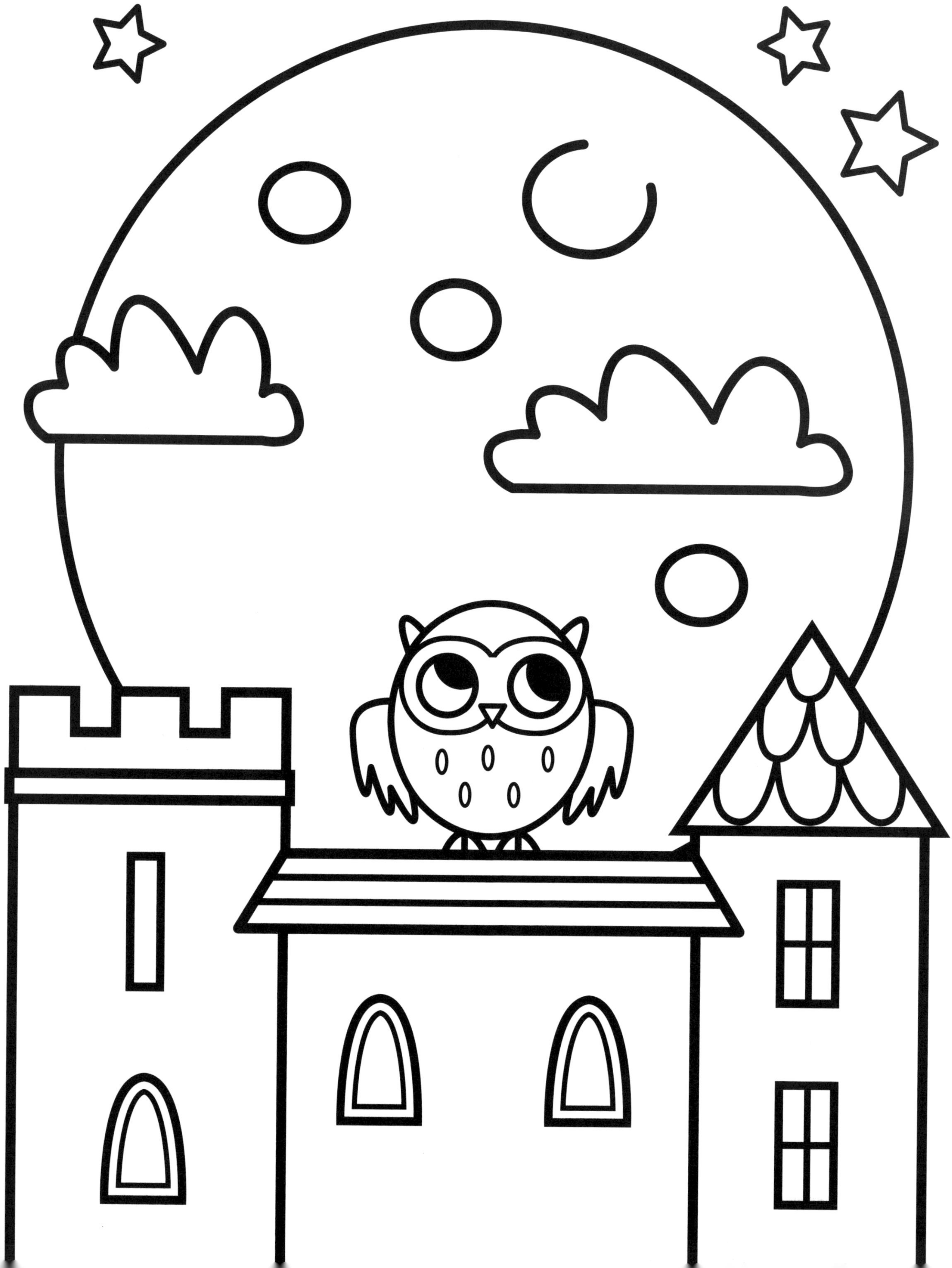

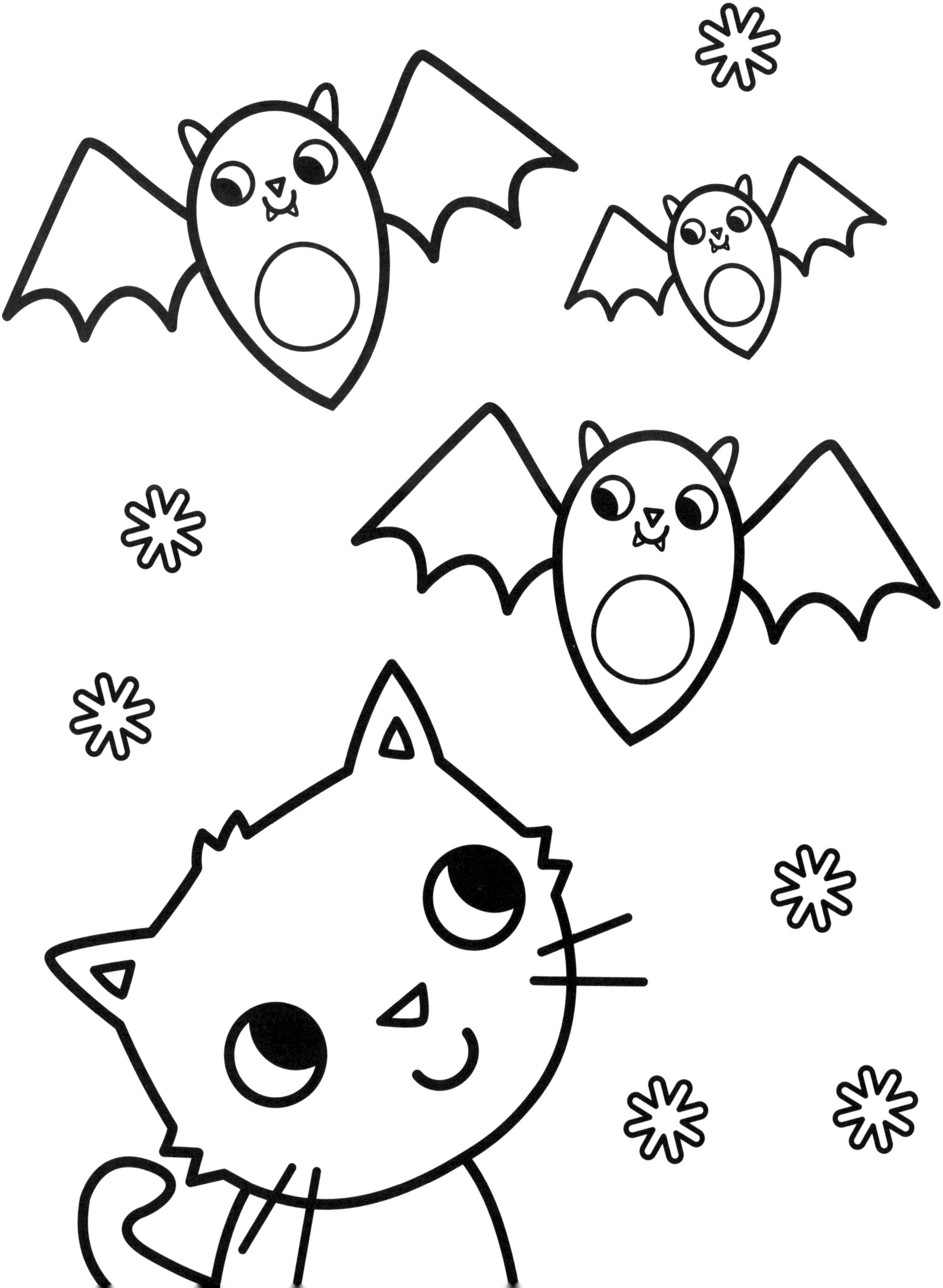

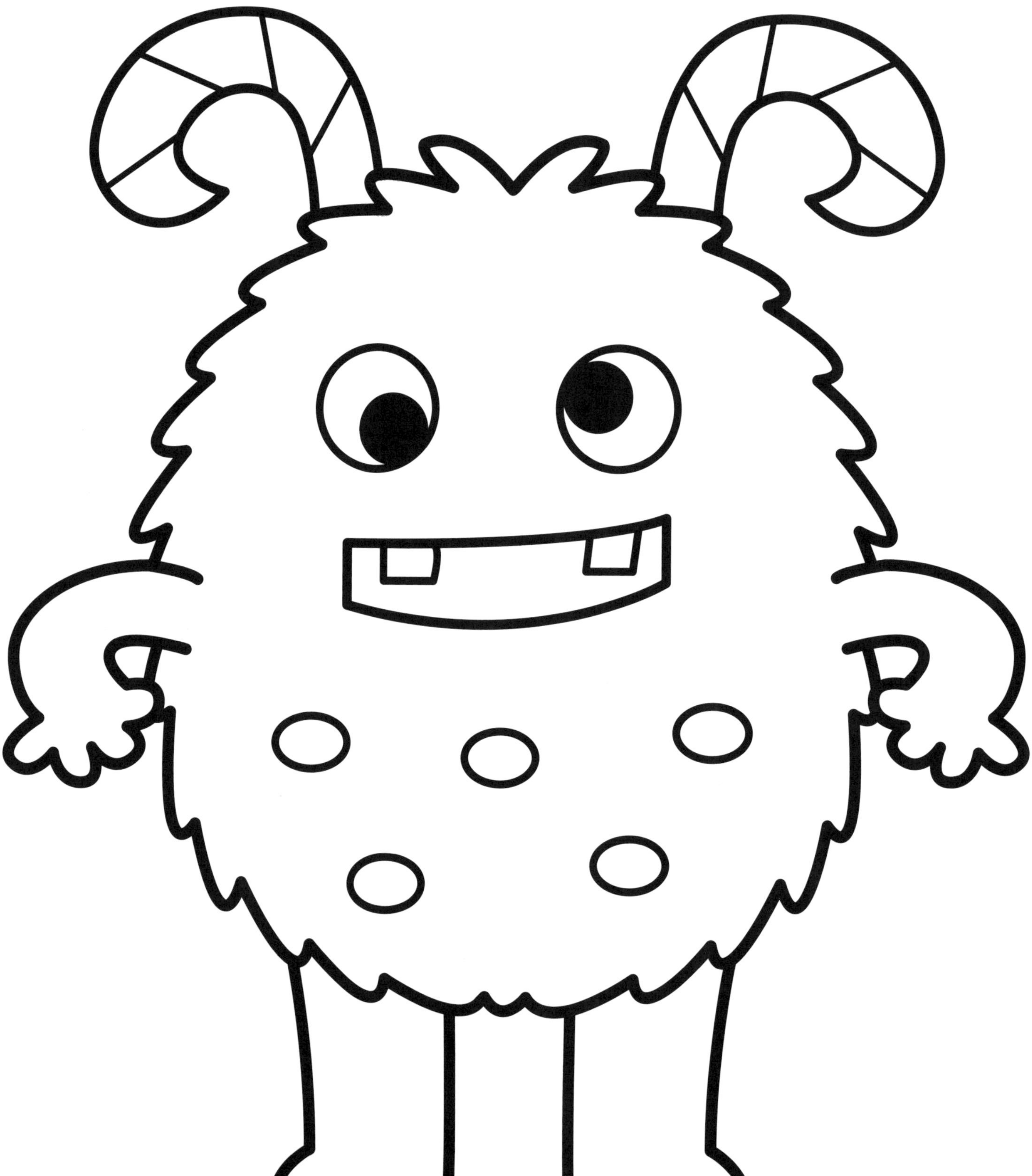

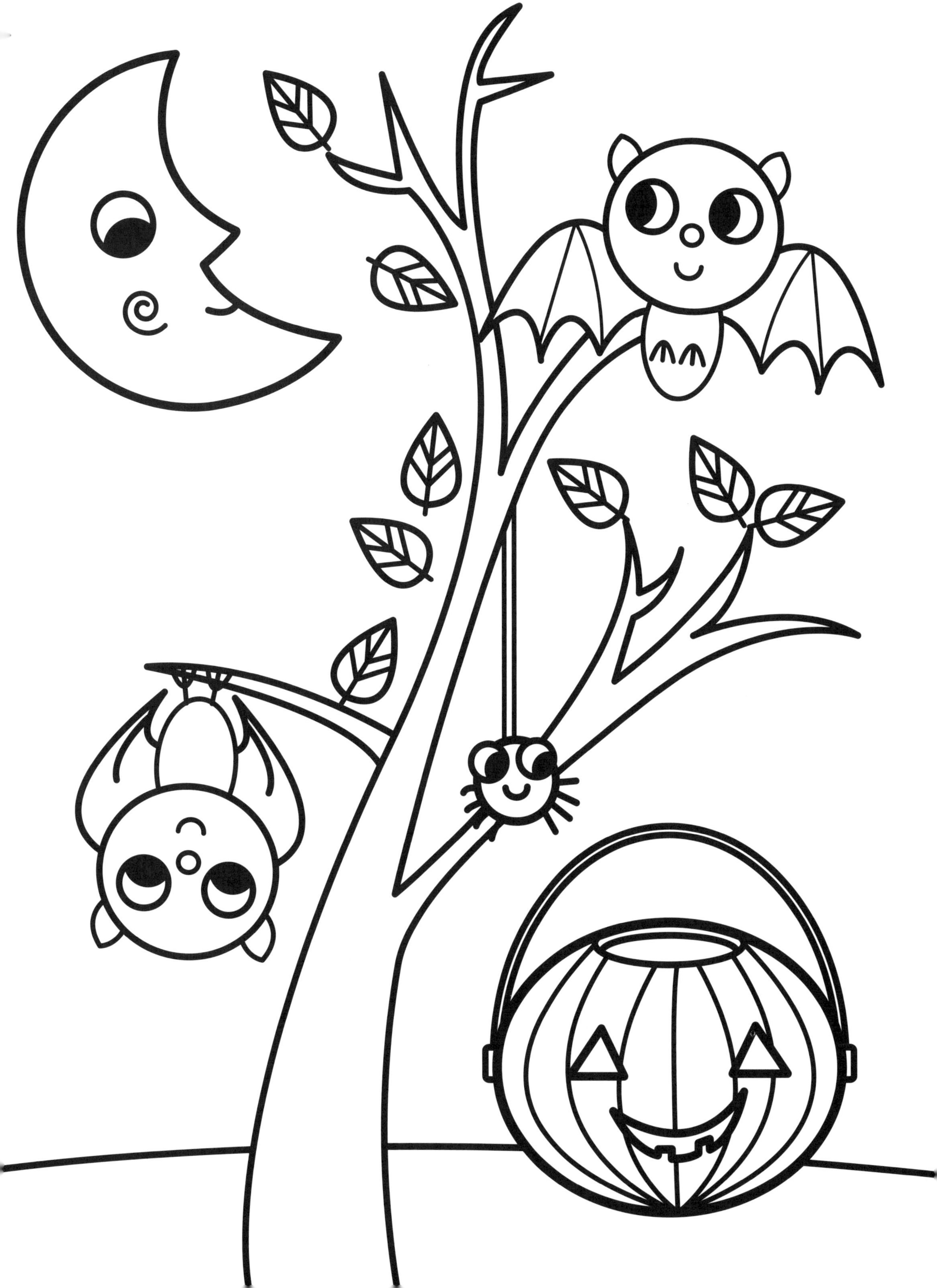

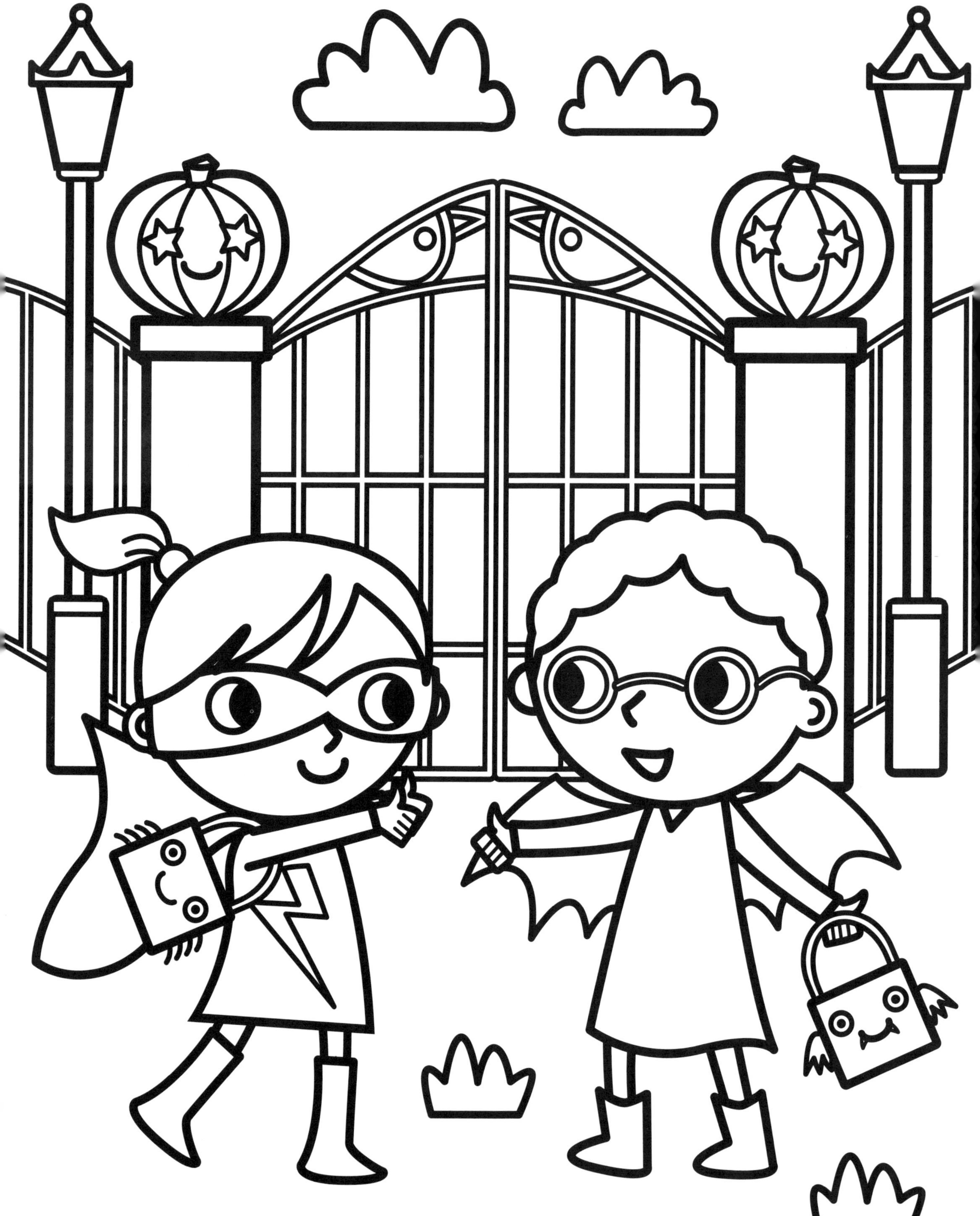

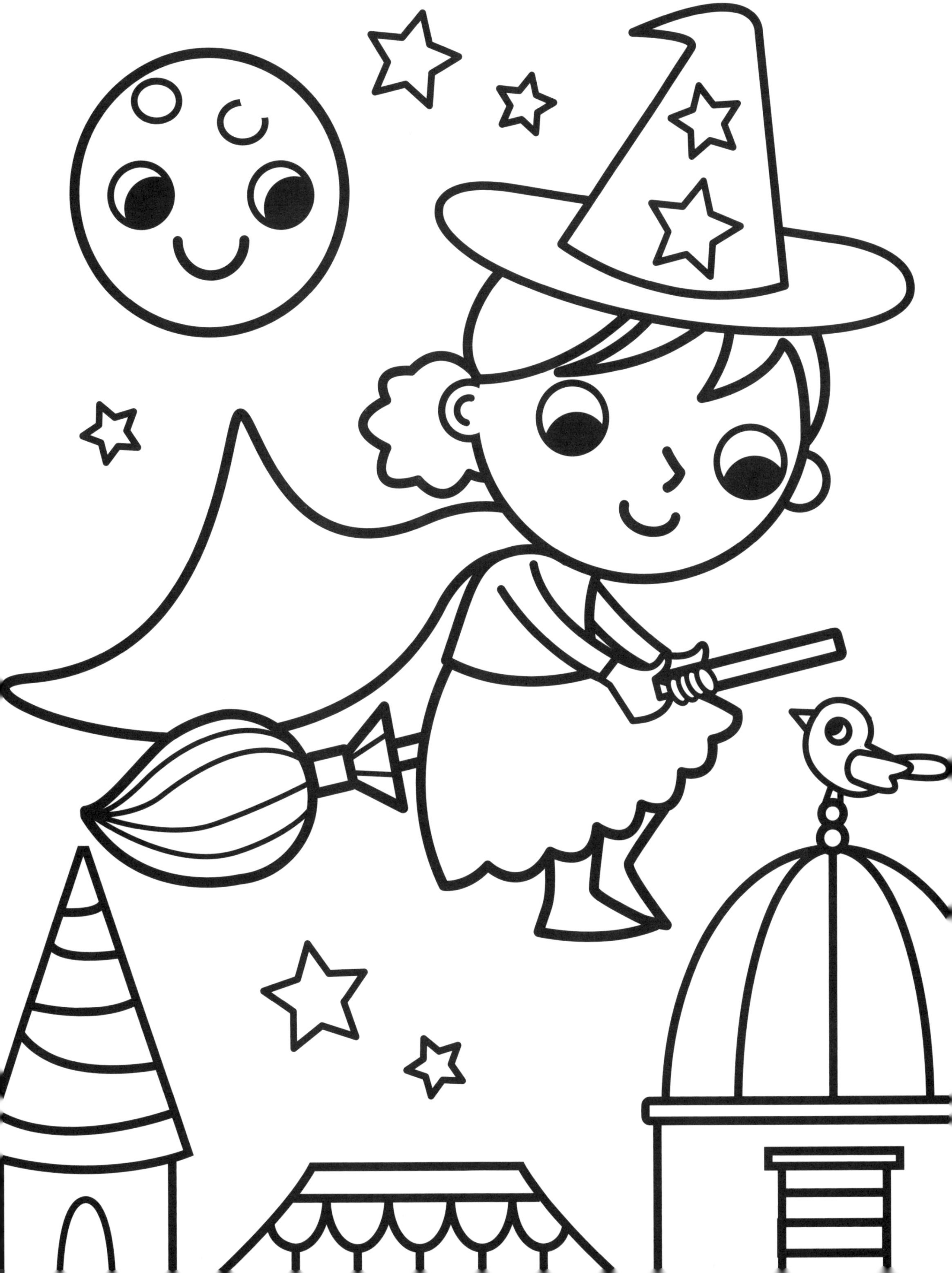

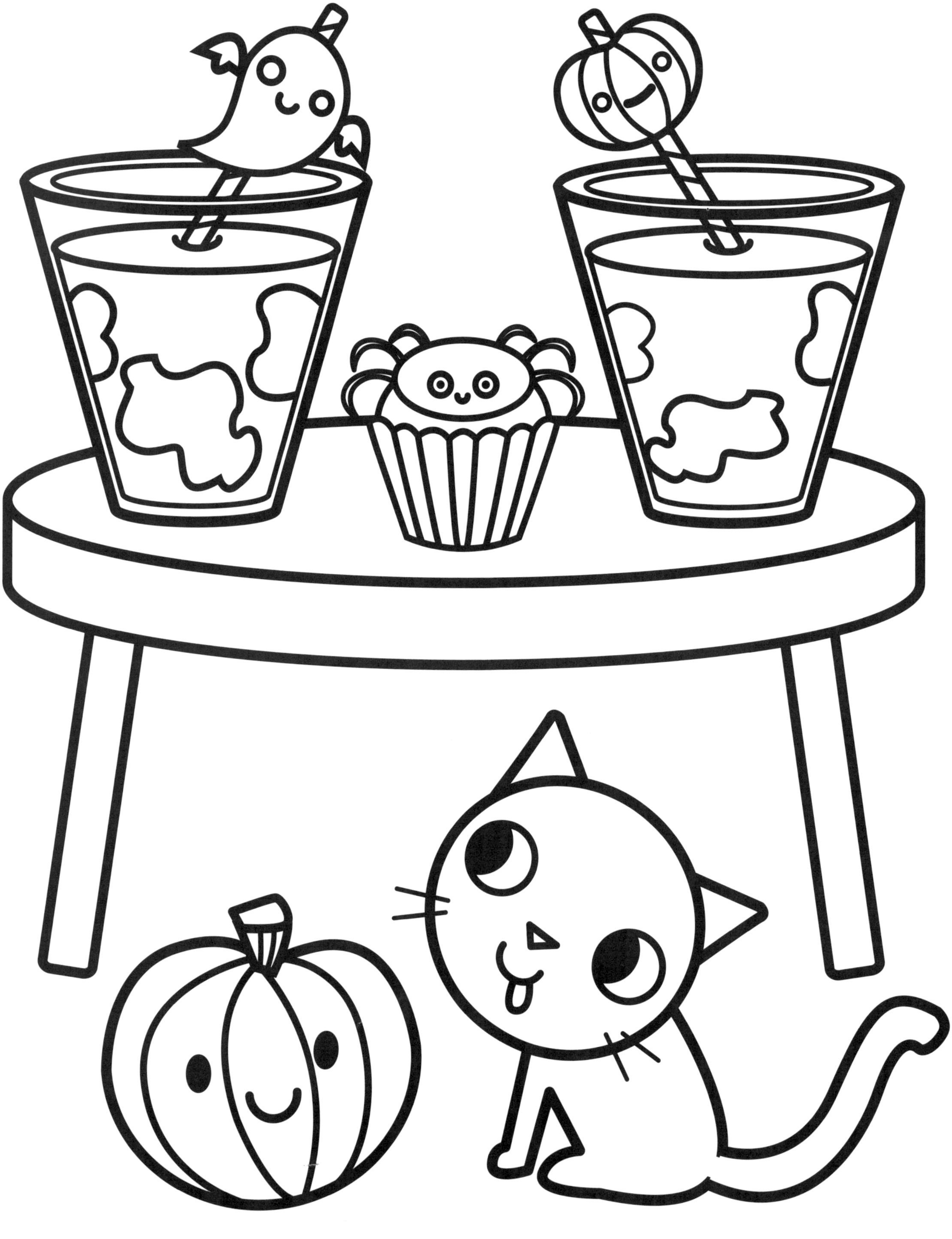

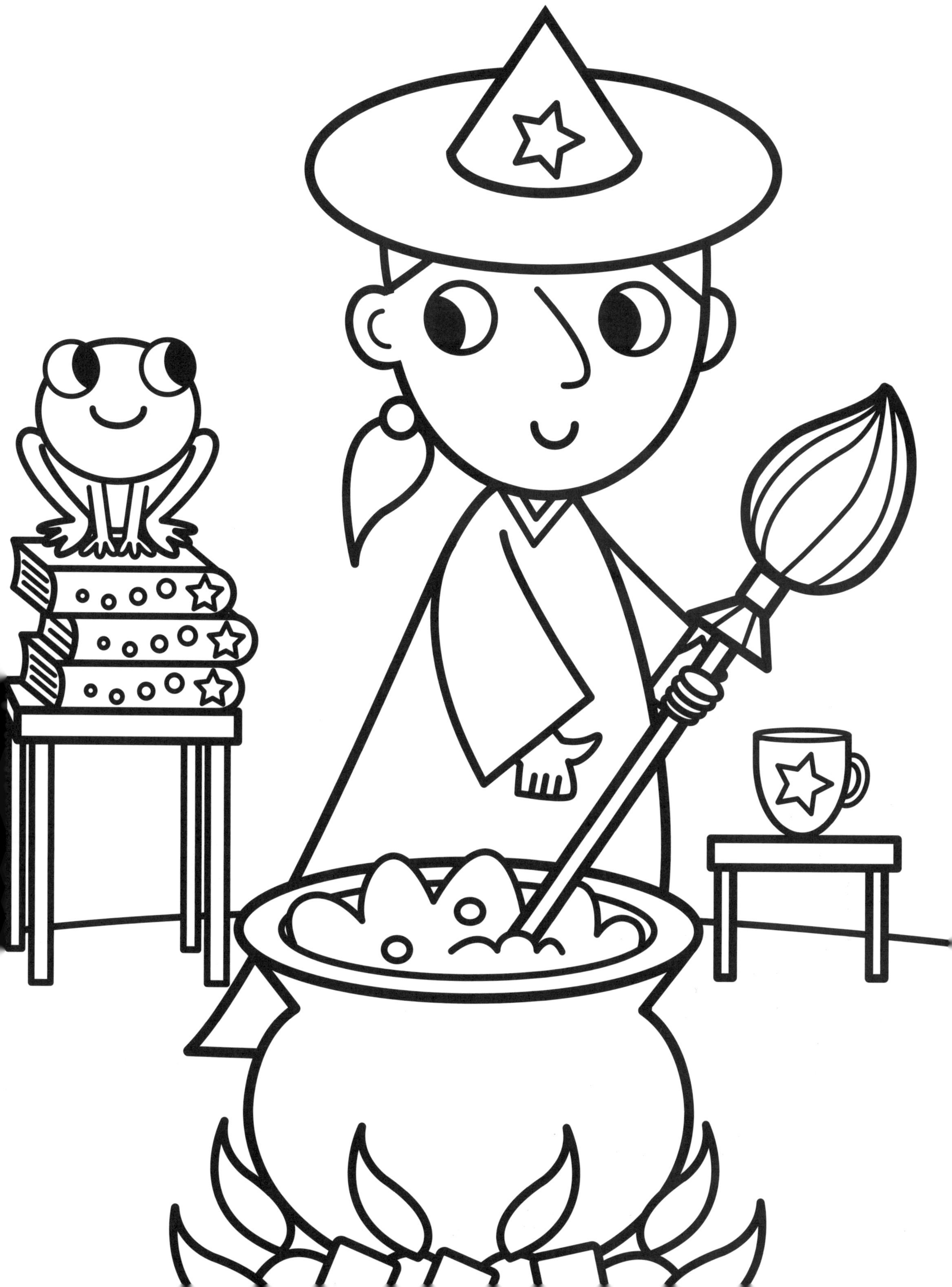

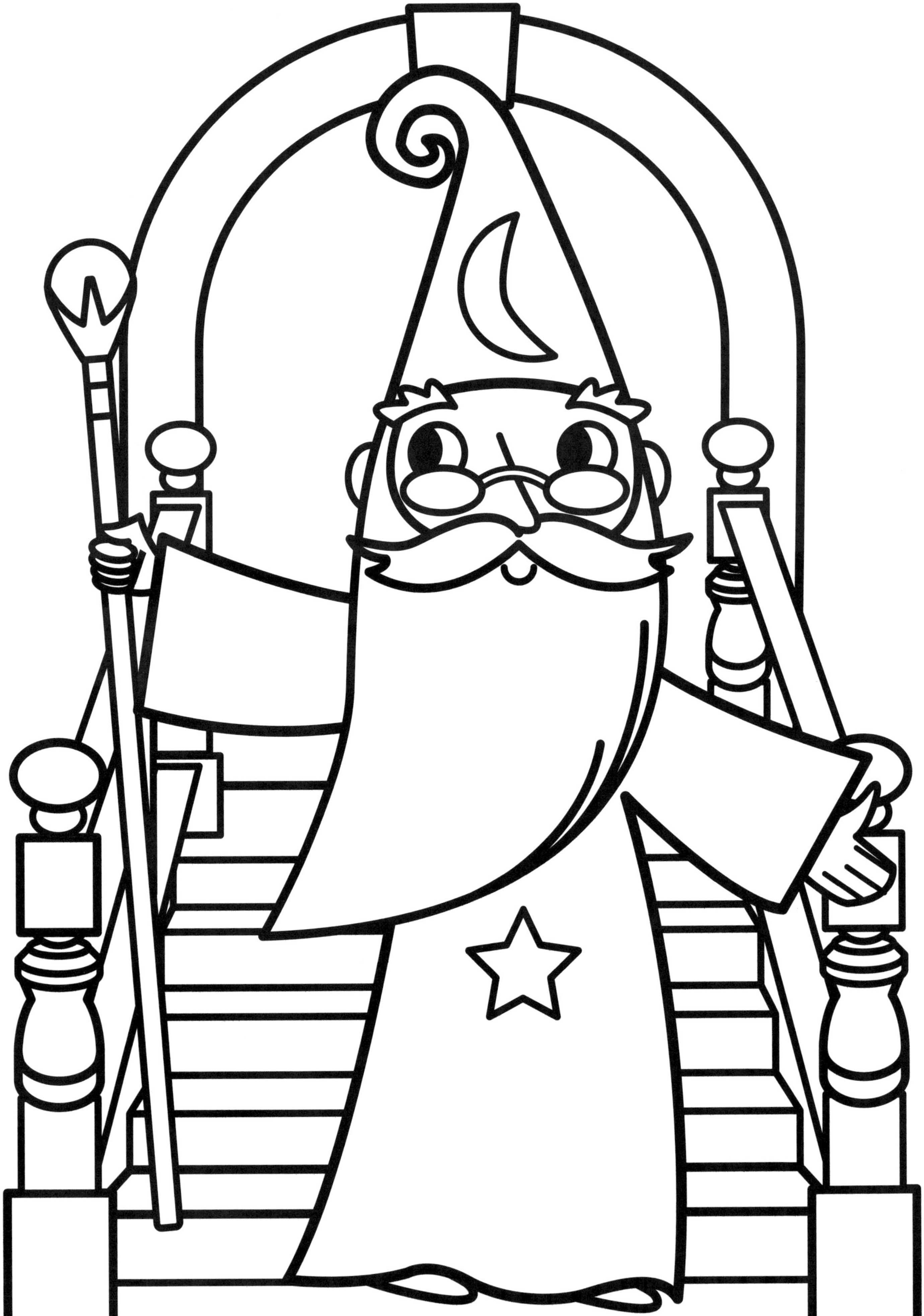

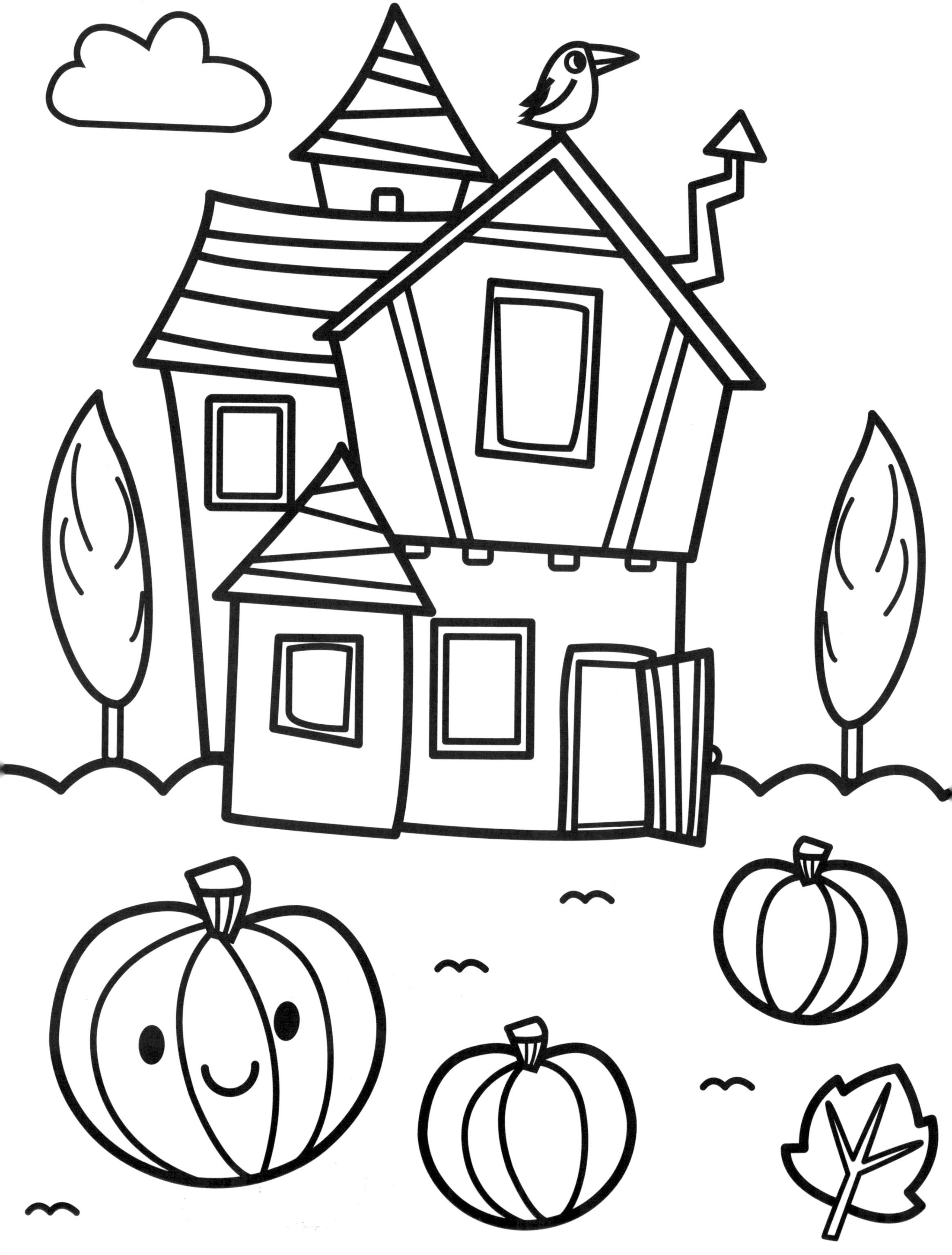

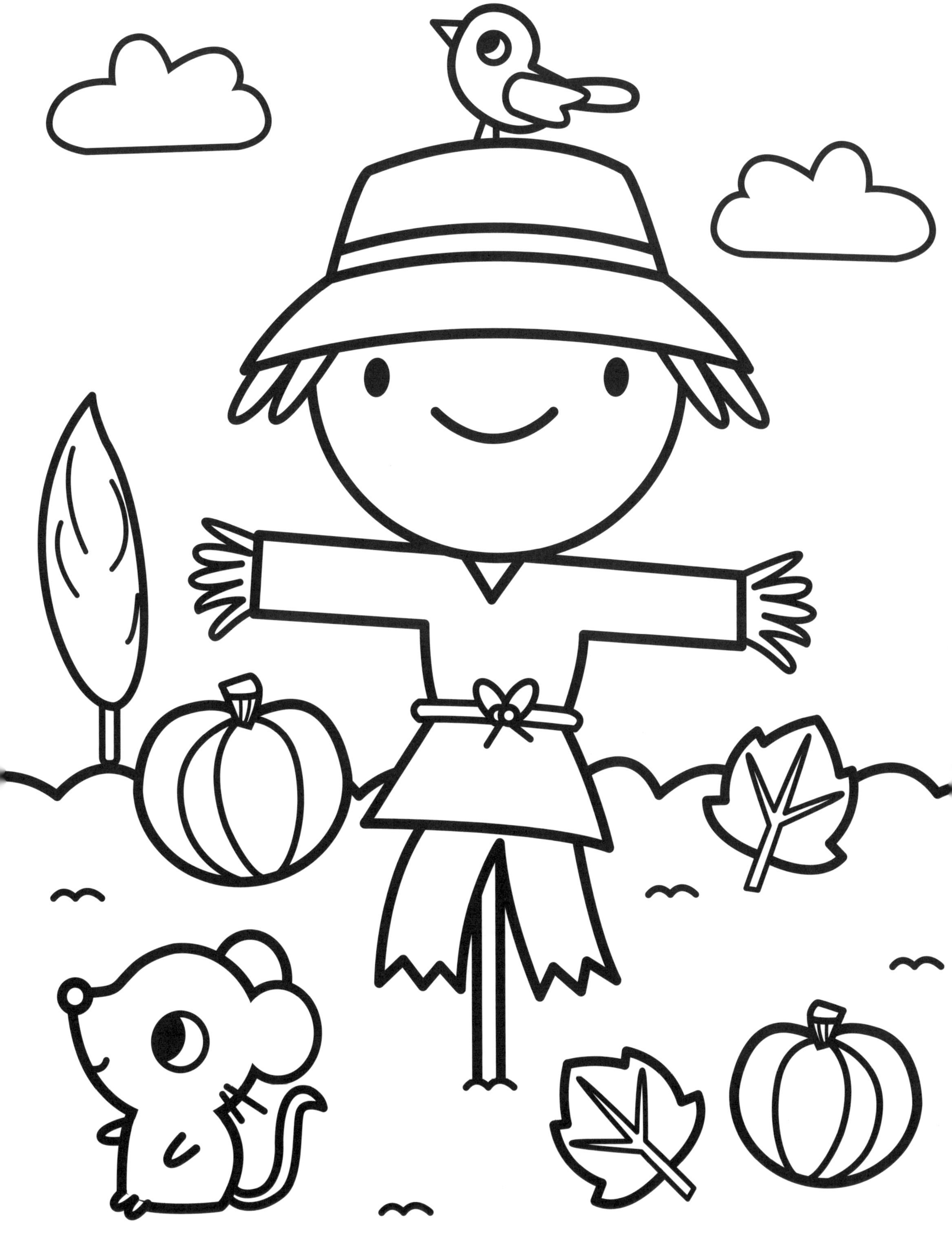

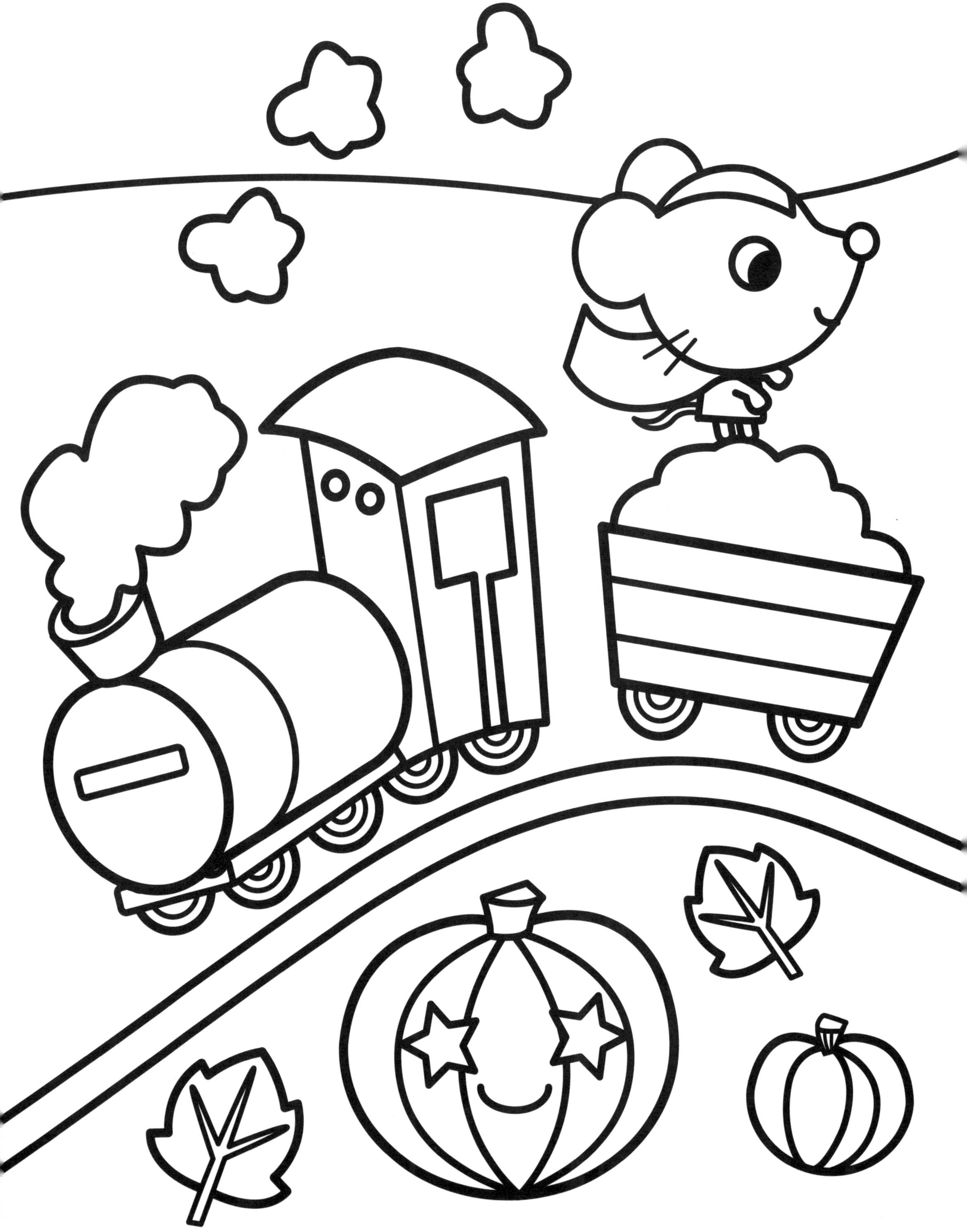

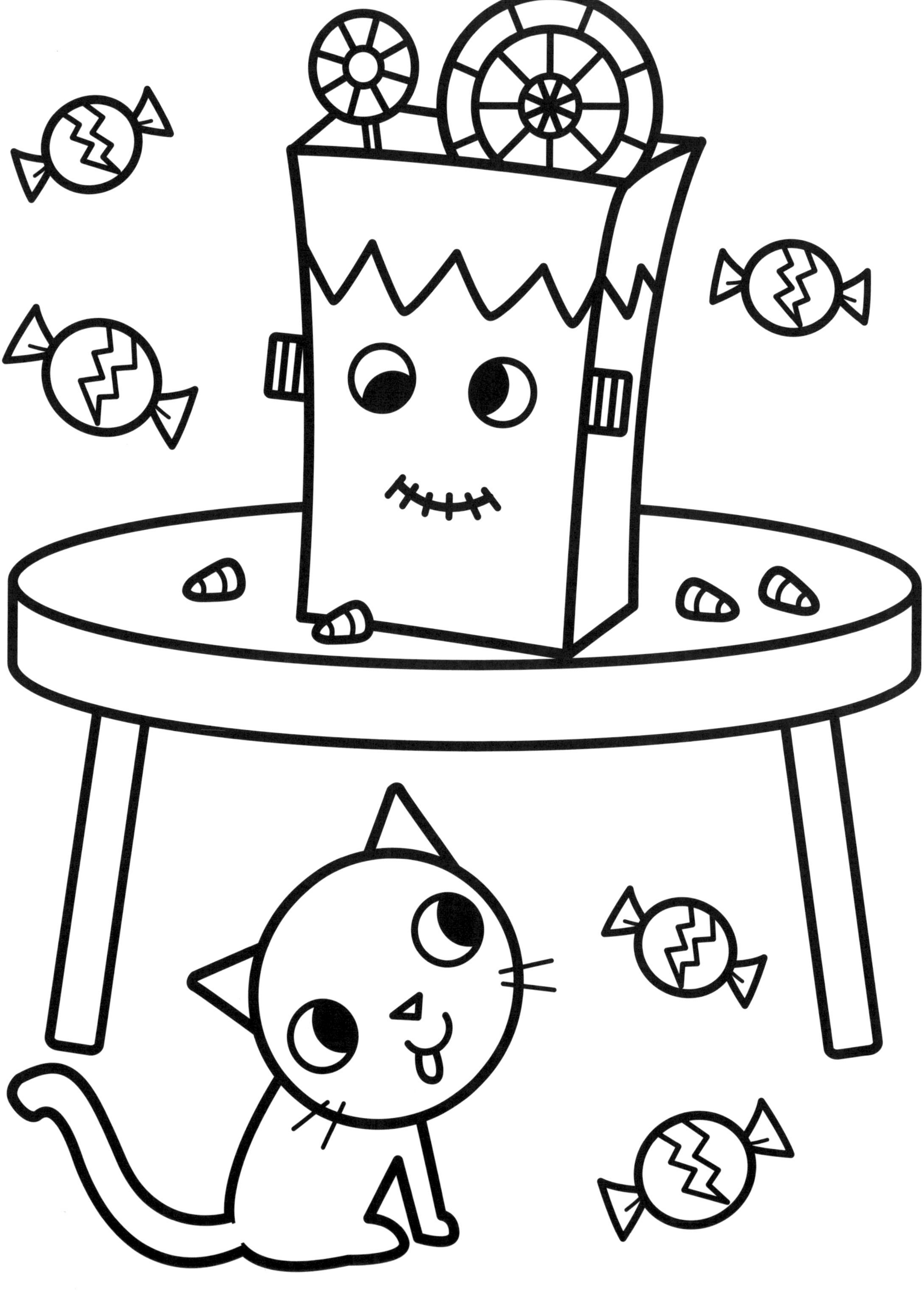

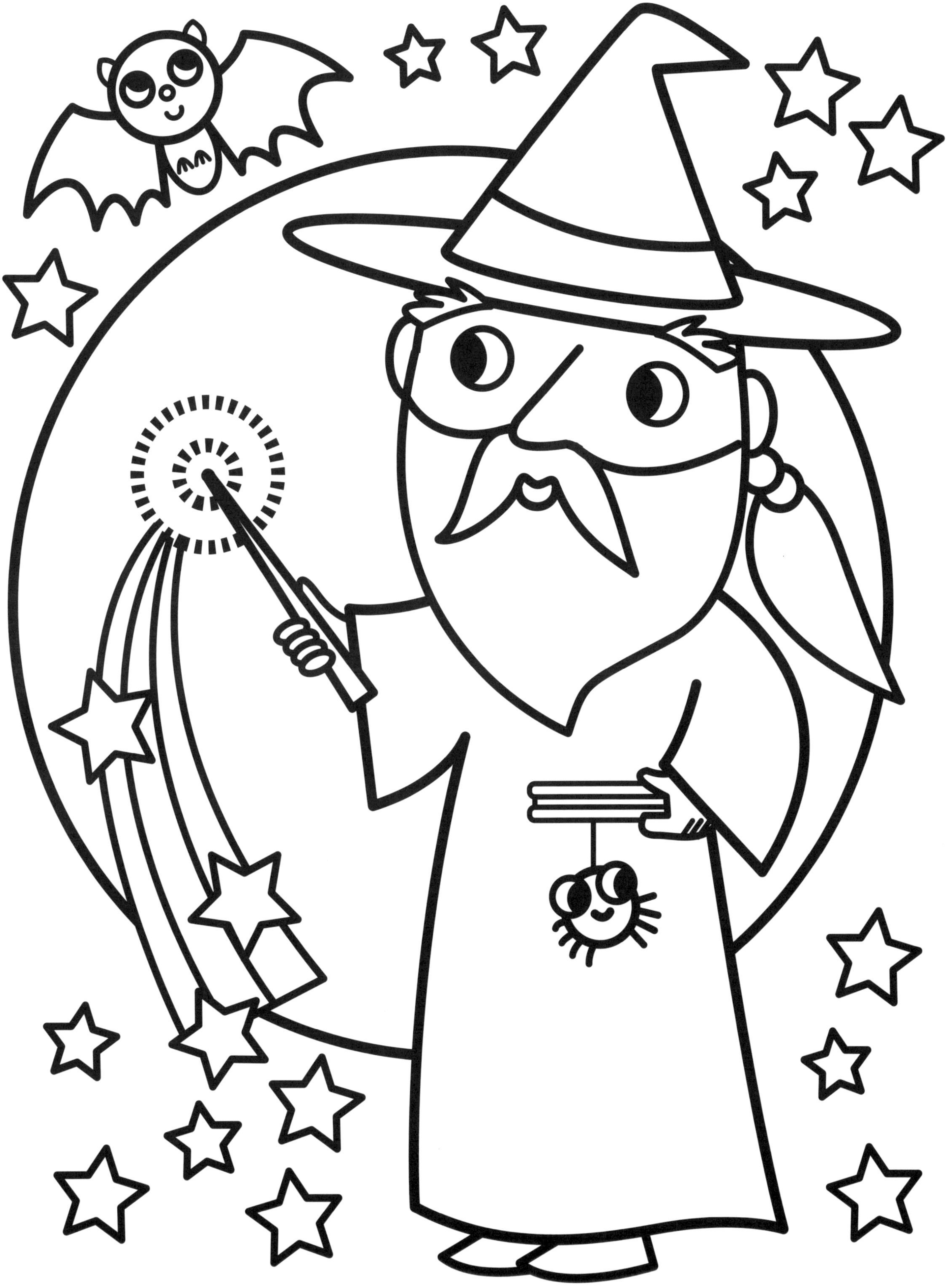

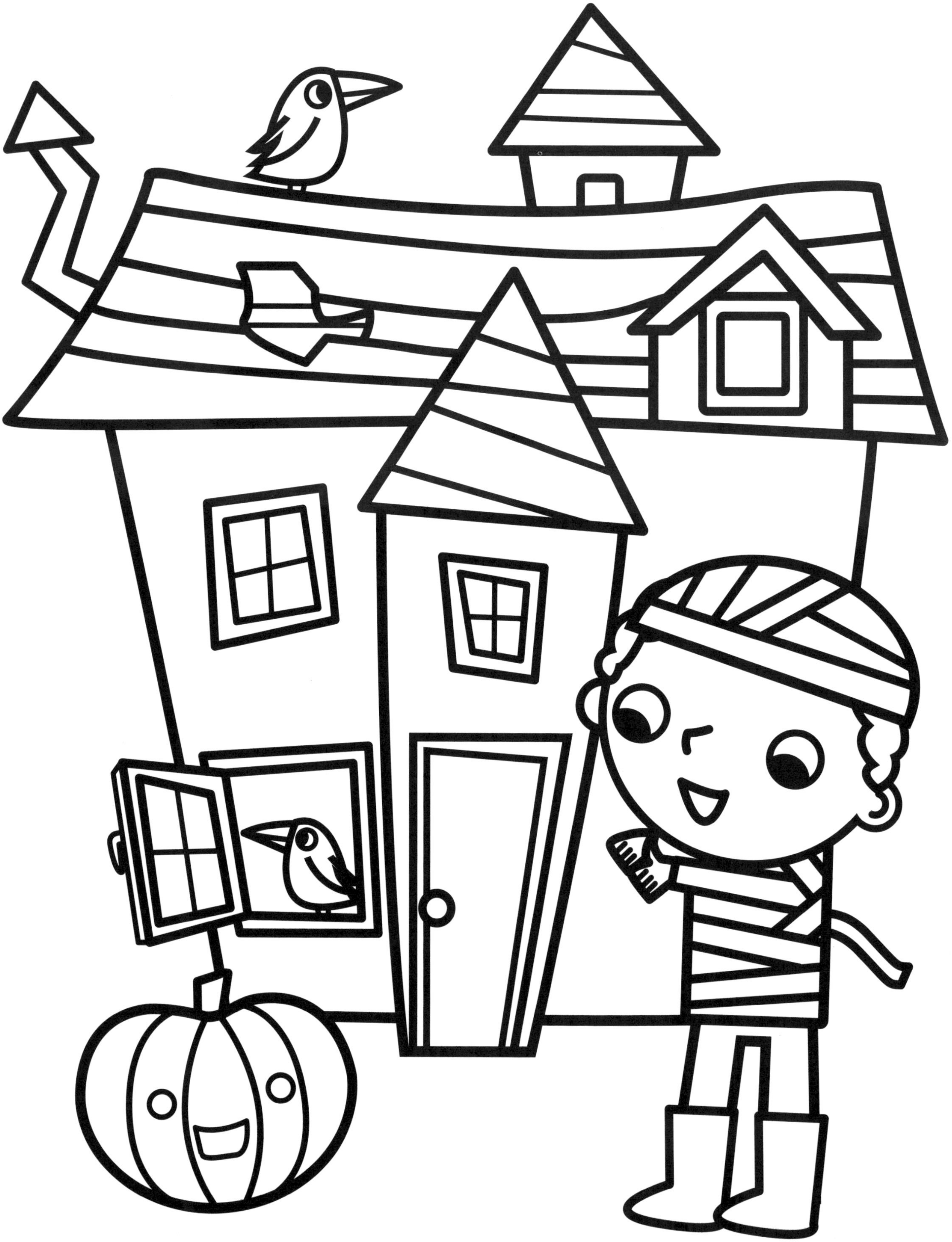

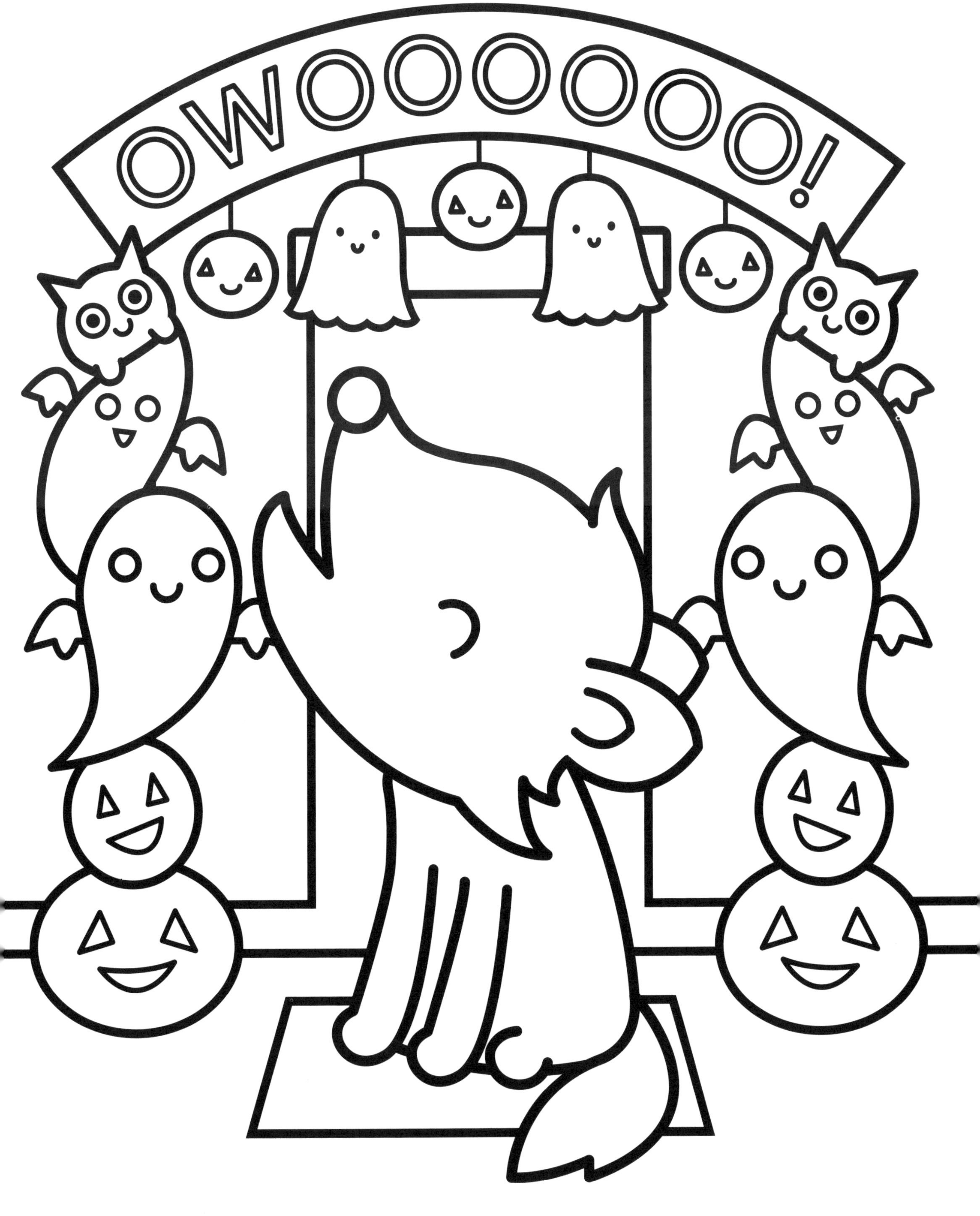
OWOOOOOO!

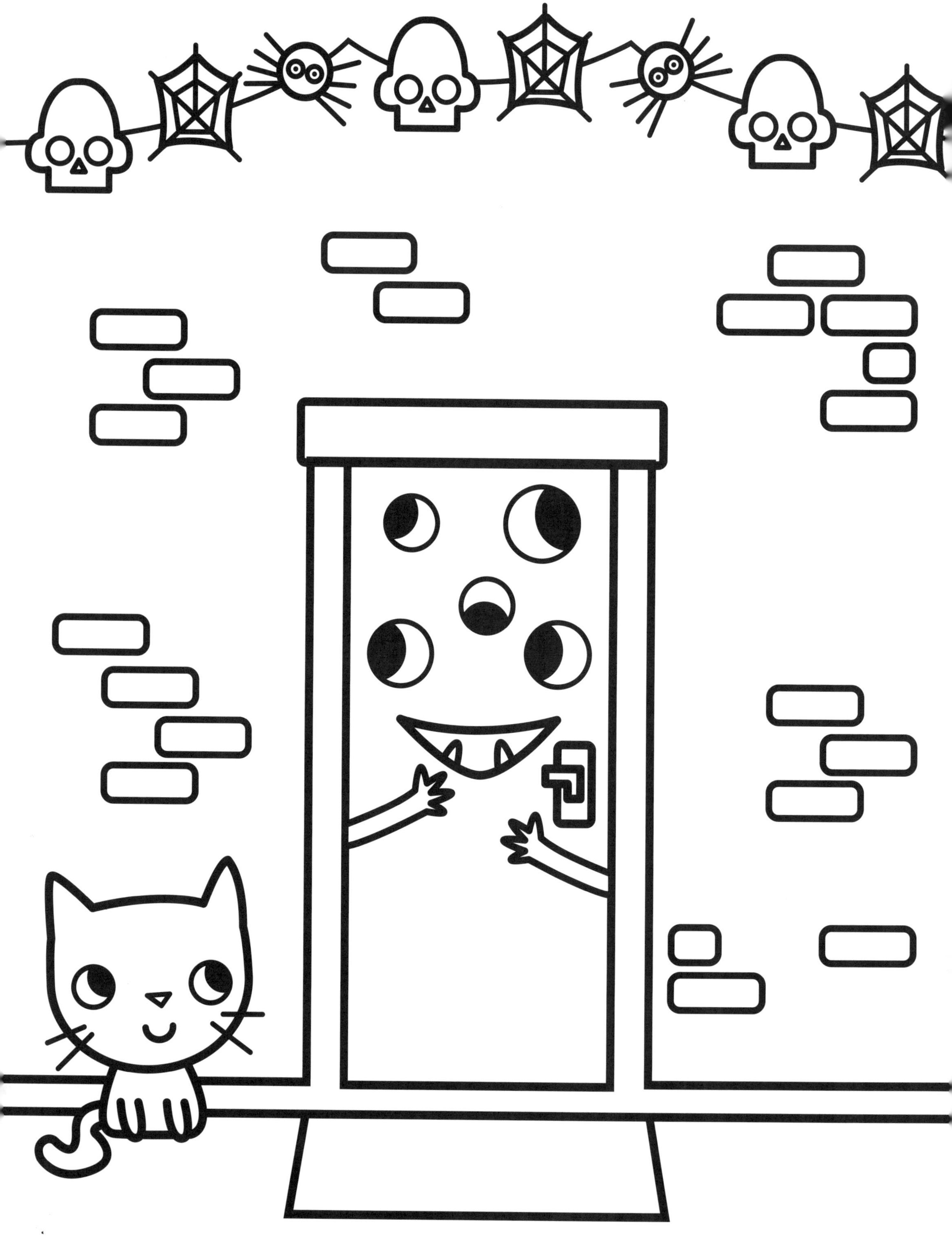

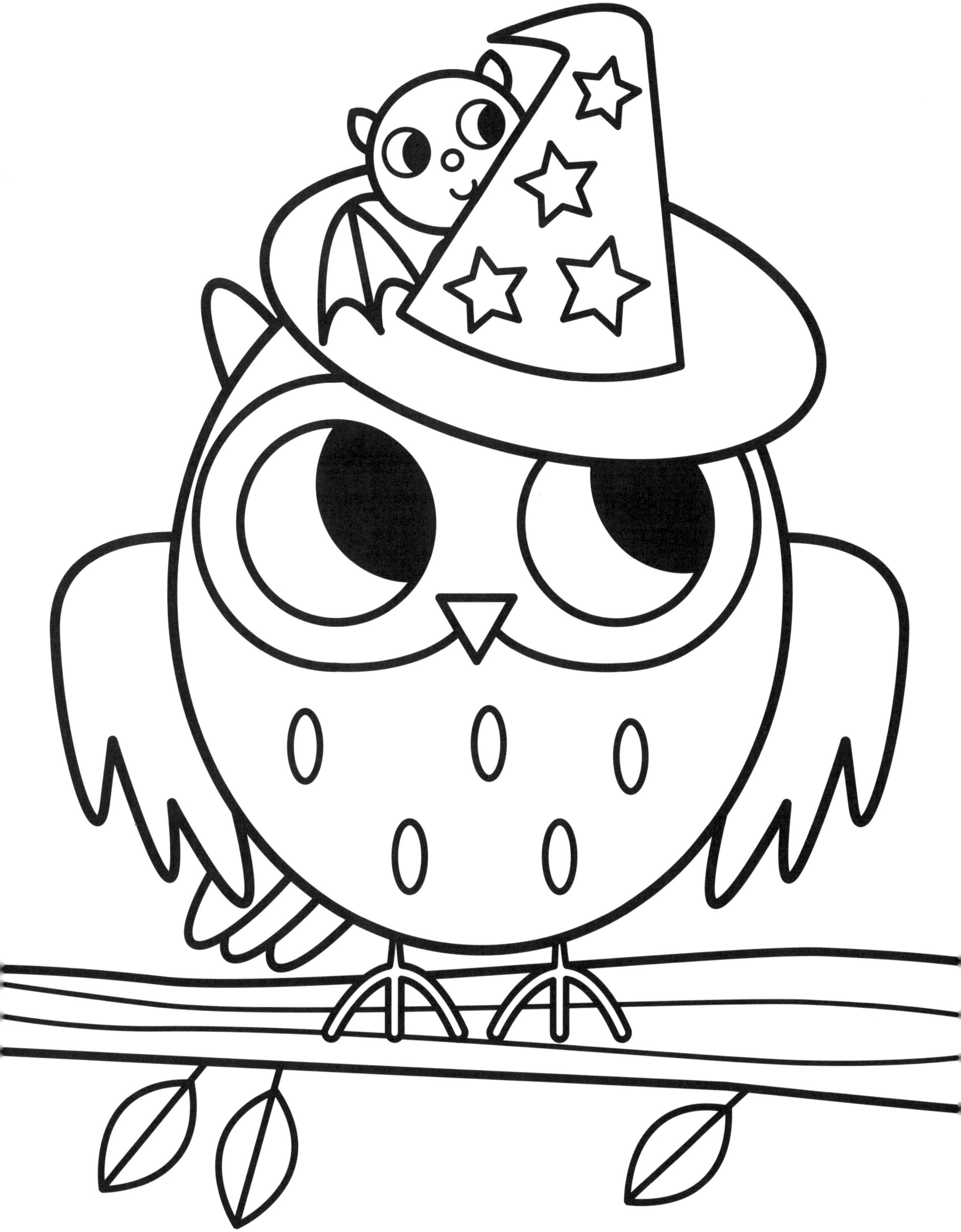

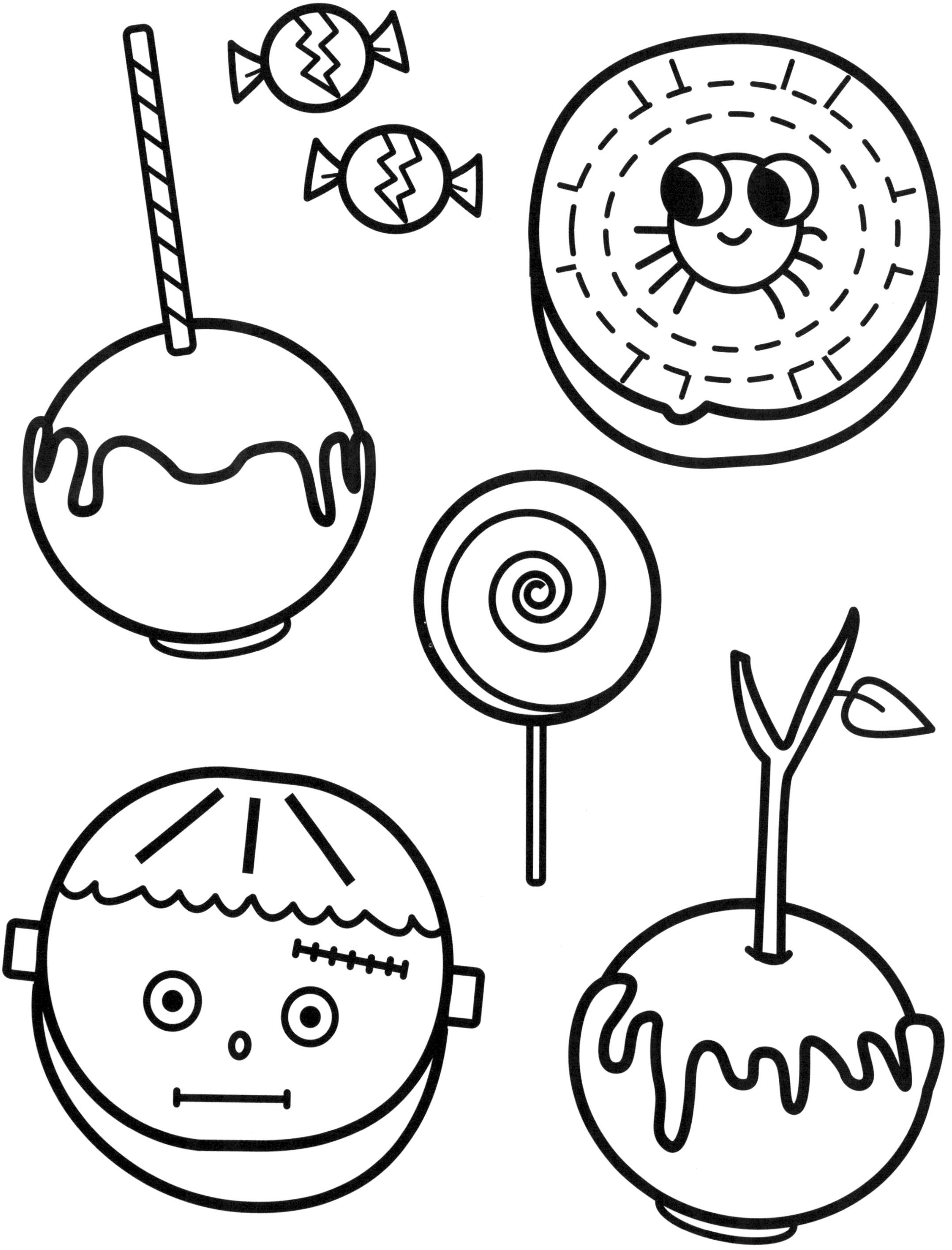

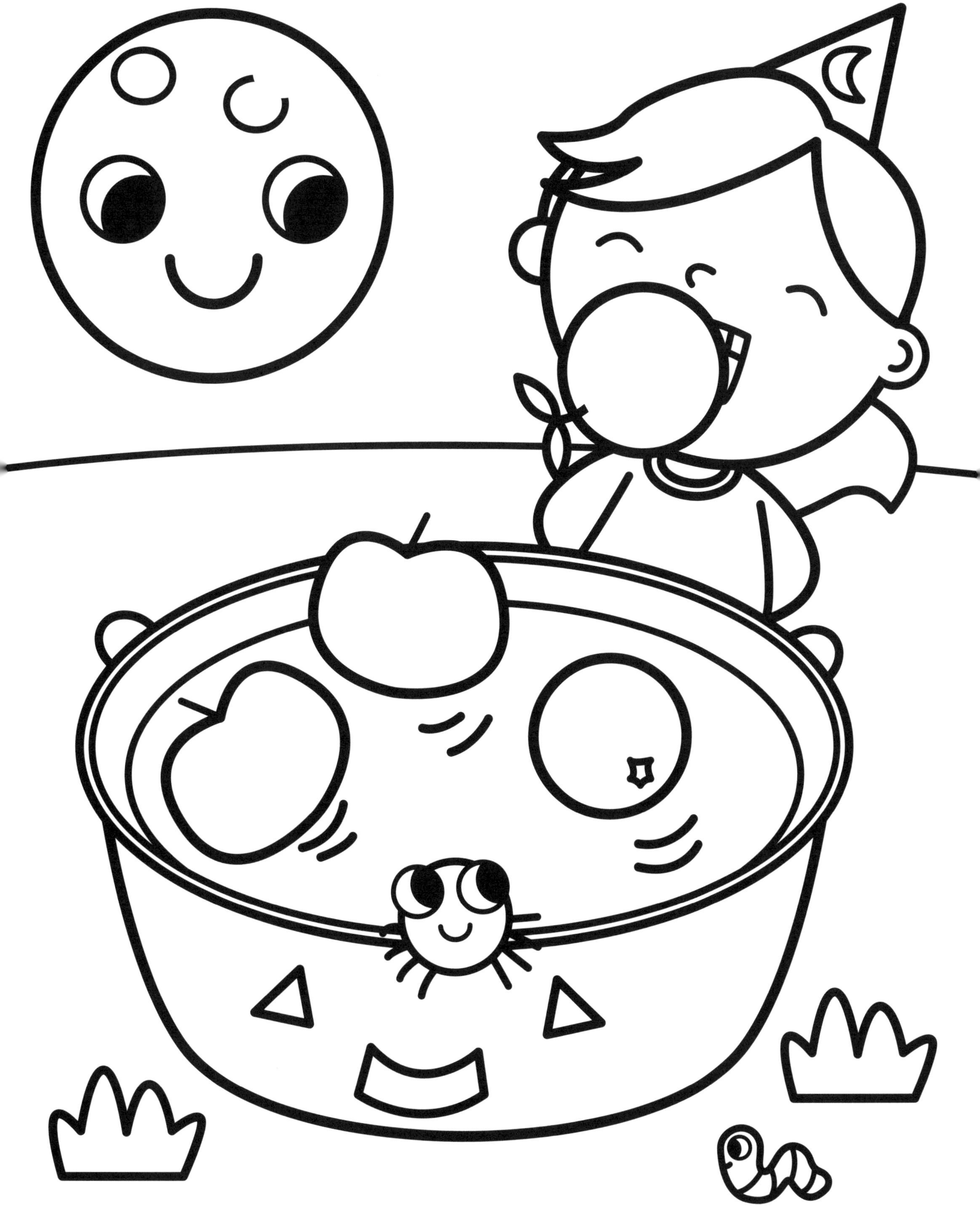

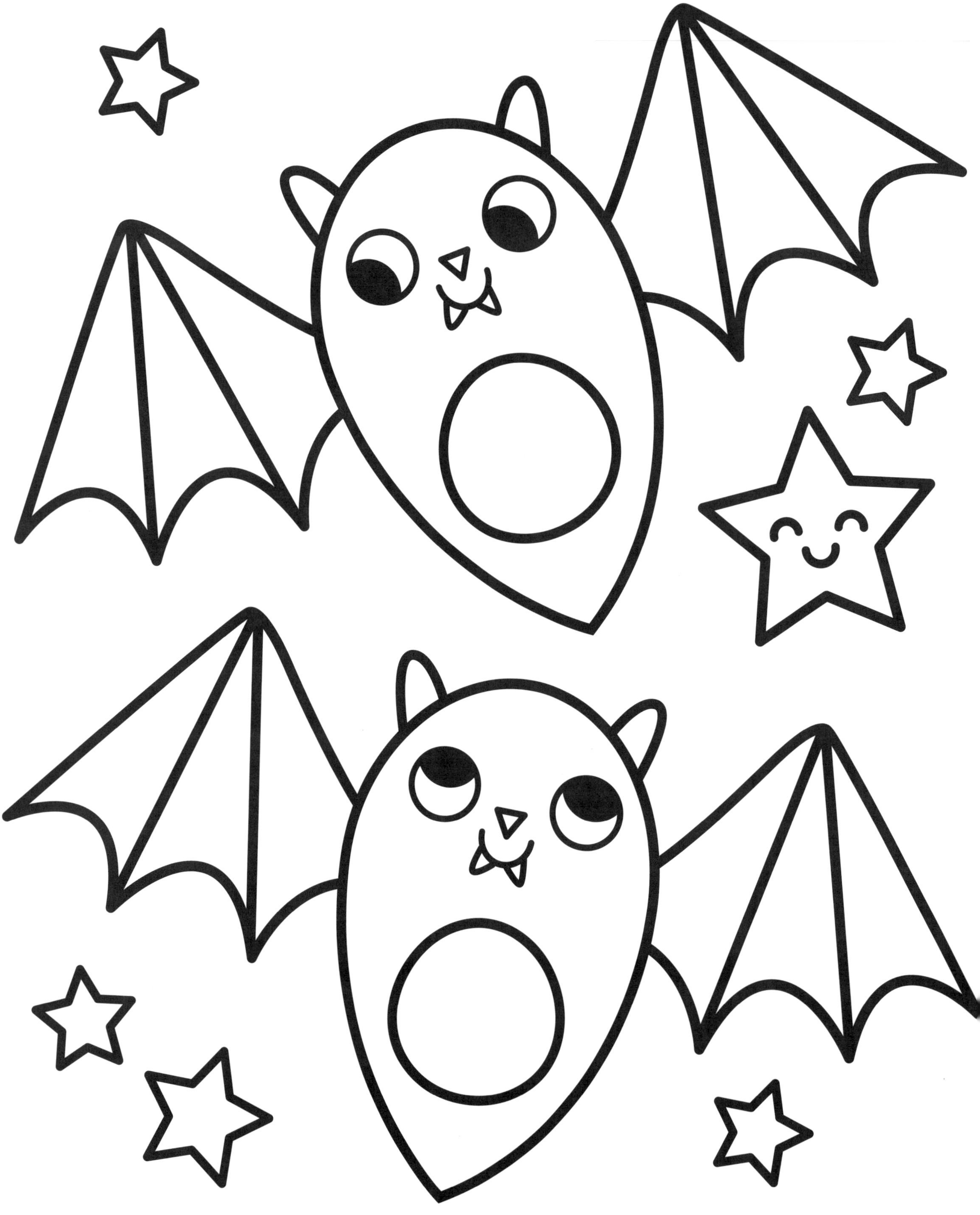

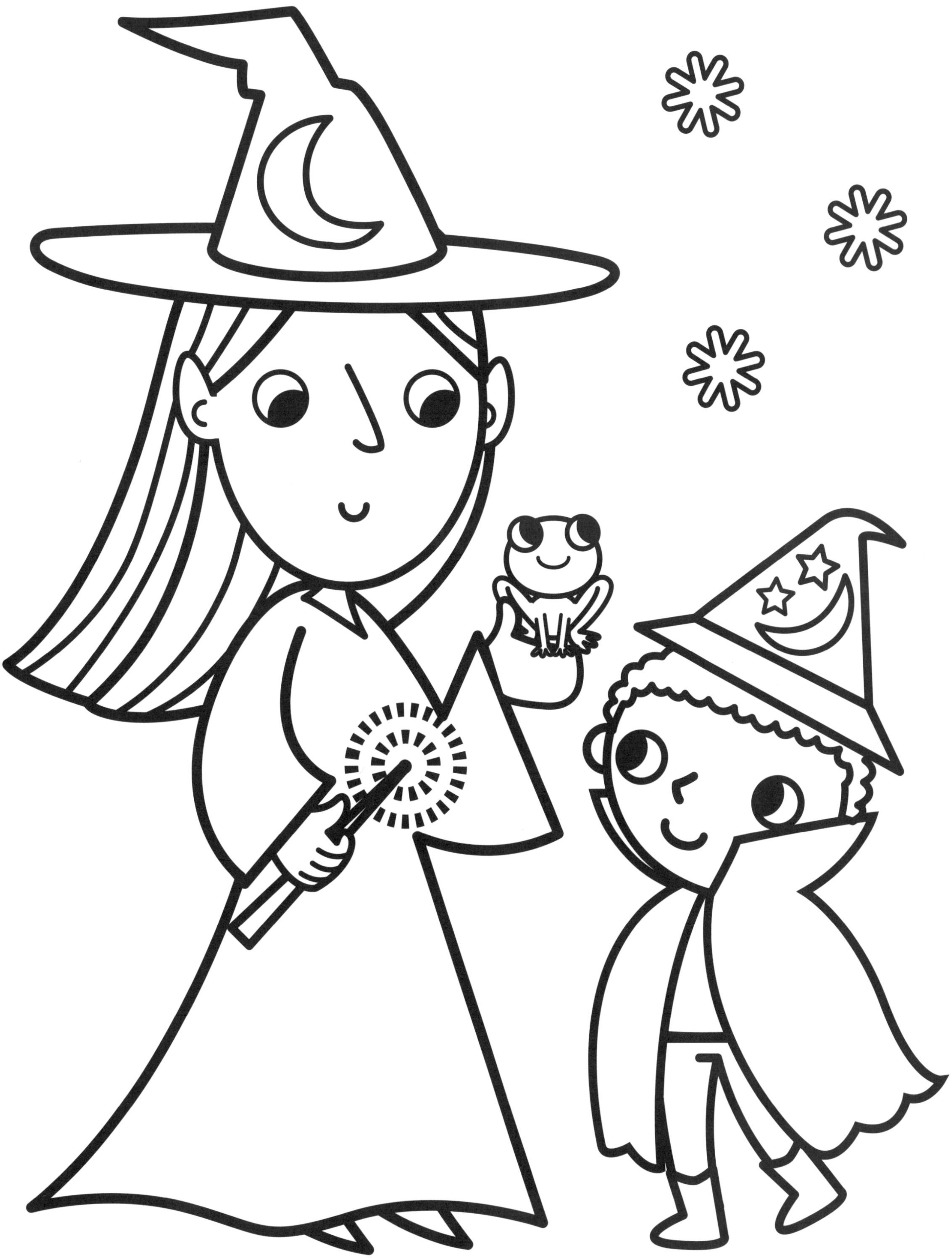

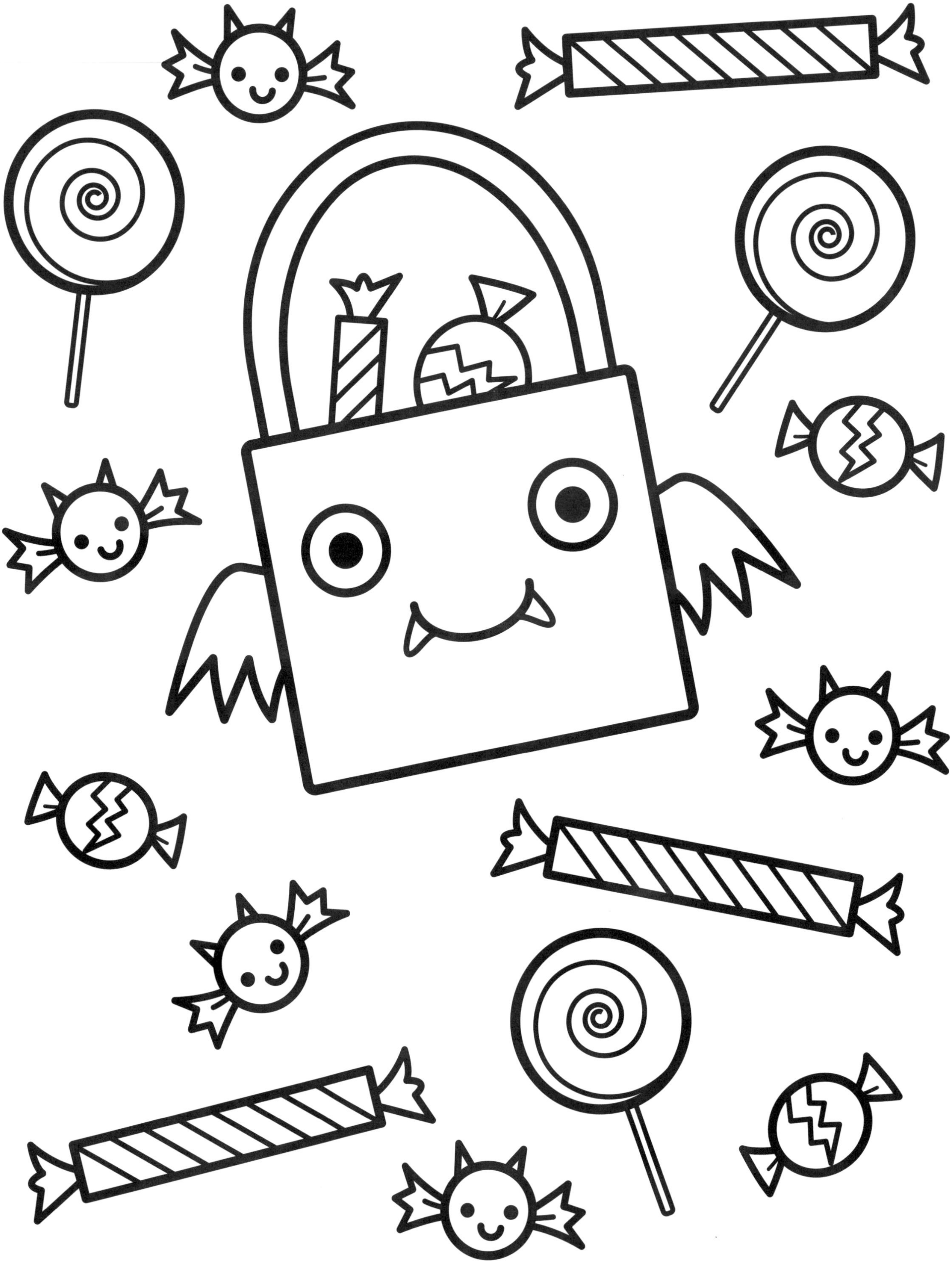

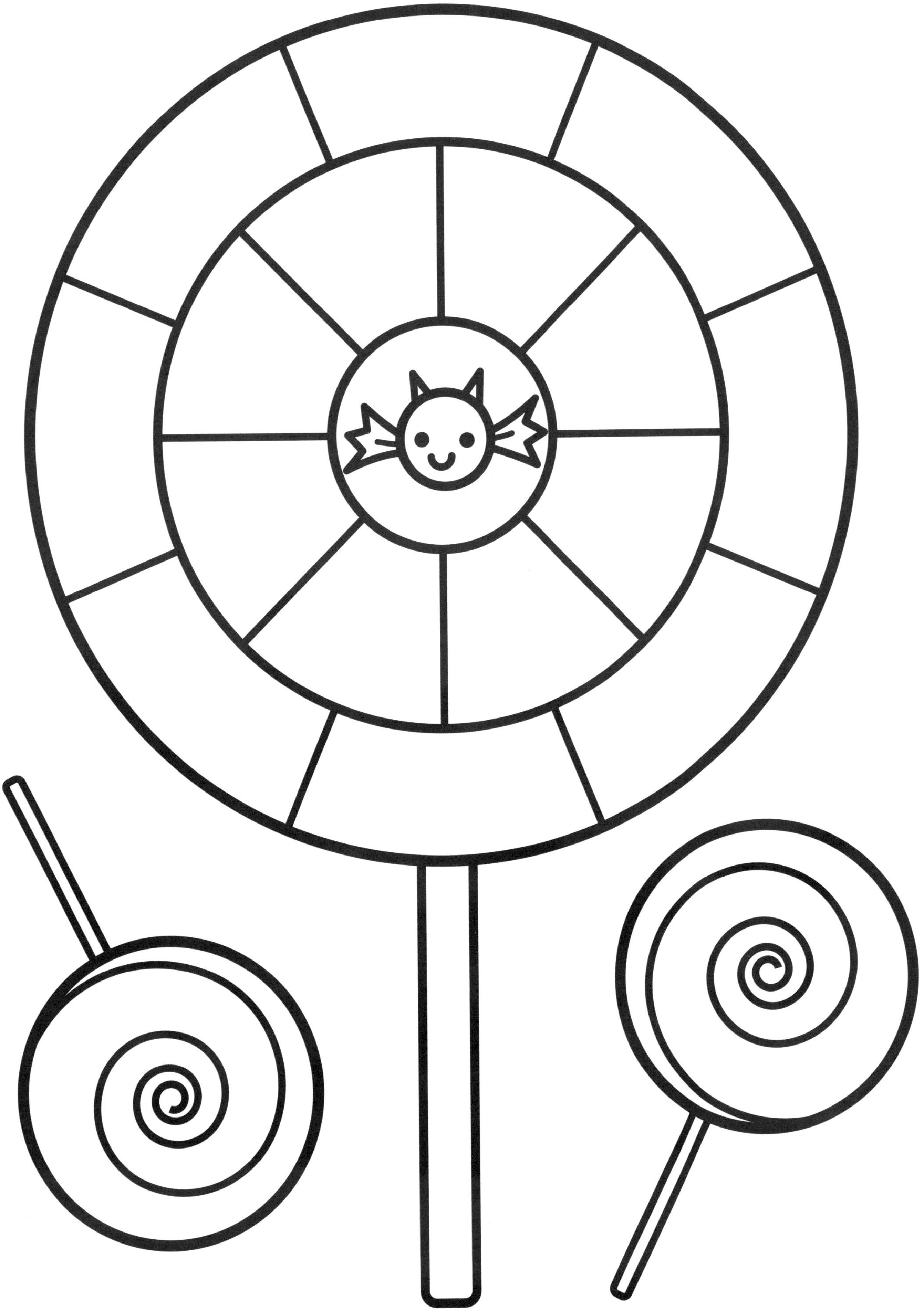

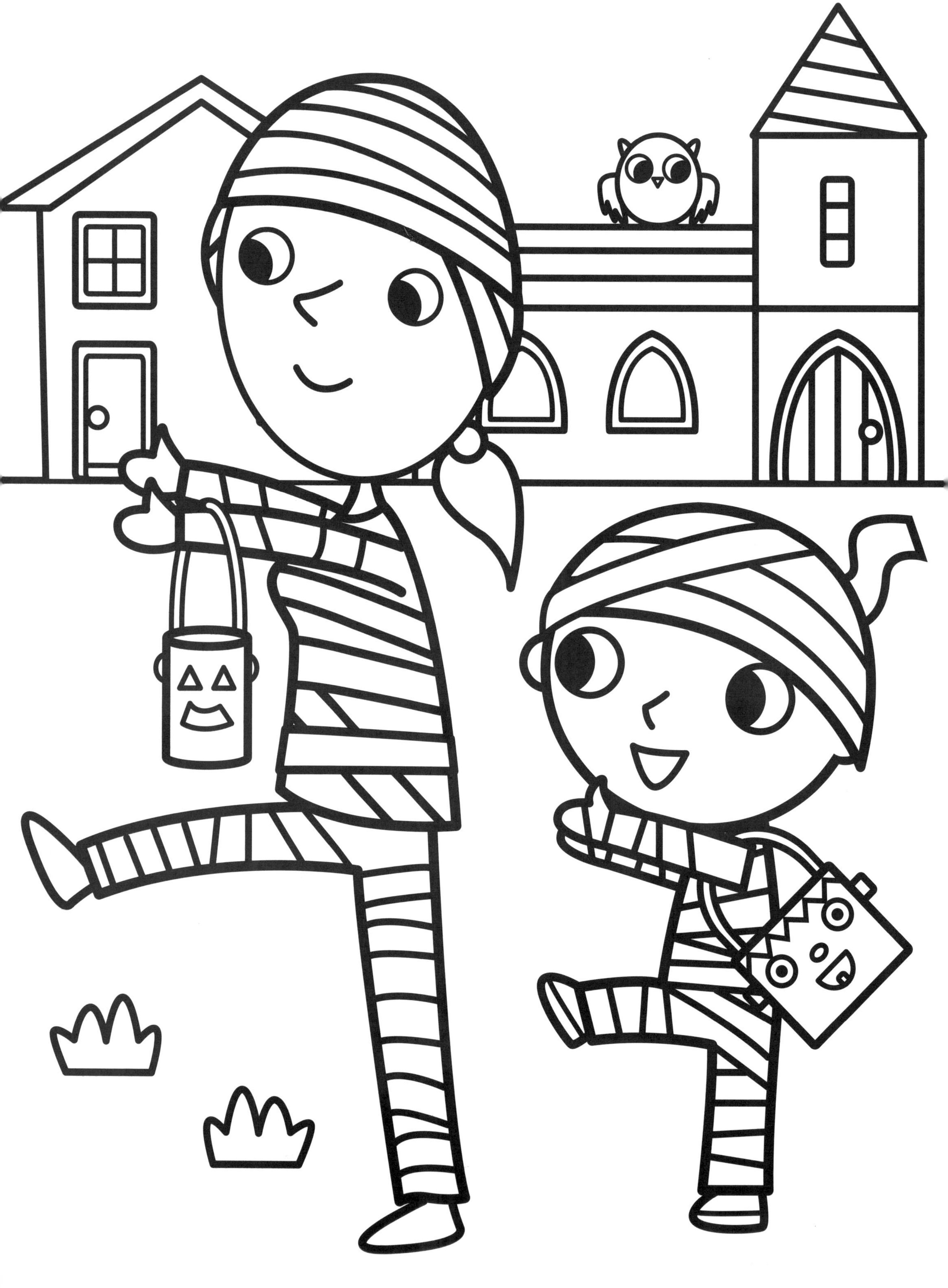

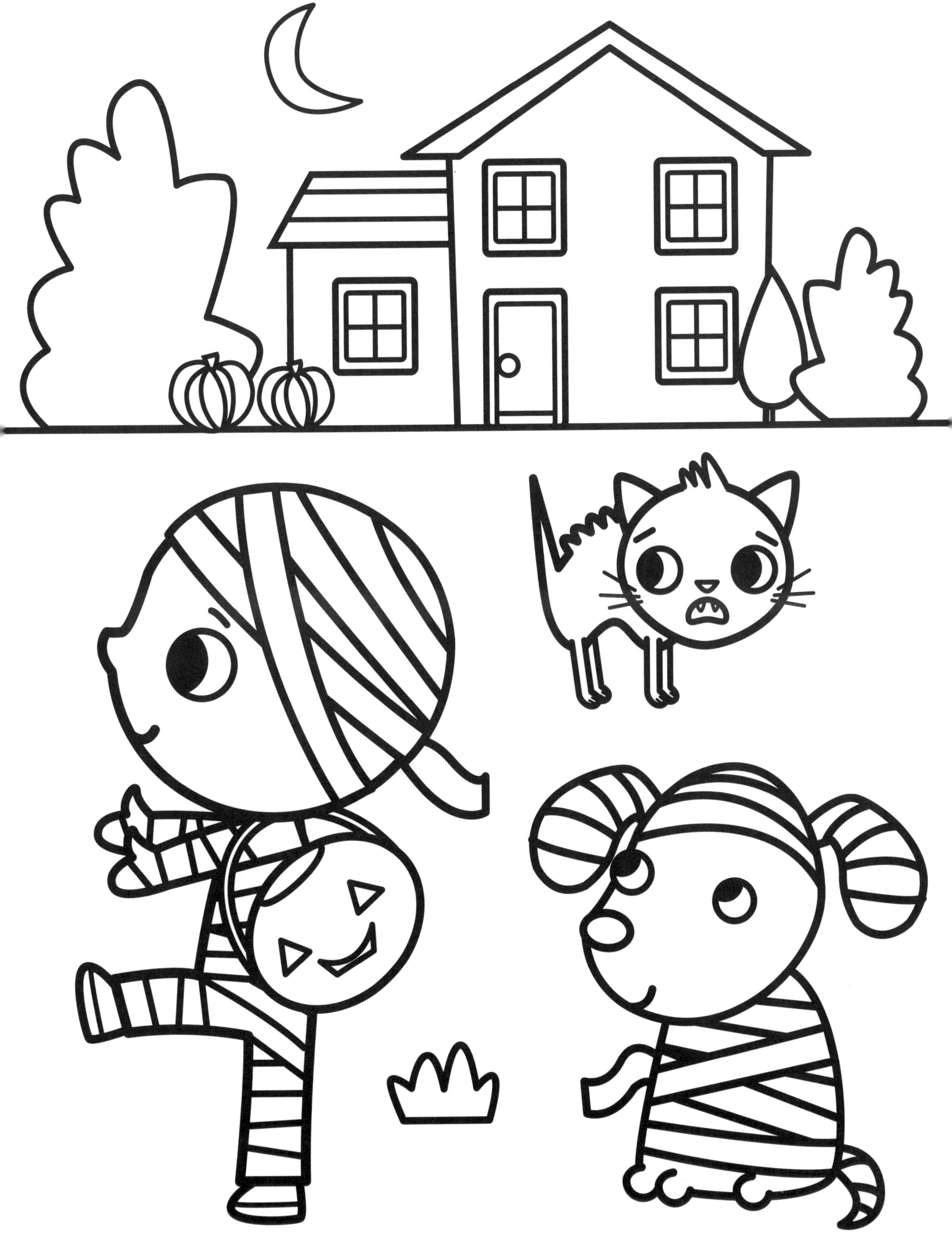

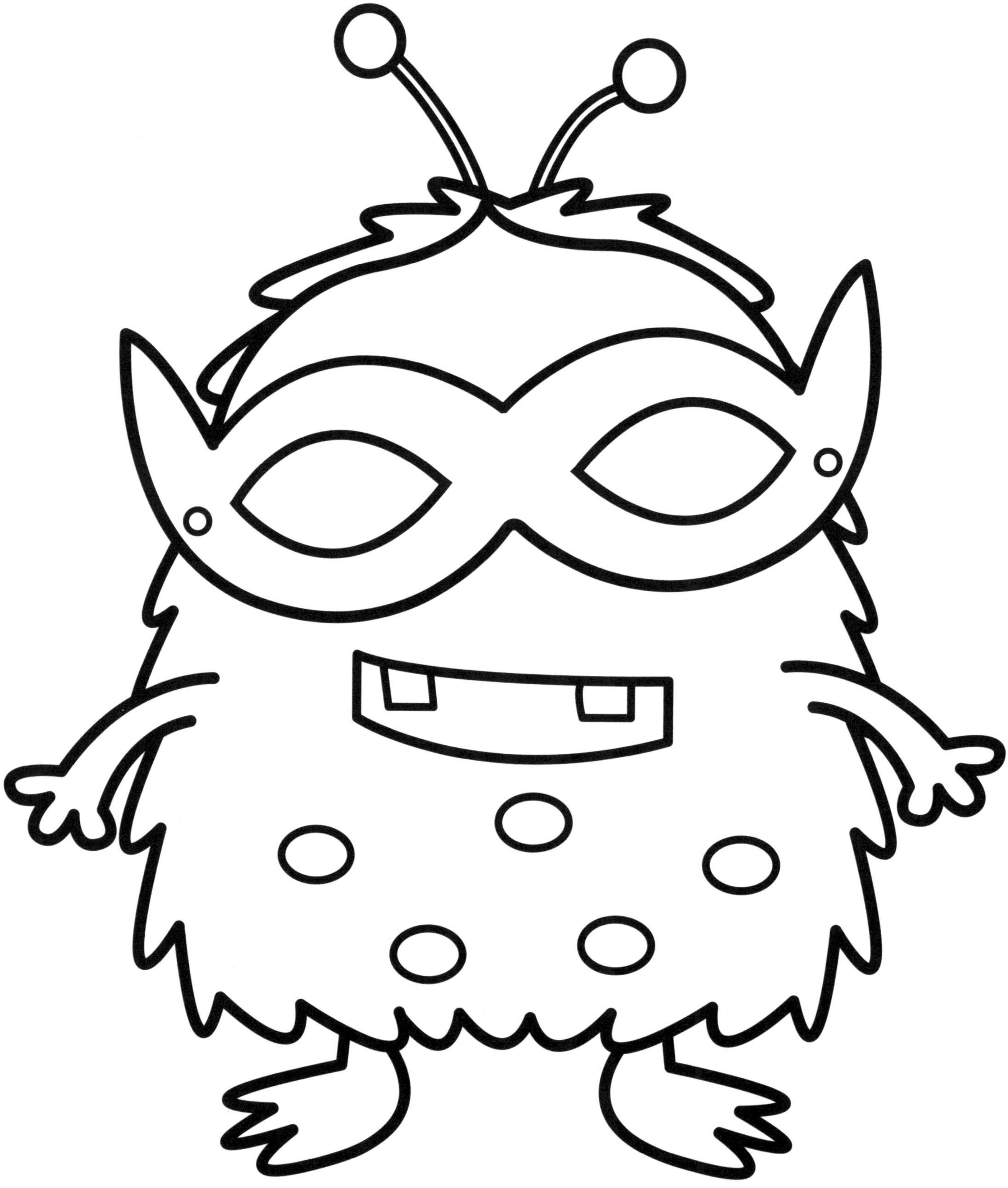

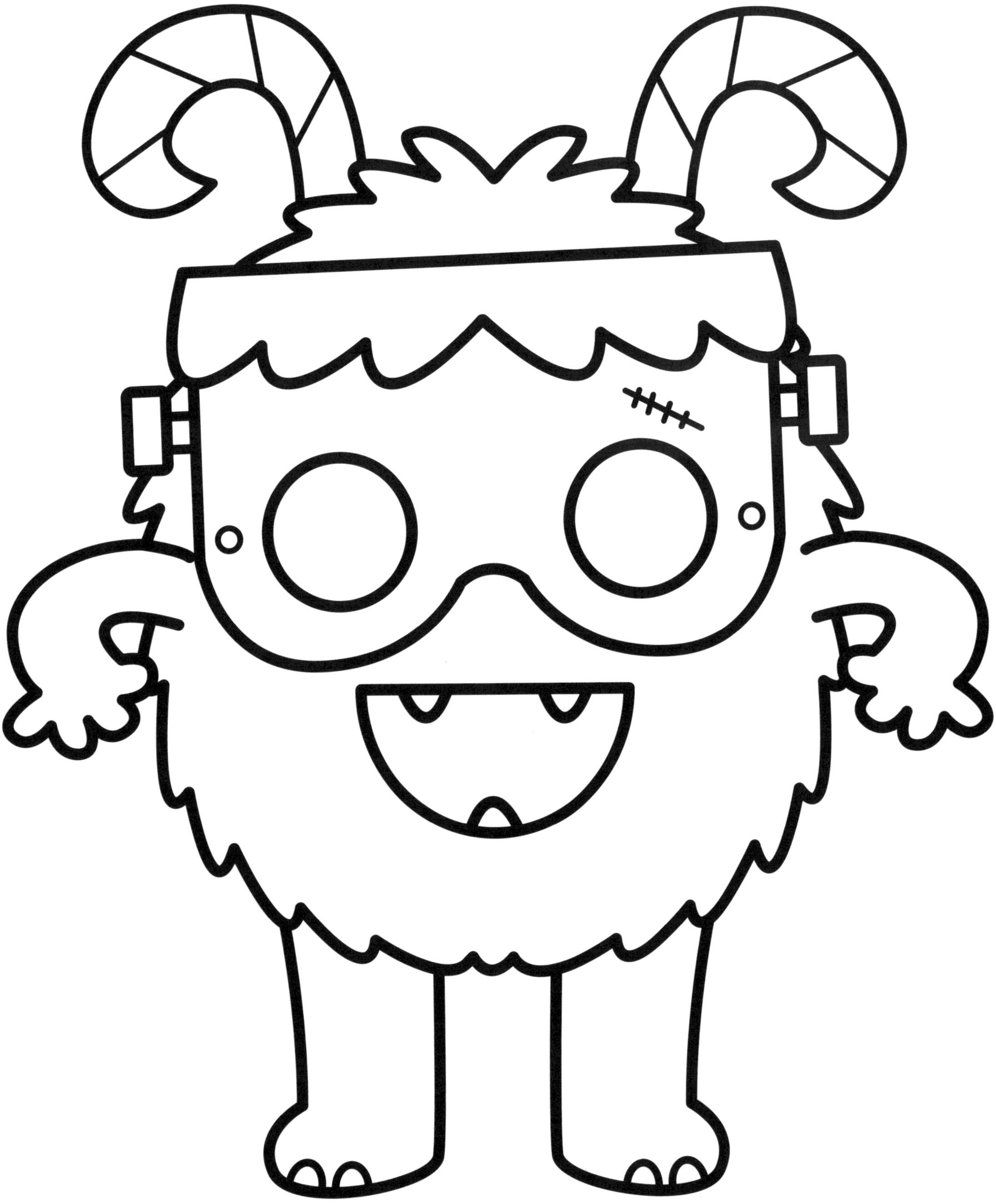

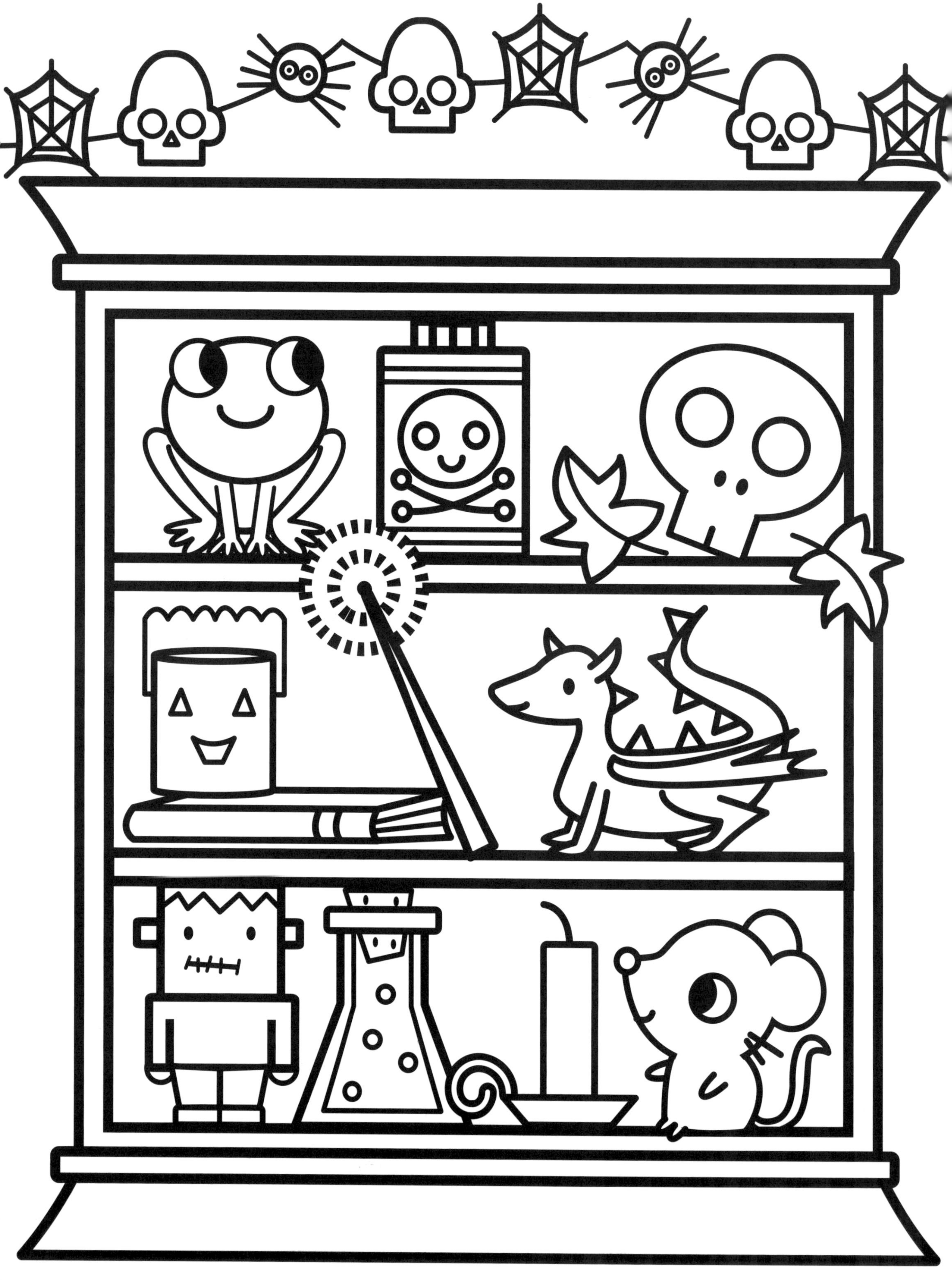

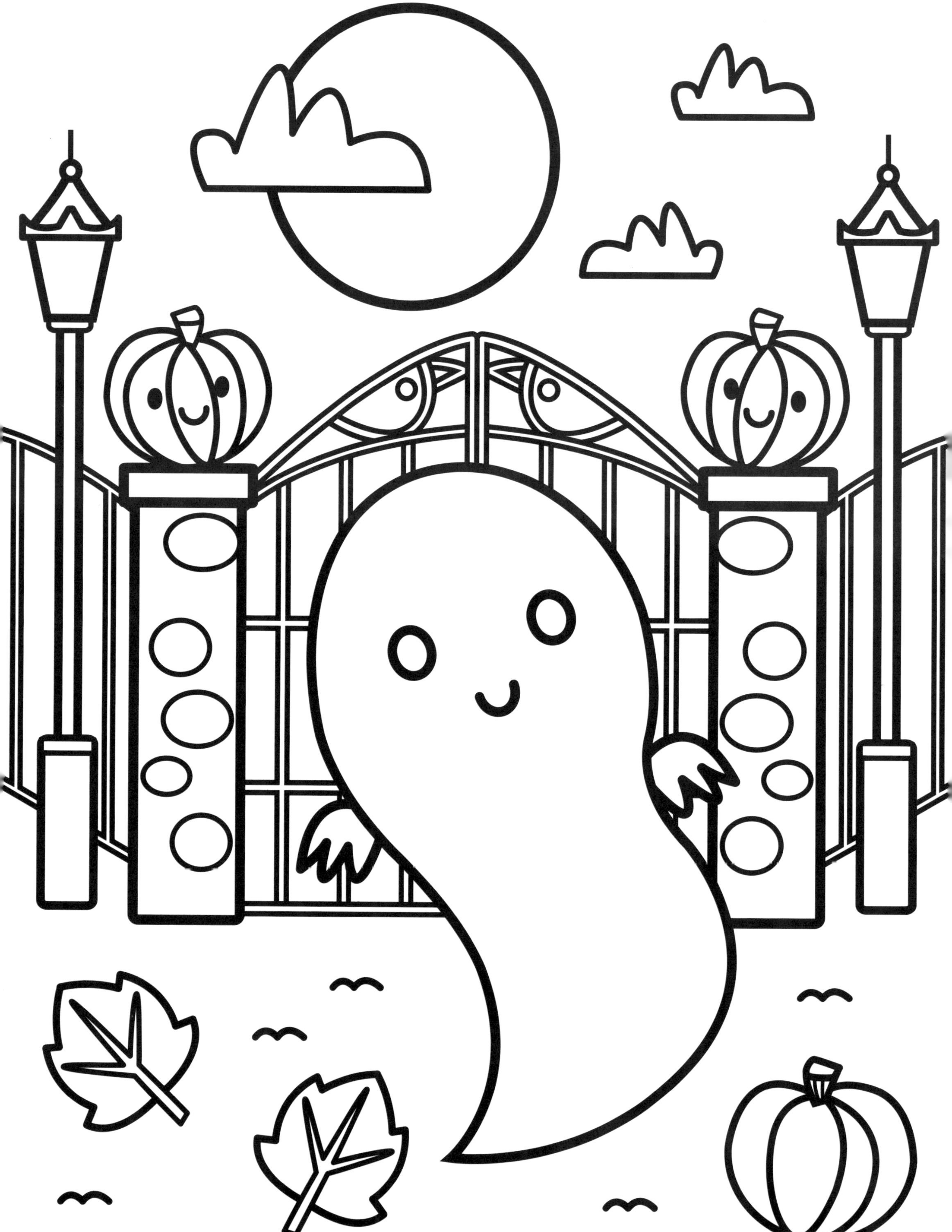

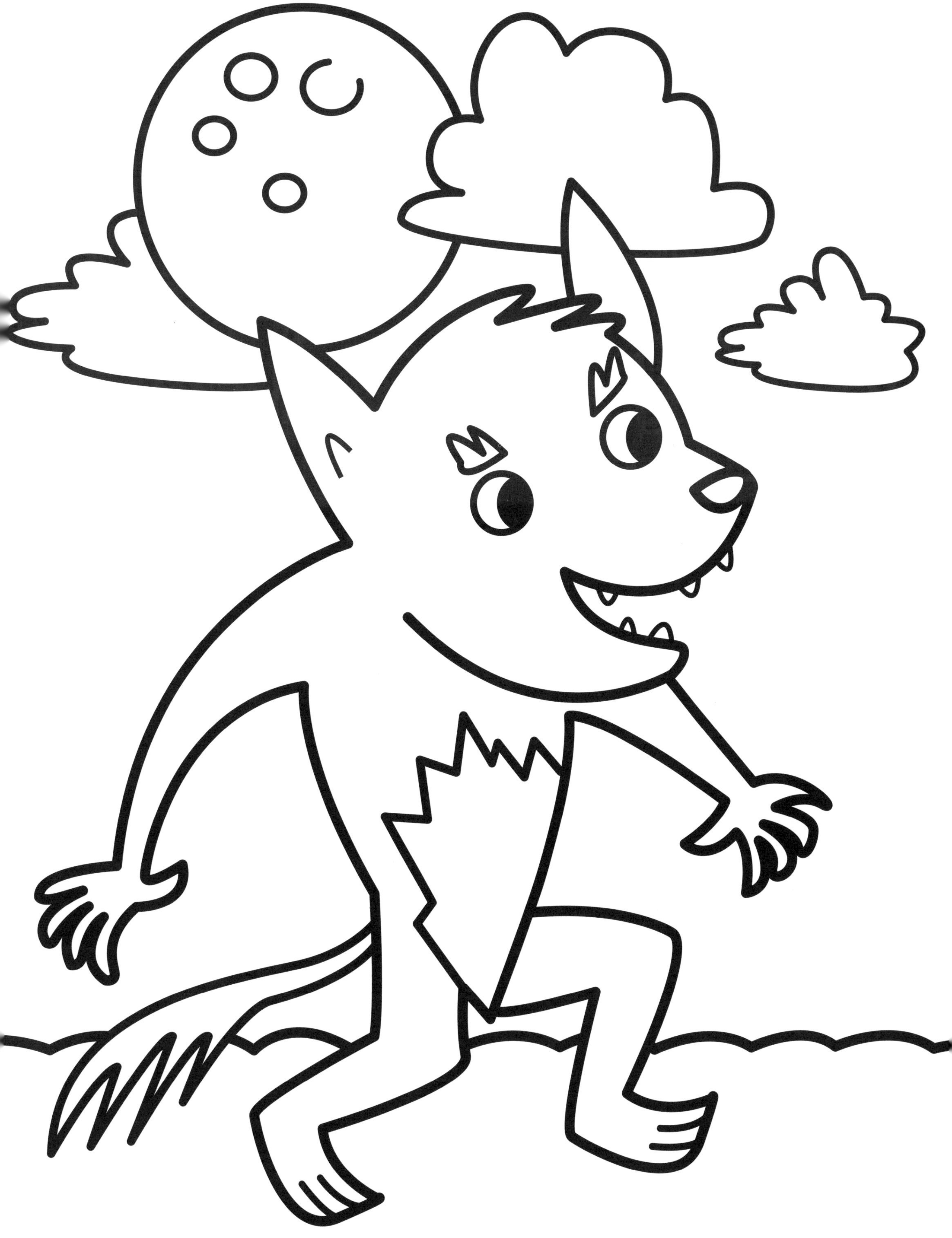

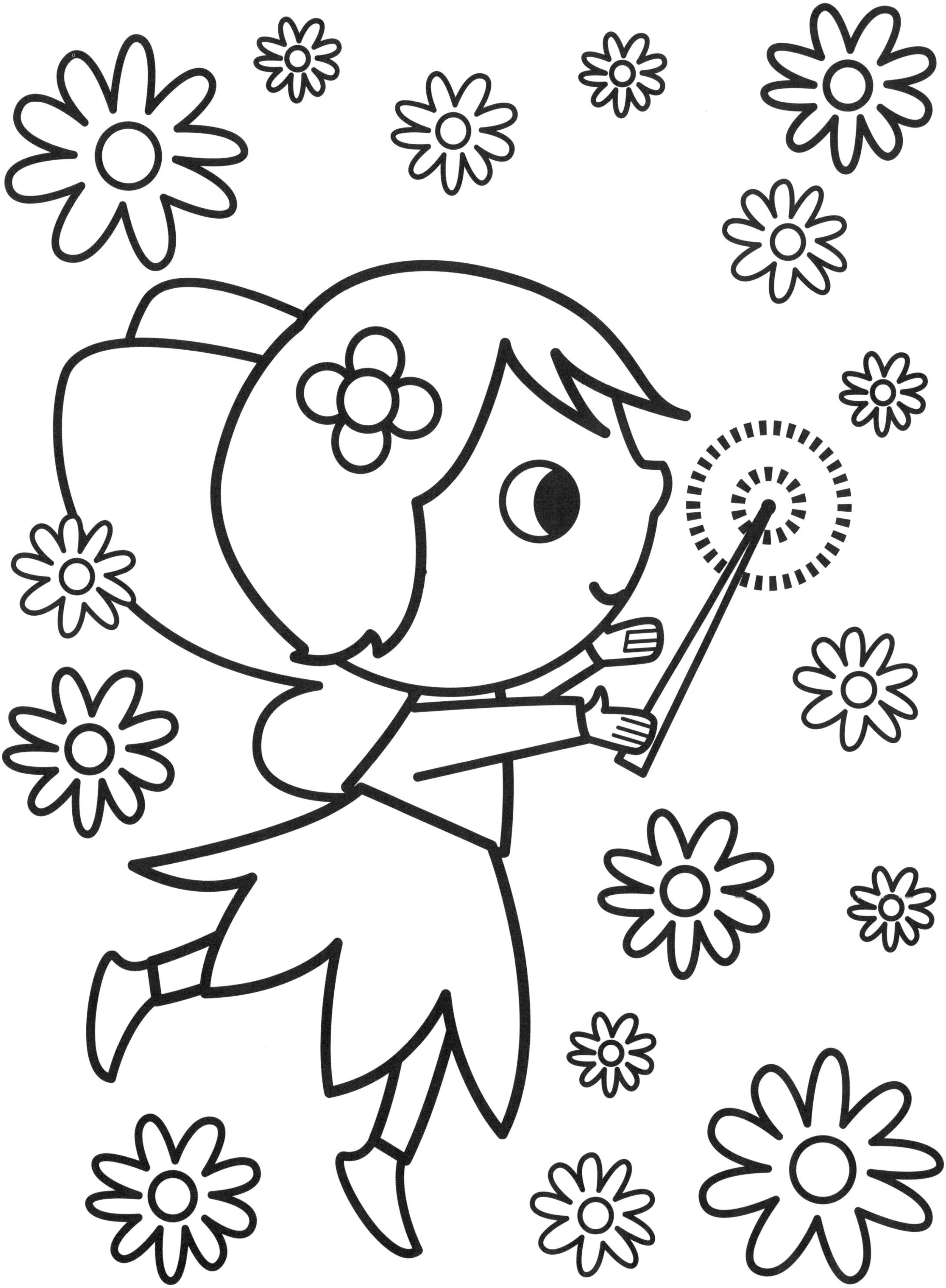

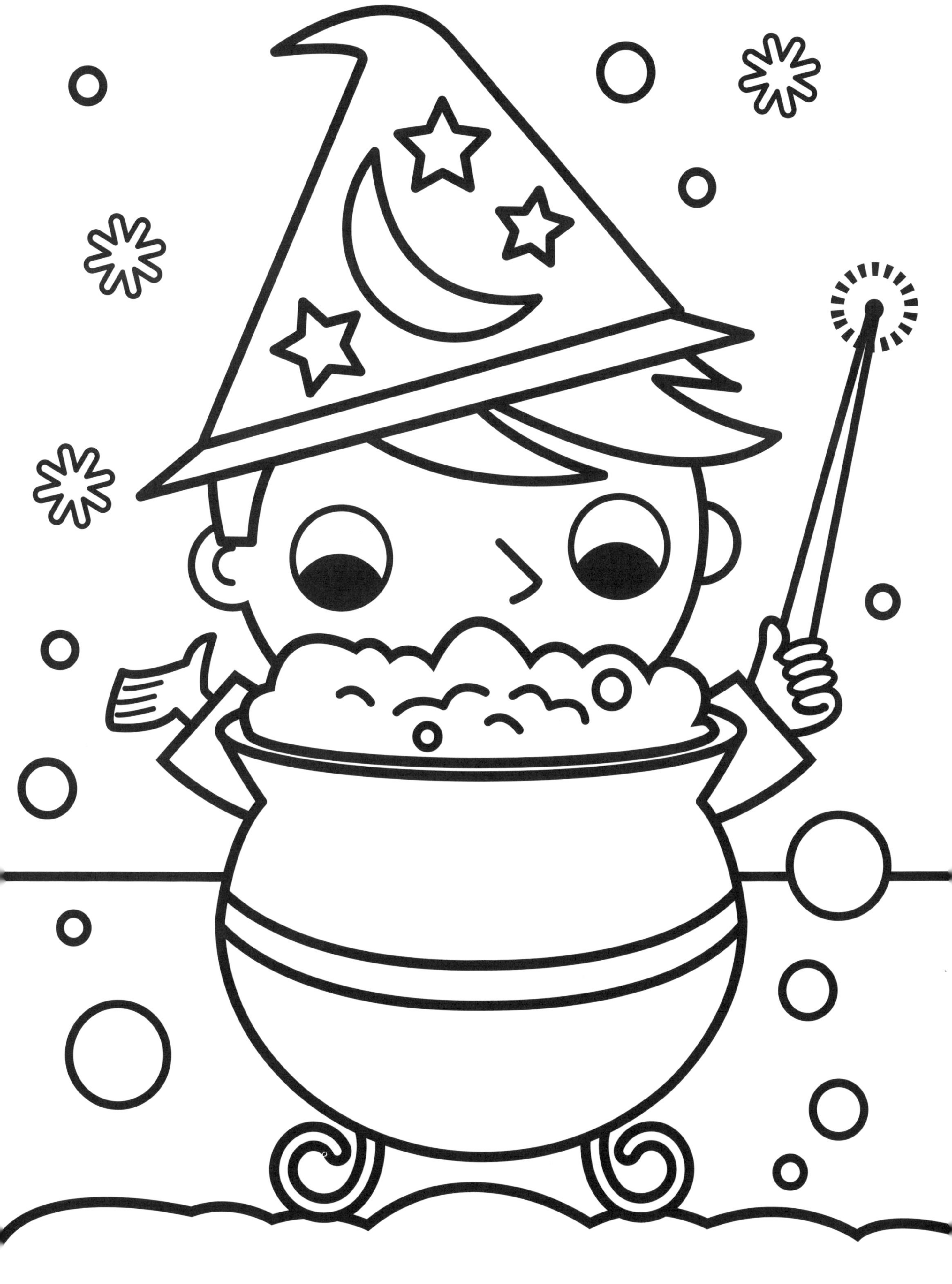

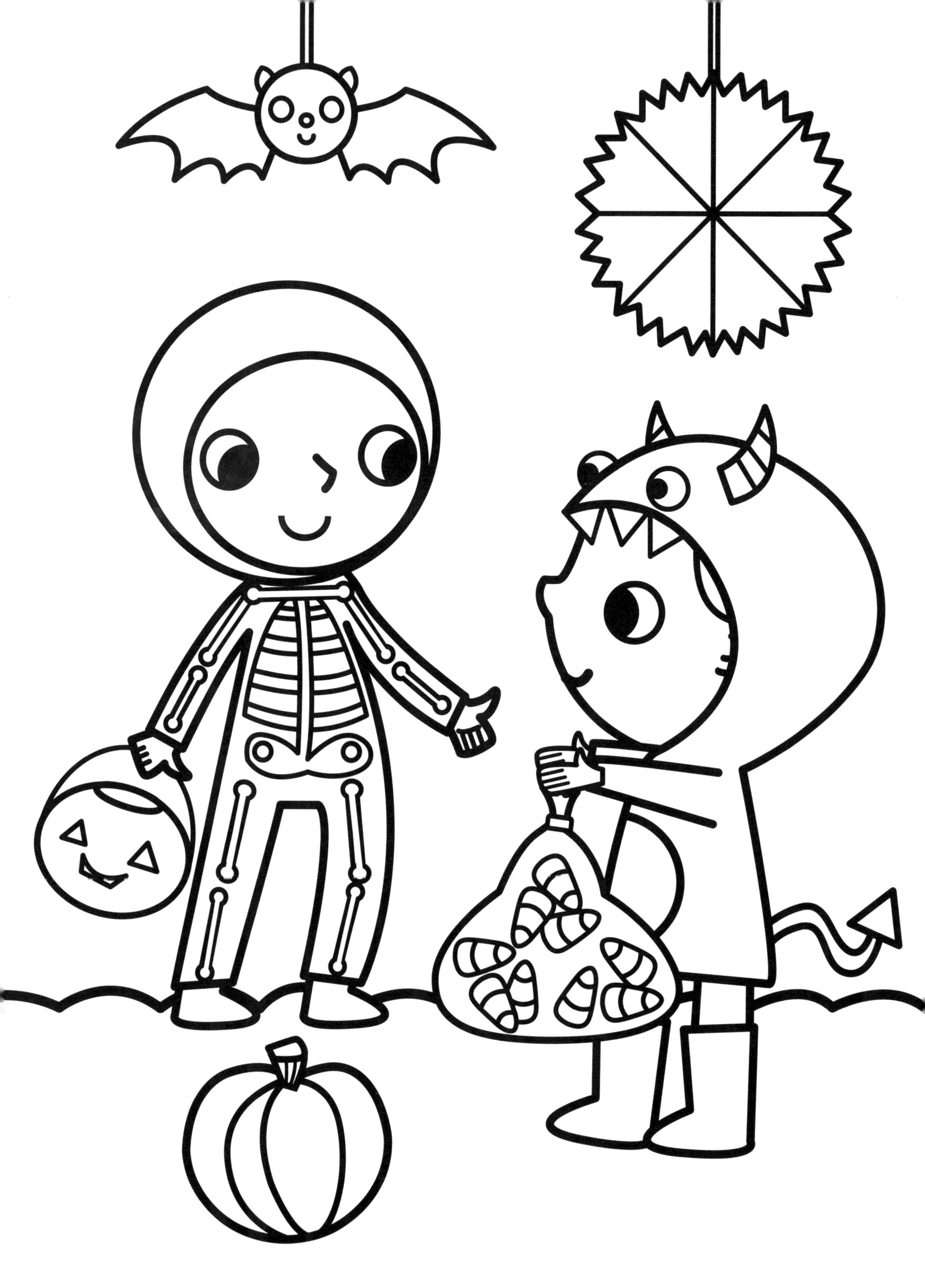

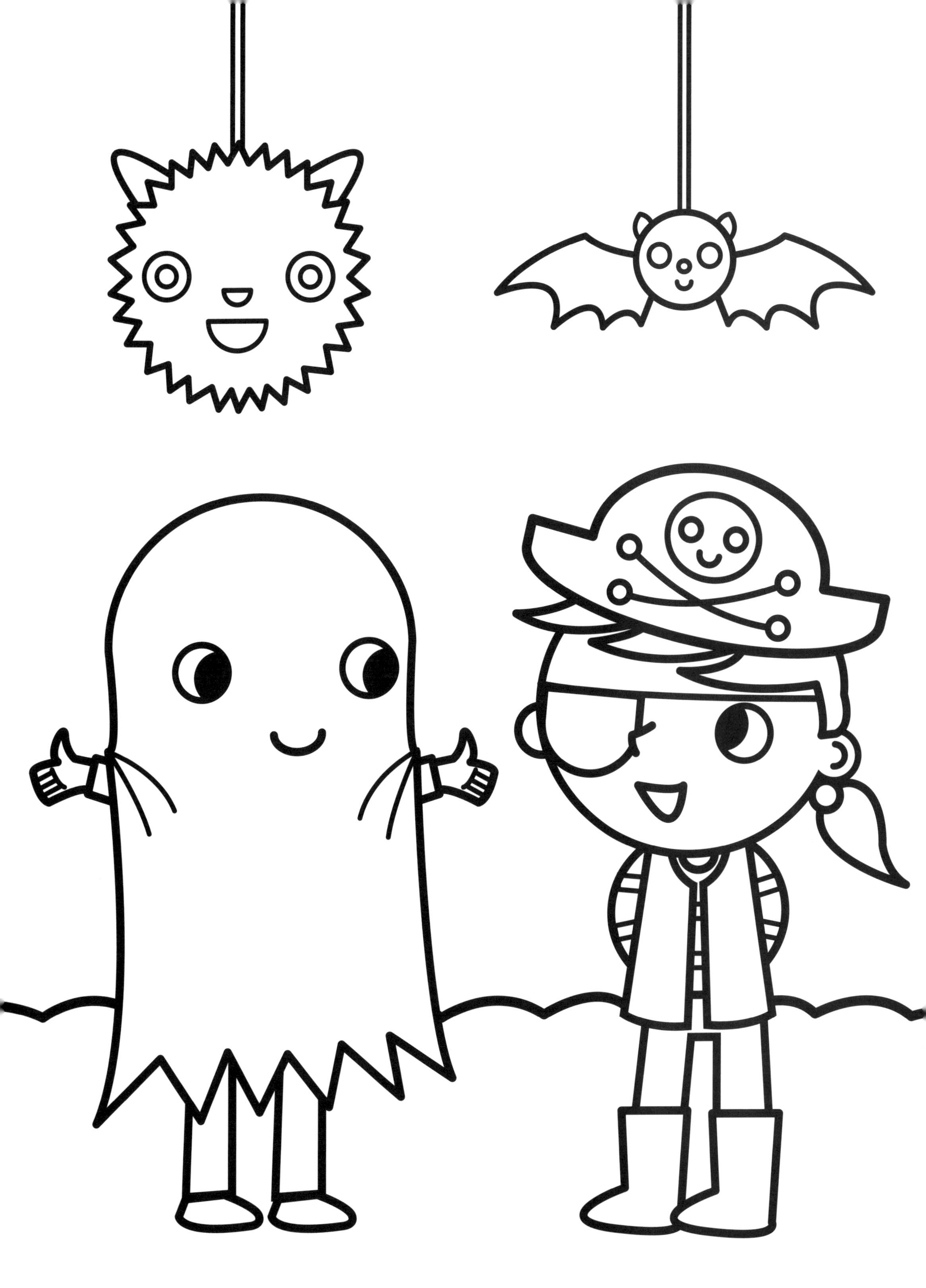

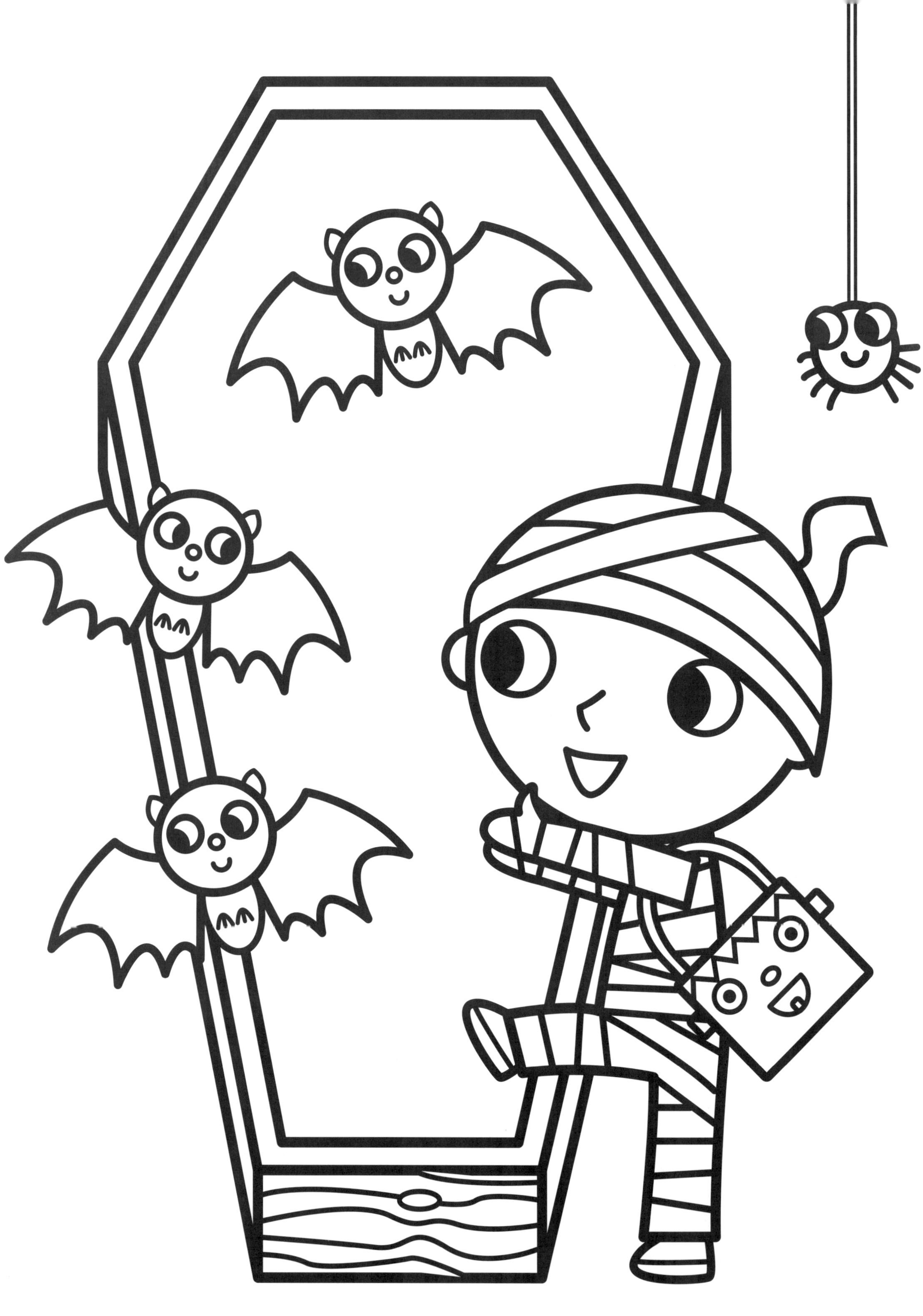

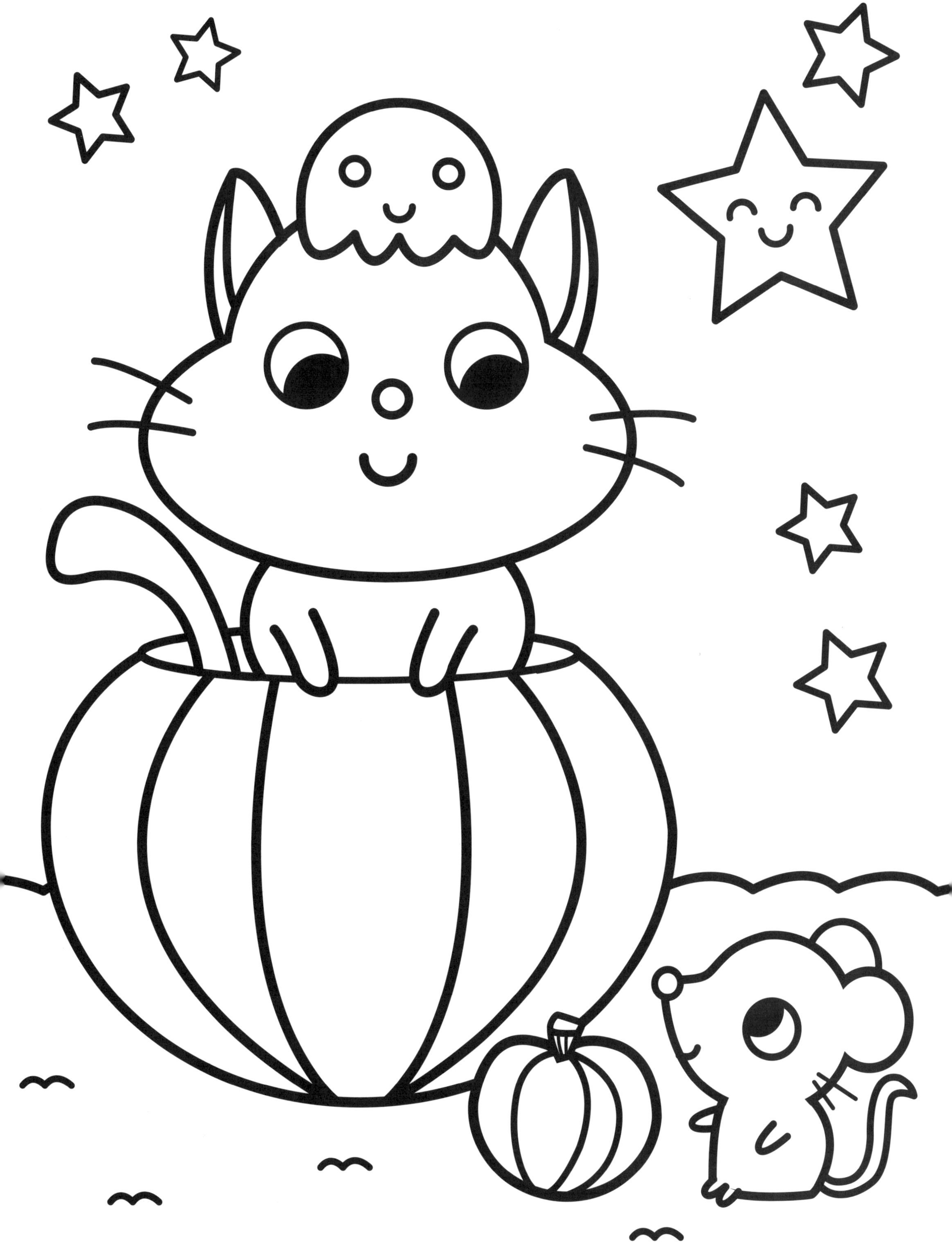

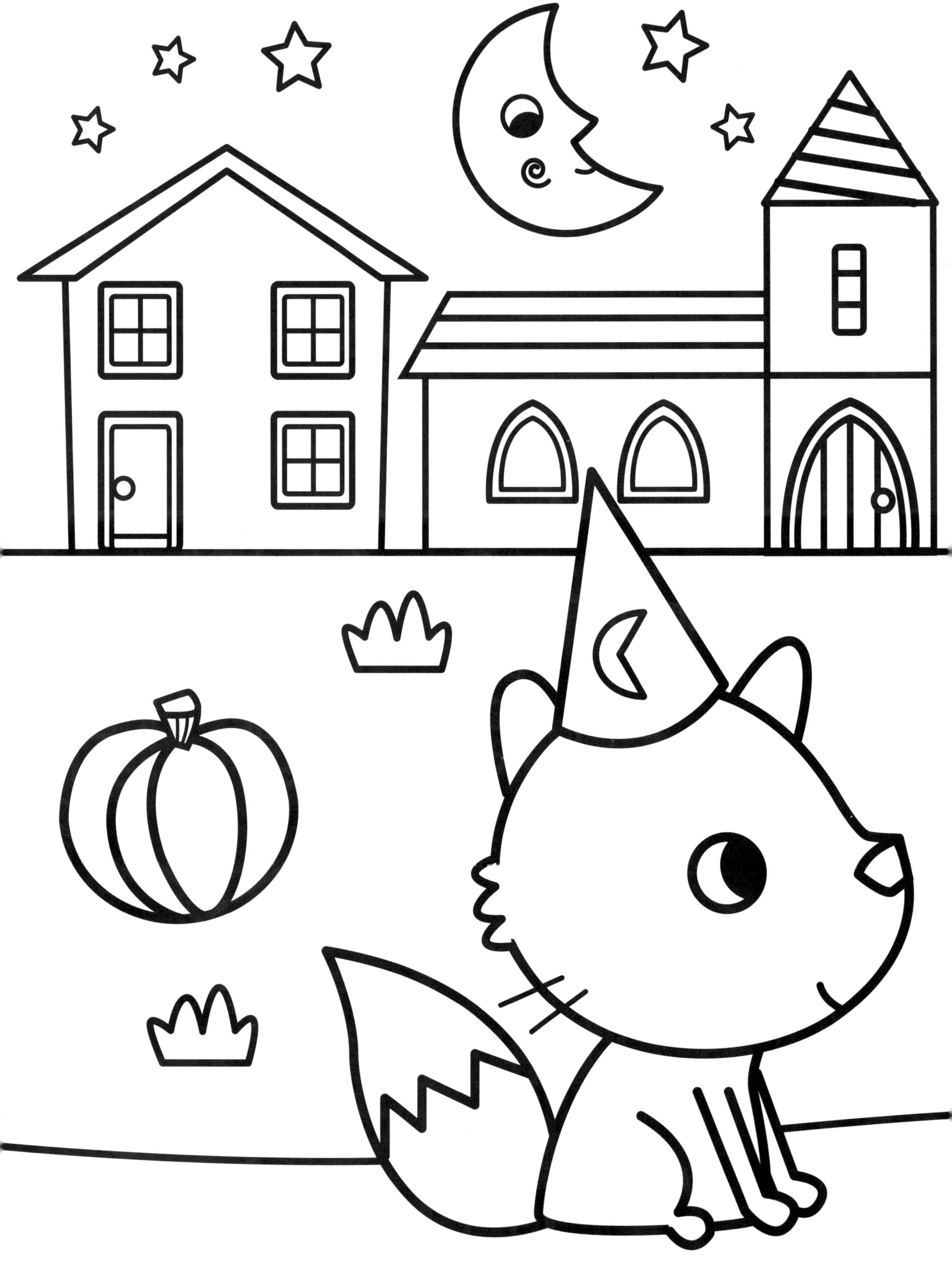

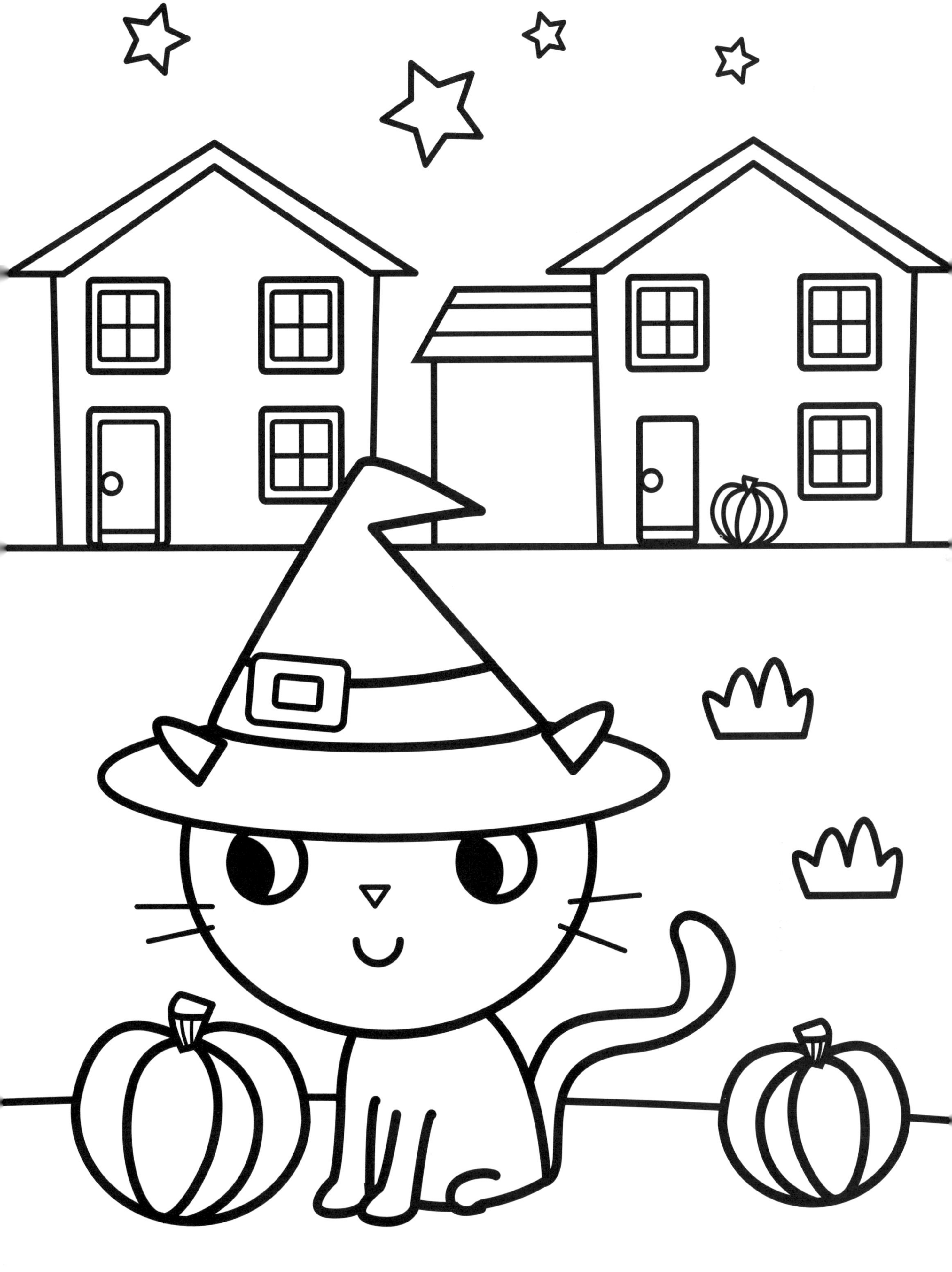

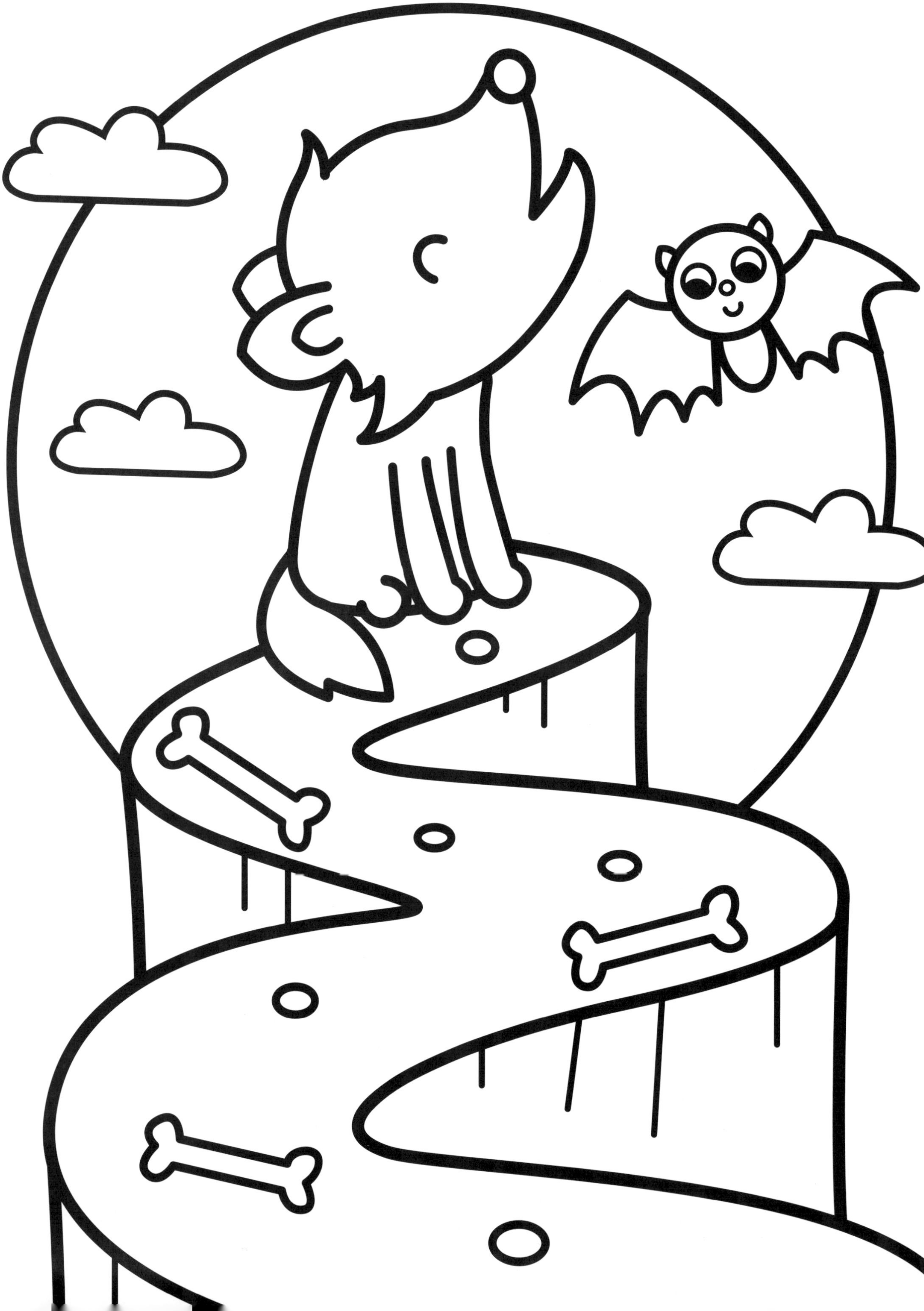

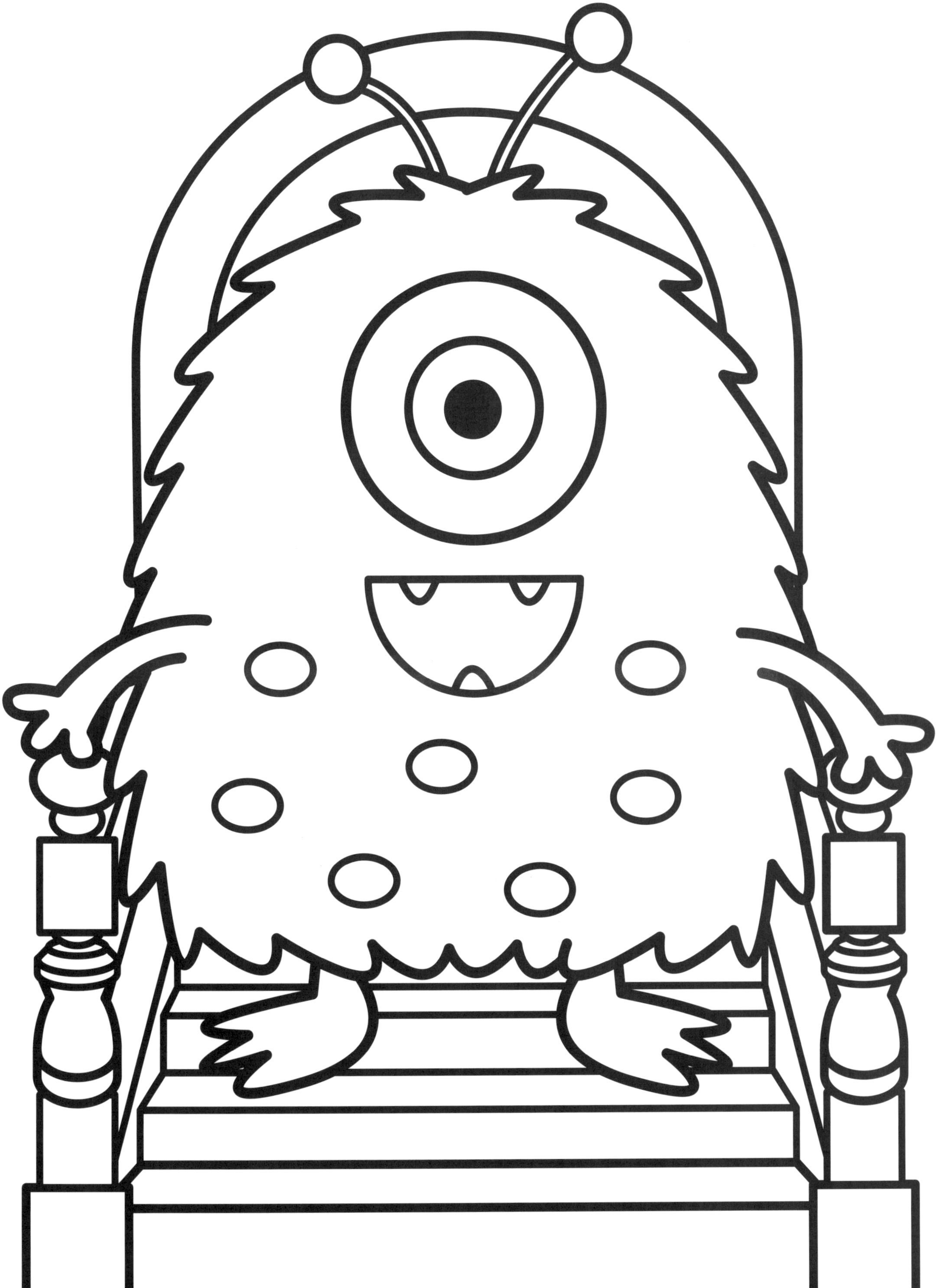

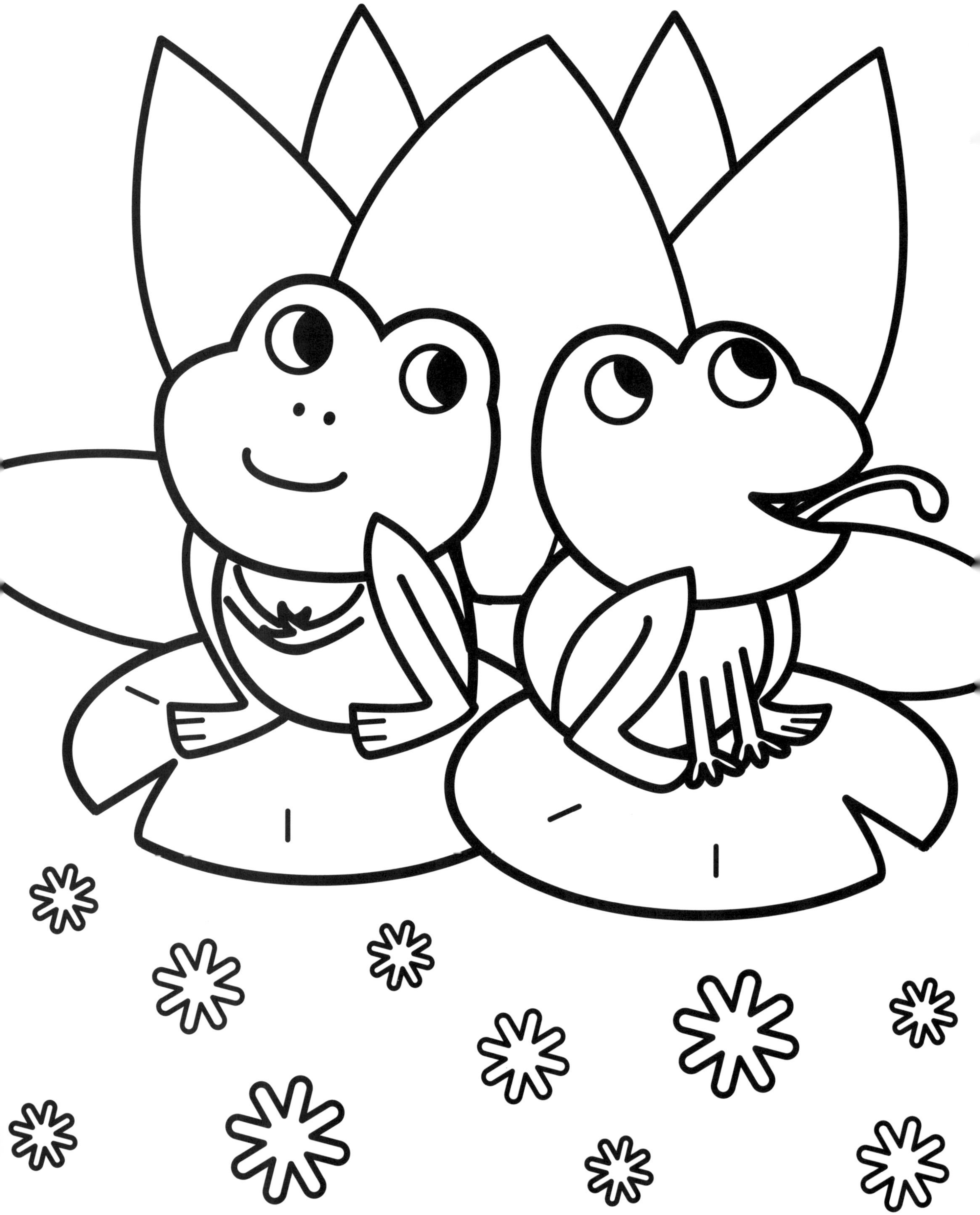

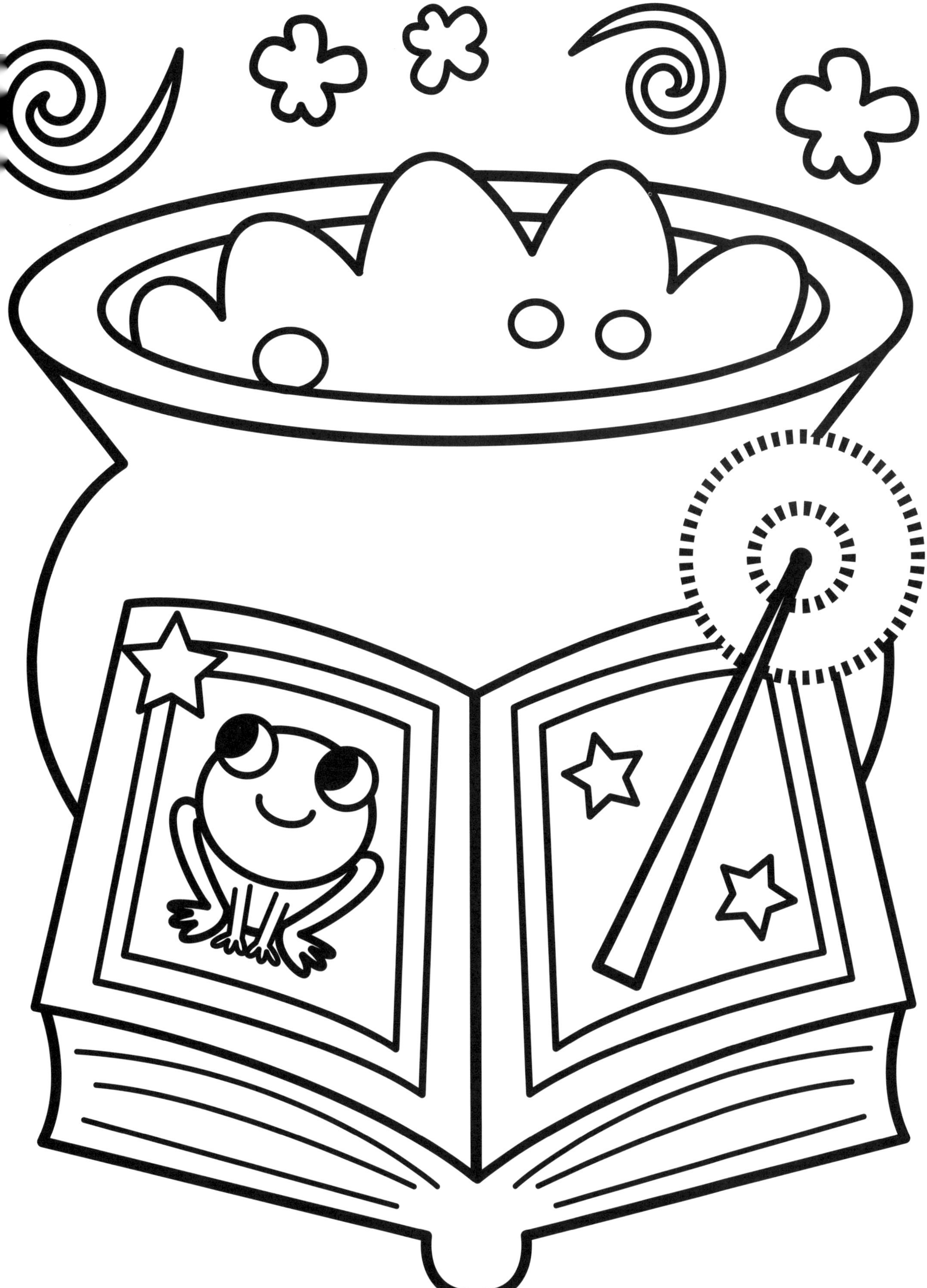

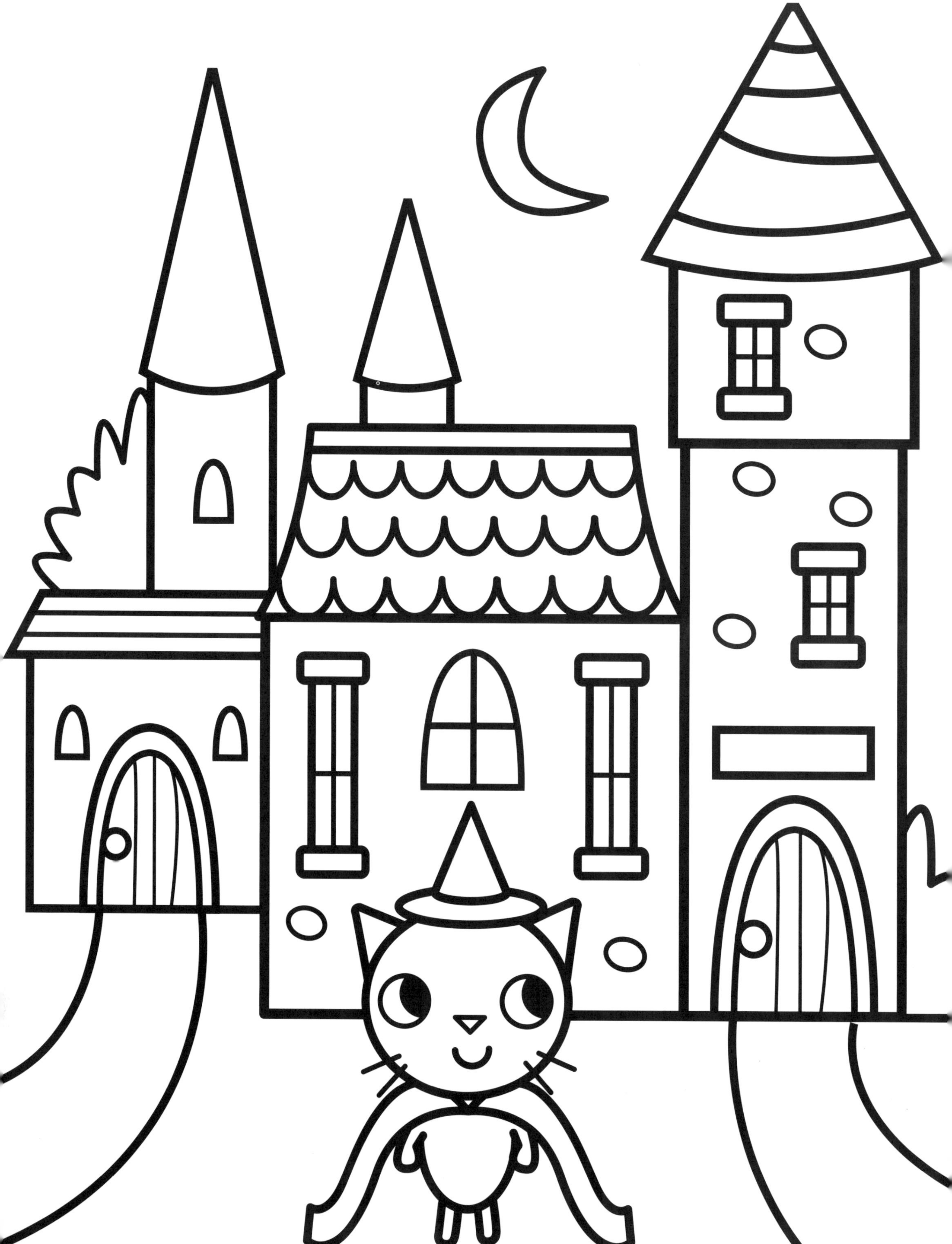

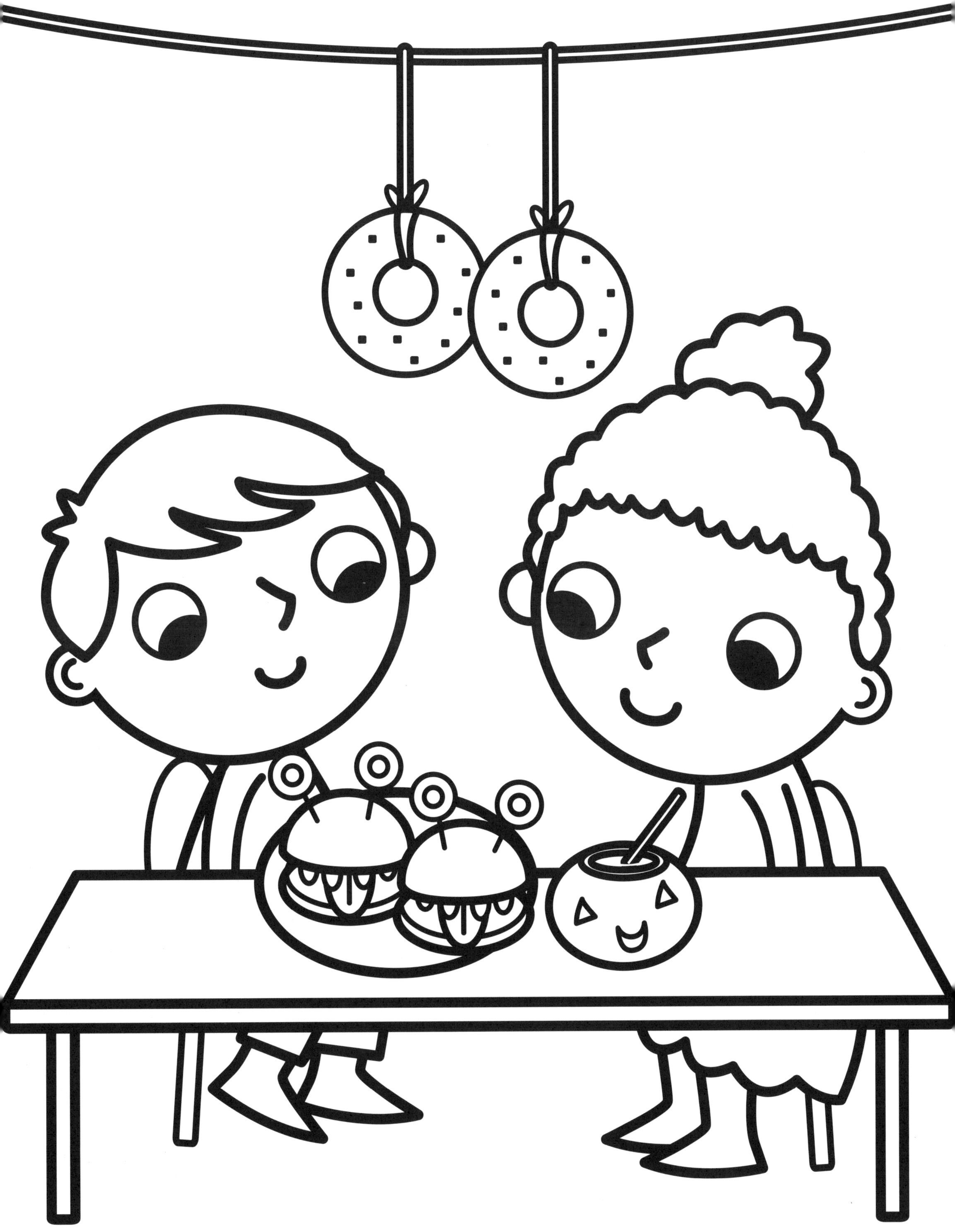

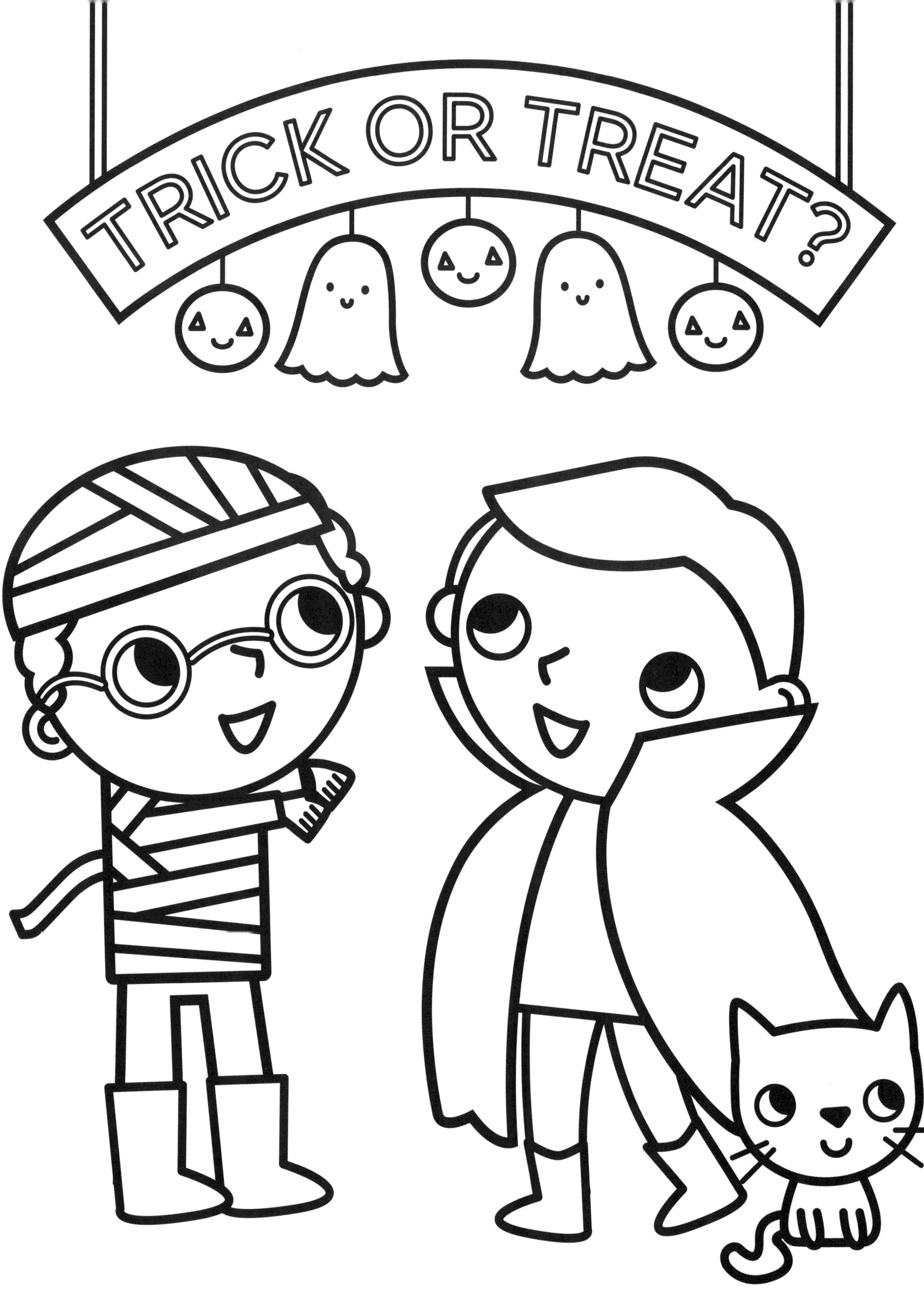
TRICK OR TREAT?

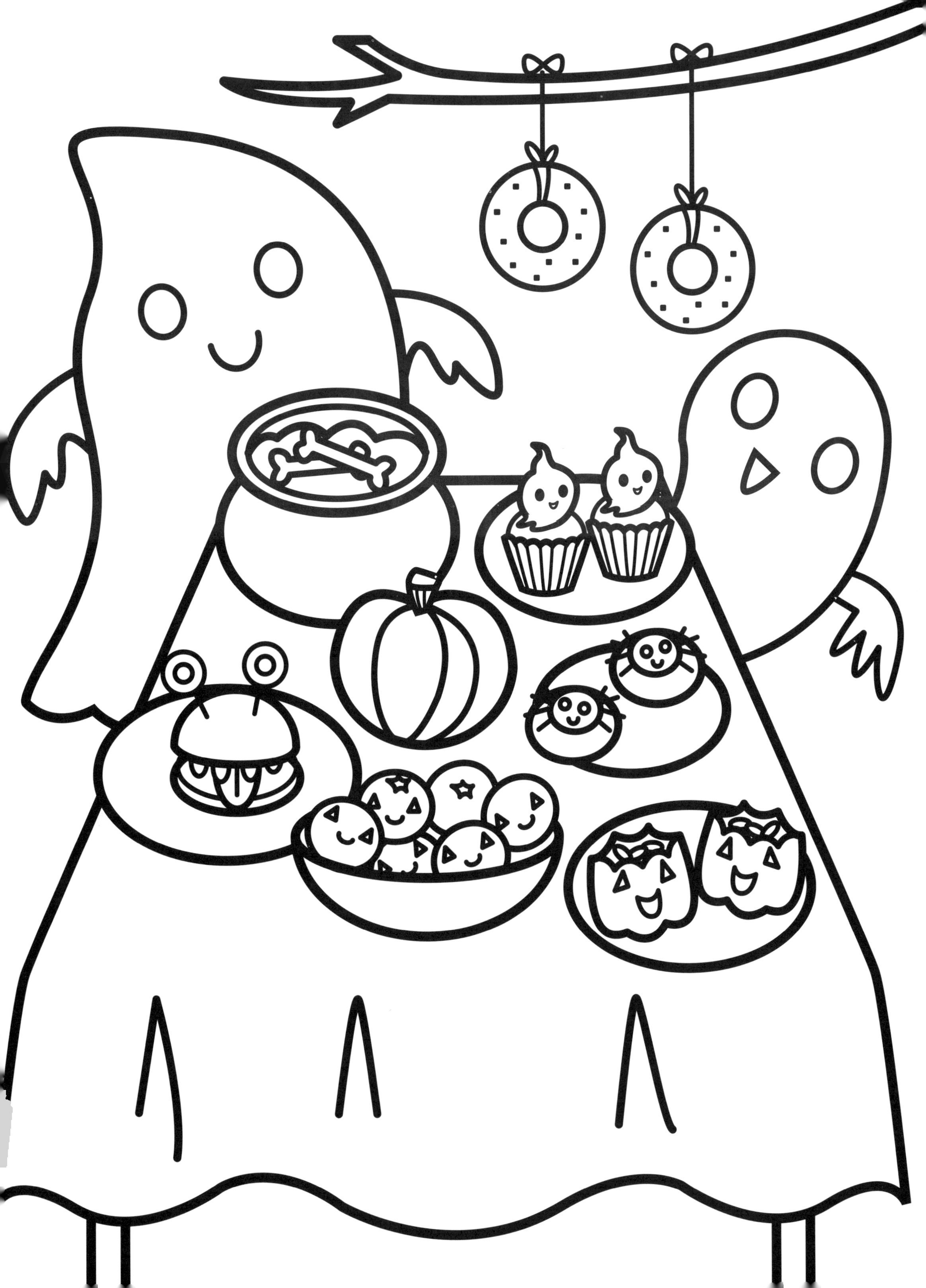

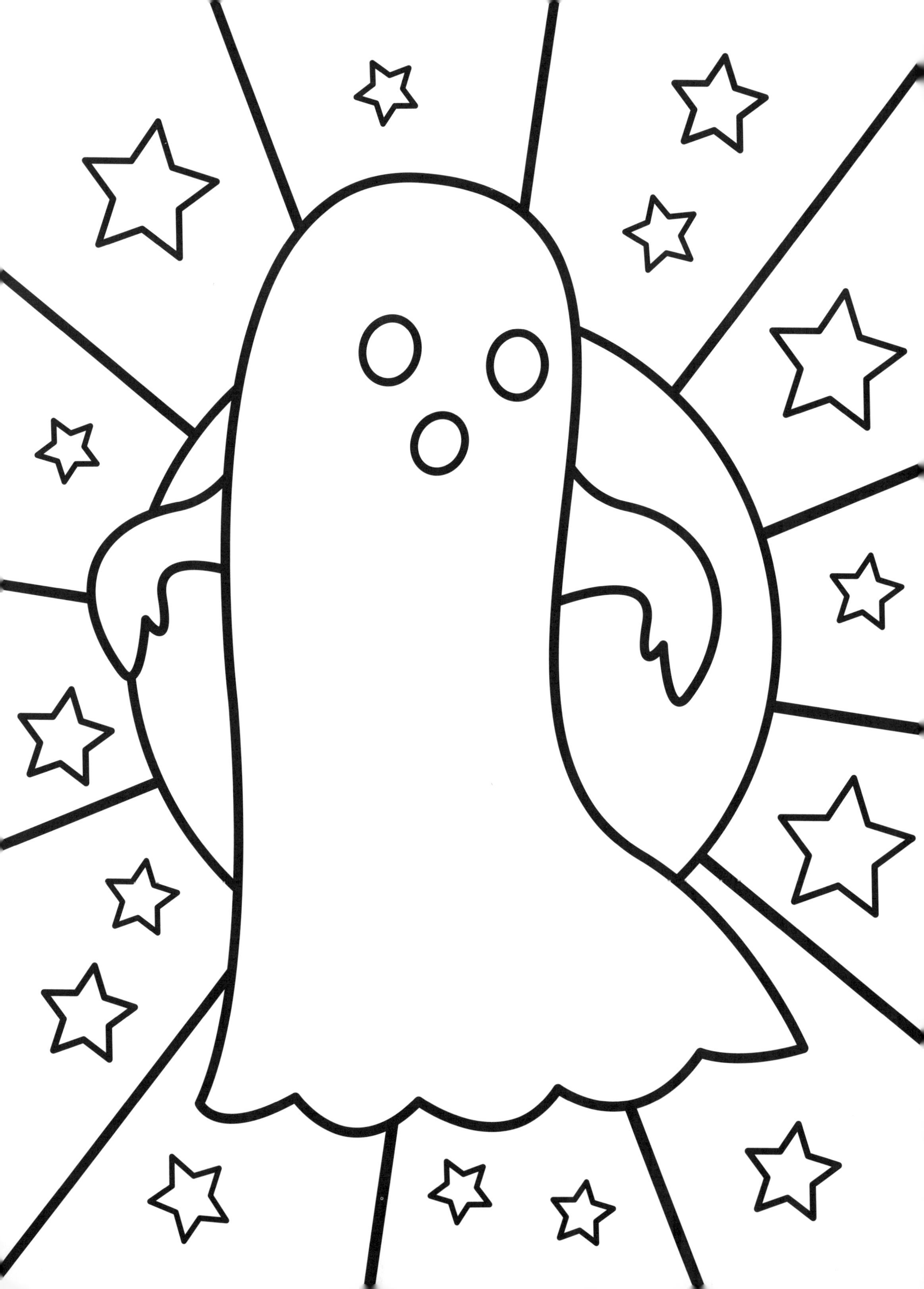

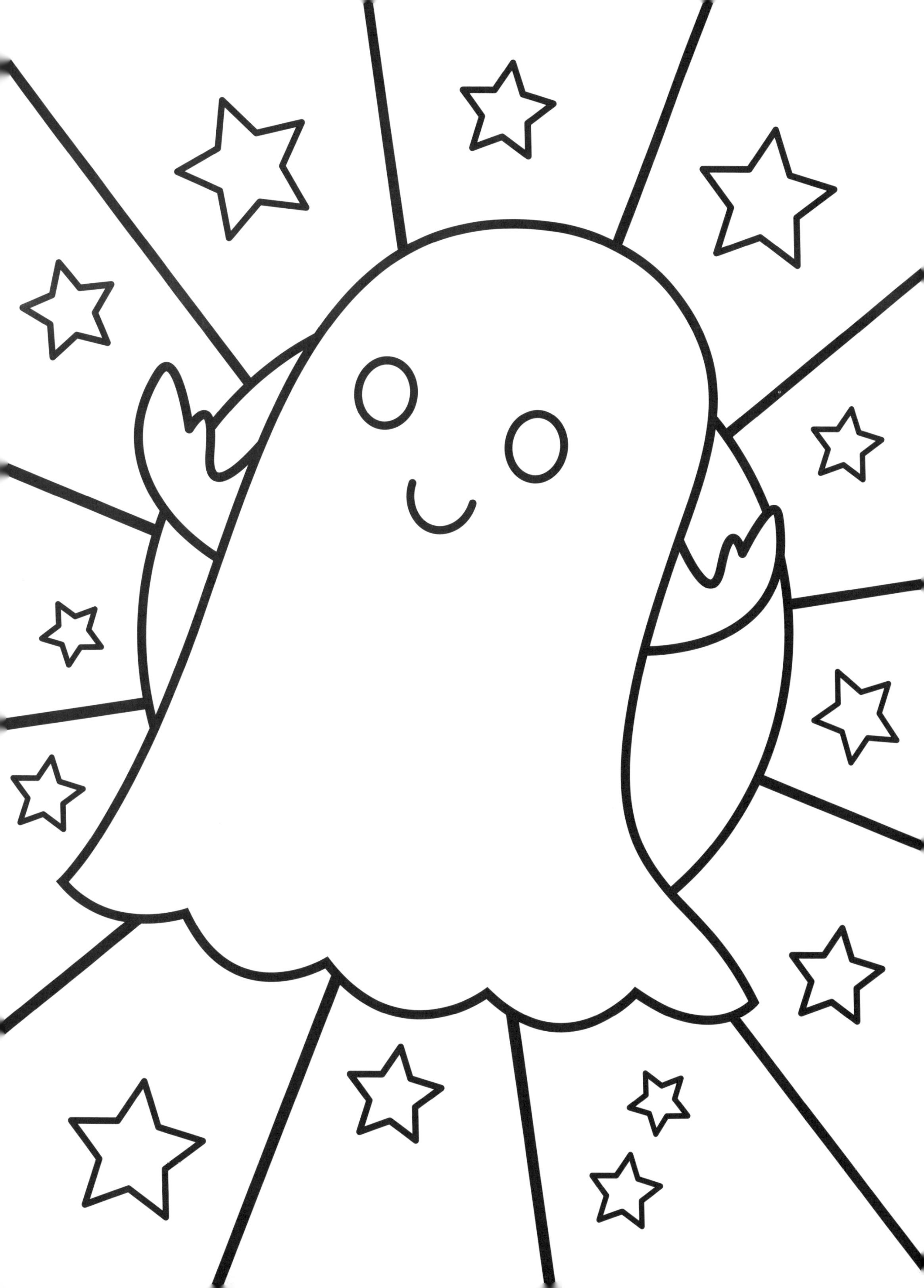

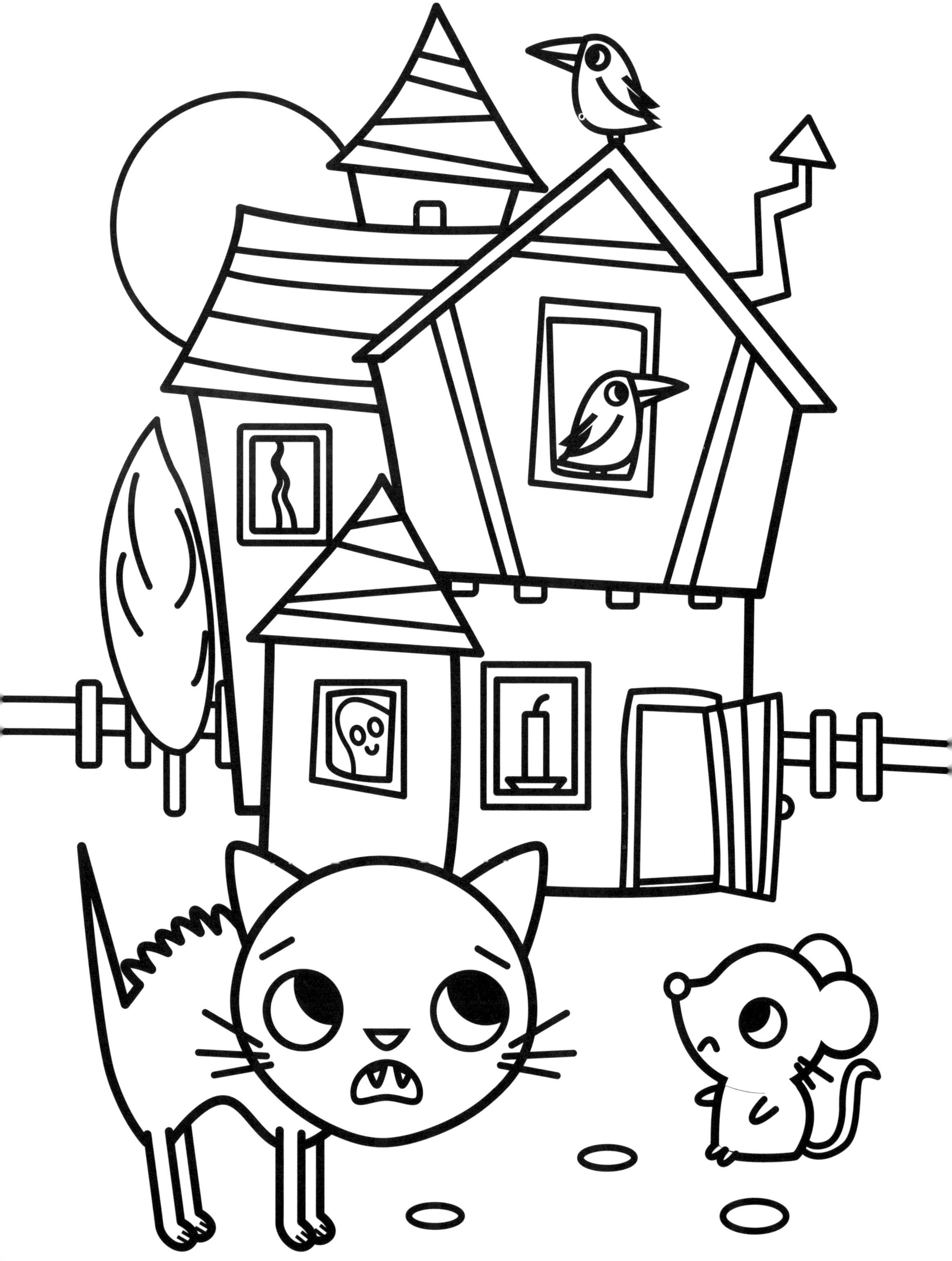

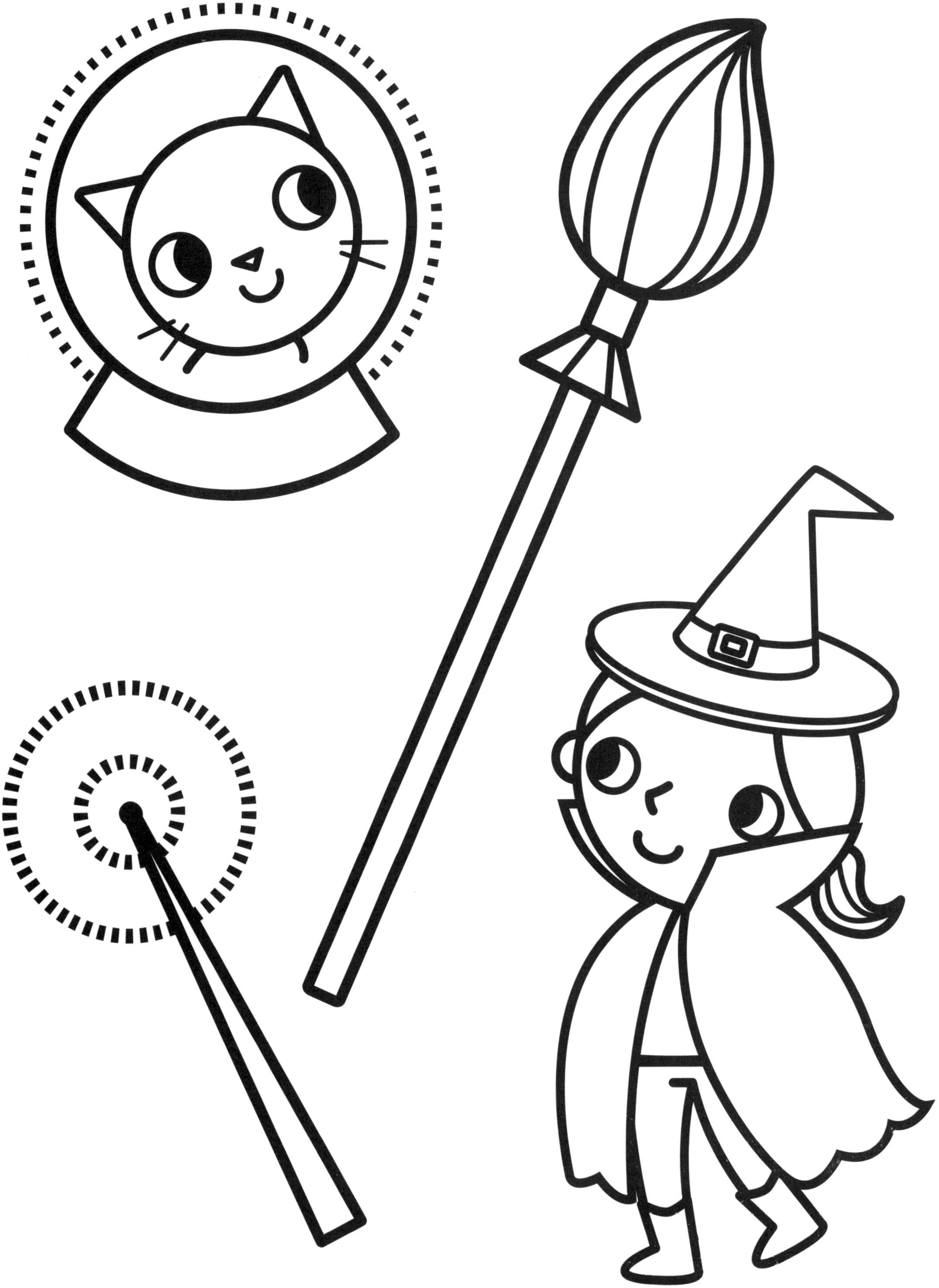

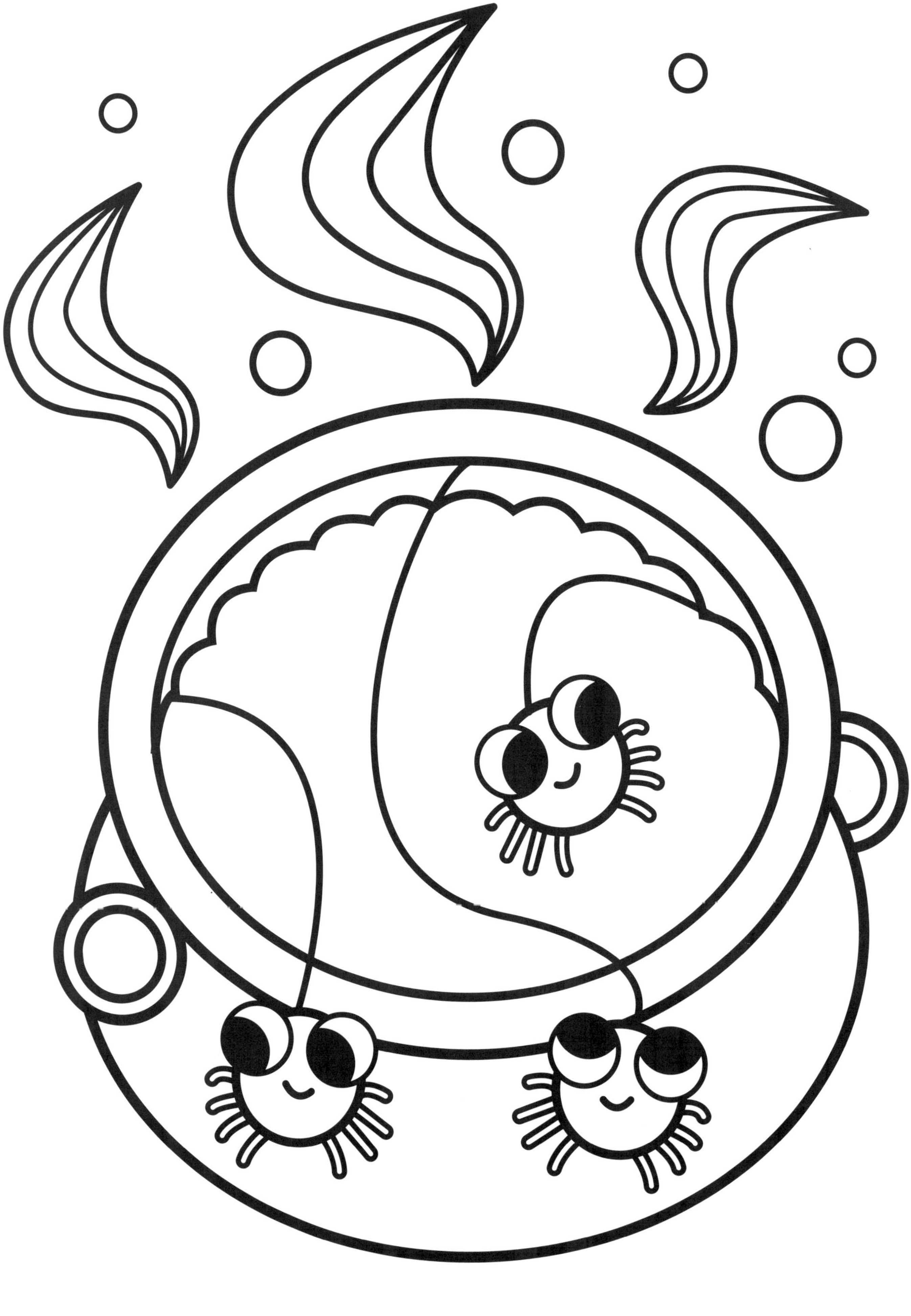

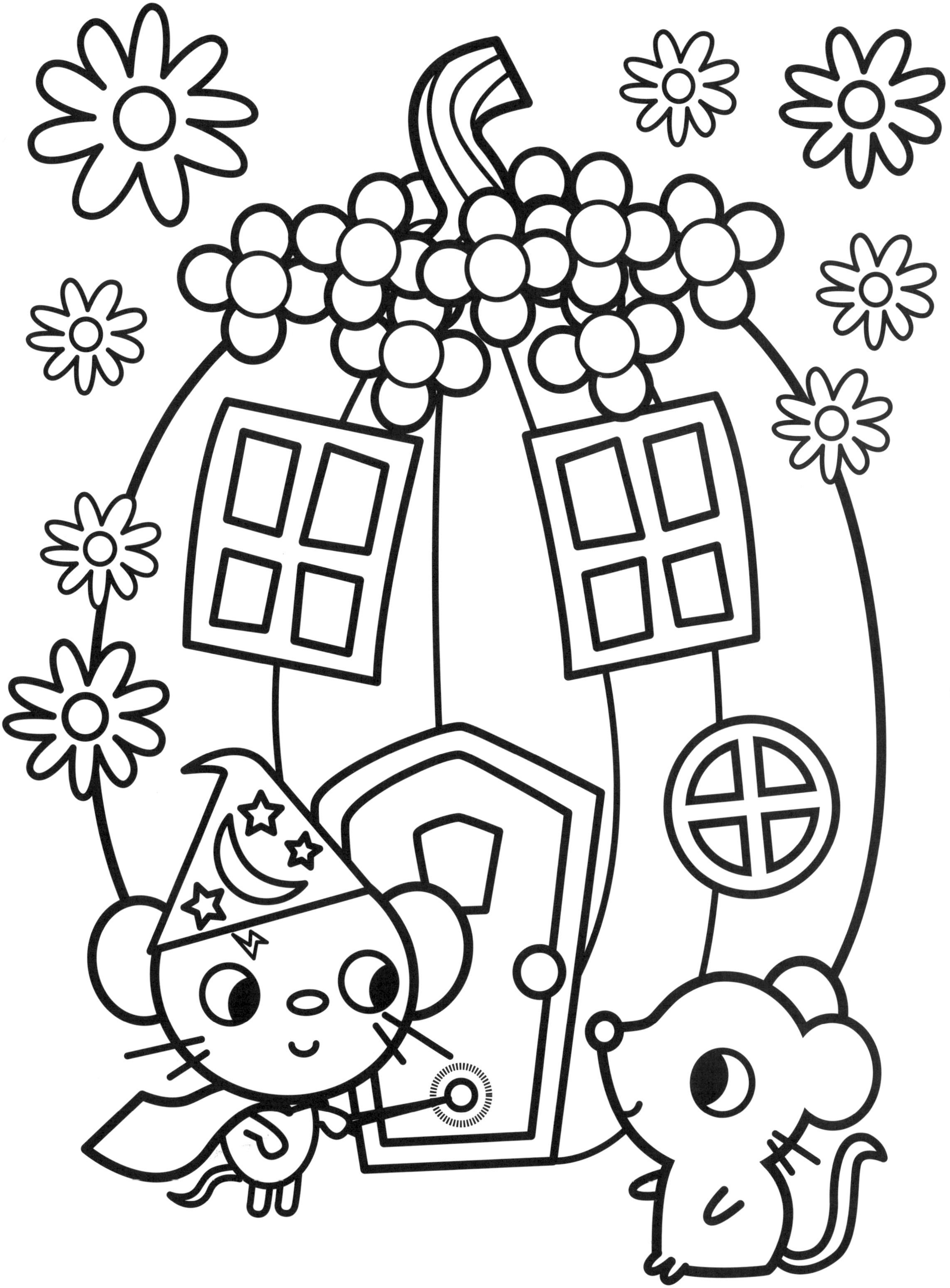

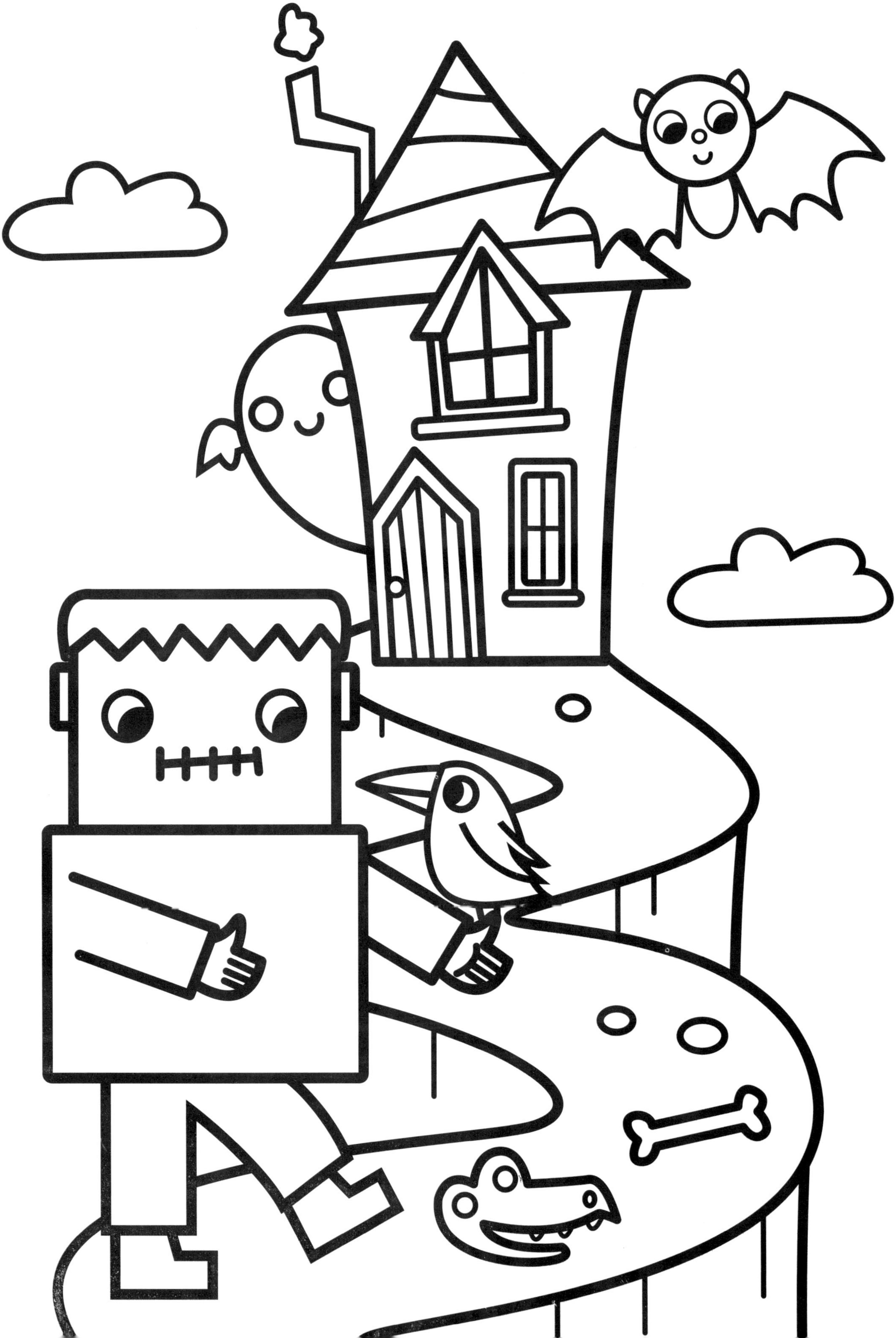

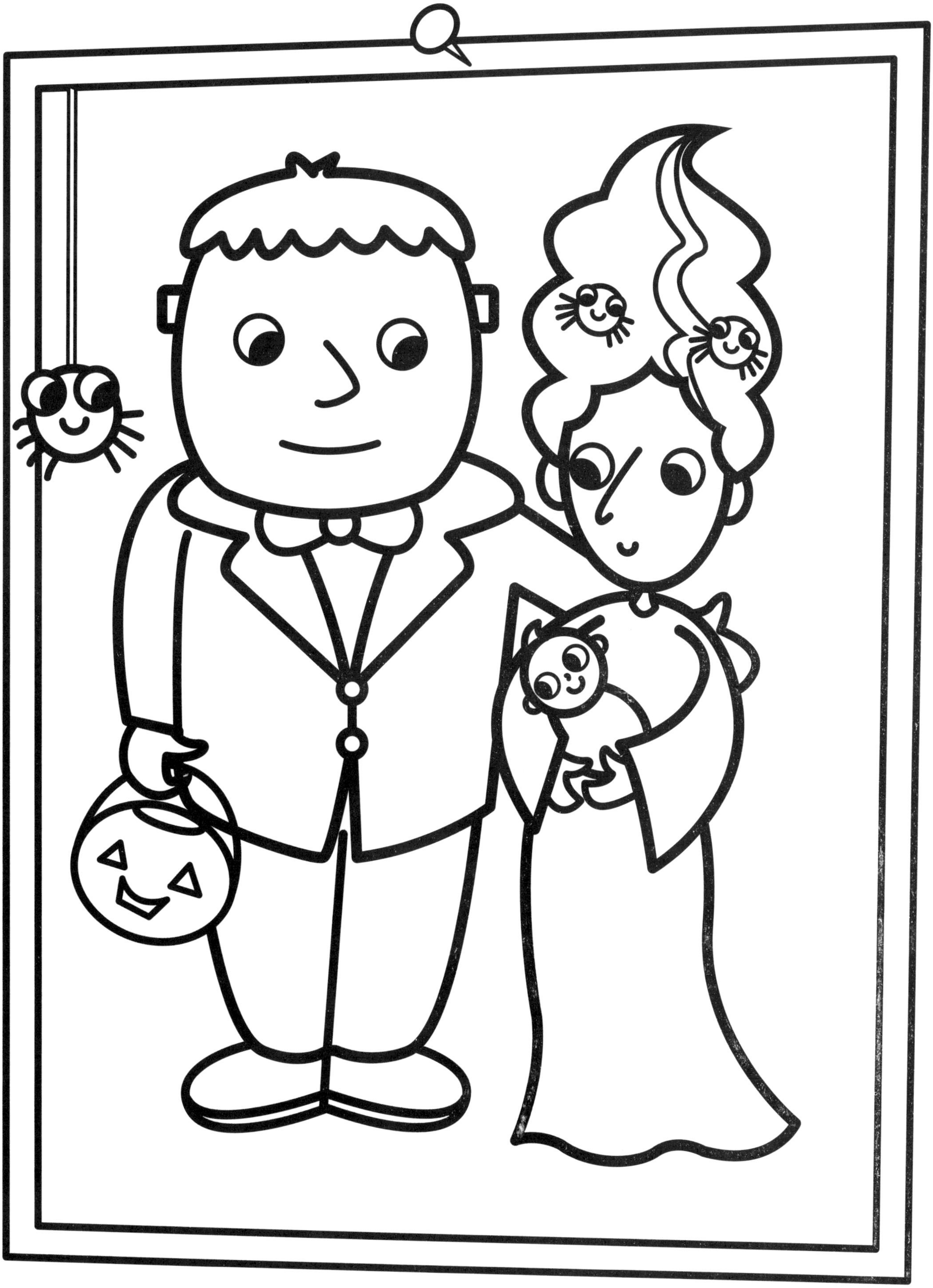

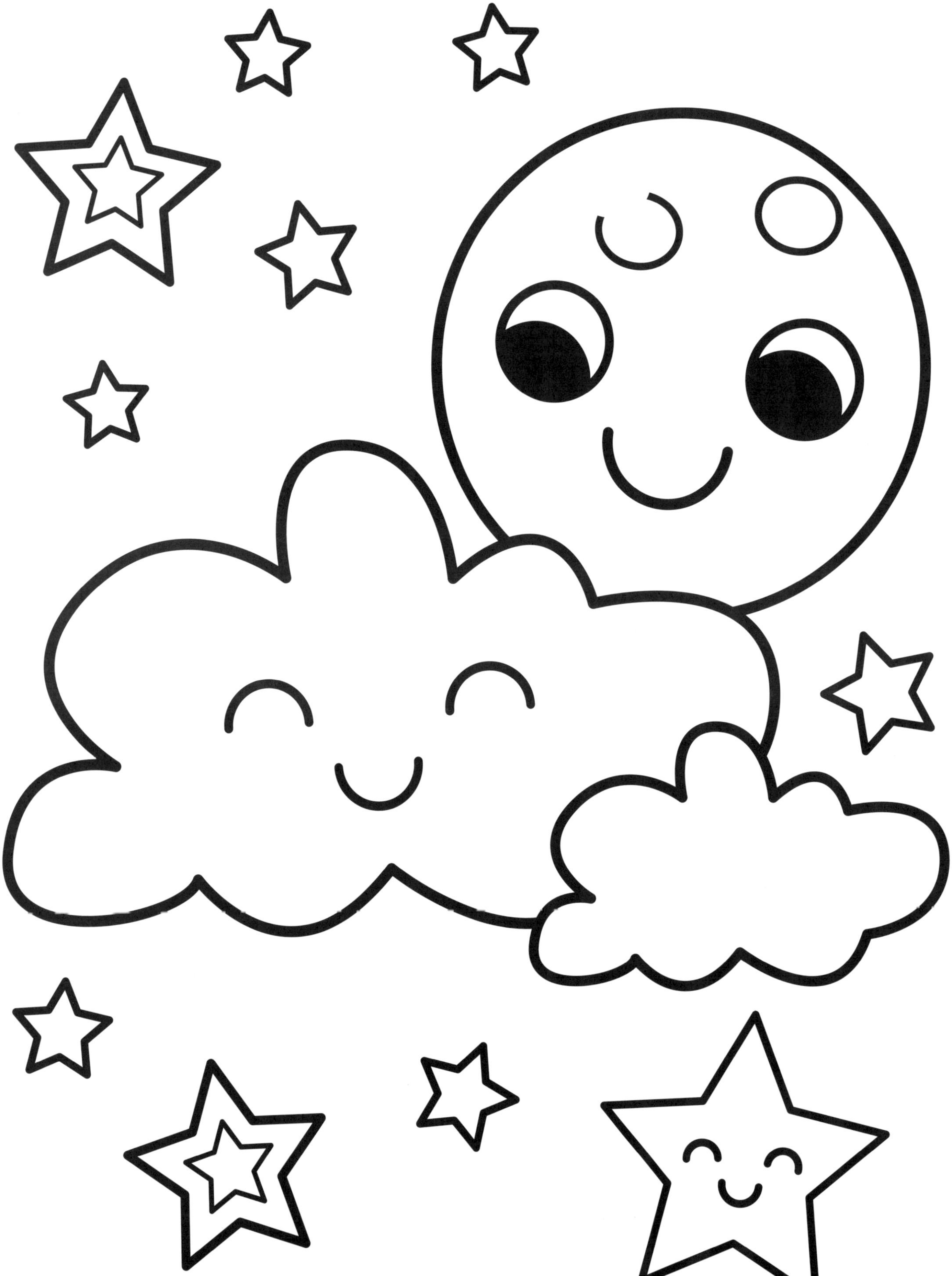

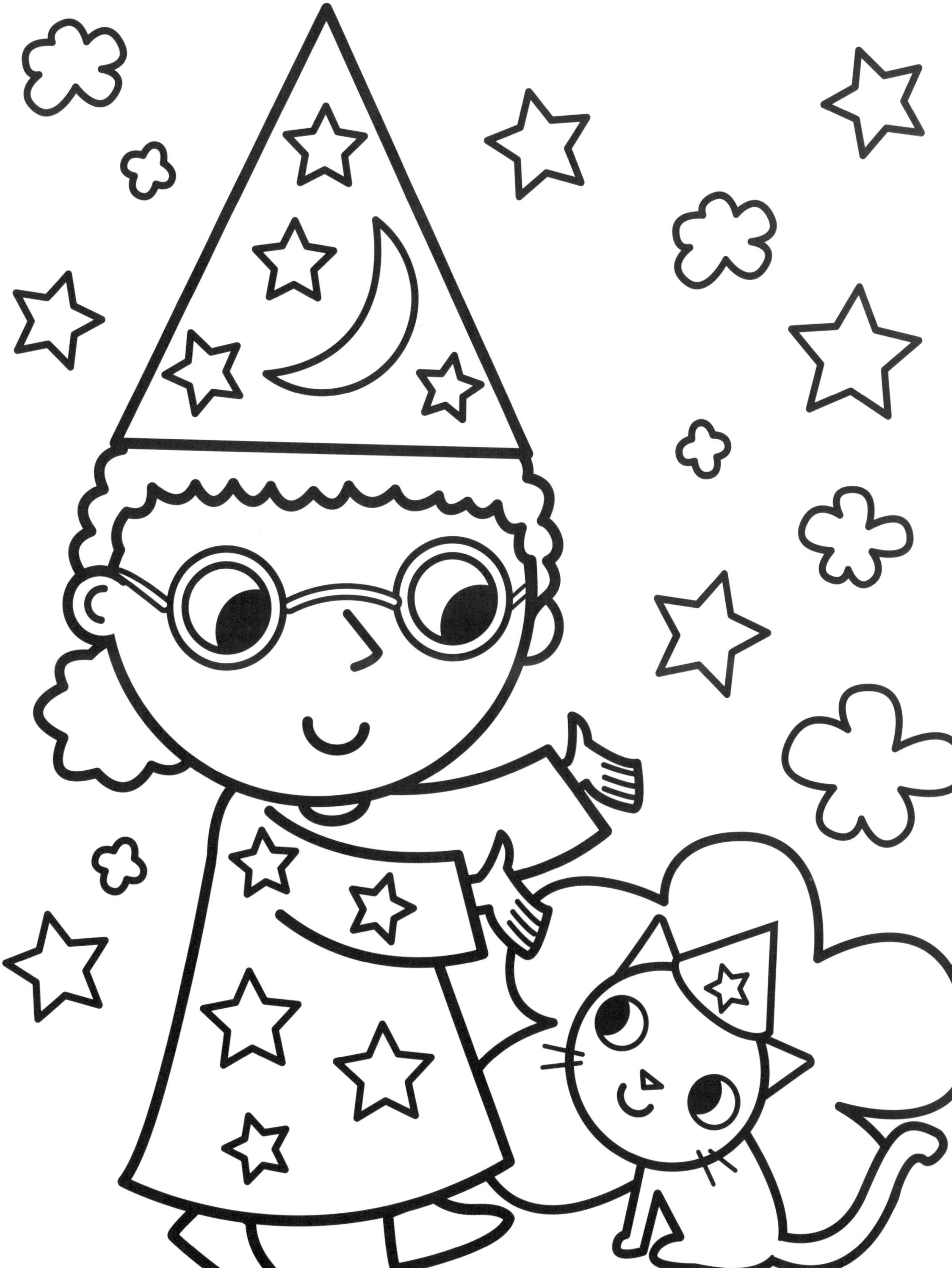

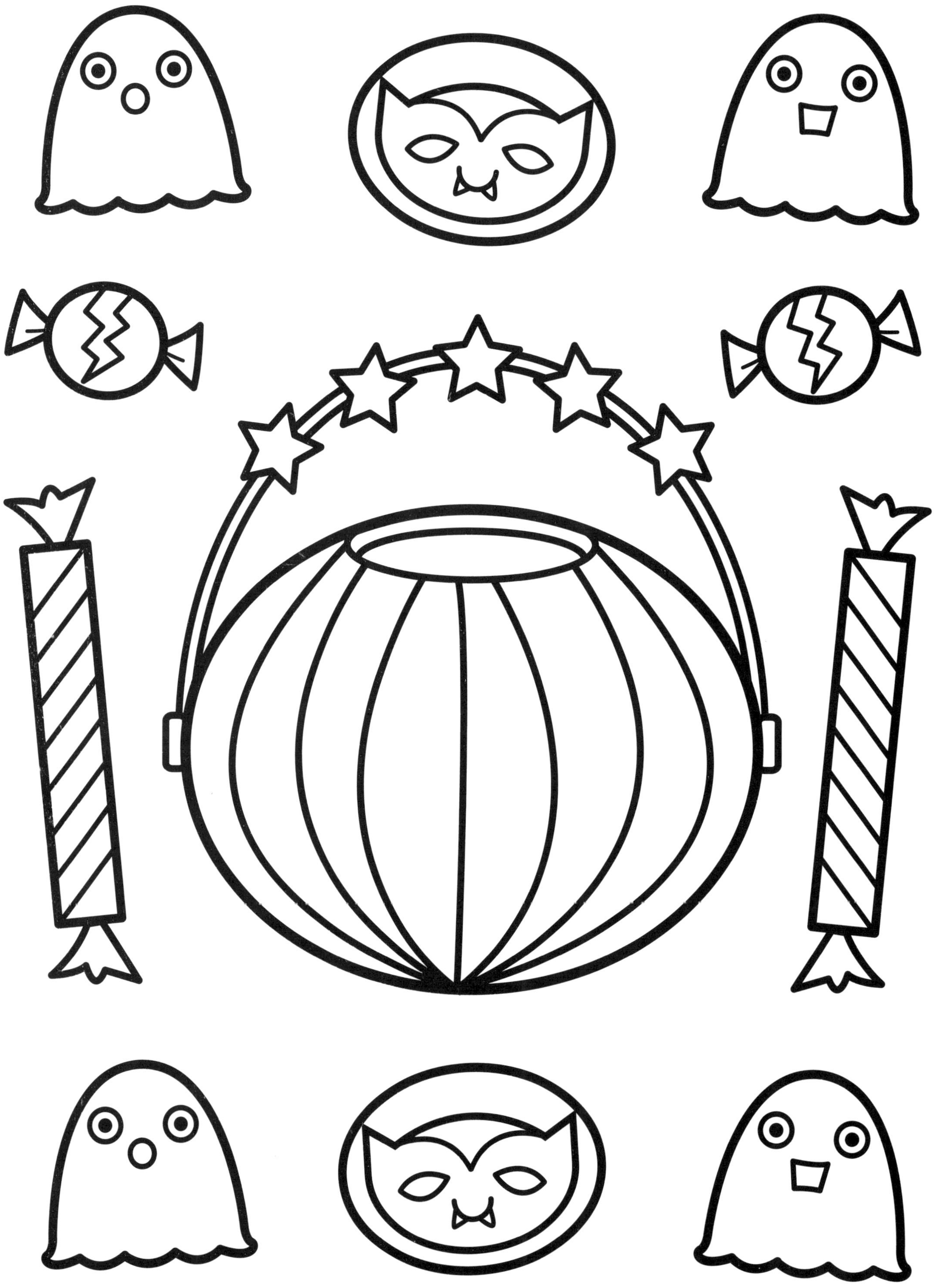

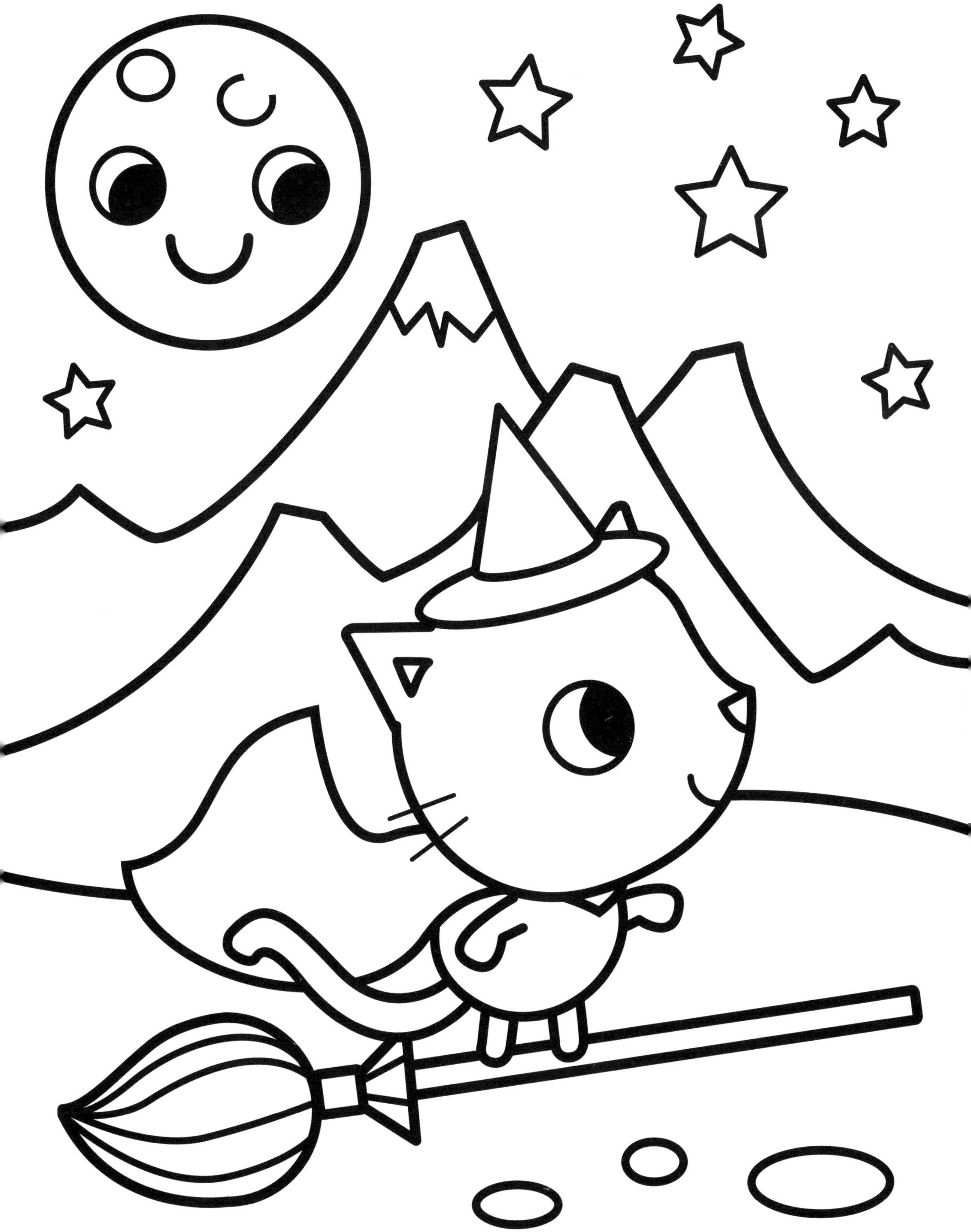

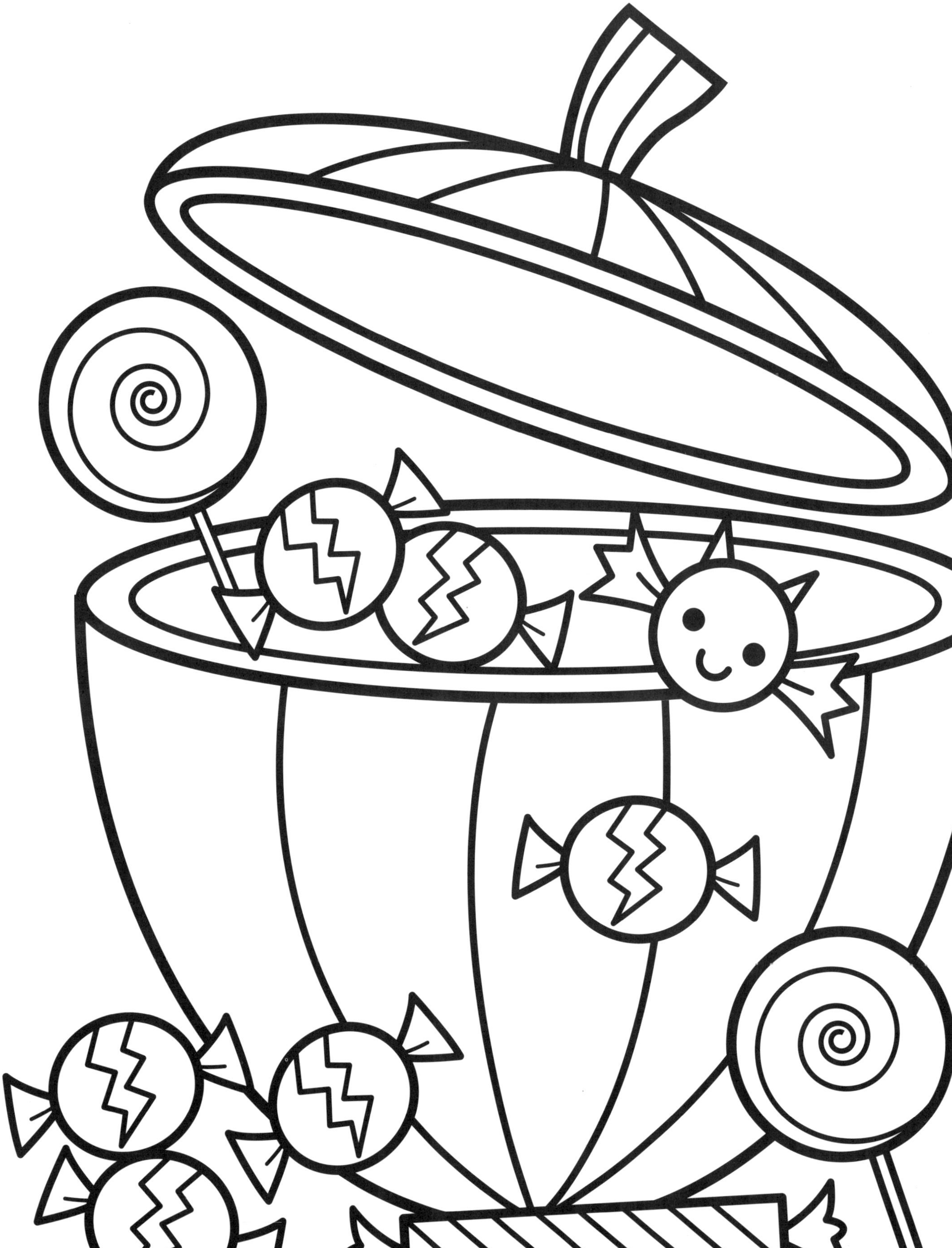

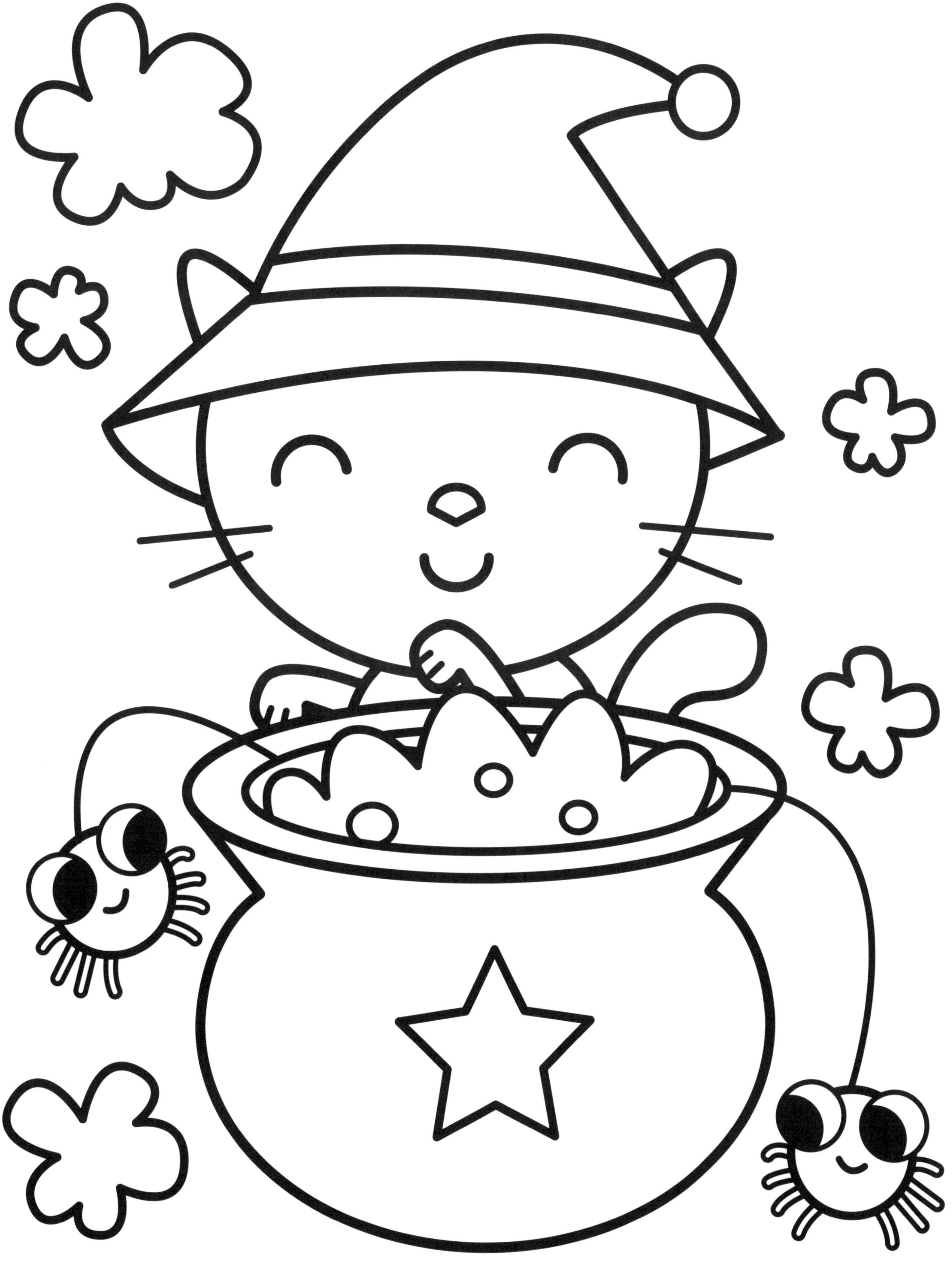

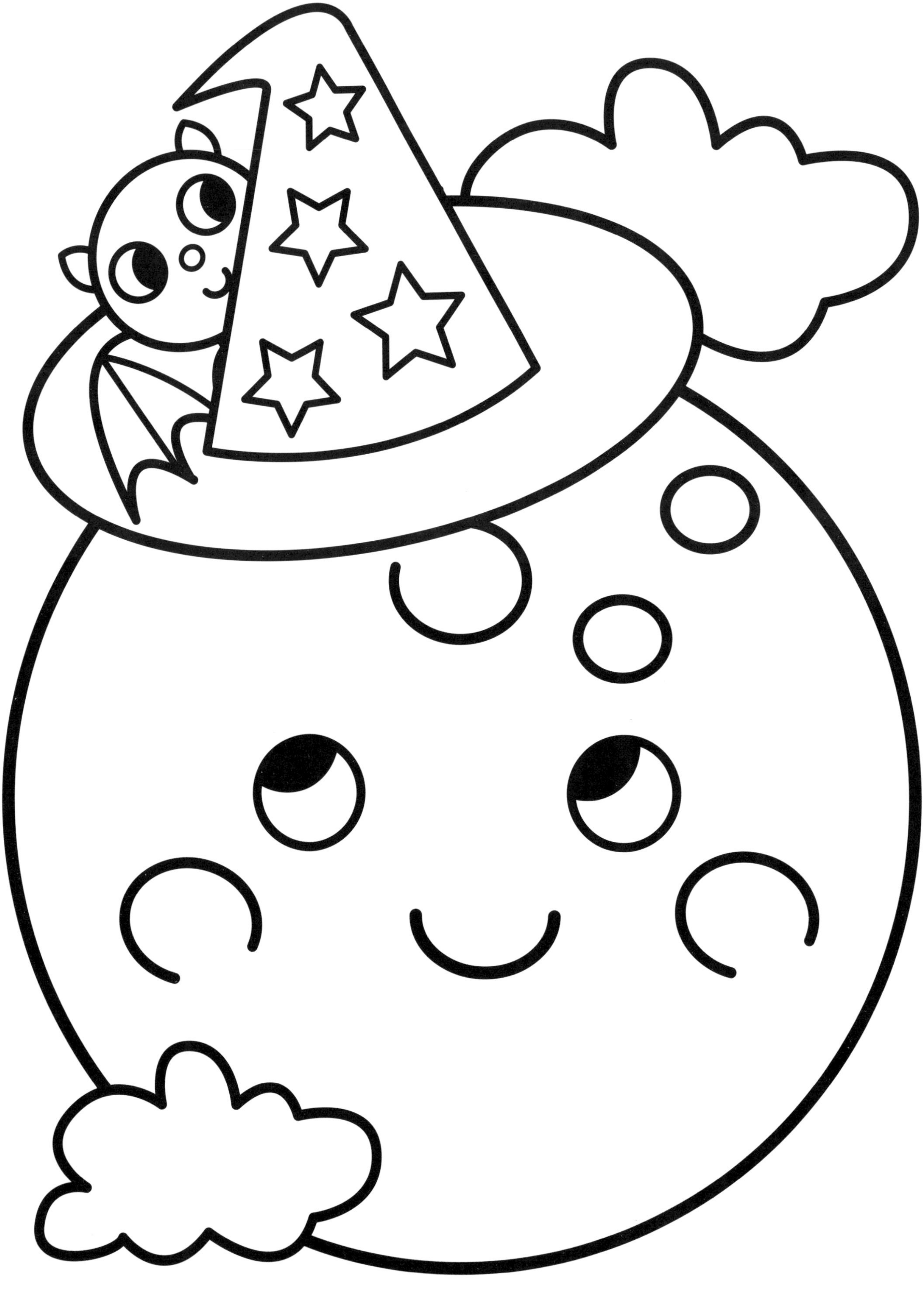

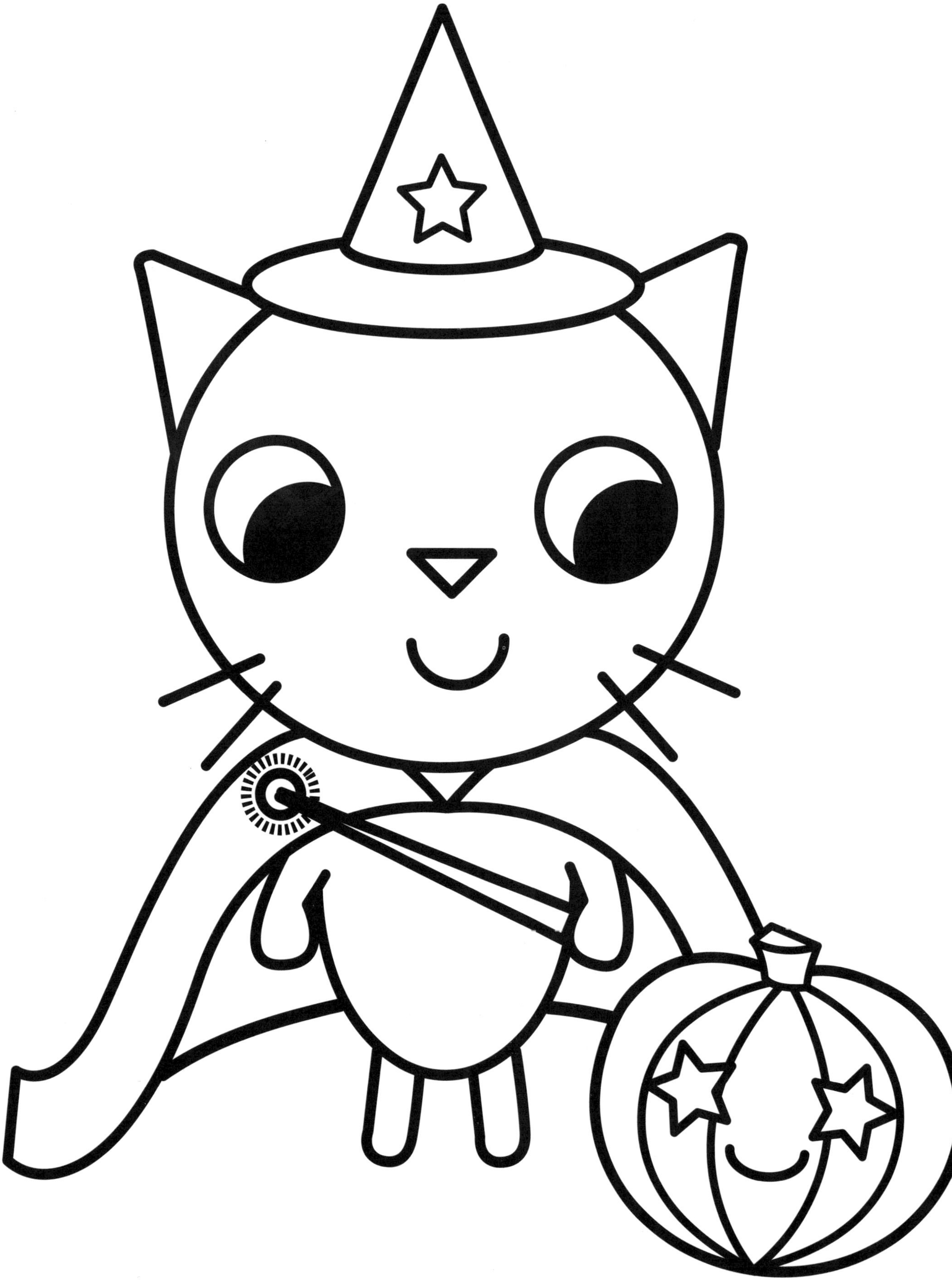